NEW YORK REVIEW BOOKS
CLASSICS

THE ORPHIC VOICE

ELIZABETH SEWELL (1919–2001) was born to British parents in Coonoor, India. During the Second World War, she worked for the Ministry of Education in London and attended Cambridge University, where, in 1949, she earned her doctorate in modern languages. That same year, she traveled for the first time to the United States, which she would later make her home, teaching at Vassar College, the University of Notre Dame, Fordham University, and the University of North Carolina at Greensboro. Sewell is best known for her books of criticism, which explore the formalist verse of Valéry and Eliot, the nonsense verse of Lear and Carroll, and the links between literature and science. She is also the author of four novels, three poetry collections, and a memoir.

DAVID SCHENCK is a writer and bioethicist. He is the coauthor of *Healers: Extraordinary Clinicians at Work* and *What Patients Teach: The Everyday Ethics of Health Care*, and is currently at work on a new book, *Into the Field of Suffering: Transformation and the Healer's Vocation*. A friend and colleague of Elizabeth Sewell's for over twenty years, Schenck now serves as her literary executor.

THE ORPHIC VOICE
Poetry and Natural History

ELIZABETH SEWELL

Introduction by
DAVID SCHENCK

NEW YORK REVIEW BOOKS

New York

THIS IS A NEW YORK REVIEW BOOK
PUBLISHED BY THE NEW YORK REVIEW OF BOOKS
435 Hudson Street, New York, NY 10014
www.nyrb.com

First published as a New York Review Books Classic in 2022.

Library of Congress Cataloging-in-Publication Data
Names: Sewell, Elizabeth, 1919–2001, author. | Schenck, David, 1951– writer of
    introduction.
Title: The Orphic voice / by Elizabeth Sewell ; introduction by David Schenck.
Description: New York: New York Review Books, [2022] | Series: New York
    Review Books classics | Published previously by Yale University Press in 1960
    and by Harper Torchbooks in 1971.
Identifiers: LCCN 2021014417 (print) | LCCN 2021014418 (ebook) | ISBN
    9781681372181 (paperback) | ISBN 9781681372198 (ebook)
Subjects: LCSH: Poetry. | Literature and science. | Orpheus (Greek mythological
    character)—In literature.
Classification: LCC PN1031 .S475 2021 (print) | LCC PN1031 (ebook) |
    DDC 809.1/936—dc23
LC record available at https://lccn.loc.gov/2021014417
LC ebook record available at https://lccn.loc.gov/2021014418

ISBN 978-1-68137-601-1
Available as an electronic book; ISBN 978-1-68137-602-8

Printed in the United States of America on acid-free paper.
10 9 8 7 6 5 4 3 2 1

CONTENTS

Introduction to the 2022 Edition · vii
Preface · xxiii

PART I · 1
Introduction

PART II · 53
Bacon and Shakespeare: Postlogical Thinking

PART III · 169
Erasmus Darwin and Goethe: Linnaean and Ovidian Taxonomy

PART IV · 277
Wordsworth and Rilke: Toward a Biology of Thinking

PART V · 407
Working Poems for The Orphic Voice

Notes · 422
Index · 455

INTRODUCTION

"POETRY is a form of power." This, the first sentence of Elizabeth Sewell's *Orphic Voice*, lets you know immediately that what you have in hand is nothing that can be conveniently labeled "literary criticism." This is another voice entirely, one ranging from Bacon and Shakespeare to Erasmus Darwin, Linnaeus, and the scientific works of Goethe; from Pico to Vico; from Novalis to Hölderlin to Rilke; with side trips to France for Hugo on Shakespeare, Renan on evolution, and Mallarmé on Orpheus. You find yourself confronted at every turn with a mind of great power investigating the origins of the powers of the mind. A suitably Orphic movement, as you will learn.

This is an investigation of thinking, guided by poets and biologists, keyed off myth—the myth of Orpheus. Better: It is a "being read" *by* Orpheus and his poets. Not just a study *of* said poets, or of Orpheus. Literary criticism could be considered the domestication of poetry; *The Orphic Voice*, to the contrary, would be its liberation. *The Orphic Voice*, first published in 1960, can be profitably read alongside works on evolution, like Gregory Bateson's *Mind and Nature* and Jesper Hoffmeyer's *Biosemiotics*, and works of literary critics, like Walter A. Strauss, Charles Segal, and Ihab Hassan on Orpheus, his myth, and its metempsychoses.

In an early review, George Steiner spoke of *The Orphic Voice* as "a difficult, maddening book," before concluding with the simple declaration: "It is a great work." And it is indeed both. The book's introduction will dash you along on one of the more extravagant intellectual courses ever; it's intoxicating, demanding, exuberant. But immediately after, you find yourself plunged into thickets of technicalities with Lord Bacon and his seconds and their foes, likely wondering what in the world has happened. The truly maddening nature of the book, its difficulty, however, lies not in these overt challenges. Rather, it is this: *The Orphic Voice* is a book designed and written to force your mind to work in Orphic fashion. Sewell insists that the reader trained in linear, logical methods must go postlogical, to work in clusters and concentric circles. Simultaneity and analogue are watchwords; linearity and logic are not. Primary evidence in this inquiry into the mind is poems—not just "poetry" as an activity but specific works. This is where the Orphic taxonomy is focused, and rightly so.

> The aim is general, as befits a discipline of investigation into the biology of thinking, a study of the development of the mind-body in the world of nature alive and dead. Of this *The Prelude* and the *Sonette an Orpheus* are textbooks, and in their thinking and validity akin to, and coequal with, every branch of biology, in the widest possible sense including psychology and anthropology, having a similar aim and field.

Poetry is to take the lead as *method*:

> Orpheus, who is poetry and myth and postlogic thinking about itself, is not subject to interpretation by other disciplines; he is himself interpretation, the specific instrument of the poet's researches.

Indeed, it is crucial to science, Sewell argues, that biology reexamine its own mythology, its proper method:

Biology has mistaken its mythology. It needs poetry rather than mathematics or language-as-science to think with; not an exclusive but an inclusive mythology to match the principle of inclusion inherent in all of its living and organic and synthetic subject matter.

For there is here a careful effort to stress the continuity of intellect throughout natural history, one of Emerson's—another of Sewell's Orphic heroes—great themes.

We have to think of the Orphic mind as a natural phenomenon.

[Human language is]...the making explicit of something implicit in life from the beginning. All striving and learning is mythologizing; and language is the mythology of thought and action, a system of working figures made manifest.

The core questions that will organize inquiry in *The Orphic Voice* are two:

What power and place has poetry in the living universe?
What is the biological function of poetry in the natural history of the human organism?

In this time of the sixth extinction and climate emergency what could be more important than these two questions about the relationship of poetry and biology, of the human to the biosphere?

The startling thesis of *The Orphic Voice* is that myth itself is an active power, as well as a depiction of its own power. As such, myth shapes poets, and poets shape myth. Myth as an evolving, living power, with its own autonomy.

> It is Orpheus' function to mark out the essential poetic tradition in any period by indicating those who are at work on the peculiar question and task of poetry in their time; also, to make plain the nature of that questioning endeavor.

The claim is that certain myths, Orpheus preeminent among them, guide as well as elucidate the history of culture and thought.

> It is going to be the theme of the rest of this book that for the last 400 years, with the coming of what one might call the modern age, poetry has been struggling to evolve and perfect the inclusive mythology on which language works and all thought in words is carried on, and that this type of thinking is the only adequate instrument for thinking about change, process, organisms, and life.

All this is entailed in focusing on myth as method.

Sewell tells us that the story of Orpheus can be divided into three main components, and it is this division that provides the framework for her text:

> The first period, Shakespearean and Baconian, will fall under the first part of the story, where Orpheus exercises his power over rocks and trees and animals. Eurydice and the journey to love and death will uphold the Goethean stage, and the Romantics; and with Rilke there will be the final high and mysterious figure, the severed prophetic head unconquered even in its destruction, and the human music

among the stars, by the help of which we shall have to set poetry's face forward if we can.

What I want to suggest to the reader is that the death and dismemberment of Orpheus may well be a promising figure for us to use in thinking about the Anthropocene. Shortly, we will turn to those who could be considered to be extending the Orphic work today, and will suggest that it is the scientists, not the poets, who are doing the most essential work. Sewell herself says that the third portion of the myth is the least explored, and it is that portion that is crying out now for concentrated attention. We can agree, I think, that we are, in fitting Orphic fashion, in the shadow of descent into darkness, now impelled to investigate the destruction of human culture by an infuriated nature.

I offer now three briefs, which I hope will be of use to the reader of *The Orphic Voice* at its most maddening moments: 1) A précis of the textual lineage this work stands in, and where it rests in Sewell's own oeuvre, which was considerable. Like her aunt, the novelist and educator Elizabeth Missing Sewell, she was at home in many genres, and was remarkably prolific: six works of criticism, four novels, three books of poetry, one collection of essays, and a memoir (which features, oddly but unsurprisingly, Bacon and Coleridge). 2) Biosketches of the two scientists who influenced *The Orphic Voice*, whom Sewell knew well and deeply loved. 3) A description of an organizational strategy that Sewell herself used in her teaching to utilize, if in extremis, to help hold the various players straight in the three main chapters of *The Orphic Voice*.

But first a few quick facts about the life. Sewell was born in

1919 in India of British parents, subsequently educated in England, taking her BA, MA, and PhD at Newnham College, Cambridge. She died in 2001 in Greensboro, North Carolina, after having come to the United States in 1949 and spending much of the 1950s and '60s in and around New York City. Sewell had a knack for being where the action was. She saw war service in London during World War II. She was, amidst considerable controversy, one of the first women graduating from Cambridge to be awarded an actual PhD, as opposed to a "certificate of PhD." She taught in historically black colleges at pivotal moments and places during the civil rights era—at Bennett College in Greensboro in 1961, the year of the sit-ins, and at Tugaloo College in Mississippi, amidst the violence of 1963. In her later life, whenever the Ku Klux Klan marched in Greensboro, she was always present in a countermarch. "Never forget," she would say, "Hitler was elected."

Though thoroughly British, Sewell was British with a difference. She was born and raised in India, and spent the bulk of her life in the United States, "this wild, violent, beautiful country." The change in citizenship came several years after having been, in her words, "shown the door at Cambridge." She was, overtly, permanently displaced, staying in no job for more than three years, and living out in her last decades a pledge to keep all jobs to six weeks or less. And yet, in another sense, she was never displaced, being preternaturally attuned, one might say, to Ovid's *Metamorphoses*—always prepared for change, always alert for signs, always ready for the next opening.

One: The key figure for placing Sewell as a critic—or, rather, as a "poet-critic," she would have vehemently insisted—is Samuel Taylor Coleridge. And, in particular, the Coleridge of the essays on method in *The Friend*. This is the Coleridge who recognized immediately, who sponsored and nourished and honored, the greatness of his friend William Wordsworth. Indeed, *The Orphic*

Voice is itself a continuation and deepening of Coleridge's reading of Wordsworth; it was while reading a new edition of the 1805 *Prelude* that the whole plan for *The Orphic Voice* came to Sewell. Whenever you get lost, think Coleridge and Wordsworth. This from Coleridge is a perfect description of the project undertaken in *The Orphic Voice*:

> O! few have there been among critics who have followed with the eye of the imagination the imperishable yet ever wandering spirit of poetry through its various metempsychoses, and consequent metamorphoses...

And this likewise from Coleridge gives the essential clue to how Sewell chose to focus on the key figures we find in *The Orphic Voice*:

> The poet is not only the man made to solve the riddle of the universe, but he is also the man who feels where it is not solved.

More specifically, *The Orphic Voice* is a continuation of the inquiry Sewell began in her rather controversial dissertation at Cambridge, which was later published as *The Structure of Poetry*. Her marvelous memoir of the time of the writing of this work is entitled "A Cautionary Tale," and in it she recounts her discovery that, despite her Cambridge education, she didn't know what thinking was. So she began to read logicians and poets, philosophers and psychologists—indeed, she studied anyone and everyone. Which is precisely what her Cambridge committee objected to. *The Orphic Voice* is a continuation of that line of research, but this time under the sponsorship of Michael Polanyi, who had a total and complete appreciation of his young protégé.

Two: Which brings us to the two scientists so critical for Sewell's development: her father, R. B. Seymour Sewell, a zoologist and Fellow of the Royal Society, and her mentor, Polanyi, a chemist and likewise Fellow of the Royal Society. Both initially were trained as physicians and both served in that capacity—on opposite sides—in the first world war. Seymour Sewell was trained at Christ College, Cambridge, during the time William Bateson was championing Mendelian inheritance and helping to establish the discipline of genetics.

Seymour Sewell was associated with the Indian Medical Service for more than twenty-five years. He made many oceanographic research voyages as a surgeon-naturalist, which culminated in his selection as the chief scientist of the acclaimed John Murray Expedition to the Indian Ocean of 1933–1934. After leaving India, he returned to England and worked in the Department of Zoology at Cambridge until his death in 1964. Between 1903 and 1958 he published more than seventy scientific papers across a variety of disciplines—including taxonomy, oceanography, marine biology, evolutionary biology, geography, ecology, and physical anthropology.

Polanyi is a far more prominent figure—a chemist, social philosopher, and, most important for our purposes, philosopher of science. His major work, *Personal Knowledge*, is easily one of the most important books of the twentieth century on the epistemology and philosophy of science. He was also deeply interested in the philosophy of biology, and particularly in the emergence of life and intelligence. Sewell spent two years in Manchester on a Simon Fellowship where she worked directly with him. She is named in the acknowledgments to *Personal Knowledge* as one of the four people who worked through the entire manuscript with Polanyi as he was preparing it for publication.

So we find Sewell at the time she began to write *The Orphic*

Voice, working as an established and esteemed critic, poet, and novelist, collaborating with one of the great scientists and philosophers of the twentieth century in the writing of his magnum opus—and carrying with her proudly the heritage of being the daughter of an eminent zoologist, as well as being the niece of an eminent Victorian author.

Three: To the American reader, to the twenty-first-century reader, Part Two of *The Orphic Voice* on Bacon and Shakespeare is likely to be tortuous. Partly it's the unfamiliar names—and then there's the awkwardness to our ears of Renaissance English argumentation and diction. (Not to mention the untranslated passages of Latin!) But mostly the trouble is the deep conflictedness within Bacon, which Sewell is determined to follow in infuriating fidelity.

But do not despair! I encourage the discouraged reader to move about freely in *The Orphic Voice*. Treat it as a work of architecture, as a memory palace. After you have read its Introduction—surely one of the most marvelous pieces of writing ever about method and thinking—you have the key in your hand. Feel free now to leap around in the text; I have jumped, for example, from the introduction to Rilke to Erasmus Darwin and back to Shakespeare with great profit. After all, myth, as Sewell teaches us, opens backwards and forwards. Often there are no linear steps to follow; confusion is to be expected. This is a land of simultaneity. My advice is to plow on ahead and expect that after ten or so pages, you will find yourself saying, "Oh, *that's* what that was." This sort of unexpected discovery—and recovery—being one of the pleasures of enigmatic texts.

Steiner says, quite helpfully, that *The Orphic Voice* is "a book by a poet for poets . . . being itself a kind of sustained argumentative poetry." Sewell would add that we are all poets (though not necessarily very good ones, she would inevitably put in, wickedly), because poetry is how the mind works. Indeed, going further with the Ovidian undercurrent, poetry is how the *universe* works. Neither we—nor perhaps Orpheus and his poets—have begun really to grasp the nature, the full capacity, the power of language.

And now for the promised organizational strategy: As an experiment in what Sewell came to call "cluster thinking," take a blank sheet of paper, turn it sideways (landscape view) and write Bacon just above the middle of the page, Shakespeare just below that. Put Pico della Mirandola to the left and down, Ovid to the left and up; Hölderlin, Novalis, and Goethe to the right middle; Coleridge and Victor Hugo to the right and up, along with Edgar Allan Poe, and then drop Teilhard de Chardin with a dotted line down to the right and in parentheses. Go farther into the lower right and put D'Arcy Thompson and Ezra Pound. Now put Milton near Bacon and Shakespeare, to the right middle, and Giambattista Vico to Milton's right. Over Bacon and Shakespeare, Sir Phillip Sydney and his foil Thomas Sprat; and under them George Puttenham and Henry Reynolds. Now stare at what you've done. *This* is how she is thinking. And all of this is unfolding Orpheus.

For the next cluster, out of *The Orphic Voice* Part Three, on a fresh sheet of paper begin with Erasmus Darwin and Goethe in the center, reach back left to Ovid once more, and forward right to Coleridge and Emerson, once more, and on to D'Arcy Thompson and Polanyi—and note the constants. Add in Charles Darwin and T. H. Huxley to the right and up, and Novalis and Charles Augustin Sainte-Beuve below them. Go to the left and up for Bishop Warburton and Thomas Taylor, and left and down for Carolus Linnaeus and his critic Michel Adanson. Left middle for Swedenborg and Vico, and still farther to the left for Pico and Bacon. For Part Four, you have a simpler task, as this section is completely dominated by Wordsworth. But you will also want Rilke in the center, with Coleridge, Hugo, and Ernest Renan to the right. Again, reach back left to Ovid, and indeed Milton. Add in Shelley and Goethe, below left, and you're done.

In sum, whenever you feel yourself getting lost in *The Orphic Voice*, stop and do a cluster diagram. Not on lined paper, however—and never, never on (Cartesian!) grid paper. You want an open page for the imagination; lines that loop are likewise encouraged.

But now, if you really want to challenge your mind, place your three cluster diagrams in a pile so that you have, in effect, a three-layered map. Then imagine that pile blown up into a three-dimensional space. *This* is the mental space of *The Orphic Voice*, and on any given page, Sewell is likely to jump to any given point within that space. This would be one definition of a maddening—and transformative—text.

If, to close these reflections, we ask who is doing Orphic work today, I would answer that one of the most promising places to look is to the biologists—more specifically to those developing the discipline of biosemiotics. I think especially of the work of Jesper Hoffmeyer and Kalevi Kull, both of whom build on the Thomas Sebeok's reading of Charles S. Peirce. This progression would have pleased Sewell greatly in one way and deeply distressed her in another. That semiotics and the investigation of language should become central for biology would have made total sense to her. That nature was itself language, and human language fully nature and biological, also would have made total sense to her. But that biology had gone to philosophy rather than to poetry for guidance—this she would have found distressing, in a curiously partisan fashion, almost as if she had found her friends cheering for the wrong soccer team. For in the quarrel between the poets and the philosophers she was, despite her love for Polanyi, always reflexively and passionately on the side of the poets.

Also deserving mention here is that cluster of disciplines investigating the Anthropocene, geographers and geologists in particular (geosemiotics). Which is especially interesting given that Orpheus returns to the elements at the last. And of course Ovid begins the *Metamorphoses* with the world emerging from the elements—a mythic symmetry here, as we will, by the end of *The Orphic Voice*, expect.

> Before land was and sea—before air and sky
> Arched over all, all Nature was all Chaos,
> The rounded body of all things in one,
> The living elements at war with lifelessness;

But then:

> As God unlocked all elemental things,
> Fire climbed celestial vaults, air followed it
> To float in heavens below; and earth which carried
> All heavier things with it dropped under air;
> Water fell farthest, embracing shores and islands.
> —Ovid, *The Metamorphoses*, Book 1,
> translated by Horace Gregory

Orpheus is alive and stirring among the sciences; very well. But what about poetry? Where are the poets continuing the Orphic line of research in the twentieth century? We have D. H. Lawrence and H.D. quite literally captured by the Orpheus and Eurydice portion of the myth—and to a much more bitter end

Ted Hughes and Sylvia Plath as well. But it is hard to see a poet who has taken up after Rilke left off. In America, we have A. R. Ammons soaked in science, drawing imagery and frameworks from biology. We have our nature poets W. S. Merwin, Mary Oliver, and Wendell Berry; and we have a new wave associated with ecopoetics who are explicitly addressing the Anthropocene, Evelyn Reilly, Ed Roberson, Forrest Gander, Juliana Spahr, and Jorie Graham among them. But do we have any truly Orphic poets, in Sewell's sense? I suggest this as an inquiry for the reader to take up after completing *The Orphic Voice*. For my part, I would say the answer to that question is "Not yet."

If myth is in some sense, or any sense, shaping the development of our minds, then, it can be argued, as Sewell does, that it has a prophetic dimension—an anticipatory component. The Orphic poet is reading and rewriting or extending a pattern that is already there.

Let us take this up as an invitation, then, and ask what prophecy can be read in the next phase of Orphic unfoldment, if we follow Sewell and take Rilke as the last major Orphic voice, and look at the century that has passed since his final songs. Might we want to say that the Anthropocene is included in the prophetic dimension of the Orphic myth? Or maybe be more precise and note that "metamorphosis" might be a more fruitful mythic frame to approach this enormous shift in the geological record and viability of the biosphere than the term "Anthropocene." For the inner structure of the Anthropocene is finally that of a myth of the fall. Not hard to imagine, really, that we would be better served by a myth of transformation, of metamorphosis.

Take the Orphic severed head as marking a crisis for our species, maybe even our endgame, but—according to the myth—not the end of Orpheus. How can we imagine such a metamorphosis? No Orphic poet has gone that far—or maybe, more chillingly, they have, and the music is so inhuman (and inhumane) as to be as yet unheard.

Maybe the next Orphic poet is the river itself. Or the wind. The clear truth, I would propose, is that Nature has always been the composer and Orpheus the musician. How does the song go on after the singer returns to the elements? Not hard to grasp, if Orpheus was simply their instrument from the beginning, elements singing through the human. And so the transformation—the emptying out—of Orpheus into the elements, and the return of the song to sky and cave, is actually the restoration of song to its origin point. Song, on loan to Orpheus, now back into the Cosmos: music of the spheres.

And if this is so, the trajectory of our inquiry must shift. We go *from* "How did human intellect arise from natural history?" *to* "How does nature use human intellect to express herself?" And perhaps the end of the myth means that nature will find new ways to express herself, once the human singer is gone. Which is surely true. Humanity is not the capstone song but one set of singers along the way. One way station in a series of Ovidian metamorphoses.

All the world—every bit and parcel, every planet and galaxy, every crustacean and ameba, every lichen and fungus—is open to, and communicating with, all that constitutes its *umwelt*. This communicating is the voicing of the universe that Orpheus taps into and manifests. This is why the trees and animals listen. Yet this much new and concentrated power is a dangerous thing—there is no more constant theme in all mythology than this. Has the *sparagmós* portion of the Orphic myth not as yet been fully addressed because it prefigured the unimaginable—prefigured the Anthropocene? Metamorphoses brought humans and Orpheus into being. And, as result of metamorphosis, nature will phase us out.

This is a deeper truth of the myth that Sewell's poets, for the most part, did not move into, as she says, but of which biology and geology are making us most aware. There are clues to this in the apocalyptic mind of Milton. And in Rilke, and definitely Mallarmé. But perhaps Lawrence (an Orphic voice much of his life, I would argue) captures the truths of radical metamorphosis better than anyone else in the Orphic line in this totally amazing passage at the end of *Women in Love*:

> Whatever the mystery which has brought forth man and the universe, it is a non-human mystery, it has its own great ends, man is not the criterion . . .
>
> The fountain-head was incorruptible and unsearchable. It had no limits. It could bring forth miracles, create utter new races and new species, in its own hour, new forms of consciousness, new forms of body, new units of being. To be man was as nothing compared to the possibilities of the creative mystery. To have one's pulse beating direct from the mystery, this was perfection, unutterable satisfaction.

Huge events we are witnessing: the recognition of Gaia and the Anthropocene, the acknowledgment of the biosphere and the climate emergency. One way to speak of them is to say that they mark *the discovery that it is nature that is signing/singing, not Orpheus*. And now we wait for next major Orphic poet to come forward, the one who will see/foresee the next metamorphosis! This would be the poet the Anthropocene calls for. The poet who grasps that song is now on the verge of being dispersed into the elements—to the air, water, earth, and fire—Orpheus's breath going out of him, his head into the river, his limbs scattered across the earth, his lyre rising to join the fiery stars. Perhaps that poet is out there. Perhaps *The Orphic Voice* can encourage her to come forward.

Sewell closes *The Orphic Voice* with a set of working poems. In turn, I take the liberty of closing this introduction by offering the reader my figured image of this Orphic poet to hold on to while making your way into this maddening, intimidating, nourishing, enlivening book:

Set Again to the Wheel
Do you read time both ways, old woman,
Eyes fixed on the eternal round?
Show the single imaging power,
Memory and prophecy as one.
Raise before us the wall of fire.

—DAVID SCHENCK

THE ORPHIC VOICE

TO

MICHAEL POLANYI

Preface

I HAVE HAD financial help from three sources while writing this book, and it is with deep gratitude that I now acknowledge what I owe to each of them and say "thank you" for it. To take the latest first: the Department of English at the Ohio State University and its Chairman, Robert Estrich, who invited me to come and talk about the work as Mershon Lecturer for the spring quarter, 1958. Next, the Christian Gauss Seminar in Criticism at Princeton University, which I was invited to give by Richard Blackmur and E. B. O. Borgerhoff during the early part of 1957. Last and most of all, the University of Manchester, which gave me a Simon Fellowship for 1955–56 with which to begin the work and extended it most generously later; and my Chairman there, Dorothy Emmet, for her kindness and support. To Michael Polanyi, also of Manchester University, I owe a debt of a kind that does not go into words. To him, as a small enough return for his understanding, encouragement, help, and inspiration, my love and this book. If I were to begin naming here all the friends who have helped me with it by talking and listening about it, suggesting what to read, and arguing for and against the findings, the list would be impossibly long. They will know how much the book is indebted to them, and will, I hope, recognize their faces in it where and if they choose.

I want to say one word about the notes. I have put them at the end so that they will be out of the way, though the references are there if anyone wants them. I have put into them also a certain amount of indirect material and comment, and they can be skimmed through for that.

My grateful thanks are due to the Director of the Insel-Verlag for permission to quote the poems by Rilke and extracts from his correspondence; to Messrs. W. W. Norton for permission to quote from the translation of Rilke's Letters by Jane Bannard Greene and M. D. Herter Norton; to Messrs. Faber and Faber for permission to use extracts from two works by G. R. Levy, *The Gate of Horn* and *The Sword from the Rock;* and to the Syndics of the Cambridge University Press for permission to quote a passage from Dover Wilson's notes to *A Midsummer Night's Dream,* New Shakespeare Edition. Full particulars are given in my Notes in every case.

E.S.

PART I
Introduction

1

For the misapprehensiveness of his age is exactly what a poet is sent to remedy

POETRY is a form of power. It fell to early thought to make that power visible and human, and the story of Orpheus is that vision and that mortality.

The story, as it will be taken here, falls into three parts. First, Orpheus makes rocks and trees move and subdues the beasts by his voice, music being wedded to language and poetry by natural right; next, after the death of his wife Eurydice he goes into the underworld to find her, gaining admittance and the granting of his request by his poetic powers but losing his prize by looking back at her at the mouth of hell, in disobedience of the conditions laid down; lastly, he is torn in pieces by the Maenads, his head floating down the river still singing, in Ovid's cross-echoes,

> flebile nescio quid queritur lyra, flebile lingua
> murmurat exanimis, respondent flebile ripae.

The head came to rest in a cave, where it prophesied day and night till Apollo himself bade it be silent. The lyre was taken up to heaven to become one of the constellations.

This story seems to say that poetry has power not merely over words and hence over thoughts, but also in some way over natural objects and their behavior, be they animate or inanimate; and to some extent, in conjunction with love, power over life and death as humans know and suffer them; that this power is almost indestructible and may turn, even in its own disaster, to something akin to prophecy. This is not a clear statement. It does not leave the mind resolved, it leaves it wondering: is the claim made by the story in any sense true? if so, in what way? what is the nature of the power and what are its limitations? Mythological statements lead to questions. Then follows something rather strange, for to these questions only the story itself can make an answer. The myth turns back upon itself because it is a question that figures its own reply, and it is that inner movement or dynamic which makes it feel obscure. This kind of unclearness is not muddle or mystification, however, but an indication of method. The myth of Orpheus is statement, question, and method, at one and the same time. This is true of every myth.

The challenge of the Orphic statement, question, and method has not yet been taken up. It seems possible that we may have now, in the context of twentieth-century thought and knowledge, an opportunity to let Orpheus speak. The conditions for this are as follows: first we are to think of myth and poetry, under the figure of Orpheus, as an instrument of knowledge and research. Next we have to formulate the question contained in the myth which that myth is to answer. This can be done in two ways:

> *What power and place has poetry in the living universe?*

or

> *What is the biological function of poetry in the natural history of the human organism?*

Third, we must believe that the Orpheus story has probably been directed this way from the beginning, its constant reappearance forming a tradition of inquiry into this very question, reaching from the time of mythological beginnings to where we are now. We shall not deal with very early times, nor, with one exception, with classical literature. For our own purposes we shall begin with the Renaissance in England and advance from there, following the line of those who mention Orpheus in a significant context. This will not be a catalogue of the myth's appearances; it consists simply of the references to Orpheus I have happened upon, ranging from major works to a single pregnant sentence. These are the main people: Bacon, Shakespeare, Milton, Hooke, Vico, Linnaeus, Swedenborg, Erasmus Darwin, Goethe, Novalis, Coleridge, Wordsworth, Shelley, Emerson, Renan, Hugo, Mallarmé, Rilke.

Language and mind, poetry and biology meet and bear on one another in the figure of Orpheus. This myth asks a great question about poetry in the natural world, the central area where language works with and on that most astonishing of biological phenomena, the human mind. The myth provides, in its narrative, a method by which to pursue the inquiry, and each of those great minds just mentioned is, in its relation to Orpheus, a stage in the history of this inquiry. The series consists, duly and properly, of poets and biologists, and it is this series, in their double discipline, that we shall try to follow.

2

Poetry agrees with science and not with logic

LANGUAGE is perhaps the greatest single gift and achievement of the human organism in the natural order. Consequently what we do with language—how we regard it and how we use it—is never indifferent. It shapes our thinking and our attitudes, powerfully and quietly. That is partly why I formulated the Orphic question in two ways, to draw attention to the fact that nowadays we have almost two languages on our hands. I shall call these for the present "language-as-poetry," and "language-as-science."

In its beginnings, language is acknowledged by scholars to have been essentially figurative, imaginative, synthesizing, and mythological rather than analytical and logical. Schelling, for instance, says, "Is it not evident that there is poetry in the actual material formation of languages?" [1] And other writers have said the same. Myth and metaphor, living instruments of a lively speech, are not ornaments and artifices tacked on to language but something in the stuff of language and hence of the mind itself. Language is poetry, and a poem is only the resources of language used to the full.

We have come to believe, however, that there is another kind of language, not figurative but literal or logical. It

6

is widely accepted that with advancing civilization comes a progress from imaginative and mythological and poetic turns of speech toward the logical, precise, nonfigurative.[2] Within our own culture, philosophers, logicians, and scientists seem to have striven for this for nearly 400 years, anxious to purify language, in the name of precision, from this very element of unclearness we have glimpsed already, from myth, metaphor, and poetry. Analytical thinking—logic and mathematics, in unison—has been set up as the model to which word-thought was to conform. Recent endeavors to develop languages which are mathematical structures of propositions are the outcome. This is language-as-science, in its more or less extreme form.

At first sight this looks like another aspect of the general split between arts and sciences which the modern world acquiesces in. Goethe, writing in 1820, says of his own time that poetry and science seemed then to be in absolute opposition to each other, and this has persisted as the official view, despite the noble and authoritative voices raised to the contrary. Yet it is not as simple a division as it looks, for if we examine poetry and criticism we shall find here also a trend toward language-as-science, in the form of a positive desire for mathematical precision or a negative nostalgia for language-as-poetry which is being ousted by its rival. Erasmus Darwin draws a distinction between the looser analogies suitable for poetry and the stricter ones which alone are suited to science.[3] "Why preyest thou thus upon the poet's heart?" asks Poe in his early sonnet to Science, continuing after a line or two, "Hast thou not dragged Diana from her car?" anticipating by a hundred years the view put forward by I. A. Richards in his essay *Science and Poetry* (1926), which is still the classic modern statement on this theme. So Stephen Spender speaks of it in "Inside the Cage," in *The Making of a Poem* (1955), and of the modern world as a place where it is believed that "all knowledge is in the minds of scientists. The walls of such a world have no ears for the songs of Orpheus."

But the walls never did have ears: it was the poetry that had the power. To reject language-as-poetry or to bewail its loss of power is to affirm language-as-science. There has been wholesale withdrawal from mythological or metaphoric or poetic thought, now relegated to the emotive, the imprecise, symbolical, metaphysical-nonsensical. Neither linguistic philosophers nor critics nor, a far more serious matter, poets, trust language-as-poetry any more. Valéry reviles words for being unreliable and inexact; unscientific, one might say. T. S. Eliot does the same. Arnold was already deeply uneasy about poetic thought, and there are suggestions of such an uneasiness even in Goethe. One result has been the general tendency in modern poetry toward the dry, ironic, self-deprecating conversational tone, the deliberate ascetical abdication from that power which language-as-poetry wields, a tendency broken only by occasional despairing incursions of language-as-poetry into the world of magic. Criticism today shows similar tendencies, particularly the "New" criticism, which in its turn is directed toward logic and analysis by its preoccupation with the text of a poem as an abstract, self-contained, timeless system of formal relations; it is hampered in addition by something it shares with a number of scientific areas as well—a tendency toward dogmatism.

If contemporary poetry and criticism find themselves in a contradictory position, perhaps science has pursued a more logical course, taking logic as the model for scientific thinking and mathematics as the ideal "language" for that thought, to which word-language, when used, should strive to conform? Up to a point, it has; and it, too, is in difficulties. Science no less than letters has a suppressed civil war on its hands in this matter of language and thinking.

In science the friction occurs along the boundary where the exact sciences border upon those which are not "exact" in quite that sense. The line divides the areas where thought can be done in mathematics from those where it cannot. If you cannot think in mathematics, you have to think in words; but with words comes Orpheus, the poetic and metaphoric power of language operating on the mind. The scientists suppose they do not want these powers. Here are five examples of scientists saying so:

1. "Well, this is a fantastic description, perhaps less becoming a scientist than a poet. However, it needs no poetical imagination but only clear and sober scientific reflection to realize . . ."

2. "The analogies which the human mind perceives have an almost universal trend towards vitiating the abstract relations by presenting them in terms of sense-relations; we cannot help craving for the relief from mental effort which is provided by 'picture thinking.' "

3. "An account of what happens rendered in dramatic terms is far more primitive than that which is rendered in scientific terms . . . We now relegate the answers to myth or poetry . . . In a scientific or natural interpretation . . . we take the order of nature as we find it under observation and experiment."

4. "Metaphors, for example . . . at best are makeshifts . . . Science demands great linguistic austerity and discipline."

5. "Köhler has defended his hypotheses against the criticism that they were purely speculative, mere brain mythology."

A physicist writing on the nature of life, a botanist, two biologists, a Gestalt psychologist [4]—these can represent the boundary regions. From these regions Orpheus is to be exorcised, even by such liberal scientists as are all of these.

Biologists generally agree that mathematics is not suited, as a unique intellectual instrument, to the kind of subject matter they deal with. This is partly because time and change are of the essence of living organisms whereas mathematics is essentially a timeless discipline; partly because it is often impossible to reduce biological subject matter into units suitable for mathematical or logical manipulation. Buffon mentions this. So does Cuvier.[5] It is Goethe's main theme as a biologist. Even those biologists who are mathematical in their approach take account of the difficulty. D'Arcy Thompson mentions it in the first chapter of *On Growth and Form* (rev. ed. 1942). Von Bertalanffy picks it up,[6] maintaining that mathematics is a universal instrument but saying that there are areas of biology which at present lack their proper mathematical tools, and speculating whether the answer may not be what he calls a nonquantitative or *gestalt* mathematics.

But now comes the difficulty. If thought cannot be done in mathematics, there is only language left to think with. Scientists reject language-as-poetry as an instrument of thought. There remains language-as-science. This attempts to make language approximate to the conditions of analytical precision which are characteristic of logic and mathematics. And it is generally agreed among biologists that mathematics by its nature is not suitable as an instrument for use on biological subject matter.

The vicious circle can be seen particularly well in the fate of Gestalt psychology. This school, which became influential in the 1920's, recognized the difficulty, in part at least, as a problem affecting not only psychology but the whole of modern thinking. It was this clarity which gave the movement its considerable influence; there is much gain in the clear statement of a problem, and hope for an answer. The answer which Gestalt psychology gave is inadequate, but like all mistakes of such a kind, it is very helpful.

The need, as Gestalt psychologists saw it, was to find "whether a logic is possible which is *not* piecemeal." In the ancient controversy between analysts and synthesists (one might call them more briefly, as taxonomers do, "splitters" and "lumpers"), Gestalt theorists insisted on the priority of wholes over parts: "the comprehension of whole-properties and whole-conditions *must* precede consideration of the real significance of parts." They applied this, with great thoroughness and logic, to their subject matter and their method alike.[7]

At the first level, the study of how perception in organisms works, they put forward the idea that our senses, particularly the sense of sight, work not analytically but synthetically, so that we perceive in simultaneous wholes or groups or *Gestalten,* in figures or forms, which is what the German word means.

(There is an interesting passage in Goethe where he picks up the word and discusses it: "Germans have a word for the whole complex of existence in a living thing, the word *Gestalt* . . . But if we observe *Gestalten,* particularly organic ones, we find nowhere anything permanent or static or segregated. On the contrary, everything seems to hover in a perpetual change."[8] This shows one of the difficulties inherent in the term and concept of Gestalt: it is spatial rather than temporal.)

At the second level, the Gestalt theorists claim that the organism must be observed as a whole, by any methods which will allow of this, unconventional though they may be from the strictly scientific point of view. At the third level, they insist that the observer is part of the whole which he observes and he must take account of this fact.

Opposition to Gestalt theory came from the behaviorists, who wished to establish in psychology the impersonal rigor of observation and quantitative analysis applicable in the exact sciences. Gestalt theory came close to offering an alternative instrument for thought, and it was the failure to appreciate the need for this, in whatever terms, which was the undoing of the Gestalt movement, for it meant that there was no positive standard to offer against the opposing demand for mathematics, logic, and language-as-science. The only possibility seemed to be to make Gestalt psychology more precise, in the opponents' terms, and so to fall back on language-as-science, and the movement petered out.

The history of this school is valuable because it is an example of what is happening inside the boundary sciences which cluster around biology, and also inside poetry and criticism. An antithesis of two terms is set up, or acquiesced in, and then an attempt is made to fashion and develop an instrument of thought which will fuse the two. Thus Gestalt psychology chose to operate in terms of wholes and parts, admitting the antithesis first and then trying to make language-as-science adequate for some new kind of thinking in wholes. The attempt may have been new, but the premises were very old. They are part of the split we have been looking at in the biological sciences and criticism, science versus poetry and art, mathematics versus words, analysis versus synthesis. What has happened in each case, over a longer or shorter period of time, is very interesting. These antitheses produce not instruments of discovery but more of the same, a recurrence of repetition of the premises with some monotony now after 300 years. The reason is that the antitheses on which all this thinking and activity is grounded, science and poetry, analysis and synthesis, mathematics and words, are not antitheses at all. Science cannot be set against poetry because they are structurally similar activities. Analysis cannot be set against synthesis because each is the precondition of the other's working. Mathematics cannot be set against words because each is an instrument for myth in the mind.

Examples have been given of remarks made by scientists about poetry in its various aspects, and remarks made by poets and critics about science. We need to notice the assumption on which the speaker in each case bases his remarks: that he knows what he is talking about. This assumption by the speaker must lie behind any meaningful utterance, and it will be accepted similarly by the hearer; at the same time each side must accept the fact that the assumption may be unfounded. Perhaps I do not know what I am talking about after all. Both points of view are simultaneously necessary. An excess of the latter will lead to too much timidity to make any utterance at all, while an excess of the former—a much commoner symptom—will lead to laying down the law, an enjoyable but inappropriate practice if the flexible activity of conversation or thought is to be kept going.

This assumption is only an assumption in each of the two cases before us, a belief we are tacitly invited to entertain, a little myth in fact. Suppose that for a moment we withdraw our confidence; suppose that neither side knows what it is talking about. What follows from this small but quite legitimate maneuver on our part?

The first thing we shall notice is that the two sides do not seem to suffer from any lack of confidence. They think they do know what they are talking about. So we have the scientist setting science against poetry and seeing in the latter a loose, vague, drunken activity, liable to mislead thought by its procedures which are easier and less exacting than those of science, neither disciplined nor in contact with reality. No poet is going to recognize this as poetry; and quite right too.[9] The poet and critic, on the other hand, speak of science as hostile to poetry, obsessed with an exactitude which is quantitative, mechanical, niggling, pedestrian, and, unfortunately for the poet's argument, vulgarly successful. No scientist is going to accept this as science, and, again, rightly.

It seems only fair to suppose that science when it speaks about poetry in these terms simply does not know what it is talking about, and vice versa. A description of their respective activities on which, in theory at least, scientists and poets could agree might run something like this: poetry and science are activities in which thinker and instrument combine in some situation which is passionately exciting because it is fraught with possibilities of discovery. That is not meant to be an exact definition, obviously, but it will do for the moment.

This is only half the story, however. If the two activities seem to their respective practitioners to be so alike that they can be covered by a common description (even though each side may be unaware of their resemblance), may not the misunderstanding of the proceedings of the supposedly opposing discipline distort the scientist's view of science, the poet's view of poetry? To put it bluntly, suppose that the scientist does not know what he is talking about when he is talking about science in such terms, and similarly for the poet or critic and poetry? If science is opposed to poetry, it begins to look something very like what the poets damn it for being, to imitate its own caricature, and poetry likewise. So each error plays into the hands of the other side, and the whole situation is self-perpetuating. To misunderstand the nature of man's thoughtful operation with any language, scientific or poetic, seems to make the mind liable to misunderstand its thinking procedures in general.

We can cheerfully vote for admitting that poets and critics misunderstand the nature of poetry, since that is the group we belong to and so can include ourselves in the general confession. To suggest that a scientist does not know what science is must be a much harder step. But it has to be said, for I believe it to be true. Fortunately it has been said already by those who have a right to say so, the scientists themselves.[10]

The important thing now is to move ourselves out of these useless antitheses on to that common ground where science and poetry are seen as related activities of human thought, instruments toward a particular end. This is where myth comes in, for it will be the means by which we shall explore that activity. We may be ready now to have more confidence in it perhaps, for if the current views on poetry and science are out of true, the same thing may hold for myth as well. As we examine those views, we shall find that they depend on two further worn-out antitheses, and once those are out of the way we can begin to see myth for what it is, a figuring of that very activity which we spoke about just now as at the heart of both science and poetry.

The word "myth" is used nowadays almost exclusively in a negative or even a disapproving way. It is held to relate to a belief or set of beliefs which are invented by fantasy and do not correspond, except figuratively, with anything real. A mythical being is one who does not exist. A mythical event is one which in fact never occurred. The term "myth" can be used purely descriptively or as a term of abuse, a characteristic it shares with the words "fiction" or "story" (as we talk of children telling stories).

We can take as a reasonably typical example of the modern attitude toward myth the work of Ernst Cassirer.[11] Here is a scholar well enough disposed toward myth to devote much study to it, in the course of which he draws close parallels between mythological and scientific thought and claims that they have a common origin in the mind. Alongside this friendly attitude, however, goes the assumption (taken so much for granted that it is not even discussed) that a modern scholar will be bound eventually to set scientific thought over against mythological thinking and to give his allegiance to the former.

Where does this attitude spring from? We do not want to get involved in a history of attitudes toward myth; there are such statements already in existence, and it would certainly be beyond our competence. But a little background may be helpful. Cassirer himself calls Vico the discoverer of myth, and certain it is that Vico adopts for the first time an entirely positive attitude toward myth, regarding it as both subject matter and to some extent method for his *Scienza nuova,* a course which is followed up by Herder and Schelling. But Vico is in another sense less a beginning here than a development of something earlier; for before the *Scienza nuova* comes the *Novum Organum,* which Vico knew and admired, and in that an approach to myth is suggested with the germs of both future developments in it, the positive as exemplified by Vico, Herder, and Schelling, and the negative which sees in myth mere fables and toys, the prevailing attitude of the eighteenth century that was continued by Comte in his *Cours de philosophie positive,* in which he put forward his theory of the progression of humanity through the three stages of theological or fictive thought, metaphysical or abstract thought, to the final term, positivist or scientific thought.

After Comte on the one side and Schelling on the other, what happens looks like an uneasy relapse into the original Baconian ambiguity, but in fact it is not. The middle position of such a scholar as Cassirer when looked at closely proves not to be a middle position at all. The claims of logic are too strong now for a thinker to be able to affirm and deny myth at one and the same time. The result is, as can be seen more and more clearly as time goes on, an acceptance of myth as subject matter and a rejection of it as method of thinking. It is an attempt to investigate myth by means of science. It can be seen in Strauss and Renan, in the conscious superiority of tone so noticeable in *The Golden Bough,* in Max Müller's concept of myth as a disease of language, in Cassirer's divided loyalties.

It is seen most clearly of all in Lévy-Bruhl. In his classic *Les Fonctions mentales dans les sociétés inférieures* (1910) he gives the name "prelogical" to the form of primitive thinking which operates by means of myth, and then begins to wrestle with his own term, saying that *pre*logical must not be taken to imply necessarily either "earlier in time" or "less in usefulness." "It is not antilogical," he says, "neither is it alogical. In calling it prelogical I mean only that it does not have as its main aim, as our thought has, to abstain from contradiction." But the writer cannot himself abstain from contradiction, and that is what makes him so interesting and valuable, for he sees clearly that one cannot declare for science, in these terms alone, without disastrous consequences. He himself suffers from this split right up to the last paragraph of the book, which speaks of unresolved combat in the mind between these two forms of thinking, "rational" and "irrational." A little earlier he gives a warning, so clear and important I give it in full. He is talking about logical activity and the fixed concepts necessary for this kind of thought:

> But if progress is not to come to a standstill, concepts of beings and objects must remain plastic, must be modified, enlarged, limited, transformed, must separate and unite continually in the light of experience. If they become rigid and turn into a system which claims to be self-sufficient, the mind engaged in such a system will go on working inside it for ever and ever, cut off from any contact with reality which these very concepts are supposed to represent. They be-

come the object of a hollow and useless dialectic and
the source of a deathly infatuation.[12]

*L'objet d'une dialectique creuse et vaine, et l'origine
d'une infatuation mortelle*—it is a noble phrase, and we
are still trying to do what it warns us against. More of the
same. For though Lévy-Bruhl delivered the warning, he
could not act upon it, because he felt, as Cassirer did later,
that only the scientific way of thinking could be trusted
as a method of scholarly research.

This forces the mind to consider science and scientific
thinking as an intellectual activity of a specialized kind,
logical above all things, upon which intrude from time
to time those flashes of inspiration or unreason which are
responsible for discoveries. For everyone knows that dis-
coveries are not made scientifically, in this sense, at all.
They are "a seizing upon some happy idea," "some sort
of inspiration," "bridging a logical gap." [13] This aspect
of scientific thinking was first discussed by the mathe-
matician Henri Poincaré, and has since under the name
of heuristics become a separate subject of study. No sci-
entist could uphold the view that logic and logic alone
is necessary for scientific thought; the consistent preferring
of the logical over the nonlogical, which would presum-
ably have been Comte's theoretical ideal, would be com-
pletely sterilizing even if it were humanly possible. Even
from a less rigorous standpoint, however, if the underlying
assumption is that the human mind, individual or collec-
tive, moves from prelogical to logical and from mythical
to scientific, the intrusion of nonlogical activity at crucial
points must remain a slight embarrassment. Discovery,
which is avowedly the most exciting and valuable thing
in science and is in fact what science is about, must al-
ways appear an irrelevance, no matter how helpful, in
terms of the prevailing system.

This is an uncomfortable situation. It springs directly from the antitheses we have already seen, and these now can be traced back one step further to two final and more fundamental ones which concern not the instruments of thought, as those earlier ones did, but the nature of the thinker.

Modern thought supposes that human beings are capable of two sorts of thinking, the logical and the imaginative. We are endowed with the faculties of intellect and of imagination—allied, since both are mental, but distinct in their methods and fields of operation. The intellect is the "mind," properly so-called, and its essential function is abstract and logical thought. The imagination is more closely knit with the body (witness its habit, in myth, of expressing all concepts in terms of bodies, of embodying its ideas, in fact, and the close connection of myth with rite or bodily action),[14] and it operates in the more primitive forms of dreams, myth, ritual, and art.

Science and poetry, mathematics and words, intellect and imagination, mind and body: they are old, they are tidy, they are mistaken. If we can dispose of these recurring antitheses which the last 400 years have, with the best of intentions, bequeathed us, we can turn to bequests made on our behalf by other ancestors, for they are there and ready to help. We have given ourselves credit, as human beings, for rather more and rather less than we possess. The human organism, that body which has the gift of thought, does not have the choice of two kinds of thinking. It has only one, in which the organism as a whole is engaged all along the line. There has been no progression in history from one type of thought to another. We are merely learning to use what we have been given, which is all of a piece. This means too that we have to admit and affirm our solidarity with the thinking of the child and the savage. All thinking is of the same kind, and it is this we have to try to understand and to exercise.

If, as we have seen, science cannot absorb myth, we can try the other way around, taking myth as a nearer model of the activity we want to explore and letting it interpret science as no less imaginative, corporeal, figuring, than itself. Discovery, in science and poetry, is a mythological situation [15] in which the mind unites with a figure of its own devising as a means toward understanding the world. That figure always takes the form of some kind of language, and that is why we have to go more deeply into language instead of trying to escape from it. Discovery is always under Orpheus' patronage, so to speak; something that the good poets have always known.

3

Lucian . . . is of the opinion that Orpheus had already prescribed that anybody introduced to the wisdom of the mysteries should be received with dancing

OUR PROGRESS so far may seem no more than a presumptuous rejection of almost everything the present state of learning has to offer, and a preaching of a return to primitive practices. Let us try to put our course in a more positive light. We are to get rid only of that which has shown itself incapable of development, and then to go back over what we possess, looking at it afresh in the belief—for this much of an act of faith is required—that language with its workings and workers is to be trusted. Far from a general course of debunking, we shall find ourselves launched on a reaffirmation of old wisdoms, a kind of passionate conservatism (which may in its turn prove to be one of the characteristics of mythical thinking), letting these antiquities which have in them yet the seeds of newness guide and help us. The Orpheus myth is one of these, and there will be others.

Here a question arises, and it had better be dealt with first. Are we, in doing this, going to imagine into these old methods and writers all sorts of potentialities which were never there? As, for instance, a critic may find himself being blamed for reading more into a poet's work than the poet can reasonably be supposed to have put into it? The answer probably is "yes," and such a procedure is entirely justified, if we are to make any progress at all. It is of the nature of mind and language, together, that they form an instrument capable of an indefinite number of developments. It matters very little whether the particular devisers or users of the instrument saw, at the point in time when they flourished, its full implications. Any good poem surpasses its writer's powers of exegesis, and Michael Polanyi in *Personal Knowledge* (1958) has shown that this is also true of scientific hypotheses, and indeed of language in general. We always say more than we know. This is one of the reasons for language's apparent imprecision. It is no reason for refusing language our confidence.

The aim will then be to draw out certain implications in earlier forms of thinking, using the Orpheus line as a clue. What can be accurately and elegantly used for a particular purpose (that is putting our standards high, but such things have to be striven for at least) may be considered as appropriate to that purpose, whether its designers and earlier users recognized this possible use of it or not. We shall be free, therefore, to draw out from half-forgotten or ill-interpreted authors and from forms of thought fallen into disuse whatever they can offer us, not worrying (beyond the straightforward claims of integrity and logic in these matters) whether we are falsifying them in the process. Tradition is not a handing down of dead fixities, but an invitation to further development: [16] Make of it what you can. No further apologies then will be made on this score.

This does not apply solely to writings or poems or to forms of thinking. It applies, very particularly and in the first place, to language itself, as the most misunderstood and underestimated instrument of them all, with almost unlimited possibilities still before it.

The nature of language has been much studied. So has its history. We are after something else: not nature or history but something nearer what we mean by natural history, a dynamic inquiry into process, a natural history of mind and language. Language is to be conceived of not as an entity but as an activity; not in itself, for one must always avoid the metaphor of saying that language is alive, but in conjunction with a mind, with numbers and series of minds in time. Language utterances become events in this kind of thinking. Every poem and recounted myth and scientific hypothesis and theological statement and theory of politics or history and every philosophy become records of happenings at particular times, all of which, if they have any life in them at all, have the capacity to be taken further, in varying degrees, by other minds present and to come. This means giving up the right to abstract language into timeless pattern, and making the effort to grasp it not as a fixed phenomenon but as a moving event, language plus mind, subject to time and process and change—to try to think in biological terms, perhaps.[17]

We will start with words. Words (or groups of words bearing a unit of sense for the mind—there is no need to be pedantic here) can be thought of as having "natures" for abstract consideration, meanings which are reasonably fixed, both in range and as regards time. Hence they can be defined, and all lexicography and every attempt to define terms and to use them precisely subscribes to this view of words. Connected with this, words have "histories" which can be studied by etymological methods and which in normal nonspecialized use of language contribute to the whole meaning. All of us fall in with these two ways of looking at language every time we use words, although we are neither lexicographers nor etymologists, and that is right and proper.

Between these two lies the shifting field which we might call usage, and which is the proper field of the philologist. It is to this field that we need to direct our attention, but in the terms in which Vico saw it. In his *Diritto universale* he talks of philology as the study of the first beginnings of the human race (the Greek could carry the meaning of "first principles" as well) and says he hopes to raise philology by his work to the due stature of a science.[18] This was to form the basis of his New Science. Words for him are the means by which human beings carry on the specific activity which makes them humans, and poetry and myth are the proper method of inquiry into it.

Every word or group of words is at once a meaning, a history, and the occasion of activity in the mind. A word means the mental activity it conjures up, just as much as it means the object to which it refers and all the past uses to which it has been put. This activity is an essential part of language's workings, and it is as much physical as mental, the correlation of perception (which is now recognized as an active and not a passive process of body and mind) [19] with concept. The active participation of the user of the language is part of the nature of language itself.

Individual words vary in the proportion to which their meaning consists of this third element, of activity. Abstracts in particular have a great deal of it. Their major component is the active response which they call up in the mind. This is what makes the interpretation of them vary so much between one mind and another, since human beings vary widely in the forms of activity of which they are capable. "Honor" and "wisdom" and "science," even at the merely linguistic level, are things you do (and can only understand by doing). Falstaff saying "What is honour? A word!" means that he is not proposing to give the word his active cooperation. He is withdrawing from participation, and the meaning leaves the word altogether for him, as the rest of the speech shows. The expression, "He is a man for whom the word 'honour' has no meaning," carries the same idea.

The result of looking at language in this way is that the universe of discourse turns out to be a world of action and of individual minds acting in certain concordant or discordant ways. It is always necessarily a world of participation, for it is blessedly obvious that there is no objective and detached doing, no doing without a doer. This activity which upholds all of language as mind cooperates with it [20] is what we are to understand henceforward by the word "myth." Word-language and poetry are at once its highest expression and the best key we yet have to it, but this same kind of activity underlies every other kind of language activity, if we are going to stretch the word beyond word-language for a little while, and is related to all other forms of activity or behavior.

This then is our field, where everything is in action and movement, and you cannot "tell the dancer from the dance." Now one point at least can be cleared up, for it is in this field that the antitheses we have been talking about belong, all five of them: science / poetry; analysis / synthesis; mathematics / words; intellect / imagination; mind / body. On this dancing ground they are not fixed and opposing marks, but moving and interchanging figures of the dance we call thinking and knowing. They are not to be melted into a hodgepodge of sameness—that was not what was meant by saying they were, as antitheses, useless—for clearly in one sense science is not poetry, mathematics is not words, and so on. They are to be seen as a choice of operations of the dancing mind by which it can learn to understand itself and the world. The image of dancing is a good one here because it prevents us from thinking that this process is an abstract one in which the body is not essentially and passionately involved. The very word "figure" contains within itself the possibility of such a setting to partners. There are figures of speech, the instruments of poetry; but figures are also the relations of change and movement, stylized yet free, of a dance, and it is the human figure which has to lend itself to each of these modes of operation before they can come into being at all. "For he who recollects or remembers, thinks; he who imagines, thinks; he who reasons, thinks; and in a word the spirit of man, whether prompted by sense or left to itself, whether in the functions of the intellect, or of the will and affections, dances to the tune of the thoughts." That is Bacon (one of Orpheus' men) in *The Advancement of Learning*. But before coming to him and what he has to say about this activity of mind and word we shall have to go back a little beyond him, for in that earlier period lies what we need, a kind of manual of language and mind as a dance of relations, moving and not static, which may help us forward.

4

And those who have this art, I have hitherto been in the habit of calling dialecticians; but God knows whether the name is right or not. But now I should like to know. . . . whether this may not be that famous art of rhetoric?

To LOOK AT LANGUAGE as a field of activity or a form of behavior is a way of looking at the universe, and is going to widen our concept of language out beyond word-language for the present. For this field of activity or myth, where mind-bodies work and unite with figures in order to learn and to discover, is far wider than words, and wider than consciousness. It is the field of all behavior which is not wholly mechanical, in any living thing. What this means is that all ordered purposive selective behavior is potentially a language situation, which develops at the human level into the invention and use of language as we know it but which implies such a development from the beginning. If this is so, then language, once arrived at, may incorporate in itself all the unexpressed elements in simpler types of behavior, offering a special insight into living behavior in a wide context. The connection between word-language or poetry and natural history may be closer than we think. Let us consider this for a moment.

The stuff of which the world is made follows, as far as we can tell, particular patterns toward particular conjunctions. In so-called inanimate matter—the division between this and the animate seems to be going or gone—the patterns are fixed. With the appearance of living things and the individual forms of bodies which characterize organisms, the formalizing tendency continues, but it is peculiar to a body and its mind together to become its own instrument for formal operation (growth and development), and its own instrument for formal behavior (function). The organism is at one and the same time medium and instrument of its own formalizing tendencies. The intervention of self-consciousness does not check this process or falsify it. It means that the body-mind recognizes itself as part of this process. It cannot withdraw from it. But in addition to these formal operations still carried on directly upon and with itself, the mind extends the process and invents systems of forms which it can use as hitherto the body used itself—that being the only material given it—systems which will serve as media in which formal operations can be carried on, and as instruments for formal behavior, including new kinds of behavior, discovery and exploration, which a new instrument makes possible. This is the point of the invention of language, which then becomes not a huge gap but the making explicit of something implicit in life from the beginning. All striving and learning is mythologizing; and language is the mythology of thought and action, a system of working figures made manifest.

By means of language, a second term, a second universe of discourse, is brought into being; and, for the first time, formal relations can be established between this and the universe of experience. By reason of the distinction between the two universes, the establishment of relations between them becomes possible.

There seem to be five such types of formal system: (1) dance and ritual, where the body as a whole is employed formally; (2) music and rhythm, where the forms come to the mind-body through the ear; (3) plastic art and all forms of visual pattern, where the form comes to the mind-body through the eye; (4) mathematics; (5) word-language. This is so far all we have. All are arts, and all are capable of serving as the second term in a relation in which the universe of experience is the first term.

The invention of a language entails the seeing of a distinction between the form constructed and used by the mind-body and the form as perceived in the material of experience to which the language is to correspond. This may have been a gradual process, perhaps akin to the perception of a self distinct from surroundings though remaining intimately linked with them, which is the nature of self-consciousness. Once the distinction is made, it alters the whole situation; in it, for instance, lies the difference between a bird's music and human music. Only when the two are separated can they be correlated. Such a correlation is the ultimate purpose of language as an instrument of thought and comprehension. This is why language is capable of generating and transmitting ideas, an idea being the perception, by the body-mind of an individual, of a correlation between a structure it has itself invented or received and a structure perceived in the universe of which it is itself a part.

Notice how, in what we have been saying, one of our original pairs of antitheses has been doing a quiet dance on its own: analysis and synthesis. For this situation is an intimate mixture of twoness and oneness. What other relations than those of contradiction can we discover for distinction and union, our first pair of dancers? The na-

ture of our approach means that these relations need to be
expressed in linguistic terms. Our cultural tradition can
provide us with what we need, an instrument which asks
only to be put to use again. It was originally, very suitably,
an instrument of education, concerned with language.
This is the medieval trivium, the first three liberal arts,
dialectic, rhetoric, and grammar: dialectic the art and
operation of argument and distinction, rhetoric the op-
eration of figurative speech directed toward persuasion,
grammar, a much more difficult operation to define but
we could think of it as those principles of movement and
conjunction on which words operate in their use by the
mind.

These three differing sets of relations are themselves
activities. Here all the oppositions which made up our
former antitheses will dance their individual dances under
observable conditions, and so throw light on more things
than just words. For what the medievals had here, whether
they realized it or not, was a triple art of thought concerned
with living behavior in general.

Since the antitheses have come in again, we will now
deal with three sets of them, analysis and synthesis, science
and poetry, intellect and imagination, considering them
by means of dialectic and rhetoric. Then we will move
on to grammar and the last two pairs, mind and body,
mathematics and words, and then we shall be ready for
other things.

It looks almost as if dialectic and rhetoric are only an-
other form of language-as-science and language-as-poetry.
We have now, however, a means of finding out what hap-
pens in each of these two fields of activity.

Dialectic is the art or science of logical argument. Its
working method is logic. It proceeds by the sharpest pos-
sible distinction and analysis, by discovering logical flaws
in its opponent's case where there is an external opponent,

or by constructing its own argument with no less care in logical analysis where the division is a purely internal one; one divides oneself in order to think, as Valéry says. This procedure is familiar to us in many settings, in the law courts, in politics (at least in theory), in all forms of scholarly and scientific controversy and discussion. This type of thinking has been extensively developed since the days of Aristotle and Plato. It is only perhaps in the comparatively recent past that we have glimpsed the odd turns it could take when overpursued to the exclusion of other no less valid forms of thought: the impasses of dialectical materialism, the rigid narrowness of much so-called scientific thought, Lévy-Bruhl's *dialectique creuse et vaine,* nonsense literature; and what might Charles Darwin have done if he had had the other two branches of the trivium at his disposal and in his confidence?

Rhetoric is a field in which we have as yet much less confidence, so that whereas dialectic is a simple technical term, rhetoric can also be used as an insult. This is the field of figurative speech, of language allowed to follow, develop, and even luxuriate in its inherent capacity for metaphor. Metaphor is not an analytic procedure; it sets up two terms only to unite them, drawing in the cooperation of the thinking mind in the process. It can never work in detachment; it is not objective. Shelley in the opening paragraph of the *Defence of Poetry* speaks of it as "mind acting upon those thoughts so as to colour them with its own light" and goes on to distinguish between reason and imagination, consigning poetry to the latter. This is the usual view. If dialectic seems to be the playground of the intellect, rhetoric is the place where the imagination may run riot.

Here then our antitheses seem to reach further expression. But now let us look at dialectic and rhetoric more closely and see what their first principles are. In so doing

we find that each has to call in the working principle of
the other apparently opposing system before it can get
started at all. It has now been put forward, by a scientist,
that science with its distinctive form of logical thought
depends on an act of affirmation by the scientist, person-
ally, in what he is doing, and that this basic assertion of
personal commitment can never be verified by any logical
means. This is the theme of Polanyi's *Personal Knowledge,*
and to this the reader is referred. It is the restoration of
science once more to the company of the arts, giving sci-
ence for its foundation the mythic or metaphoric or poetic
situation where figure and agent become one and the same.
Analysis, then—logic, dialectic—rest on a fundamental
act of confidence and synthesis (or call it faith and love).

Now for rhetoric and metaphor. It in its turn cannot
function without sharp discrimination, selection, and anal-
ysis in the separating out of the two terms of which the
figure or metaphor is to be made. This is the exact science
of the poet. It is described by Mallarmé, "Instituer une
relation entre les images exacte, et que s'en détache un
tiers aspect fusible et clair présenté à la divination." [21]
Mallarmé's syntax is as individual in his prose as in his
verse, and it must not seem officious if I point out that
the reader must construe "exacte" with "relation," not
with its immediate neighbor. If metaphor is a synthesis,
it nonetheless begins with analysis into the separate units
with which logical thinking works. Because things are per-
ceived to be clearly and sharply and exquisitely separate,
metaphor becomes possible. Indeed on the recognition
of twoness, with the possibility of constructing from it
certain forms of oneness, depends the whole operation of
consciousness and of learning and discovery by language
which we mentioned a little earlier.

What we have in the end is a situation where dialectic
depends on synthesis and rhetoric on analysis (the process

can go on backward indefinitely, so impossible is it to segregate these two). This holds good, by extension, for science and poetry and for reason and imagination. Each depends on the other for its very existence; and since they are so closely interdependent, we can resolve to hold to both of them and to be prepared to see in rhetoric no less than in dialectic a way in which the world of living forms may be thought about.

5

Man being no more, properly speaking, but intelligence, body and language, and language being as it were the mediator between the two substances of his nature

GRAMMAR, in one sense the most familiar member of the trivium, proves to be the hardest to grasp. This is not a weakness in the word, but a strength, an indication that we have here, as with philology, an essentially mythological, poetic, active field, which still awaits its due inquiry. The word has a considerable range of meanings (Renan says of the ancients that they were not dismayed by the extremely complex sense of their word for grammar),[22] and those meanings are all in movement: a choreography of language and mind, a pattern of action and behavior as Newman uses the word in *The Grammar of Assent* (1870). It is one of the dynamic forms of mind and words working together, that word "form" bringing with it an interesting doubleness, meaning both complete abstraction and bodily shape. With the help of grammar and form we will discuss our last two pairs of antitheses, mind and body, mathematics and words.

Inside the moving structures of mind and language,

there is a hint in grammatical theory and practice that the body is part of the working instrument active here. In other words, the body thinks. We are curiously inclined to think and speak as if the mind thought somewhere away by itself, and the body inside and through which it is doing its thinking could be ignored. Grammar does not treat language processes in this way. It treats them as bodily, and as sexual. There are general references to bodily life, such as the fact that verbs have "moods" and "voices," but the majority of references of this sort are to bodily fertility, as if it were the chief contribution of the body to language activity and thought: in "copula" and "conjugation" in grammatical terminology, and most of all in the phenomenon of gender in nouns, where not necessarily just the object referred to but the noun itself will have a gender, and the two may be independent of one another.

This can be regarded as a relic of a primitive age when all thought was "mythical" in the imperfect sense of that word, and every object was endowed with a life and personality of its own, masculine, feminine, or neuter. This may be true but the notion that myth stopped, and ought to stop, ages ago will blind us to something supported by language in other ways as well, that the fertility of the body cooperates in the processes of thinking with language. There remains a great unsolved problem behind this, as behind the use of such words as "fertile" or "pregnant" of ideas, of the verb "to conceive" in intellectual terms. To relegate these simply to metaphor is to miss the whole point, for they are clues to something that is going on in this field of myth we are exploring. Grammar maintains that the body is operative there as much as the mind.[23] The human organism thinks as a whole, and our division of it into mind and body is the result of overemphasis on logic and intellect in near isolation which has led us into so one-sided a view of the activity of thought, so gross an underestimation of the body's forms of thought and knowledge. This is where mathematics enters in also, for it has come to be regarded as an almost disembodied universe of discourse, wholly mental, intellectual, all the things which words and the body are not, the most abstract and advanced expression of pure form that we know. But perhaps form in mathematics and words can be thought of rather differently.

The formalism and rigorous necessity of mathematics make it more rather than less akin to those formalizing tendencies of matter and of body as body which we were thinking about a little while ago. If a system of necessary form is something we share with matter, logic or mathematical process may be thought of as an inherent characteristic of matter itself in its own progress toward form. If mathematical activity is a development and prolongation by the human mind of those activities by which matter, inanimate and animate, operates on itself, this might explain why the results of mathematical thinking can be referred back to matter with such signal success. The extent of the correlation between mathematics and physical reality in contemporary physics might be not an astonishing correspondence of apparent opposites but the family agreement of two terms of a similar progression. Mathematics may be the evidence not of man's emancipation from the material world but of his absolute solidarity with it.

If, for the living individual, the body is the original generator of forms, first its own form in structure and behavior, then forms which are in varying degrees separated from itself and which accordingly offer the mind-body scope for *its* formalizing tendencies, it may be true to say that all formal activity in the human mind has its origin and roots always in the physical. The mind-body may generate forms as languages or terms for metaphoric activity by which to understand itself and its experience; but all form, no matter how apparently abstract and intellectual, may never lose its connection with, its message for, the body. It seems possible that all forms observed by or constructed by the so-called mind are *Gestalten* or figures or forms in the recurring double sense of all those terms: that a figure is always an image; that a form, how abstract soever, calls forth from the body a physical response, is perceived as an image, if that is the right word, by the body which is the source of all forming activity.

Suppose that all forms are, whilst they are perceived as pure form by the mind-body, simultaneously perceived and enjoyed as images by the body-mind, if I may be allowed to shift that term so as to suggest a shift of emphasis. I do not mean that the body translates form, abstractly perceived, into pictures; rather, that all form addresses itself no less to the body than the mind, the former perceiving it by virtue of its own formalizing tendencies and uniting with it. The body mates with forms no less than the mind does. The more abstract they are, the more specialized, rarefied, perhaps even concealed an image they offer to the body; but that image is always there. This means that such constructions as logic, syntax, fugue, algebra, are enjoyed by the body as its own kith and kin. Those who do not respond to these webs of pure relation—the unmathematical, the unmusical—are no exception: they simply have not perceived the form in the first place, and consequently cannot respond to it with any part of themselves. The perception and glimpse of pure form—for instance, the moment when one first realizes, possibly very belatedly and in the teeth of all the education one has ever had, something of the point of mathematics—is accompanied by the double enjoyment of mind-body, the latter uniting itself with its fellow forms, even in that abstract state, no less surely than the former.

If the body always actively participates in all formal activity, including the most apparently abstract, the whole organism of self is equally always involved, as an open or hidden factor, in any of the figures by which we try to make sense of the world. At the level of myth which is that of the discovering, learning, thinking organism, the agent is never detached from the figures used. Indeed the agent frequently is the figure itself, and the notion of objectivity ceases to be useful. All formal operation is myth. Logic, under which we include all the highly developed forms of apparently purely formal mental activity, is a specialized form of mythologizing activity in which attention is not paid to the participation of the body, which is nonetheless, tacitly, part of the process and a vital part. That mathematics, for instance, is not a detached activity may be seen from the passion with which it is pursued and the use of such terms as "elegance" or "beauty" in connection with its workings. The relation between the organism and this purest of pure forms is in the end one of love, a function of mind and body jointly; and this is true of all the other forms which the human being can perceive, at whatever level. This suggests once again how mistaken is the notion that we progress, as individual or race, from metaphorical or poetical thinking to logic. The only choice for the mind lies not between mythology and logic but between an exclusive mythology which chooses to overlook the body's participation and an inclusive mythology which is prepared in varying degrees to admit the body, the notion of the organism as a whole, as a partner in that very odd operation known as thought.

Word-language, in the course of its development, has itself acquired two modes of operation, a more exclusive and an inclusive one. The first is prose, which does not necessarily recognize the agent's participation in the system of words and ideas under construction; the more it does so, the closer it may approach to poetry. Prose has as its aim to establish a form of words which shall be equivalent to experience, the self participating in the construction being disregarded. To examine an inclusive mythology we must turn to language's other mode, poetry. Here the inclusion of the participating self (poet or reader, it is all one) is open, deliberate, an active ingredient in what goes on. Poetry is the most inclusive form of thought we have yet devised, a conscious call upon those resources of myth which underlie all language and all thinking. If the self is involved in any working system of thought, whether it is recognized or not, poetry, with its recognition of the self's cooperation, is in fact nearest to reality. Exclusive mythology, in its preoccupation with abstract form, embarks on a wholesale game of make believe by the exclusion of the self. Poetry, metaphor, mythology are highly realistic and down to earth. It is logic and mathematics which are the imaginative and fantastical exercise.

With mathematics man invented, and goes on inventing, a mythology which could be regarded as nothing but form, by which to explain such forms in nature and experience as were patient of this approach. Word-language too has certain formal properties of its own, grammatical and other, as if it were a kind of mathematics. But it brings with it a new factor which alters the whole situation, making things at once much more difficult and full of greater possibilities. Words provide content as well as form. This is their incalculably great contribution to the five languages we spoke about earlier. By virtue of their content or meaning, words provide a double system of images and forms for the body and mind to work with in seeking to understand one system by another. Language has, as well as its own inner system, all the relations of the external world as connections between its elements, since words have the job of making sense, or truth. Thus form and content in

word-language—grammar and syntax together with sig-
nification—cannot be separated from one another, any
more than can mind and body in the individual. The re-
sult is that grammar becomes an area of constant inter-
change between form and content. Each of the two ele-
ments, form and content, reflects back on the other, and
both together make up the history of the mind. It seems
to be a recurring process in this field, and small wonder
after all—for what we have really just said is the tautology
that reflection is reflexive.

Grammar embodies and exemplifies this process. There
are certain classes of words in grammar, notably pronouns
and verbs, which are called "reflexive" by virtue of the
trick they have of reasserting the agent, doubling the ac-
tion back on the doer while at the same time carrying the
meaning forward. French has a good many such verbs;
so does German. There are not very many left in English.
"To enjoy oneself" is an example; so is "to bethink one-
self," and though I do not want to make such a word, al-
ready slightly archaic, bear more than it should, there
may be a clue here to the nature of mythological activity
in thought, to be arrived at through grammar and lan-
guage. Everything that thinks thinks about its thinking
while also thinking about all sorts of other things. All
arts may set the mind moving in this way; language and
poetry will pursue it through the special contributions of
meaning and the inclusion of the body and the self, "while
biology itself appears in its turn as a process of life reflect-
ing on itself" (Polanyi, *Personal Knowledge*).

We can now, after a long detour, come back to Orpheus,
with an added reason for abiding by him. It might be
asked, why Orpheus in particular? Would not any mythical
figure serve for the exploration of myth? Yes, probably;
but in this particular story, mythology is considering, in
the person of the poet, the power and the fate of poetry

or thinking or myth. In the Orpheus story, myth is looking at itself. This is the reflection of myth in its own mirror. It promises to give Orpheus a special significance: for myth as living thought and the very type of thought in action, and for all those other reflexive or self-reflecting forms; for the human organism as an indivisible whole trying to understand itself and its universe; for language and poetry reflecting back to the organism its own countenance and activity; for biology reflecting on the whole span of life in which thinking man appears as the last enigmatic development.

6

Consciousness, life, and thought are not far from winning the right to a scientific existence

MOST BIOLOGISTS would deny that their science can possibly keep such questionable company. That is absolutely all right, just as it is perfectly all right for anyone who finds them helpful to go on using the antitheses we have thrown out. No one opinion excludes or invalidates others in these speculative fields. It is only necessary to make clear what principles one proposes to work with oneself. All that has been and will be said about biology here is said from the poet's point of view. This has its disadvantages, for one is of necessity an outsider. Perhaps this is not entirely a disadvantage, however, for we are in danger of forgetting that sciences and arts and poetry and all the occupations of man are directed not toward specialists but toward ordinary people. So we can give ourselves ordinary people's scope here and make our own constructions and mistakes.

Biology's own attitude to itself is, for the poet, one of the most interesting features of this whole area, for it is next to impossible to discover. The outsider looking at biology not for the facts it has to offer but for its methods of selection, classification, and general principles is bound to be struck by the real difficulty of finding out any of these things. One gets no help from the discipline itself —with one or two exceptions, of which Lamarck is the most outstanding; and perhaps his incursion into *Philosophie zoologique* did him no good in the rigorists' eyes. Biology seems to show a marked apathy or resistance to formulating the principles on which its thinking works. There has been a good deal of interchange between biology and philosophy in Germany, much of it rather confusing, accounting for the ill-repute into which *Naturphilosophie* fell in the later nineteenth century. But there is no equivalent in this branch of science of practitioners of first-rate importance who were themselves concerned with self-examination, seeking to assess the principles of their discipline, its scope and potentialities. Here biology differs widely from mathematics and physics. The outside reader has therefore to do a good deal of groping in the dark, looking for methodological principles implicit in the works themselves but never clearly stated at any length.

This characteristic of biological thinking, a refusal of self-consciousness, may provide a clue to something that is going on. There is a very real problem at this spot. Biology has, as we have already discussed, adopted as a model for itself the conventional exact scientific methodology, with its exclusion of the observer as anything other than transparent or invisible mind, so to speak, observing processes which can be figured by that detached mind as determined mechanisms. His body, which he thinks inside of, or with, and his language, which he thinks inside of, or with, are to be excluded—that is to say, ignored or pretended out of existence. The desirable end product of this maneuver would be, for biology, wholly intellectual mind thinking about, ordering, and comprehending wholly material body.

So the very continuity which biology so splendidly affirms in the sweep and organization of its subject matter, the continuous development and process in time, is broken by awkward intrusions such as thought, consciousness, speech, which are left out of account—science holding them to be, as Sherrington said of just these phenomena, "none of her business," while at the same time saying a little earlier in the same book, "Nature and Evolution deal with the individual, body and mind together, as a unity." [24] Nature and evolution may, but biologists do not; and to have one's method totally different, in form, from what one is investigating leads to considerable difficulty. For all ways of thinking at their best establish a relationship between the formal properties of the system of thought being employed and certain properties in the subject matter. This is the central problem; there are other minor difficulties too, such as, for instance, the fact that the body is not so easily pretended away in biological studies which frequently demand a very high degree of skill and coordination of eye and hand as well as more abstract mental dexterities.

Biology has mistaken its mythology. It needs poetry rather than mathematics or language-as-science to think with; not an exclusive but an inclusive mythology to match the principle of inclusion inherent in all of its living and organic and synthetic subject matter. Its failure has added to the difficulties of the other boundary sciences we were talking about, for biology occupies a key position among them and its refusal to think fully with language has clamped down on the whole area, imprisoning us, as Teilhard de Chardin says, in old habits of thought which try to restrict the world to their own narrowness. Its fellow disciplines have for a hundred and fifty years or so been asking it for a lead. But biology had nothing to offer but an unsuitable method which it held as a dogma, and which even then and still more so now, is out of date, as Goethe already saw.

To turn poetry toward biology and to suggest a closer relationship between them is only to follow in a long line of similar suggestions made by other disciplines. Lamarck says as early as 1809 that the zoologist is bound to think about thought, an extension which is pleaded by outsider after outsider, without further response. Comte claims that all the analytical work of biology is only the preamble to its essential activity which has to do with man, and man as a social being. Renan in 1849 tries in *L'Avenir de la science* to move toward some more general synthesis of disciplines beyond those ordinarily accepted by the professionals, putting in a particular plea for an evolutionary point of view and an inclusion of language, poetry, and religion. Sainte-Beuve asks in his turn for an extension of biology to "l'homme morale," as a help in the development of his own art of literary criticism. Later there is Lévy-Bruhl, whose doubts about scientific method we have already considered, and Bergson; and we will consider in a moment what has been happening in the last twenty or thirty years. There is no doubt about the need, a need which Gestalt psychology tried and failed to satisfy.

There is comedy in this spectacle of biology, itself very uncertain where it stands, being solicited on all sides and urged toward greater inclusiveness by disciplines whose status, as pure and respectable science, was shakier even than biology's own, and whose attentions could only be highly compromising. But if biology's dilemma and absolute lack of response to these requests is amusing, it is at the same time a perfectly proper and honorable position. Had it accepted the exact science's figure of exactitude, and thrown in its lot with mathematics wholeheartedly, there would be no problem, and no hope of advance. The recognition and acting out of a difficulty, even if the recognition is only implicit and finds little expression beyond hesitation and negation, is in itself a contribution. After all, biology is a comparative newcomer among the disciplines. Like most of our thinking it goes back to the Greeks, but did not really get started till the Renaissance, and even then was a slow starter. It has as yet no equivalent to the long magisterial tradition of mathematics and physics, and this is just what we might expect. The problems of biology in finding its instrument depend on the fact that that instrument, language, is the hardest of all and is only being developed slowly, with a long way still to go. Biology has lacked the kind of fully developed instrument of thought needed for its own special organic subject matter.

We are still only in the early stages of knowing how to make use of the very complex instrument which language offers us, with its double nature of form and content and its inclusion of the working agent as part of the process. But in language lies the possibility of elaborating an inclusive mythology by which to understand all those areas of experience not suitably figured by mathematics and exclusive mythology or by the other three arts or languages we have at our disposal. It is this instrument which is needed for thinking about living material. And it is poetry's task to learn how to manage this kind of thinking and then to teach it. Poetry puts language to full use as a means of thought, exploration, and discovery, and we have only so far just about made a beginning and no more on its potential usefulness.

The argument put forward here may result merely in estranging both sides. For if to a biologist it may seem ludicrous to suggest that poetry has a vital bearing on his discipline, it will be no less shocking to those who dwell in the—as they suppose—opposite camp to suggest that poetry is highly useful and is bound, in nature, to justify it-

self biologically.[25] It has become customary to exempt po-
etry and the arts in general from having to be useful.
Indeed, their uselessness has at times been raised to the
virtue almost of a principle of conscience.[26] This is gen-
erally the view of those who set art in opposition to utili-
tarian science as they conceive of it. We prefer to think
that both are useful, varying mythologies or figures for
the mind, interdependent at every step, with poetry as the
most perfect development of word-language to which is
allotted the task of empowering as medium and instrument
all the middle ranges of our thinking, including thinking
about living things and ourselves. Poetry is one of our
most practical inventions, but it is not completed and
never will be. The poetic tradition to date is the record of
what we have done and are doing with it, and in that tra-
dition lie the seeds of further development along these
lines.

It is going to be the theme of the rest of this book that
for the last 400 years, with the coming of what one might
call the modern age, poetry has been struggling to evolve
and perfect the inclusive mythology on which language
works and all thought in words is carried on, and that this
type of thinking is the only adequate instrument for think-
ing about change, process, organisms, and life. The history
of this struggle and evolution is occasionally explicit, more
often implicit. This is where Orpheus comes in: for Or-
pheus is poetry thinking about itself, and every significant
mention of Orpheus by a poet or scientist may bring the
working methods a little nearer the surface, make them
easier to grasp than they will be when they are bound up
with all the other things poets think and write of. For we
are not saying this is poetry's sole task; poetry has not one
task but many, which is why all approaches to it are allow-
able. We shall hear what the Orphic voices have to say on
this matter. One of these is Linnaeus, the man who de-

cided to name and classify the organic world by means not of a new symbolic formula but word-language, perhaps a decision whose significance has been overlooked, suggesting as it does a recognition, even if only half conscious, that living things can only be dealt with in their organic relationships by means of words. It is this man whom we find saying, in one of the addresses called *Amoenitas Academici* (1790), "Deberem dicere de . . . Orpheo, ejusque voce divina," I ought to speak of Orpheus and his divine voice —this among the *Deliciae Naturae*. Here is a point at which the naturalist and Orpheus, natural history and poetry, had not parted company, and it only remains to try to bring them, after their long and wintry estrangement, back to one another.

7

Poetry was no longer a strange and irrelevant loveliness in a chaotic world; it was a necessary and consummate flowering on the great tree of life; it was the immanent purpose of the universe made vocal

THE TASK is becoming not the invention of something new but a revaluation and a making explicit of a long tradition. For that reason it will be helpful to gather up the voices in the immediate past which belong to this tradition too, all of whom have been saying, from their widely differing standpoints, that thinking needs rethinking on lines other than those currently accepted in the various academic disciplines, if modern thought is to reach out to its living material in dynamic ways and overcome the artificial barriers which have been allowed to hedge it in, the division between arts and sciences, for instance.

Things have been moving this way fairly steadily since the twenties. Names which come to mind are Agnes Arber, Teilhard de Chardin, Evelyn Hutchinson, Suzanne Langer, John Middleton Murry, Michael Polanyi, Herbert Read, Rebecca West, Lance Whyte. The disciplines involved range from archaeology and anthropology, botany, chemistry, zoology, and physics through philosophy and social thought to plastic art and literature. These are our immediate masters. Past these and past Gestalt psychology the principal line of descent goes back to the Romantics. George Boas, writing of *Our New Ways of Thinking* in 1930, points out the foreshadowing of this type of thought in "certain Romantic Germans, notably Schelling." [27] Jacques Barzun calls the shift of outlook which Romanticism brought about "a Biological Revolution." [28] Middleton Murry, describing the origins of his *Metabiology* says, "I became conscious that I was working towards a new theory of Romanticism." [29] And alongside Murry's own work on Keats may be ranged Herbert Read's *Studies in Romantic Poetry*, while in his turn Evelyn Hutchinson invokes Blake to elucidate the vision of Rebecca West.[30] In Cassirer the Romantics appear as the rediscoverers of mythology and of Vico's work. Goethe, as biologist and artist, is frequently mentioned (in Arber, Murry, Whyte, Polanyi, for instance). And it is Murry who takes us back one stage further, to the point at which we ourselves shall begin. "The Renaissance . . . is the beginning of modern Romanticism. Shakespeare is its prophetic voice." [31]

It is interesting to see that this tradition coincides fairly closely with the Orpheus lineage we drew up for ourselves in Section 1, and we can begin to draw up our own plan for tracing, above the surface and below, the work done on mythology, this flexible and exquisitely adjusted instrument for biological thought. We shall stick to the Orpheus line, starting with Bacon and Shakespeare, with a look backward at Sidney and forward at Milton; then move through Vico, Swedenborg, and Linnaeus to Erasmus Darwin and Goethe; then to the Romantics; and so through nineteenth-century France to Rilke, whose *Sonette an Orpheus* are the most recent statement of the theme.

Before we move ourselves back 400 years, however, there is one more point to be made. Our own method has to be mythological if it is to work properly, and so we shall use Orpheus and his story not merely as a guide but as an imaginative framework as well for our own constructions, figuring that there may have been a progression in this kind of thinking over the period we shall traverse, and the progression of the story may help us with it. The first period, Shakespearean and Baconian, will fall under the first part of the story, where Orpheus exercises his power over rocks and trees and animals. Eurydice and the journey to love and death will uphold the Goethean stage, and the Romantics; and with Rilke there will be the final high and mysterious figure, the severed prophetic head unconquered even in its destruction, and the human music among the stars, by the help of which we shall have to set poetry's face forward if we can. For poetry's task, for all of us, is to be not the nostalgic and complaining thing it has become in so many quarters, as if the modern air did not suit its delicate constitution, but what it has always been meant to be, an instrument of immense power with a scarcely foreseeable but wholly positive future.

PART II
Bacon and Shakespeare: Postlogical Thinking

1

To think of nature as a poem hidden in a secret and mysterious writing

IN ENGLAND something happened to thought between 1600 and 1610. It happened in the persons of Bacon and Shakespeare, our two great thinkers at that time. The results of what happened can be seen in their work. This transformation of thinking was effected and suffered (the two in this kind of operation being one and the same) by two minds apparently different yet fundamentally so similarly directed that their names have kept cropping up together ever since, in opposition, conjunction, or even identification. What they accomplished was a "Renaissance" action in the best sense, for they drew, out of a classical tradition as old as poetry, which is as old as language and thinking, the lines of possible development for the future. So they are balanced between new and old, men at once profoundly traditional and also, perhaps because of that, even more profoundly prophetic and forward-looking.[1]

With this new stage in a long development we begin our natural history. The evidence consists of the writings of the two men, but we should be clear from the start about what is happening. We are not observing in detachment a clearly defined, rational event. We are assisting at a metamorphosis.

The first figure of the Orpheus story calls up such a transformation. It is so well known, Orpheus playing to beasts and the mountain tops that freeze and plants and flowers and so on, in the words of that song from *King Henry VIII*, that it seems overfamiliar and banal, like those tasteless Bible pictures where lions lie down with lambs in an impossible countryside, and the imagination is not moved to recognize any sort of reality. It is curious but I think true that we always picture the scene, perhaps because of the "sun and showers" of that best-known of Orpheus lyrics, as taking place in the clear light of day. It will help the figure to help us—by waking a jaded imagination and incidentally by producing a much closer image of our own state in this inquiry—if we shift the happening from day into night. Imagine, then, something happening in a night which includes ourselves, the singer in almost complete darkness in which his reordering of creation has just begun, but as if it were a dream he is having, or that of the beasts whose masks, fierce or gentle, appear suddenly like emblems or heraldic devices out of the darkness only to puzzle the mind catching at beauty and significance which vanish again from moment to moment; or even the still less explicable dream of the moving trees and stones, sliding to a pattern not their own. Nothing is seen except in glimpses, a phantasmagoria out of which nevertheless a world of new order is shaping, half unknown to the one who wields the power and suffers the terror that accompanies all transformation.

Orpheus and myth are the methods for our natural history, and they warrant a figure of darkness for they are in themselves riddles, dark sayings, hieroglyphics, in that field where minds and language engender their productions of thought. We shall meet Orpheus and classical myth explicitly in Shakespeare and Bacon and elsewhere in this period, for Greek and Roman mythology flourished in Renaissance England, and Orpheus is one of the favorite figures. Bacon discusses, retells, and interprets myths; Shakespeare is steeped in Ovid (either direct or at secondhand by translation only, as critics discuss).[2] One part of our task is to see what Bacon and Shakespeare make of Orpheus and classic mythology, and this leads on to that wider field which I am calling "myth," the activity between mind and language in poetry whereby the mind invents new models and methods to understand new things.

I am going to assume that the *Magna Instauratio,* of which the *Novum Organum* forms part,[3] is just such a living myth, that it can be explored in poetic and mythological terms and compared with works such as *King Lear.* One of the aims of such works (which does not exclude others) is the discovery, fostering, and development of poetic and mythological thought. I shall call this postlogical thinking or, more briefly, postlogic.

In the first stage of the Orpheus story we shall be restricted to thinking about natural phenomena, those three great orders of stones, plants, and animals which are drawn in the myth under Orpheus' power. It may be that the method of thinking which Shakespeare and Bacon propose is designed to draw the mind and body into a closer working relationship with these things, and to help it to understand its own nature by means of them. To limit Bacon and Shakespeare to this range would be absurd; it is ourselves we shall limit, for we have enough to cope with as it is, groping about in the dark with our own beginnings. Thinking about human nature must wait until Orpheus can carry us forward to it. But even at this stage, and even though in darkness, Orpheus will help, standing as he does for the reflection of myth upon its own nature.

From that time Orpheus betook himself to solitary places . . . where, by the same sweetness of his song

and lyre, he drew to him all kinds of wild beasts, in
such manner that . . . they all stood about him
gently and sociably, as in a theatre, listening only to
the concords of his lyre. Nor was that all: for so great
was the power of his music that it moved the woods
and the very stones to shift themselves and take their
station décently and orderly about him.

This is Bacon's description of the scene, in *De Sapientia
Veterum*, published in 1609.[4] Its grave dignity is charac-
teristic of its writer. If nature is set dancing by Orpheus,
in Bacon's scheme of things that dance is stately and meas-
ured. It takes quite another form in Shakespeare, who
speaks of Orpheus as one

Whose golden touch could soften steel and stones,
Make tigers tame, and huge leviathans
Forsake unsounded deeps to dance on sands,
                    (*The Two Gentlemen of Verona*, III.2)

We have here two differing conceptions of the Orphic
activity. Bacon, who recounts the whole of the myth, be-
gins by offering his interpretation. "The story of Orpheus,"
he says, "which though so well known has not yet been in
all points perfectly well interpreted, seems meant for a
representation of universal Philosophy. For Orpheus him-
self,—a man admirable and truly divine, who being master
of all harmony subdued and drew all things after him by
sweet and gentle measures,—may pass by an easy metaphor
for philosophy personified." Shakespeare's introduction
takes the form of one marvelous line:

For Orpheus' lute was strung with poets' sinews.

These two visions of Orpheus suggest that here we have
two things to think about. First, the two passages fall in
quite naturally with the distinction we make nowadays

between poetry and philosophy. Secondly, each writer identifies himself—as he sees himself—with Orpheus. To the poet, Orpheus' instrument is the poet's body. To the philosopher, Orpheus is the embodiment of philosophy.

Shakespeare's figure is, in a sense, simple. In that splendid, painful metaphor he unites himself, as poet, immediately with the Orphic power and becomes the myth he is describing, that inclusive myth we were talking about earlier where instrument and agent are one. The image holds also a muted anguish at the notion of being strung, fiber by fiber, on something. It almost suggests the rack in those tight, drawn sinews, with a further hint of intimate dissection, for sinews used as lute strings can come only from a body that has been unpicked. It is as if the finale of the Orpheus story were present also, poets sharing of necessity the dismemberment of their master. Orpheus draws from Shakespeare the declaration that, body and mind, the poet is his own instrument; and when we look for Shakespeare's own myth in his work, the active moving principle of organism and language in form and content, we shall find there a complete integrity, the moving-all-of-one-piece which befits such a poet. This simplicity makes our task doubly difficult. The more perfect and unitary a system, the harder it is to find your way in.

This is why we shall turn our attention to Bacon first. For Bacon is not simple. His Orpheus is already doubled back upon itself. Orpheus is philosophy, says Bacon—that is, poetry and myth are philosophy; but Bacon is in his own eyes a philosopher, and so by his metaphor he is made one with the Orpheus myth—and the imaginative fusion of self and instrument and subject matter is a poetic, not a philosophic, way of thinking.

Doubleness, ambiguity, and contradiction are the essential characteristics of this man and his work. We think we know, by virtue of general knowledge and often without reading him, what Bacon was about. He is ranked as a philosopher, the innovator or supporter of inductive reasoning and the experimental method in science, opponent of Aristotelian logic, forerunner of utilitarianism and the development of technology,[5] a figure in the history of scientific and social philosophy. Yet this widespread image of Bacon proves, when looked into, to be completely untrustworthy.

There is controversy about the nature of his method, about his crucial contribution to thought, about his importance or the reasons for it. Some maintain he was not himself clear on these matters.[6] The volume of disagreement must be almost without parallel in literary history. Here are some examples: Bacon is the Moses of the new experimental science (Cowley), a spiritual ancestor of the founding of the Royal Society (Sprat), a genius in the history of science (Macaulay), the prophet of modern science (James); he is the most terrible enemy science has ever had (de Maistre), a dilettante insufficiently informed in scientific matters (Fowler). He was interested in method, but his inquiries proved fruitless (James); we do not really know what his method was (Dean Church, Ellis); he tries to shift logic into time (Farrington); he is deficient in logic (Macaulay). He insists on the importance of abstract ideas (Ellis); he can think in no form but the concrete (de Maistre). His notion of a natural history is what is most important (Spedding); it is unimportant (Ellis, Robertson). His doctrine of forms is his most important contribution (James), a forerunner of modern concepts of matter (Farrington, Whyte); it is quite extraneous to Bacon's system (Ellis).[7]

It seems we know next to nothing about Bacon. He is held to be important, although it is not clear why. He is concerned with a new kind of thinking or method, which has to do with power over nature, with natural history and an understanding of forms, whatever he means by that; this can be gathered from his work. And that work vibrates with a passion of excitement which he communicates, unexplained, to his reader. On one point all those who write about him agree: he has a marvelous power of words.

A man dealing with the moving and changing forms of natural things, organic and inorganic, who enchants us without our knowing why by thought and words, which are also what he is thinking about—this suggests not a philosopher in the modern sense at all but a myth-maker. It is Bacon's most implacable opponent, de Maistre, who throws him this very title: "his writings, considered as fables, are still very entertaining." [8] The qualified title of poet is allowed to Bacon by several of his critics and biographers,[9] but it is to the poets themselves to whom we turn for ratification of the title, to Shelley and Poe.

The Orpheus line of descent among the poets establishes its own subsidiary lines of spiritual heredity, whereby later Orphic voices recognize and acknowledge their ancestors. So it is Shelley who in his *Defence of Poetry* says, "Lord Bacon was a poet." We shall take this to be true, and consider Bacon from now on as a dark, riddling, emblematic poet, struggling with a metamorphosis of his own thinking and of man's power over the universe, a counterpart of the darkling Orpheus with whom we began. Poets of this kind are not common, and a second example will be helpful, the mind that struggles to interpret itself and the universe in Poe's *Eureka*. In his essay Poe mentions Bacon, but with his characteristic wrongheadedness (equaled only by Bacon's own) mentions him only in derision, rejecting Deduction and Aristotle, and Induction and Bacon, and going on to exalt imaginative speculation as the true form of scientific thinking. The first part of the passage exhibits Poe at his most vulgar, and he must have had a particular liking for it, since it appears twice in his work, in the story *Mellonta Tauta* as well as in *Eureka*. One strongly suspects that Poe knew Bacon only by hearsay, for even he could hardly have failed to recognize in the *Magna Instauratio* a mind attempting the same kind of task as his own in *Eureka,* a reshaping of thought about the universe, a suppressed excitement, a splendor of language, a preoccupation with science, and a feeling that the poet has a new way of thinking about the world. Bacon and Poe resemble each other, too, in that each found and displayed something other than he thought he had found. Poe through a vast cosmology displays the workings of the poetic mind. What Bacon displays we have yet to work out.

For all his unevenness, however, Poe's endeavor has greater unity than Bacon's. He took the precaution, or had the insight, to preface *Eureka* with the injunction, "Nevertheless, it is as a Poem only that I wish this work to be judged after I am dead." Bacon knows no such unity of purpose. It is not that he was a poet who thought himself a philosopher, as his version of Orpheus at first sight suggests. He was a poet who did not trust poetry.

2

They contain some haunting beauty that is mysteriously knit up with some vaguely apprehended truth . . . They are not merely beautiful, or they could be admired and let us go; they are not merely true, or they could be understood and put away

THE FIRST ORPHEUS figure we are using, the singer who moves a world in darkness, is a figure of movement and change. We are hoping by it to see what Bacon and Shakespeare will tell us of a poet and his powers, but we shall learn nothing unless we are ready to submit to it and to change ourselves; and we have to begin here and now.

We have first to recognize the disadvantages of twentieth-century minds in coming to an understanding even of conventional mythology. Our rigidity of mind and a sense of superiority are bred and educated into us. To connect mythology and science seems to us unlikely enough, while to go back to Bacon for help in that quest after the "Wisdom of the Ancients," which will take us yet farther back —into fable and myth—may seem absurd. Yet we have to do both these things now; and possibly each stage in this inquiry may challenge our conventionalisms. We have to believe that the "ancients," Bacon among them, meant what they said, and, at least as much as we ourselves, talked sense. It is not a question of abdicating from any knowledge which modern minds possess. It is more a matter of new beliefs.

A second disadvantage has to do with history. We have two great periods of interest in mythology behind us. The first was the Renaissance, when mythology meant classical Greek and Roman mythology. The second was the nineteenth century, when the scope of mythology was broadened to include the myths of the world. Each period has a similar shape. In its opening, one Orphic voice proclaims what is necessary for understanding and developing mythology as an instrument of inquiry. A few later minds can hear what this voice has said, but the instrument ends each time by being broken in prolonged battles. By the end of the first period myths had become mechanical ornament, affronts to desirable common sense,[10] or even burlesques. At the end of the second period, where we now find ourselves, myth, ill-comprehended and isolated from its fellow disciplines, has gone from poetry and is consigned uneasily to two branches of science, anthropology and psychology.[11]

If we are to learn about myth, we must first of all go back to those two Orphic harbingers. They will tell us what to believe. We are not going to ask them what myth is, not being yet in a position to put that question. What they can suggest is how we must modify ourselves in order to find out; they can give us back the instrument they originally offered, since broken in our hands.

The first voice, back in the late fifteenth century, is Pico della Mirandola. Bacon knew and quoted his work.[12] The second, nearer, voice, more anguished but unanimous with that serene predecessor 300 years earlier, is Hölderlin, the contemporary of Goethe and Schelling, who has been only recently restored, as if out of the darkness into which his mind fell in the latter half of his life, to his due rank as a prophetic poet of the first order. What is the message of these two?

What Pico della Mirandola set out to do, in his *De Dignitate Hominis,* was in the first place to show how mythology, Christian theology, and natural philosophy could be regarded as a unity. By a gesture of high intellectual courtesy he gives to pagan myths the title of the theology of the ancients, and seeks to establish correspondences between these mysteries and those of Moses and Christ. For Pico, however, it is not just a question of reconciling two theologies; there is a second step in the process, for these mysteries are connected with natural philosophy and the secrets of nature. Where we should speak of science, Pico speaks of magic, as a name for that high knowledge and power which he was seeking (as Bacon was), but which he distinguishes meticulously from evil magic. Pico's "magic" is this, in his own words: "Altera nihil est aliud, cum bene exploratur, quam naturalis philosophiae absoluta consummatio." Theology, mythology, and natural philosophy are, in conjunction, the means to this end, tending toward "profundissimam rerum secretissimarum contemplationem, et demum totius naturae cognitionem." For Pico, Orpheus and his mysteries are veiled theology and natural philosophy, while Apollo is philosopher as well as poet and the true Apollo is Christ. He does not argue, though arguments on this score were ancient even in his day. He simply unites the three disciplines on a footing of mutual charity, as forms of inquiry into the better understanding of the world.

Hölderlin, in the different language of his time, says the same thing. In his late poem *Der Einzige* he unites, though with a troubled questioning which is absent in

Pico, the Greek gods with Christ in a common bond of
love and in relationship with the world of nature. In an-
other, shorter, poem, *Die scheinheiligen Dichter* or seem-
ing-holy poets, he makes a great protest against myth being
used simply as empty ornament; here, too, belief in the
gods, in a due and loving sense, is joined with a turning
toward nature and our need to understand it. Here is a
rough translation:

> Cold lying mouths, how dare you name the Gods!
> Reason's your line. You never gave belief
> To Helios, the Thunderer, the Sea-God.
> The earth is dead—and shall we thank you for it?
>
> Take comfort, Gods! for still you bless the song
> Though from your names the soul of life is fled;
> And should we need a high and reverent word,
> All-mothering Nature—that shall serve our turn.

Each voice says that myth as a discipline of inquiry is
to be united with theology and science (as I shall call nat-
ural philosophy for the present) in the endeavor to dis-
cover and comprehend the universe; and so for Pico Or-
pheus is a bearer of secret and mysterious teaching. Also
we have in some sense to believe in myth as in those other
two disciplines, before we can learn from it; and so for
Hölderlin, Orpheus is the bearer of a love which embraces
the whole universe and runs from heaven to hell.[13] I pro-
pose that we should accept this, seeing myth as part of the
corpus of learning and giving it its meed of belief, as a
means to truth and reality. But in that case we had better
think about what this implies.

Christian theology in its speculative aspect, mythology
or poetry, and science are three disciplines of discovery
and learning. They differ in their subject matter; they are
united in their structure and aim. Thought of in this way,

they may all three appear less as a body of knowledge, something you possess, than as a particular activity founded on an appropriate set of beliefs. Much of religion, apart from dogma, seems to fit with this. Myth we have already thought of as an activity, and are inquiring into the beliefs behind it; and it is becoming gradually clear that, as Goethe saw, science too can be regarded in this way.[14] These three disciplines do not merely have a common structure. They have a common aim. That is truth, taken in its most simple everyday sense.

For each of these disciplines, to deny its obligation to truth is to deny its whole existence. It is fatal to say of myth and poetry that it is beautiful but a lie; or to say of religion that it is morally useful even if only symbolic; or of science that its first duty is to practical or political ends and not to truth. When this is done, beauty and moral expediency and practical usefulness disappear, for they are inseparable from the obligation to truth. With myth and poetry, no truth, no beauty, as was found out in the eighteenth century [15] and as we are finding out in our own wasteland nowadays. The denial of one discipline's truth usually took place because another discipline was claiming truth as its own private monopoly. This meant the loss of the charity in which they are founded and in which Pico and Hölderlin rooted them. When they fight each other, the whole endeavor of learning is maimed, each discipline is weakened by isolation, and in the end, as we have learned in the last forty years, all three are liable to be laid waste by an external aggressor in the form of a state system which denies freedom to literature, science, and religion alike, and admits no obligation to truth at all. If the three disciplines had not been so busy fighting one another for hundreds of years, they might have seen this danger more clearly. But in this respect our history is one long noisy battle.

In the more recent period science was the main aggressor, claiming, as it still does in many quarters, an exclusive primacy of certainty and truth. In the first period religion was on the attack, the Catholic establishment tussling with Galileo, the Puritan *franc-tireurs* battling with myth.[16] In each period there is a great Orphic casualty in the battle. In the modern period, it is Renan. Renan, in adopting science, feels he must renounce religion and myth, but he cannot cure himself of his love for them, and in *L'Avenir de la science* argues in favor of a reunion of the disciplines, as Newman was to do from a different standpoint. Renan goes further, for he hints that belief, in some sense, is necessary if we are to understand myth at all, and is indeed the true scientific attitude toward it. But he sees this as a task for the future, saying of the synthesis, "Alors il y aura de nouveau des Orphée."

The Orphic casualty of the first period is Milton. He, like his counterpart Renan, espouses the discipline which is on the attack, in this case religion, and supposes that it excludes him from admitting myth as well, except as ornament secularly hallowed by classical traditions and scholarship. By Milton's time there was already a history of attacks by Puritans, on religious grounds, against poetry—particularly poetic drama—and myth. It begins with Gosson's *Schoole of Abuse* in 1579, to which Sidney replies in his *Apologie for Poesie*. (But even for Sidney the religious question was so ticklish that the theologian is omitted from the great list of disciplines of learning which he gives in the *Apologie;* similarly Bacon insulates his religious beliefs, which he firmly held and nobly expressed, from his thought on science or myth, and even so did not escape the charge of atheism.) The attack reaches a climax in *Histriomastix* (1633), with a marvelous prodigal wealth of invective. There are various counts in the indictment. One is that of immorality, "the very Rapes, Adulteries, Mur-

thers, Thefts, Deceites, Lasciviousnesse, and other exe-
crable Villanies of Dung-Hill, Idole, Pagan-gods and God-
desses," as Prynne puts it. The other two accusations are
those of idolatry and lying. They frequently occur together,
and continue for a surprisingly long time.[17]

Milton raises the question of the truth of myth in his
latest Orpheus reference, the opening of Book VII of *Para-
dise Lost*. The progress of Orpheus through Milton's work
is interesting. In *L'Allegro* and *Il Penseroso*, which are
primarily secular and have no deep bearing on the nature
of the poet or of poetry, Orpheus can come and go freely,
in connection with music, as if he were freed from content
and could appear as pure form. In *Lycidas*, as Rachel
Trickett has pointed out (in *Essays and Studies*, 1953),
Orpheus represents the poet's task and its agonies, and in-
troduces the passage where first Apollo and then Saint
Peter make their appearance in a rather uneasy sequence.
In *Paradise Lost* Orpheus embodies Milton's thought
about the poet's vocation in the great invocation to Urania
as heavenly muse: "The meaning, not the name I call."
The poet is in darkness which is not merely Milton's
blindness, that great allegorical suffering, nor the threaten-
ing of outward circumstance, though both these are pres-
ent,

> In darkness, and with dangers compast round
> And solitude;

it is also the darkness of an Orphic mind torn from its
proper synthesis of religion and myth and knowledge of
the universe. As in *Lycidas*, the singing and wonder-
working Orpheus becomes the dismembered corpse,

> In *Rhodope*, where Woods and Rocks had Eares
> To rapture, till the savage clamor dround
> Both Harp and Voice; nor could the Muse defend

Her Son. So fail not thou, who thee implores,
For thou are Heav'nlie, shee an empty dreame.

Is myth, then, an empty dream? It is a question which exercised many minds in Bacon's time, and rightly, for it is profoundly important. An immense theme lies here: the relation of the world of creation, and of poetry, to the Logos. It is out of reach of the theme to which this study will be limited. But upon theology and what it stands for depends that charity of learning which Pico and Hölderlin proposed for us, and in the end the appeal to truth returns there. It is a moral and religious issue, and it tacitly upholds and binds together poetry and natural philosophy or science, in the sixteenth or any other century.

3

Thus you see that poets may lye if they list *Cum privilegio*. But what if they lye least of all other men? what if they lye not at all?

AN AGE in its own eyes and in ours may look very different. We think of the Elizabethan period as almost a golden age for poetry and plays and myth. To the Elizabethans it did not seem so. "In this iron and malitious age of ours . . . it is hard to find in these days of noblemen or gentlemen any good Mathematician, or excellent Musitian, or notable Philosopher, or els a cunning Poet." That is Puttenham in *The Arte of English Poesie* (1589). Sidney complains that poor poetry is fallen to be the laughingstock of children. Bacon says of myths that they are left commonly to boys and grammarians and held in slight repute (*De Augmentis Scientiarum*, Bk. II, chap. 13); he adds of the stage plays of his time: "of corruptions in this kind we have enough; but the discipline has in our times been plainly neglected." (The probable date for the writing of this, Spedding conjectures, is 1605.)

The tone tends to be polemical: poetry and myths are felt to be under attack. As early as 1545 Ascham is saying in his *Toxophilus*, "Even as I am not so fonde but I knowe that these be fables, so I am sure you be not so ignoraunt,

but you knowe what suche noble wittes as the Poetes had,
ment by such matters: which oftentimes under the cover-
ing of a fable, do hyde and wrappe in goodlie preceptes
of philosophie, with the true judgement of thinges."
Ascham hits off the point exactly. It concerned the con-
nection between poetry and philosophy and the universe.
This is why Bacon's poetical-philosophical Orpheus is so
central a figure. Poetry and myth had to be justified. The
appeal to antiquity, though strong in an age which
had so much veneration for tradition, was felt to be
insufficient. Why had the ancients so written, and
what value was there in their "fables" and in poetry in
general?

Orpheus accompanies the discussion. He appears in Sid-
ney's *Apologie,* and in Bishop Thomas Sprat's *History of
the Royal Society of London* written in 1665–66. Here, it
seems, is poetry ranged against science, and one might ex-
pect the writers to differ widely on the relation of poetry
to philosophy, science, reality, and truth. In fact they
agree to a surprising extent, as a set of parallel passages
will show:

Sidney	*Sprat*
Orpheus, Linus, and some oth- ers are named, who having been the first of that country that made pens deliverers of their knowledge to posterity, may justly challenge to be called their fathers in learning.	Hence it came to pass, that the first Masters of Knowledge amongst them, were as well Poets as Philosophers; for Orpheus, Linus, Musaeus, and Homer first softened Man's natural rudeness.

Sidney a little earlier had spoken of philosophy used to
the defacing of poetry, "with great danger of civil war
among the Muses." Both writers then agree on the original
unity of poetry and philosophy. Each accepts the fact
of their more recent separation, and on this each com-
ments:

Sidney	*Sprat*
After the philosophers had picked out of the sweet mysteries of poetry, the right discerning true points of knowledge, they forthwith, putting it in method, and making a school-art of that which the poets did only teach by a divine delightfulness . . . were not content to set up shop for themselves, but sought by all means to discredit their masters.	When the fabulous Age was past, *Philosophy* took a little more courage; and ventured more to rely upon its own strength, without the Assistance of *Poetry*.

So the two disciplines are separated. Sidney regrets it, resenting the claims of a philosophy weaned from its nursing-mother, poetry; Sprat applauds it as progress (and behind Sprat one hears Comte and all the voices down to the present day). Sidney claims knowledge as a part of poetry and its mysteries, but he wavers in his claim, as we shall see, by presenting the poet as exceptional, aloof from the general endeavor of knowledge and justified on other grounds. He thus plays straight into Sprat's hands:

Sidney	*Sprat*
There is no art delivered unto mankind, that hath not the works of nature for his principal object . . . [Sidney here ties in the astronomer, geometrician, arithmetician, musician (Quadrivium); the natural philosopher, lawyer, historian; grammarian, rhetorician, logician (Trivium); the physician and metaphysician.] Only the poet, disdaining to be tied to any such subjection . . . doth grow, in effect, into another nature . . . Now, for the poet, he nothing affirmeth and therefore never lieth.	The poets began of old to impose the Deceit. They to make all things look more venerable than they were, devis'd a thousand false *Chimaeras;* on every *Field, River, Grove,* and *Cave* they bestow'd a *Fantasm* of their own making . . . The *Wit* of the *Fables* and Religions of the *antient World* is well-nigh consumed; they have already serv'd the poets long enough, and it is now high time to dismiss them, especially seeing they have this peculiar *Imperfection,* that they were only *Fictions* at first.

Sprat at least is logical: poets are liars, and the sooner scientists and other true minds are free of them the better. Sidney is illogical: poetry is philosophy and the source of true knowledge, but it is not to be classed with natural philosophy and the other branches of true knowledge; it says nothing about the real world and so is neither true nor false. (What a modern view it sounds when put that way!) This logic and illogic, however, are not the product of a scientific and a poetic mind respectively. Neither voice is scientific, and neither voice is poetic. Sprat is saying half a thing; Sidney is saying two things at once which contradict one another. Sprat's half-statement and half of Sidney's statement agree: poetry is not true and is not concerned with reality and nature. The results are equally unfortunate for any vision, whether it be of science or poetry. Sprat is not troubled by any sense of inadequacy; it is we who must feel that his presentation of science is glaringly inadequate: humdrum pedestrian collecting, arranging, and experimenting, without imagination of any sort. Sidney in his turn does not seem troubled by the contradiction in his work. He was regarded as the mirror of his age, and in the *Apologie* he mirrors the muddle his century was in (the quotation at the head of this section, dated 1591, shows it clearly) about the connection between poetry and philosophy, myths and truth. We shall meet the same contradiction in Bacon.

Sprat claims Bacon for his ancestor, or for the ancestor of the Royal Society and its scientific proceedings as Sprat presents them. That he is so, in part, is undeniable. Bacon and Sidney agree upon this: that if poetry is not true, and is still to be justified, the justification will have to be in terms of moral effect, or of idealizing escapist beauty. "It raises the mind aloft," Bacon says in *De Augmentis* (Bk. II, chap. 13), "accommodating the shows of things to the desires of the mind, not (like reason and history) buckling and bowing down the mind to the nature of things." Such a view is the result of separating reason and imagination. Bacon assigns philosophy to reason (Bk. I, chap. 1) and poetry to the imagination. So poetry becomes (Bk. III, chap. 1), "a dream of learning; a thing sweet and varied, and that would be thought to have in it something divine; a character which dreams likewise affect. But now it is time for me to awake, and, rising above the earth, to wing my way through the clear air of Philosophy and the Sciences."

If this were all there were to Bacon, or to poetry, we should be left with vain dreams on the one hand, and Sprat's deadly science on the other. But Bacon's essential vision was of neither of these two inadequacies, but of a synthesis, inspiring the cry in the "Plan of the Work" which precedes the *Novum Organum:* "God forbid that we should give out a dream of our imagination for a pattern of the world." To this any good scientist and, no less, any good poet, will say Amen. Poetry is true knowledge, and about the real world. Sidney also says it, and others before and after him. This note is already there in Ascham (it is of course part of Pico's view). Sandys, the translator of the *Metamorphoses,* voices it in 1632, in his introductory verses:

> Phoebus Apollo, (sacred Poesy)
> Thus taught: for in these ancient Fables lie
> The mysteries of all Philosophie.
> Some Nature's secrets shew; in some appeare
> Distempers staines; some teach us how to beare
> Both Fortunes, bridling Joy, Griefe, Hope, and Feare.

This is Bacon's Orpheus, the union of poetry and universal philosophy. Bacon is not clear about the relations between the two. He shares his age's fondness, as does Sandys, for moral allegory, where we shall not follow him; but even when this is left out of account, he is in two minds about the nature of the instrument he is working with.

There are two minor Orphic voices of this period, one earlier than Bacon and one later, which show a remarkable grasp of the dilemma. The first is Puttenham, whose *Arte of English Poesie* deserves to be better known. Puttenham denies implicitly Sidney's exclusion of the poet from the study of the works of nature, and Bacon's division between reason and imagination. Poets, he says, "were the first that entended to the observation of nature and her works, and specially of the Celestiall courses . . . they were the first Astronomers and Philosophists and Metaphysicks . . . and historiographers." Orpheus is behind all this, and is "first musitien" as well, arts and sciences converging, "so noble, profitable, ancient and divine a science as Poesie is." [18] When Puttenham turns his attention to the imagination, he produces one of the great passages in English literature on this subject:

> So is that part well affected, not onely nothing disorderly or confused with any monstrous imaginations or conceits, but very formall, and in his much multiformitie *uniforme,* that is well proportioned and so passing cleare, that by it as by a glasse or mirrour, are represented unto the soule all manner of bewtifull visions, whereby the inventive parte of the mind is so much holpen, as without it no man could devise any new or rare thing. . . . and of this sorte of phantasie are all good Poets, notable Captaines stratagematique, all cunning artificers and enginers, all Legislators, Polititiens and Counsellours of Estate, in whose exercises the inventive part is most employed and is to the sound and true judgement of man most needful.

Puttenham here comes to the root of the question, considering the mental activity which informs all living thought, under whatever discipline, as one. When he turns more specifically to poetry, he connects it with power, saying that poets by their works, "setting them with sundry relations, and variable formes, in the ministery and use of words, doe breede no little alteration in man. For to say truely, what els is man but his minde? which, whosoever have skil to compasse, and make yealding and flexible, what may not he commaund the body to performe?" The altering of the mind, power over bodies, by imaginative power and vision: this was Bacon's Orphic vision too, but clouded by indirection and ambiguity.

Our second minor Orphic writer, Henry Reynolds, complains of this very thing in his essay *Mythomystes* (1632),[19] a remarkable little work. This is his accusation against Bacon: "What shall we make of such willing contradictions, when a man to vent a few fancies of his own shall tell us first, they are the wisdom of the Ancients, and next, that those Ancient fables were but mere fables, and without wisdom or meaning till their expositors gave them a meaning; and then scornfully and contemptuously (as if all Poetry were but Play-vanity) shut up that discourse of his of Poetry with *It is not good to stay too long in the theatre*." The criticism depends on Reynolds' own understanding of poetry and of its connection with natural philosophy. He first disposes of the Sidney-Bacon view of poetry: "Nor expect here any Encomium or praise of any such thing as the world ordinarily takes Poesy for: that same thing being, as I conceive, a superficial mere outside of Sense, or gay bark only (without the body) of Reason: Witness so many excellent wits that have taken so much pains in these times to defend her; which sure they would not have done, if what is generally received nowadays for Poesy were not merely a faculty or occupation of so little consequence." Poetry then is a serious endeavor of some kind; and poets and philosophers are both engaged in it: "I put them together, as who are or should be both professors of one and the same learning, though by the one received and delivered in the apparel of verse, the other of prose."

Reynolds complains that modern poets are not scientific enough: "The last and greatest disparity, and wherein above all others the grossest defect and maim appears in our Moderns, and especially Poets, in respect of the Ancients, is their general ignorance, even throughout all of them, in any the mysteries and hidden properties of Nature, which as an unconcerning Inquisition it appears not in their writing they have at all troubled their heads with. Poets I said especially, and indeed only, for we have many Prose-men excellent natural Philosophers in these late times . . . So nowadays our Philosophers are all our Poets, or what our Poets should be."

We are directed next to the myths of the ancients. "The Ancients . . . were Authors of Fables . . . True; but sure enough the meanings were of more high nature, and more difficult to find out, than any book of Manners we shall readily meet withal affords; else they had not writ them so obscurely, or we should find them out more easily, and make some use of them." Reynolds renounces the view of myth as moral allegory, and makes the suggestion that in their obscurity lies their method which relates to nature and her secrets, a hidden method lost through inattention or a falsely utilitarian concept of science:

> Suppose a man should . . . be at the pains of running through all the Fables of the Ancients, and out of them shew the reader, and lead him by the Finger as it were (who yet can discover nothing but matter of Manners in them) to the speculation of the entire Secret of our great God of Nature in his miraculous fabric of the world . . . I would fain know who they

are that would be . . . fit readers nowadays of such a Treatise? because what one of a million of our Scholars or writers among us understands, or cares to be made to understand, scarce the lowest and trivialest of Nature's ways, much less seeks to draw (by wisely observing her higher and more hidden workings) any profitable use or benefit from them, for their own or the public good, than perhaps to make an Almanac or a diving-boat to take butts or crabs under water with or else some Dutch water-bellows, by rarefying water into a compressed air to blow the fire withal?

So the practical Sprat, as well as the Bacon-Sidney underestimation of poetry, is put out of court, and the way is open for Bacon himself, once we are past his own contradictions.

There is an art suggested here which Reynolds sees as lost, an art the ancients once possessed, the wisdom of the ancients in fact. (He uses Orpheus' loss of Eurydice as a figure for the modern world bereft of it.) That Reynolds probably conceived of this art as magical and cabalistic, as Pico in part seems to have done also, need not disturb us.[20] That method of inquiry, still open in the seventeenth century, is so no longer, but what Reynolds says still makes sense. The *Sortes Virgilianae* are not the best use to which a poet can be put, but poets do have uses and powers which are to be uncovered and set to work. "So Orpheus within the folds and involvements of fables, hid the mysteries of his doctrine, and dissembled them under the poetic mask." Poetry is an Orphic hieroglyphic by which nature may be interpreted. Reynolds uses the word "hieroglyphic." So does Sandys in the preface to his version of the *Metamorphoses,* and each writer cites Ovid in this connection. Sandys speaks of "these fables of Ovid, if I may call them his, when most of them are more antient than any

extant Author or perhaps than Letters themselves; before
which, as they expressed their Conceptions in Hiero-
glyphickes, so did they their Philosophie and Divinitie
under Fables and Parables." [21] Reynolds adds, "Of which
beads the ingenious *Ovid* has made a curious and excellent
chain, though perhaps he understood not their depth."

Myth and poetry as a hieroglyphic art by which the mind
might interpret the mysteries of nature, an art going back
to the dawn of language and rooted in it—this is the vision
which is emerging, and it is right that Ovid should come
in thus early. His *Metamorphoses* are one of the principal
sources of the Orpheus myth itself, and his influence over
Orphic poets has never failed.[22] He was a master to Shake-
speare, Milton, Erasmus Darwin, Goethe, Wordsworth,
Rilke. In our day Ezra Pound includes this work (in Gold-
ing's translation, the one Shakespeare knew) among the
five needful literary works. The persistent devotion of
great poets is not paid to a mere compiler of mythological
narrative. It is paid to genius which chose metamorphosis
for subject matter; a brilliant shot and assuredly not, as
Reynolds suggests, a shot in the dark. Change and process
and transformation become in this poem a means of relat-
ing the inner workings of the mind with the workings of
nature. Goethe will catch up this theme in his *Metamor-
phose* (of which we shall have more to say when we dis-
cuss Goethe and Ovid below, Pt. III), maintaining that all
fixed forms in nature are merely momentary crystalliza-
tions of a reality which is in perpetual change, and which,
if we are truly to understand it, must be the model for our
methods of thought. These have to be as flexible and
plastic, *beweglich und bildsam,* as nature is.

Of this kind of thinking Ovid has given us an example,
and to get clear about it is part of Bacon's purpose. He
speaks of it in that remarkable passage on Poesy Parabol-
ical which concludes, and quietly turns upside down, his

chapter on poetry in the *De Augmentis*. To parable he adds hieroglyphic, which we have met already, in Ovidian company, in Sandys and Reynolds. Bacon says, "In a word, as hieroglyphics were before letters, so parables were before arguments." [23] Parables before arguments, poetry before dialectic—is this Lévy-Bruhl's prelogical thought, or something else?

4

Videmus nunc per speculum in oenigmate . . . wherein nevertheless there seemeth to be a liberty granted, as far forth as the polishing of this glass, or some moderate explication of this oenigma

AN AUTHOR can do three things with myth. He can study its nature and its origins, in its traditional form; interpret myths according to his own theories; or mythologize himself, either by thinking himself into existing myths and using them as instruments for his own thought, or by inventing new myths and using them in the same way. The first activity may be poetical, although it need not be. The third must be poetical. The second is wholly nonpoetic, indeed antipoetical. It is typical of Bacon that he should apparently choose the second mode in which to work in his *De Sapientia Veterum*.

The body of the work consists of thirty-one classical myths, preceded by two letters of dedication and a substantial and remarkable preface. Bacon retells each myth and then proceeds to interpret it. (This is where his "Orpheus" is.) The interpretations fall into three groups. Nine fables are interpreted in terms of political philosophy; ten are given moral interpretations; and the remaining twelve are expounded in terms of natural philosophy. Bacon's would-be philosophical Orpheus seems to preside over the whole work; Bacon ascribes to him two kinds of singing, the one relating to natural, the other to moral and civil, philosophy.

As we have seen, such attempts at interpretation were not uncommon in Bacon's time. Bacon himself remarks at the end of the preface, "That the thing has been attempted by others I am of course aware, but if I may speak what I think freely without mincing it, I must say that the pains which have been hitherto taken that way, though great and laborious, have gone near to deprive the inquiry of all its beauty and worth . . . Here, on the other hand, it will be found (if I mistake not) that though the subjects be old, yet the matter is new; while leaving behind us the open and level parts we bend our way towards the nobler heights that rise beyond."

Subsequent editors and critics allow Bacon his originality, but they allow him very little else in respect to this work. The earlier nineteenth century saw in it an elegant irrelevance to the whole corpus of Baconian achievement. The later nineteenth century was uneasy about the fallacious beliefs on which, it was supposed, the whole attempt rested, and tried to present the work as on a par with the *Essays*, "replete with good sense of the best quality." It remained for the twentieth century to see in it a naive waste of time and ingenuity. Only one commentator of those I am familiar with, writing in 1951, gives it its due consideration, seeing in it a key to the *Magna Instauratio* and a serious and interesting work in its own right.[24]

The work covers all three possible uses a writer can make of myth. That they were mutually contradictory did not worry Bacon. In the preface he writes of myth partly poetically, partly antipoetically. In the individual myths his allegorical approach is unpoetic and unhelpful in itself. But in the myths of natural philosophy, especially "Orpheus," "Daedalus," "Erichthonius," "Deucalion," "Atalanta," "Prometheus," and "Sphinx," he cannot prevent himself using them to further his lifelong passion, his own method of thinking, and the result is that he cannot sterilize them into mere representations of philosophical ideas. They become figures for exploring his own method, and this keeps them alive, for this is what myths are for. His Orpheus insists on being a dark poetry and not just philosophy in the clear light of reason. The question in Baconian terms is whether Orpheus, or myth, is a hieroglyphic or a cipher.

The progression from hieroglyphic to cipher, as a range of knowledge having to do with tradition and language, occurs twice in Bacon's work, in Book II of the *Advancement* and in the equivalent passage in the *De Augmentis* (Bk. VI, chap. 1). (The latter is more extensive, but I am drawing, on the whole, on the *Advancement* version, because there we have Bacon's own English instead of a translator's.) [25] The fourth kind of rational knowledge which Bacon speaks of "is transitive, concerning the expressing or transferring our knowledge to others; which I will term by the general name Tradition or Delivery." He goes on to say that the organ of tradition is Speech and Writing. There follows a list of Notes of Cogitations having to do with communication. Here we move from hieroglyphic, which includes gesture, to grammar, literary and philosophical; then to poetry, with which is associated the dance; then cipher. Bacon goes on immediately to talk about method. The whole passage is important, but I must hold the more general questions for the moment. The point is: given a "dark" saying, a riddle or myth or enigma, or a poem perhaps, what is the nature of that darkness? We may remember that Orpheus is for us, in this first phase where he exercises his power over the lower orders of creation, in darkness, and we need now not a rejection but a diagnosis of that darkness. This is not a fanciful figure. To know the nature of your own darkness, your own mystery or problem, is the first stage of any intellectually imaginative inquiry. Is the nature of the Orphic darkness, then, that of hieroglyphic or that of cipher?

Bacon would rather like the answer to be in terms of cipher. He has a fondness for it; he gives a number of examples in his work and obviously rather fancies himself in this connection. In this too he resembles another poet, by rights emblematical, who had a fondness for ciphers— Edgar Allan Poe.[26] The attraction of ciphers lies in their ability to be "disciphered," as Bacon calls it. A code is subject to, indeed demands, a single clear decoding or interpretation. It stands for something which can be worked out with certainty and presented in rational form. Such a possibility is bound to attract poets of this sort, who have a strong feeling for pure intellect and analysis. Bacon was as impatient of darkness as Valéry was. Caroline Spurgeon has pointed out how whenever Bacon thinks of intellectual activity, he uses images of light.[27] Yet he is large-minded enough, or poet enough, to know that hieroglyphics—with which he couples emblems, enigmas, and fables—are of another kind. You cannot crack a myth as you can crack Minoan. In hieroglyphic the meaning is embodied in the figure itself. The reason the word "symbol," that favorite of modern criticism, is so unsatisfactory an instrument is that it never makes its position clear between the two.

Bacon is not the only one in his day who tries to understand dark sayings in terms of both hieroglyphic and cipher, and whose splendid practice with the former denies their rationalism about the latter. An exact contemporary of Bacon's, George Chapman, is in the same predicament.

The man who, I think, was clear about it was Shakespeare.
Let us see what they can offer. Chapman, like Bacon, works
at all three levels of mythological activity: statement upon
myth, interpretation of myth, invention of myth. Shake-
speare simply embodies cipher and hieroglyphic, and sets
them side by side, that we may see the un-poetry of the
former and the power of the latter.

Chapman, in *A Justification of Perseus and Andromeda*
(1614), says:

> As Learning hath delighted from her cradle to hide her-
> self from the base and profane vulgar, her ancient
> Enemy, under divers veils of Hieroglyphics, Fables,
> and the Like, so hath she pleased herself with no dis-
> guise more than in mysteries and allegorical fictions
> of Poesy . . . ever held in high reverence and au-
> thority as supposed to conceal within the utter bark,
> as their Eternities approve, some sap of hidden Truth:
> as either some dim and obscure prints of divinity, and
> the sacred history; or the grounds of natural or rules
> of moral Philosophy . . . ever, I say, enclosing within
> the rind some fruit of knowledge, howsoever dark-
> ened; and, by reason of the obscurity, of ambiguous
> and different construction . . . This ambiguity in
> the sense hath given scope to the variety of exposi-
> tions.

Chapman is himself addicted to darkness, not least in his
prose style. This had its disadvantages. His *Perseus and
Andromeda*, for instance, had to be publicly "justified"
because he wrote it so darkly that readers gave it all sorts
of political and scurrilous meanings which, he protests,
it was never meant to have. Nonetheless, such a turning
toward a hieroglyphic darkness need not be simply ob-
scurantism. Certainly Chapman is a magnificent hiero-

glyphic—which is to say mythologizing—poet in his own
right. Witness *Bussy D'Ambois,* where the darkness of
the play is emblazoned by what are almost heraldic images
of mysterious splendor, as for instance in the famous pas-
sage which begins with the "silently gliding exhalations";
or this, at the beginning of the play,

> Man is a torch borne in the wind: a dream
> But of a shadow, summ'd with all his substance,

an image to be caught up in the play by a wandering torch
which indicates the presence of a demon; or this, from
Bussy's dying speech,

> Fly where the evening from the Iberian vales
> Takes on her swarthy shoulders Hecate
> Crown'd with a grove of oaks; fly where men feel
> The burning axletree: and those that suffer
> Beneath the chariot of the snowy Bear.

Here is emblematic poetry of a wonderful kind. Yet this
is what the same poet could do to classical myth and to
Orpheus when he set about interpreting it: [28]

> So when ye hear the sweetest Muse's son
> With heavenly rapture of his music won
> Rocks, forests, floods and wind to leave their course
> In his attendance: it bewrays the force
> His wisdom had, to draw men grown so rude
> To civil love of art and fortitude,
> And not for teaching others insolence
> Had he his date-exceeding excellence
> With sovereign poets, but for use applied,
> And in his proper acts exemplified.
> And that in calming the infernal kind,
> To wit, the perturbations of his mind,

And bringing his Eurydice from hell
(Which justice signifies) is proved well.
    ("Hymnus in Noctem," in *The Shadow of Night*)

If I say that this is oddly reminiscent of something in
Shakespeare, I am drawing no textual or bibliographical
conclusions but simply making a connection for my own
purposes, irrespective of known or surmised points of con-
tact between Chapman and Shakespeare.[29] What it recalls
is the verse of the Pyramus and Thisbe interlude in *A Mid-
summer Night's Dream*.

When Bottom and his company finally appear before
the royal lovers to act their play, their verse has just this
same ring of helpful explanation for the mind in dark-
ness:

Gentles, perchance you wonder at this show;
    But wonder on, till truth make all things plain.
This man is Pyramus, if you would know;
    This beauteous lady, Thisbe is certain . . .

Thus have I, wall, my part discharged so;
And, being done, thus wall away doth go.

Now the method which the rude mechanicals adopt, with
the best of intentions as they make plain during their re-
hearsal in Act III, is the method of cipher. They do their
very best to translate the darkness of their subject (which
is mythical and Ovidian and set in a summer night) into
the light of plain common sense. They provide the inter-
pretation as they go. Every actor is "representing" some-
body or something; he is the cipher who deciphers him-
self.

This man, with lime and rough-cast, doth present
Wall, that vile Wall which did these lovers sunder.

> This lantern doth the horned moon present;
> Myself the man-i'-th'-moon do seem to be.

In cipher, the figure and the meaning are quite separate, and this separation is insisted on:

> You, ladies, you, whose gentle hearts do fear
>   The smallest monstrous mouse that creeps on floor,
> May now perchance both quake and tremble here,
>   When lion rough in wildest rage doth roar.
> Then know that I one Snug the joiner am,
> No lion fell, nor yet no lion's dam.

Here, too, myth is being interpreted. Bacon's and Chapman's interpretations were philosophical. Shakespeare shows myth being interpreted dramatically as cipher, and the utter inappropriateness of the deciphering method. But instead of turning the myth into dead boredom by this method (though this threatens the stage audience at least, for Hippolyta complains, "I am a-weary of this moon; would he would change!" and even the courteous Theseus implores finally, "No epilogue, I pray you"), as Bacon and Chapman do unwittingly, he turns it to burlesque and laughter.

And then he does a marvelous thing. For at the end, when the lovers are gone to bed and Puck returns to bring back the fairies and so wind all up, Shakespeare—who is beyond question mythologizing in the whole of this play —takes back, as it were, his own mythological material into his own hands and out of those of the "hard-handed men, that work in Athens here," and recreates as hieroglyphic and myth and poetry all the elements which the cipher has annulled. Shakespeare is strong enough to admit a parody of mythology and drama into his own mythological play, and then to restore everything at the end.

What are the elements in the Pyramus and Thisbe inter-
lude? Darkness first; and if you ask "Of what nature?" the
answer is Pyramus-Bottom's invocation of it,

> O grim-lookt night! O night with hue so black!
>   O night, which ever art when day is not!
> O night, O night!

After darkness, there is classical mythology. There was
sorrow and death and a tomb, or more than one. There
was a lion, who with moonshine was "left to bury the
dead," and with whom, as in the old fables, a mouse is
associated: "Well moused, lion." Last of all, there are
the hempen homespuns themselves. Now recall Puck's
speech almost at the end of the play,

> Now the hungry lion roars,
>   And the wolf behowls the moon;
> Whilst the heavy ploughman snores,
>   All with weary task fordone.
> Now the wasted brands do glow,
>   Whilst the screech-owl, screeching loud,
> Puts the wretch that lies in woe
>   In remembrance of a shroud.
> Now it is the time of night,
>   That the graves, all gaping wide,
> Every one lets forth his sprite,
>   In the church-way paths to glide:
> And we fairies, that do run
>   By the triple Hecate's team
> From the presence of the sun,
>   Following darkness like a dream,
> Now are frolic: not a mouse
> Shall disturb this hallow'd house:
> I am sent, with broom, before,
> To sweep the dust behind the door.

The shift from palpable-gross ciphering back to hiero-glyphic is perfected in twenty lines, so swiftly that the mind has no time to remember that these are the same elements it has been invited to make merry with when they were being subjected to the wrong method. Shakespeare is clearer about the right and wrong handling of myth than either Chapman or Bacon. He employs interpretation only to demonstrate its absurdity, but his method of bringing the myth back to life is to unite the figuring mind with the myth again. After showing us what might almost seem the fundamental absurdity of myth and drama, Shakespeare then shows that the absurdity is because we are not far enough into either. So he draws us out of a mis-managed play-within-a-play back into his own play, which is so perfectly managed that we do not even notice the transition, nor remember that Puck who now takes the stage is no less fabulous than Bottom's Pyramus.

The exact equivalent happens in Bacon's interpreta-tions of the natural philosophy myths. Of these twelve, seven are directly concerned with method, and the remain-ing five touch on it; not keys to natural phenomena them-selves but keys to ways of thinking about them or work-ing upon them. Bacon's triple passion, for facts about na-ture, for method in the mind, and for the just relating of those two, finds here, as it does in the rest of his work, a unified expression. So each man identifies his own voca-tion, the passion of his mind, with the mythical figures he is using. We are back, in fact, to the Shakespearean and the Baconian Orpheus.

A Midsummer Night's Dream begins to assert itself as an early, shadowy, yet convincingly Orphic statement of exactly the kind we are looking for. (Orpheus makes a fleeting personal appearance in the play, or almost makes one, for one of the entertainments offered to Theseus and Hippolyta by Philostrate is "The riot of the tipsy Bac-

chanals / Tearing the Thracian singer in their rage"; but
it is not chosen for presentation.) Orphic statements, it
will be remembered, are reflexive, comment on themselves,
and thus this play becomes also an experimental essay on
myth and mind and universe. This may help us with
Bacon's poetic-philosophic Orpheus in the *De Sapientia
Veterum*, to which we now turn.

In his dedication to Lord Salisbury, Bacon defends or
explains his subject matter of myth on the following
grounds: "For if time be regarded,—primaeval antiquity
is an object of the highest veneration; if the form of ex-
position,—parable has ever been a kind of ark, in which
the most precious portions of the sciences were deposited;
if the matter of the work, it is philosophy, the second grace
and ornament of life and the human soul." The preface
expands these three ideas; and we are likely to think them
commonplace enough until we begin to ask just what he
meant by each of them. For antiquity proves to be not
classical antiquity, but something far older. Parable is
not just classical myth, nor any work of the poet. And
philosophy is not classical philosophy, nor any philosophy
that has followed it. Yet in these three, antiquity, parable,
philosophy (or call them time, poetry, and science), we
have the key to the whole of Bacon's speculative work.

The opening sentence gives us the mystery and the
method at one and the same time.

> The most ancient times (except what is preserved of
> them in the scriptures) are buried in oblivion and
> silence: to that silence succeeded the fables of the
> poets: to those fables the written records which have
> come down to us. Thus between the hidden depths
> of antiquity and the days of tradition and evidence
> that followed there is drawn a veil, as it were, of fables,

which come in and occupy the middle region that separates what has perished from what survives.

We who live in the latter days of tradition and evidence have to penetrate records, poetry, myths themselves, if we are to arrive at what Bacon is calling wisdom. The search is a serious one. Bacon makes this clear at once, realizing how fantastic such an endeavor may seem. "Now I suppose most people will think I am but entertaining myself with a toy, and using much the same kind of license in expounding the poets' fables which the poets themselves did in inventing them." He adds, "But that is not my meaning." By implying his own seriousness, by the parallel he draws between his own endeavor and that of the poets, he implies the seriousness of their task also, and sets his task and theirs side by side. He is realistic about the dangers of this:

> Not but that I know very well what pliant stuff fable is made of, how freely it will follow any way you please to draw it, and how easily with a little dexterity and discourse of wit meanings which it was never meant to bear may be plausibly put upon it. Neither have I forgotten that there has been old abuse of the thing in practice; that many, wishing only to gain the sanction and reverence of antiquity for doctrines and inventions of their own, have tried to twist the fables of the poets into that sense.

He gives an example or two of this distortion, but then he speaks his mind: "I do certainly for my own part (I freely and candidly confess) incline to this opinion,—that beneath no small number of the fables of the ancient poets there lay from the very beginning a mystery and an allegory." This is, fittingly, a profession of faith in a hypothesis. He now gives the grounds for his opinion. The first is the inherent absurdity of so many myths: "they may be said to give notice from afar and cry out that there is a parable below." (They are even more monstrous than dreams, Bacon says; once again myths and dreams are neighbors in his thought.) The second reason is this:

> But the consideration which has most weight with me is this, that few of these fables were invented, as I take it, by those who recited and made them famous,— Homer, Hesiod, and the rest. For had they been certainly the production of that age and of those authors by whose report they have come down to us, I should not have thought of looking for anything great or lofty from such a source. But it will appear in an attentive examination that they are delivered not as new inventions then first published, but as stories already received and believed. . . . so they must be regarded as neither being the inventions nor belonging to the age of the poets themselves, but as sacred relics and light airs breathing out of better times, that they caught from the traditions of more ancient nations and so received into the flutes and trumpets of the Greeks.

So, for Bacon, behind myths are figures (he uses that word himself in *The Advancement of Learning*, where he discusses whether fables are pleasure or figure). These figures are of deep antiquity, older than their embodiments in the known myths; in these are laid up "the most precious portions of the sciences," coming down from "better times." It is these figures or meanings which are the Wisdom.

Then, after that lovely statement—an echo of another passage of Bacon's, as so often in his work—and just when we seem to be moving toward a real unification of science and poetry, his doubleness reasserts itself and he scuttles back on his tracks.

Nevertheless, if anyone be determined to believe that the allegorical meaning of the fable was in no case original and genuine, but that always the fable was first and the allegory put in after, I will not press that point; but allowing him to enjoy that gravity of judgment (of the dull and leaden order though it be) which he affects, I will attack him, if indeed he be worth the pains, in another manner upon a fresh ground.

Parables have been used in two ways, and (which is strange) for contrary purposes. For they serve to disguise and veil the meaning, and they also serve to clear and throw light upon it. To avoid dispute then, let us give up the former of these uses. Let us suppose that these fables were things without any definite purpose, made only for pleasure. Still there remains the latter use. No force of wit can deprive us of that . . . On this account it was that in the old times, when the inventions and conclusions of human reason (even those that are not trite and vulgar) were as yet new and strange, the world was full of all kinds of fables, and enigmas, and parables, and similitudes: and these were used as a device not for shadowing and concealing the meaning, but as a method of making it understood.

The argument now stands thus: There is an essential contradiction in the function of myth. It can be used to "retire and obscure" the knowledge or learning it bears, something significant having been deliberately hidden within it, to be discovered by investigation. Or it can be used to "demonstrate and illustrate" it (the phrases are from the discussion in the *Advancement*). Here, myths, the product of pure chance, can be employed as similitudes by which knowledge can be made impressive and memorable; there will be no intrinsic connection, however, between the knowledge and the figure serving as visual aid or mnemonic. Bacon then tries to affirm both halves of the contradiction he has himself set up: "Upon the whole I conclude with this: the wisdom of the primitive ages was either great or lucky; great, if they knew what they were doing and invented the figure to shadow the meaning; lucky, if without meaning or intending it they fell upon matter which gives occasion to such worthy contemplations. My own pains, if there be any help in them, I shall think well bestowed either way: I shall be throwing light either upon antiquity or upon nature itself."

Bacon is faced with two dilemmas here. The first is his inability or unreadiness to decide—when confronted with a series of forms in which his mind perceives symmetries, related patterns, and hence significance—whether to ascribe the origins and propagation of this series of forms to accident or design. We are in no position to be superior about this difficulty, for it is parallel to the modern problem, unsolved, of the nature of evolution. Bacon's second difficulty is that he mistakes the basis of his own thinking in this preface, the "concealment versus illustration" theme. He supposes he has been arguing on the basis of concealment, and turns at the end to take up the case for illustration. This is not so. All the first and positive part rests on the tacit assumption that such an antithesis in myth between concealment and enlightenment is unnecessary.

There is something deep in Bacon which assents to concealment and hence to this antithesis, an urge to make his work deliberately dark, to keep it from the vulgar. Chapman had it too, to a more marked degree, and perhaps it springs from that lack of self-confidence and that intellectual pride to which poets are peculiarly liable. There is a hint of it in Bacon's *Valerius Terminus* (speculatively dated 1603), an early work on knowledge. In the notes for chapter 18—the work was never completed—Bacon says, "That the discretion anciently observed . . . of publishing part, and reserving part to a private succession, and of publishing in a manner whereby it shall not be to the capacity nor taste of all, but shall as it were single and adopt his reader, is not to be laid aside." More revealing still is the remark from the "Epistle to the Reader" by which Dr. Rawley, Bacon's chaplain and biographer, introduced Bacon's fragmentary natural history, *Sylva Sylvarum:* "I have heard his lordship say also, that one great reason why he would not put these particulars into any exact method (though he that looketh attentively into them shall find that they have a secret order) was because he conceived that other men would now think that they could do the like." On the other hand, light or enlightenment for Bacon is never just a function of the pedagogue only. "Therefore do thou, O Father, who gavest the visible light as the first fruits of creation, and didst breathe into the face of man the intellectual light as the crown and consummation thereof, guard and protect this work, which coming from thy goodness returneth to thy glory." The beauty of such passages—this is from the "Plan of the Work" preceding the *Instauration*—bespeaks a vision beyond that to which he tries to restrict myth's second function in this perverse end to his preface.

This is the struggle between the cipherer and the hieroglyphic poet in Bacon. He ascribes to myth a double function, but the two functions turn out to resemble one another, each depending on "This stands for that," which is cipher and not myth. Deliberately to encode knowledge so as to hide it from the vulgar is the task of cipher but never of myth or poetry. Nor is it part of poetry's task

to supply chance pictures which will make ideas or bits
of learning memorable. Bacon does not have the option
he allows himself here of saying something either about
nature or about the ancients, according to which way you
take his supposed antithesis. He has the option of saying
nothing whatever about either because he is using the
wrong instrument, or of saying something about both. A
bid each way is hopeless. The stakes are very high: all or
nothing. Bacon playing safe is a sad spectacle, for there
is another Bacon who is a monumental gambler, as a poet
must be: "Certain it is that all other ambition whatsoever
seemed poor in his eyes compared with the work which
he had in hand; seeing that the matter at issue is either
nothing, or a thing so great that it may well be content
with its own merit, without seeking other recompense."
That is the final sentence of the "Prœmium" to the
Magna Instauratio.

He was right. The "matter at issue" is the same in *The
Wisdom of the Ancients* and in the *Instauration,* and
it is incomparably great. It is a vision of a method of
thinking, in which enfoldment and enlightenment are one
and the same thing, in which there is no division between
figure and meaning. This is hieroglyphic, myth, and poetry,
the Orphic darkness to which Bacon, whether he would
or no, was dedicated. It is a darkness which is its own light,
or, to change the Baconian figure for a moment, a laby-
rinth which is its own clue. In the *De Sapientia* Bacon
says in the "Daedalus" fable, "the same man who devised
the mazes of the labyrinth disclosed likewise the use of
the clue," as if figure and meaning belong by right to-
gether. One of his earliest works is called *Filum Labyrinthi
sive Formula Inquisitionis.* His labyrinth is sometimes
method (as in the fable "Sphinx," where the riddling
monster is not Nature but Science), and sometimes nature
itself: "But the universe to the eye of human understand-

ing is framed like a labyrinth; presenting as it does on every side so many ambiguities of way, such deceitful resemblances of objects and signs, natures so irregular in their lines, and so knotted and entangled" (preface to the *Instauration*). Yet where the figure is the answer is.[30]

5

The best in this kind are but shadows

So the Baconian Orpheus begins to unfold, no longer as allegory but as hieroglyphic or true myth or poem, in which are exhibited those three elements which Bacon introduced in his dedication—antiquity, parable, and philosophy, or, as we paraphrased them, time, poetry, and science. Bacon's Orpheus embodies a failure: "whereupon the charm being broken that had been the bond of that order and good fellowship, confusion began again; the beasts returned each to his several nature and preyed one upon the other as before; the stones and woods stayed no longer in their places: while Orpheus himself was torn to pieces in their fury by the women." Yet this failure is not complete, "the waters of Helicon being sunk under the ground, until, according to the appointed vicissitude of things, they break out and issue forth again, perhaps among other nations and not in the places where they were before." So there is a venerable tradition and a good hope for the future in some union of poetry and science, partly achieved but waiting to be perfected.

And waiting to be perfected by Bacon. He realized this very early, and is, as a great mind must be, astonished at his vocation, but unable to gainsay it. So in the *Novum*

Organum he calls himself "a birth of Time," insisting on his election by time and luck and not by his own merits. The phrase also occurs among those hieroglyphic titles to his works which are part of his poetic genius, *Temporis Partus Masculus*,[31] the masculine birth of time, by which he meant his own system.

Like everything else in Bacon, time is not a simple matter. The word "time" in ordinary use is paradoxical, for it can mean something infinitely ancient—"A rose-red city half as old as Time"—or up-to-the-minute immediacy, as when we say, "What time is it?" So in Bacon's thoughts and in his hieroglyphic titles of works, the wisdom of the ancients is old beyond imagining, yet Bacon sees it as a most modern instrument with a great future. The *Novum Organum* is new, but it is a new version of that old instrument or *organon* of Aristotle's. In Book 1 of that work, Aphorism 84, Bacon says:

> The old age of the world is to be accounted the true antiquity; and this is the attribute of our own times, not of that earlier age of the world in which the ancients lived; and which, though in respect of us it was the elder, yet in respect of the world it was the younger. And truly as we look for greater knowledge of human things and a riper judgment in the old man than in the young, because of his experience and of the number and variety of the things which he has seen and heard and thought of; so in like manner from our age, if it but knew its own strength and chose to essay and exert it, much more might fairly be expected than from the ancient times, inasmuch as it is a more advanced age of the world, and stored and stocked with experiments and observations.

As the Aphorism continues, Bacon's thinking on time takes on the imagery of his own times:

Nor must it go for nothing that by the distant voyages and travels which have become frequent in our times, many things in nature have been laid open and discovered which may let in new light upon philosophy. And surely it would be disgraceful if, while the regions of the material globe,—that is, of the earth, of the sea and of the stars,—have been in our times laid widely open and revealed, the intellectual globe should remain shut up within the narrow limits of old discoveries.

It is, he says in *Valerius Terminus,* "as if the opening of the world by navigation and commerce and the further discovery of knowledge should meet in one time or age." This is how Bacon sees his own task and exploration. He gave the title *Descriptio Globi Intellectualis* to a fragmentary tract he wrote about 1612. But, more important, this is the notion which lies behind name and figure in his *New Atlantis.* He sees himself as the discoverer of a continent, old and yet new. Yet for Bacon, antiquity or novelty are in the end secondary. What matters is the nature of the discovery itself. He says this in *Novum Organum,* Book I, Aphorism 122:

Nor do I think that it matters any more to the business in hand, whether the discoveries that shall now be made were long ago known to the ancients, and have their settings and their risings according to the vicissitude of things and course of ages, than it matters to mankind whether the new world be that island of Atlantis with which the ancients were acquainted, or now discovered for the first time. For new discoveries must be sought from the light of nature, not fetched back out of the darkness of antiquity.

And in this same Aphorism we get a further clue to the nature of the "business in hand":

It may be thought also a strange and harsh thing that we should at once and with one blow set aside all sciences and all authors; and that too without calling in any of the ancients to our aid and support, but relying on our own strength.

And I know that if I had chosen to deal less sincerely, I might easily have found authority for my suggestions by referring them either to the old times before the Greeks (when natural science was perhaps more flourishing, though it made less noise, not yet having passed into the pipes and trumpets of the Greeks), or even, in part at least, to some of the Greeks themselves.

This passage at the end is an almost exact echo of one we have already quoted from the *De Sapientia* preface. There it was parable which breathed its ancient wisdom into the musical instruments of the Greeks; here it is science. They are, for Bacon, one and the same, as his Orpheus hints. His birth of time is to be but a renewal of them both exhibited in that most ancient tradition of all.

This doubleness of old and new, and of science and poetry, is the heart of Bacon's whole endeavor, and that is why he keeps talking about it as a restoring of knowledge rather than an innovation. In the preface to the *Novum Organum* he speaks of his task as "so great a restoration of learning and knowledge," that *Magna Instauratio* which is to give back something formerly possessed but lost or unused; "froide d'oubli et de désuétude." Bacon says of himself in the "Proœmium" to the *Instauratio:* "he thought all trial should be made, whether that commerce between the mind of man and the nature of things, which is more precious than anything on earth, or at least than anything that is of the earth, might by any means be restored to its perfect and original condition, or if that may not be, yet reduced to a better condition than that in which it now is."

The nature of this knowledge and of its restitution can best be approached by another passage from *Valerius Terminus,* chapter 1:

> To conclude then, let no man presume to check the liberality of God's gifts, who, as was said, *hath set the world in man's heart.* So as whatsoever is not God but parcel of the world, he hath fitted it to the comprehension of man's mind, if man will open and dilate the powers of his understanding as he may.
>
> But yet evermore it must be remembered that the least part of knowledge passed to man by this so large a charter from God must be subject to that use for which God hath granted it; which is the benefit and relief of the state and society of man . . . the same author [St. Paul] doth notably disavow both power and knowledge such as is not dedicated to goodness or love, for saith he, *If I have all faith so as I could remove mountains* (there is power active), *if I render my body to the fire* (there is power passive), *if I speak with the tongues of men and angels* (there is knowledge, for language is but the conveyance of knowledge), *all were nothing.*
>
> And therefore it is not the pleasure of curiosity, nor the quiet of resolution, nor the raising of the spirit, nor victory of wit, nor faculty of speech, nor lucre of profession, nor ambition of honour or fame, nor inablement for business, that are the true ends of knowledge; some of these being more worthy than other, though all inferior and degenerate: but it is a restitution and reinvesting (in great part) of man to the sovereignty and power (for whensoever he shall be able to call the creatures by their true names he

shall again command them) which he had in his first state of creation. And to speak plainly and clearly, it is a discovery of all operations and possibilities of operations from immortality (if it were possible) to the meanest mechanical practice.

A fitting together of the mind and the world which bears some relation to the story of Adam naming the animals and which is subject to love; a knowledge which is power, which is to be useful and is akin to language; a power which is to exercise itself in science—this is the vision Bacon has of postlogic.

We began with Bacon's thought about the oldness and newness of time. Time is also the intervening stretches, and Bacon is concerned with these as well. If he sees his method as almost vanishing into the extremes of antiquity and futurity, he was also well aware that poetry and science meantime had had a long history, and it is part of his task to consider this in the light of his own vision. The difficulty is that his terms "parable" or "philosophy," with all their possible variations, stand sometimes for that archaic vision where parable enshrines the most precious science now to be given back to the world, and sometimes for what has been done with each discipline meanwhile. In the first case they are one and the same; in the second they fall apart.

In his vision of philosophy or science as truth and beauty Bacon never falters. The whole recorded history of the works of philosophers and scientists is in his eyes a sad tale of mistakes and illusions, and he will belabor philosophers and scientists accordingly. But he holds always to his own vision of a philosophy, true, original, and shining with a light from Heaven, which lies behind such bunglings and which he alone can see. It was this, I suppose, which would have formed the last part of his unfinished

Instauration. He speaks of it in the "Plan of the Work": "The sixth part of my work (to which the rest is subservient and ministrant) discloses and sets forth that philosophy which by the legitimate, chaste, and severe course of inquiry which I have explained and provided is at length developed and established." If he had had a similar certainty of vision about poetry, he might have exercised a power almost without parallel.

The two sides of this vision, the strength of the philosophic and the weakness of the poetic, are apparent in the passage from Book I of the *Advancement* where Bacon discusses the position of poetry as learning. "Poesy is a part of learning," the first paragraph begins, and this is reiterated at the end: "In this third part of learning, which is poesy, I can report no deficience. For being as a plant that cometh of the lust of the earth, without a formal seed, it hath sprung up and spread abroad more than any other kind." Between these two remarks comes the "Sprat-Sidney" view of poetry which we have already talked about: then the affirmation of the antiquity of parable and hieroglyphic, myth's double function of darkness and light, the cautious hypothesis that there may be meanings behind old fables. If there is learning in poetry, it is not yet clear of what kind it is. The uncertainty is even more prolonged in the equivalent passages of the *De Augmentis.* There too poetry is said to be a kind of learning, the word being repeated in the final remark, for where Bacon's English in the *Advancement* says simply "spread abroad more than any other kind," his Latin in the *De Augmentis* says "super ceteras *doctrinas* excrevit et diffusa est." There follows a more definite statement about myth and meaning, and three examples of interpreted myths are included. Then once again Bacon wobbles, and the next passage begins, "Poesy is a dream of learning." This is the hinge between the discussion on poetry and one upon knowledge, and in this way Bacon gets back to safe ground and to philosophy. The same pattern is followed in the *Advancement,* but the hinge is different. Here occurs that remark which so annoyed the Reynolds of *Mythomystes,* "But it is not good to stay too long in the theatre. Let us now pass on to the judicial place or palace of the mind, which we are to approach and view with more reverence and attention." Poetry, where Bacon rejects it, is equated with dreams and the theater. What of philosophy?

Earlier in Book 1 of the *Advancement* Bacon speaks of something that he calls *philosophia prima.* What he seems to have in mind is some intellectual activity behind every form of learning: [32]

> Therefore it is good, before we enter into the former distribution, to erect and constitute one universal science, by the name of *Philosophia Prima,* Primitive or Summary Philosophy, as the main and common way, before we come where the ways part and divide themselves; which science whether I should report as deficient or no, I stand doubtful. For I find a certain rhapsody of Natural Theology, and of divers parts of Logic; and of that part of Natural Philosophy which concerneth the Principles, and of the other part of Natural Philosophy which concerneth the Soul or Spirit; all these strangely commixed and confused . . .

A little later he defines this: "That it be a receptacle for all such profitable observations and axioms as fall not within the compass of any of the special parts of philosophy or sciences, but are more common and of a higher stage." There follows an extraordinarily interesting paragraph in which Bacon suggests points at which different branches of learning may exhibit similarities of structure: analogies between mathematics and logic, mathematics and ethics; the idea of change in all fields; harmonic and visual effects, and so on—a web of possible relationships and analogies.

This spring or well-head of all learning (Bacon calls it in a marginal note *Philosophia Prima sive de Fontibus Scientiarum*) he reports as deficient. The fact that in the end he reports this philosophy as deficient, and poetry as not deficient, does not mean that he is reporting in poetry's favor. It is because he is going to make demands on philosophy that he is so strict with it; it is a mark of confidence which he lacks when it comes to poetry. Despite glimpses that his method has as much of poetry as of science in it, he will not trust this unified vision, just as he did not trust it in the *De Sapientia* preface. So what he does is to try to separate the two and to rid himself of poetry as he sees it in his blindest moments, as illusion, escape, and empty fantasy. He goes further than this, and here a very curious knot occurs in his thinking. He blames the deficiencies of philosophy, as recorded in history, upon poetry and poetical ways of thinking. The philosophers and scientists who failed in his eyes are cursed for being poets.

The thing appears most clearly in *Temporis Partus Masculus*. Practically everything Bacon wrote includes somewhere or other a diatribe against past philosophers, but in this tract Bacon is more aggressive than anywhere else in his work.[33] The attack, in chapter 2, centers on Aristotle and Plato, and they go down for the count in resounding Latin: "Plane autem non dissimulo (fili) mihi quopiam submovendos esse philosophastros istos poëtis ipsis fabulosiores, stupratores animarum, rerum falsarios . . . Itaque citetur Aristoteles, pessimus sophista inutili subtilitate attonitus, verborum vile ludibrium . . . Citetur jam et Plato, cavillator urbanus, tumidus poëta, theologus mente captus."[34] More fantastical than the poets, the cheap fool of words, a windbag of a poet—this comes particularly badly from one who is so much of a poet

himself. One editor after another wonders at Bacon's in-
justice to the great philosophers of the past, but it springs
from deeper roots than philosophy. Bacon the poet is
being unjust to poetry, distorting his vision of his own task
and the achievements of others.

This is a betrayal. It is not an isolated instance. Such
double-crossing runs through all his works. We can see it
in that uncertainty between poesy as learning and poesy as
a dream of learning. He saw myths, positively, as dreams
in the *De Sapientia* preface. But in the *Descriptio Globi
Intellectualis,* chapter 3, writing about science under the
form of natural history, he says: "For this is that natural
history which constitutes a solid and eternal basis of true
and active philosophy; this it is which gives the first spark
to the pure and real light of nature; and whose genius
being neglected and not propitiated, has caused us to be
visited most unhappily by that host of spectres and king-
dom of shadows which we see flitting about among the
philosophies, afflicting them with utter barrenness in re-
spect of works." Bad philosophers, then, are first, poets,
second, dreamers of dreams; but Bacon has not yet finished
with them. He has a final similitude, in which poetry is
again degraded to serve as an insult for philosophers. He
likens myth and poetry to the theater, "But it is not good
to stay too long in the theatre," and in that scornful vein
he turns the likeness against the philosophers. For the Idols
of the Theatre, the last of the four idols of the mind, are
the systems of the philosophers. So we return to Book I of
the *Novum Organum,* Aphorism 44:

> Lastly, there are Idols which have immigrated into
> men's minds from the various dogmas of philosophies,
> and also from wrong laws of demonstration. These I
> call Idols of the Theatre; because in my judgment
> all the received systems are but so many stage-plays,

representing worlds of their own creation after an un-
real and scenic fashion. Nor is it only of the systems
now in vogue, or only of the ancient sects and phi-
losophies, that I speak; for many more plays of the
same kind may yet be composed and in like artificial
manner set forth.

He goes on, in Aphorism 62:

And in the plays of this philosophical theatre you may
observe the same thing which is found in the theatre
of the poets, that stories invented for the stage are
more compact and elegant, and more as one would
wish them to be, than true stories out of history.

It is not the comparing of philosophy with poetry and
dream and the theater which matters; there is a lot to be
said for it. What matters is Bacon's injustice and insult to
his vocation of poet.

If this were all our resources and we had to work out
the remainder of Bacon's profoundly poetical system in
spite of its author's treason, the task would be a depressing
one. But there is a poet who can move in here, at the very
point where Bacon lets us down, to show what can be done
if a poet trusts poetry, if Orpheus is undivided, if poetry
and dreams and shadows and the theater are taken as a
means toward learning and even toward science. For *A
Midsummer Night's Dream* is poetic drama which handles
myth in one form after another, full of dreams and shadows
from beginning to end, as Ovidian and metamorphic in
its action and subject matter as is *The Tempest,* and, like
that play, putting forward sleep and dream as a method of
learning.[35]

What then is the play's subject matter? First, and quite
simply, love and marriage. Five times over, with five sepa-
rate couples, is this theme set out. First come Theseus and

Hippolyta, half-mythical themselves and wholly royal, whose wedding rites enclose the whole play, occasioning the Pyramus and Thisbe interlude as part of their due ceremonies, and whose steady love never wavers from first to last. Next, Oberon and Titania, mythical though of another order of myth, royal no less, whose love is troubled but will be restored during the play. These two couples are given a cross-reference of love (the *Wahlverwand-schaften* which Goethe appropriated from chemistry and used to cover cross-affinities of this kind). In Act II, Scene 1, Oberon says,

> How canst thou thus for shame, Titania,
> Glance at my credit with Hippolyta,
> Knowing I know thy love to Theseus?

Then come the four young lovers of the play, human all-too-human, who end up paired Demetrius–Helena, Lysander–Hermia, after much crossing and changing. Lastly there is the Pyramus and Thisbe couple of the play-within-the-play, mythical in origin but held firmly to earth by the mechanicals who enact their story. Yet this is not the end, for Pyramus–Bottom in his translation knits up his own earthy relationship with faery and, bypassing the young human lovers through his metamorphosis, is transported into Titania's arms and into a tenderness which if it has to be forsworn and set right later, is exquisite at the time:

> Come, sit thee down upon this flowery bed,
> While I thy amiable cheeks do coy,
> And stick musk-roses in thy sleek smooth head,
> And kiss thy fair large ears, my gentle joy.

And the mechanicals themselves have their security and their welcome in the royal courtesy of Theseus, where love shifts from love between man and woman to a love which is nearer charity in the theological sense. Though warned by Philostrate that "it is nothing, nothing in the world," it is their play which he chooses,

> I will hear that play.
> For never anything can be amiss
> When simpleness and duty tender it.

The whole passage, in Act v, Scene 1, is eloquent of a kingly heart. Hippolyta in her turn watches over the young lovers. After Theseus in Act 1, Scene 1, decrees that Hermia's failure to obey her father and marry the man she does not love will bring her "to death, or to a vow of single life," he says immediately to Hippolyta, "Come my Hippolyta, what cheer my love?" as if she needed to be distracted from inwardly taking Hermia's part; and after the return of the four lovers from the forest, it is she who believes their strange tale of change and chance, against Theseus' incredulity,

> But all the story of the night told over,
> And all their minds transfigur'd so together,
> More witnesseth than fancy's images,
> And grows to something of great constancy;
> But howsoever, strange, and admirable.

She affirms the dream—a communal dream—as learning, and she has the last word over Theseus' common sense.

Love is treated in this play as if it were not a moral phenomenon. Perhaps there is a slight censure on Titania for ungenerosity: "Why should Titania cross her Oberon?" which is followed by her enchanted beguilement with Bottom. Lysander is called, mistakenly, "this lack-love, this kill-courtesy," but here again the reproach is only for making an inadequate response to love's demands. Mistakes are made frequently, right through to the mistake by which Pyramus and Thisbe meet their ends, but the only mistake which is reproved is made by the one completely detached character in the play, the Puck ("Lord, what fools these mortals be!") who alone is held to account— "What hast thou done? Thou has mistaken quite." The other characters are in a sense compelled into their errors as one is in a dream, and therefore the play is without any moral note, as a dream is and as nature is. "I am convinced," Coleridge says, "that Shakespeare availed himself of the title of this play in his own mind, and worked upon it as a dream throughout." [36] The unmoral condition, love in the natural world, are part of the privileges which dream affords him, permitting an innocence which mirrors the innocence of nature. (Lust has no entry to this play; whereas in *The Tempest* it is admitted, only to be exorcised, as if Shakespeare made there the fuller picture without abandoning the dream).[37]

Love appears here in its variety: marriage and fertility, with their natural contrast to virginity, the constant argument of the first hundred lines of the play which set the theme; love as innocence, as tenderness, as friendship. But through this subject matter the play will explore, by a five-times repeated theme with all its cross-connections, possible relations in the world of nature as perceived by the mind, "that commerce between the mind of man and the nature of things" as Bacon said, which needs to be "restored to its perfect and original condition." In Bacon, we remember, the note of Eden, of a kind of paradisiacal state of innocent knowledge, crept in; it is there too in the *Midsummer Night's Dream*.

First, Shakespeare draws his instrument together. It consists of play, dream, and poetry, connected by countless cross-references. In Act 1, Scene 1, the theme of the play, true love, is said to be "Swift as a shadow, short as any dream." There are dreams within dreams in this work, just as there is a play within the play. Hermia's dream of a serpent in II.2; the insistence of Oberon (III.2), there called "King of shadows," that the lovers are to return to Athens in their right minds and right relationships, thinking no more of the night's events than as "a dream and fruitless vision," or, later, in IV.1, as "the fierce vexation of a dream." When at last they are restored to themselves, they leave saying, "And by the way let us recount our dreams." At the very end of the play, in Puck's final speech, this is said,

> If we shadows have offended,
> Think but this (and all is mended)
> That you have but slumber'd here
> While these visions did appear.
> And this weak and idle theme,
> No more yielding but a dream . . .

where the whole play is given dream status, the characters are shadows, and the audience involved in the dream and dreaming it. It is of plays that Theseus says, "The best in this kind are but shadows." But perhaps the best comment of all is that of Bottom, in his last speech in IV.1 when he is awakened and restored to his own shape. There he discusses his dream, and at the end says, "I will get Peter Quince to write a ballad of this dream, it shall be called *Bottom's Dream*, because it hath no bottom; and I will sing it in the latter end of a play, before the Duke. Peradventure, to make it the more gracious, I shall sing it at her death." So dream and play and love and death are drawn together here, by the fool in his own way as perfectly as by the lovers or the fairies.

Shakespeare picks up precisely what Bacon wants to reject—poetry, theater, dreams, and shadows—with an immense respect for each, and presents through them a vision of *his* method, a mythological vision of the relationship between man's mind and the natural universe. It is not an abdication from rationality but a widening of it to include the world of dreams as well. It is as if Bacon were imprisoned in that palace of the mind of which he speaks more than once; but Shakespeare, while he sets us to begin with in the palace of Theseus, as the stage directions disclose, is ready to take us out of it, "And I am to entreat you, request you, and desire you, to . . . meet me in the palace-wood, a mile without the town, by moonlight: there will we rehearse." Between these two the scenes alternate; in the palace all is clear and comprehensible, but it is in the palace wood that most of the metamorphoses take place which are the substance of the play, and at the end the creatures of the wood move into the palace to bless it.

In general Shakespeare embodies and exemplifies his method without commenting on it. There is one exception to this, however, in the *Dream,* and it is particularly valuable because it is made by a character who might represent Bacon at his most rational and antipoetic. This is Theseus, in his famous speech on imagination in lunatic, lover, and poet. He begins, in no vein of compliment:

> More strange than true. I never may believe
> These antique fables nor these fairy toys.
> Lovers and madmen have such seething brains,
> Such shaping fantasies, that apprehend
> More than cool reason ever comprehends.

One can almost hear the dry voice of Bacon appealing to the dry light of rationality. Theseus goes on to say that these three types "are of imagination all compact." He notes and dismisses the illusions of the first two, in two lines apiece. But when we come to the poet, it is as if Shakespeare forgets who is speaking for six lines and speaks himself, and there is a shift in the sense of "imagination," from negative to positive. The lines are so well known that I shall certainly give them in full, because the better known a quotation is, the less likely we are really to pay attention to it.

The Poet's eye, in a fine frenzy rolling,
Doth glance from heaven to earth, from earth to heaven,
And as imagination bodies forth
The forms of things unknown, the Poet's pen
Turns them to shapes, and gives to airy nothing,
A local habitation, and a name.

Immediately after, Shakespeare–Theseus becomes Bacon–Theseus again, with "such tricks hath strong imagination." Meantime, however, the statement stands. It gives us the universe for the poet's scope, the working imagination incorporating the intellectual figures and ideas it has perceived into shapes—that is, natural shapes such as come in a few lines later, bushes and bears and so on; and the poet's use of language gives them a place in the world and a name—one might say an ecology and a classification. Poetry's task lies somewhere between mental figures and created forms, relating the one to the other reciprocally by words. It comes down to the universe of nature, to forms and to a working method of mind and language which in Shakespeare's case will take the form of poetic drama. This is Shakespeare's method, or myth.

Is Bacon's method different? Far from it. It is, in direction and operation, identical. There are three main parts to Bacon's doctrine: his concept of *forms,* his project for a *natural history,* and his proposed reform of *logic* (i.e. of the mind's ways of working with a language). Philosopher and playwright offer corroboration, the one to the other, of the means by which postlogical thought can be realized.

6

Almost as easy as to unravel a Bottom when you begin at the right end

BACON chose to designate the three principal aspects of his new vision by terms already old and carrying many meanings. He did so deliberately, and this is interesting, for it shows Bacon acting as a poet, prepared to accept the ambiguity which words have by nature because he saw in that quality something more to his purpose than a brand-new technical term. In the *Advancement,* Book II, he says, "in this and other particulars, wheresoever my conception and notion may differ from the ancient, yet I am studious to keep the ancient terms." *Pietas* toward language is proper in a poet; so is the renewal of old words, and in Bacon the renewing of words is part of the renewing of the vision of nature itself, which he calls interpretation. So each of these three venerable terms is to be emptied and refilled. "The art which I introduce . . . is a kind of logic; though the difference between it and the ordinary logic is great; indeed immense." "Matter rather than forms should be the object of our attention, its configurations and changes of configuration, and simple action, and law of action or motion; for forms are figments of the human mind, unless you will call those laws of action forms." (This is in fact what he means to do.) "Of this reconstruction the foundation must be laid in natural history, and that of a new kind and gathered on a new principle . . . But my history differs from that in use (as my logic does) in many things,—in end and office, in mass and composition, in subtlety, in selection also and setting forth, with a view to the operations which are to follow."

All three, the living principle of the *Instauratio,* come together near the beginning of Book II of the *Organum.* Aphorisms 10 and 11 recall once more the novelty of what is being attempted, but they emphasize also the interconnection of these three. First, Bacon commends to us his Natural and Experimental History, supplemented by Tables and Arrangements of Instances to help in the management of the material supplied. Then we are to "use *Induction,* true and legitimate induction, which is the very key of interpretation. But of this," he goes on, "which is the last, I must speak first, and then go back to the other ministrations." So ends that Aphorism, and the next one begins immediately, "The investigation of Forms proceeds thus . . ." Induction, then, is to proceed to the interpretation of nature through forms, drawing its material from the natural history, which Bacon describes in the introduction to the *Parasceve* as "the primary material of philosophy and the stuff and subject-matter of true induction" (Aphorism 2).

Indeed, so closely allied were natural history and intellectual method in Bacon's mind that he could never decide which to work on first. At the end of Book I of the *Organum* (see Aphorisms 101 and 130), we find him resolving to go ahead with the art of interpreting nature; but he only carried this out in very small part, and changed his mind about the priority. In his preface to the third part of the *Instauratio,* immediately preceding the *Historia Ventorum,* he discusses this very point:

> Having in my *Instauration* placed the Natural History
> —such a Natural History as may serve my purpose—
> in the third part of the work, I have thought it right to
> make some anticipation thereof, and to enter upon it
> at once. For although not a few things, and those
> among the most important, still remain to be com-
> pleted in my *Organum,* yet my design is rather to ad-
> vance the universal work of Instauration in many
> things, than to perfect it in a few . . . It comes there-
> fore to this; that my *Organum,* even if it were com-
> pleted, would not without the Natural History much
> advance the Instauration of the Sciences, whereas the
> Natural History without the *Organum* would advance
> it not a little.

In the end he left everything unfinished.

These three together—forms, logic, and natural history
—constitute the art or science which Bacon proposes. They
can be compared, point by point, with the principles set out
in Theseus' speech; but more than this, the whole of Shake-
speare's play can be looked at in the light of these three
themes. The first theme is nature—the whole universe (ex-
cepting the moral universe of man) with particular empha-
sis on the "biosphere"; beside this we can set Bacon's
natural history. The second theme is form—the transforma-
tion, transmigration, translation of forms in nature and the
mind; beside this goes the Baconian concern with form.
The third theme is method itself, imagination in the work-
ing mind appearing here as myth, poetry, and theater;
beside this we shall put the Baconian logic or induction,
which also deals with the mind working with language.
Since the two allow of so close a comparison, I shall no
longer talk about two separate methods but about post-
logical thought as such. Bacon and Shakespeare jointly

present it as natural history, forms, and method of mind and language.

Bacon discusses his natural history in some detail in the *Parasceve* and in chapters 2 and 3 of the *Descriptio Globi Intellectualis*. As early as the *Advancement*, however, the main lines are laid down, to be repeated and expanded a little in the *De Augmentis*.

The range of the work is stated in Aphorism 4 of the *Parasceve:* [38] "In the history which I require and design, special care is to be taken that it be of wide range and made to the measure of the universe. For the world is not to be narrowed till it will go into the understanding (which has been done hitherto), but the understanding to be expanded and opened till it can take in the image of the world, as it is in fact." The scope of postlogical thought, then, is to be the natural universe.

The next question is its nature. It is not to be a mere catalogue of what is in the world. Bacon discusses this in the *Globi Intellectualis*, chapter 3, claiming that the natural histories already in existence were of this faulty kind:

> Besides, it is not of much use to recount or to know the exact varieties of flowers, as of the iris or tulip, no, nor of shells or dogs or hawks. For these and the like are but wanton sports and freaks of nature, and almost approach to the nature of individuals. And though they involve an exquisite knowledge of the particular objects, the information which they afford to the sciences is slight and almost useless. And yet these are the things which our ordinary natural history takes delight in.

Long after Bacon the debate still goes on about the usefulness to biology of "exquisite knowledge of particular objects." [39] But Bacon is laying down the principles for postlogical thought, not for specimen collecting. He has to make a shift of attention from entities to process, from the static to the dynamic; thus in the *De Augmentis*, II.2, he remarks: "Natural History treats of the deeds and works of nature." Nature is an action, to be reflected by natural history which is an activity in the mind. With this in view, we will begin looking for this natural history in two places, Bacon's *Catalogue of Particular Histories by Titles* which follows the *Parasceve*, and the scope of natural subject matter in the *Midsummer Night's Dream.*

Anyone who is interested may try an experiment with this play: Begin at the beginning and note down references to natural phenomena as they occur. The experimenter will almost certainly be exhausted before getting halfway through. The profusion is astonishing. For me the final touch came with the speech of Titania beginning, "Be kind and courteous to this gentlemen," where in six or seven lines the listmaker suddenly and finally disappears from sight under showers of apricocks and figs and dewberries, not to mention honey and butterflies and bees and glow-worms. It seemed best to say at that point *Benedicite omnia opera,* and leave it at that. Shakespeare brings into this play element after element which Bacon lists in his first eighty titles of "Particular Histories." The heavenly bodies, lightnings, thunders, winds, clouds, showers, hail, frost, snow, fog, dew, and the like, says Bacon—these are all in the *Dream;* seasons and temperatures of the year, of floods, heats, and the like—these are here, notably in Titania's long speech about the bad weather; history of earth and sea, of the shape and compass of them—"I'll put a girdle round about the earth," says Puck, and there are references to the Antipodes; of geography, of mountains, vallies, woods, sands, rivers, of ebbs and flows of the sea—these are all here. Passing over Bacon's next entries, the four elements, fire, metals, jewels, the magnet, which the play likewise produces, we come to the history of living things, of plants, trees, shrubs and herbs, and of their parts, wood, leaves, flowers, fruits—these are here, down to the red dots in the cowslips and the blades of grass. History of fishes will be matched only with dolphins, leviathans and, questionably, mermaids, but the birds flock in, doves, cocks, larks, owls, nightingales, ousels, throstles, cuckoos, wrens; and the history of quadrupeds is very wide, cats, dogs including spaniels and hounds, lions, leopards, tigers, monkeys, bears, bulls, horses, asses, boars, ounces, wolves, deer, hedgehogs—and that is not a complete list. Next for Bacon come serpents, worms, flies, and other insects, to which rather motley company the play adds newts and blind-worms, spiders, moths, snails, and beetles; then we come to man, his senses, beauty, sickness and health, limbs, flesh and blood—but we cannot pursue this any further. To lump all these together will bring us to Bacon's No. 80, with fifty heads still to come on the mechanical arts. But before we come to them and to Shakespeare's no less elegant matching of them in this play, there is one more point to be made about Shakespeare's natural history, lest this list leave us, as the play most certainly does not, with the feeling of an enumeration rather than a Baconian action.

Any account of Shakespeare's natural history in this play would be hopelessly incomplete unless it mentioned the central aspect under which nature is presented, the theme of love, or, to give it its natural rather than human name, fertility. With this theme the play begins, looking forward to the marriage of Theseus and Hippolyta which is to be its close. The discussion of Hermia's fate is in these terms,

> To live a barren sister all your life,
> Chanting faint hymns to the cold fruitless Moon.
> Thrice blessed those that master so their blood
> To undergo such maiden pilgrimage,

> But earthlier happy is the rose distill'd,
> Than that which withering on the virgin thorn,
> Grows, lives and dies in single blessedness. [1.1]

Oberon and Titania complain of ill weather in these terms
—the harvest rotted, the folds empty—repeated in Ti-
tania's lovely description of the young mother before her
boy is born, a galleon with full sails:

> Which she with pretty and with swimming gait,
> Following (her womb then rich with my young squire)
> Would imitate and sail upon the land.

It falls away in the middle of the play, only to be picked
up when the royal pair find the sleeping lovers: "Begin
these wood-birds but to couple now?" and moves to its
triumphant fulfillment in Theseus' "Lovers, to bed," and
the blessing the fairies give to each bride-bed, the children
to be perfect and the field-dew sprinkled in token of it all.

It is not only Shakespeare who gives fertility a central
place in the workings of a postlogical natural history. Bacon
does so too. In Aphorism 1 of the *Parasceve* we read:

> Natural History therefore is threefold. It treats of the
> *liberty* of nature, or the *errors* of nature, or the *bonds*
> of nature: so that we may fairly distribute it into his-
> tory of *Generations,* of *Pretergenerations,* and of *Arts;*
> which last I also call *Mechanical* or *Experimental* His-
> tory.

The term "generation" is, it should be realized, partly a
recording of fact and partly a choice of metaphor—that is
to say, it is partly subject matter and partly methodology.
Much of nature does in fact reproduce itself by generation,
but much does not, and it is worth noticing that Bacon
chooses to spread the living metaphor over inanimate na-
ture rather than figure (as is done where the image of ma-
chinery is used, for instance) the living by the nonliving.

It is clear in the *Globi Intellectualis*, chapter 4, that this is what he is doing, for there his history of generations begins with ether and meteors. This is a mythical turn of thought.[40] To see the whole of nature as a generative process is part of postlogic, and allows the thinking organism to figure in itself the processes it is reflecting upon.

Alongside generations and in unity with the whole natural process, Bacon sets down arts. He has more to say about this aspect of postlogical natural history in the *Descriptio Globi Intellectualis*:

> And I am the rather induced to set down the history of arts as a species of natural history, because it is the fashion to talk as if art were something different from nature, so that things artificial should be separated from things natural, as differing totally in kind; whence it comes that most writers of natural history think it enough to make a history of animals or plants or minerals, without mentioning the experiments of mechanical arts (which are far the most important for philosophy) . . . Therefore as nature is ever one and the same, and her power extends through all things, nor does she ever forsake herself, these three things should by all means be set down as alike subordinate only to nature; namely, the course of nature; the wandering of nature; and art, or nature with man to help. And therefore in natural history all these things should be included in one continuous series of narratives.

That makes the unity of nature and art plain enough. This is not only a Baconian doctrine, however; Shakespeare holds it too:

> Yet nature is made better by no mean
> But nature makes that mean: so, over that art
> Which you say adds to nature, is an art

> That nature makes . . . this is an art
> Which does mend nature,—change it rather; but
> The art itself is nature.

This is Polixenes in *The Winter's Tale*. The views of each man are very important, for they set up an immense continuity which is part of the conditions for postlogical thought.

"Art" or "arts" has a multiplicity of meanings. It could mean, in Bacon's period, operations of almost any sort, from the art of interpreting nature which Bacon seeks, through the liberal arts, some of which we should nowadays call sciences, to the practical arts of the craftsman, and eventually to magic, Prospero's "so potent art" or "that damnèd art" of Doctor Faustus. Practice and operation, it suggests, are unified in the general scheme of nature as process or "nature with man to help." It is this, in part, which Bacon sees. Dynamic process interested him deeply; so his forms turn into laws of motion, and the inquisition on motion was one of the first he undertook, so crucial did he hold it to be. Technology was for him part of this process, but the utilitarian Bacon, the father of the industrial revolution, does not on his own terms exclude the poet. Later centuries made that false division. If art is taken in this broad sense, as it should be, poet and technologist are connected by analogous operations but on different bits of nature, so to speak. Postlogical thinking, which accepts this over-all unity of process in nature and art, will take this into account.

As so often happens, Bacon's theory will not go as far as his practice. In the *Parasceve*, Aphorism 4, he states: "History of Arts, and of Nature as changed and altered by Man, or Experimental History . . . is drawn either from the mechanical arts or from the operative parts of the liberal arts." (In the similar passage in *De Augmentis*, II.2, he calls them "the liberal sciences.") In a fragment, *Cogitationes de Scientia Humana,* he construes these "operative parts" as music, perspective, and medicine. But his own practice goes far beyond this. A direction is already implicit in the mention of liberal arts; for these, we remember, begin with the trivium, the mind operating in figures of language which are then to be directed in the quadrivium toward the universe of nature. Because Bacon is a poet searching for the methods of postlogic, which is an operation of mind and language directed toward nature, he is profoundly concerned with the point at which nature and language meet. This would seem at first sight to be the mind, but Bacon says more than that. In fact, his interest in this meeting point of nature, mind, and language explains his preoccupation with the mechanical arts. Those who think his interest was solely practical have mistaken what he means by power.[41] He is interested in the mechanical arts because he believes that at this point nature will be more ready to give evidence and to reveal what she secretly knows. He expresses this belief in a series of metaphors.

The first and most frequent is that, by these arts, nature or matter is imprisoned and handcuffed and so made more tractable and ready to give evidence. He calls this "the vexations of art." The myth of Proteus is a favorite image of his in this connection. The metaphor goes further, however, logically pursuing the image Bacon has embarked on, the juridical processes of his own period which he knew, as an eminent lawyer, very well; one might say too well. For the second part of the metaphor is that nature is to be put to the question—that is, tortured if necessary to extort the necessary evidence. This underlies Bacon's constant use of "Inquisitio" (*Filum Labyrinthi sive Formula Inquisitionis*); the direct Englishing of that still carries a hateful sound to our ears, and "interrogation," with which Bacon concludes the *Parasceve* ("to examine nature herself and the arts upon interrogatories"), a yet worse because a more modern one.

So-called confessions extracted by torture have become so abhorrently familiar that it is hard to bring one's mind to see in this figure of Bacon's what he saw, a legitimate procedure to compel not just speech but the spoken truth from the obdurately silent. Attendance at sessions of such a kind formed part of Bacon's duties, as we know.[42] Bacon uses the metaphor about nature because in his view she could be made to speak out and to speak true if the right expedient were employed. We no longer share the complacency at the method nor the belief in it as a means to truth, and it is with relief that we can turn to Shakespeare at this very point. He too will deal with mechanical arts as part of natural history, thus matching the last fifty titles in Bacon's *Catalogue of Particular Histories* which begin with cookery and baking and continue through wood-working and weaving and the like—all, as Bacon insists, under the heading of natural history. Shakespeare, however, does not deal with them by torture. He gives us instead the *Dream* clowns, unmenaced in the freedom and folly their creator so largely bestows upon them.

The six mechanicals are no mere accident of comic relief in this play. They are Shakespeare's equivalent of Bacon's insistence on the need to observe the mechanical arts. Shakespeare does not argue the point: he presents characters. But each writer is making a case for the special status of the arts in the widest sense, human operation upon nature, as part of natural process and the point at which forms—in nature, mind, and language—interact and interpret one another. They are, for Shakespeare as for Bacon, the bridge between the study of natural history and the study of forms as such. Bacon, true to his Orpheus, directs toward philosophy whatever profit may come from the study of these arts: "My meaning plainly is that all me-

chanical experiments should be as streams flowing from all
sides into the sea of philosophy" (*Parasceve,* Aphorism 5).
Carefully, however, he keeps his own art, that of interpret-
ing, separate from the mechanical arts; the latter are to be
referred, for translation and collating, to the former. Shake-
speare, no less true to *his* Orpheus, goes much further. In
an astonishing stroke of genial generosity he unites himself
and his art with the mechanicals, lending them his own
craft of poetic and mythological drama, since if natural
process is really all of a piece and includes arts of all kind,
such a union is only logical. Where once again Bacon stops
half way, Shakespeare follows through the logic of post-
logic. His mechanicals here take on exactly the task he has
himself in hand, the production of a play on the occasion of
a wedding.[43]

What Shakespeare presents us with, in these clown scenes,
is in the best Baconian sense a "mechanical experiment."
Philostrate in v.1 makes this plain:

> THESEUS: What are they that do play it?
> PHILOSTRATE: Hard-handed men, that work in Athens
>   here,
>   Which never labour'd in their minds
>   till now.

With these simple minds, versed only in mechanical skills
and now attempting art of another kind, a mythological
and linguistic piece of work, Shakespeare conducts his own
experiment. That is why their play is so important, their
sole purpose in Shakespeare's play. All four of their com-
munal scenes are devoted to it—to its casting, its rehearsing,
its near-abandonment as marred without Bottom, and then
his return with the news "our play is preferred," and lastly
its performance. And between the first two and the last two
Shakespeare sets the obligato of Bottom's adventure, which
is an experiment of a rather different kind, though Bottom
calls it "Bottom's dream," so that we are still within the

main framework of Shakespeare's method, and we are accompanied by poetry all the way through. We shall begin with poetry in simple and essential form—the actors' marvelous names and trades.

It is clear that their names and callings are not just to be listed under *Dramatis Personae,* a mere program convention. They are built into that first scene of theirs where Peter Quince is calling the roll of his team. They are, you recall, Peter Quince; his trade is not called because he is doing the calling, but the stage directions give him a carpenter; Nick Bottom the weaver; Francis Flute the bellows mender; Robin Starveling the tailor; Tom Snout the tinker; and Snug (who is given no first name) the joiner. Now look at the names. Dover Wilson says of them that they are "technical names":

> Commentators have remarked that *Bottom* takes his name from the "bottom" or core of the skein upon which the weaver's yarn is wound; but they have not noticed that most of the other clowns have technical names likewise. Thus *Quince* is simply a spelling of "quines" or "quoins," i.e. wedge-shaped blocks of wood used for building purposes, and therefore appropriately connected with a carpenter; *Snout* means nozzle or spout (v. N.E.D. "snout" 4) which suggests the tinker's trade in mending kettles; *Snug* means "compact, close-fitting, tight,"—a good name for a joiner; and *Flute,* the bellows-mender, would of course have to repair fluted church-organs as well as the domestic bellows. *Starveling,* indeed, is the only non-technical name among them, though it is apt enough, referring as it does to the proverbial leanness of tailors, of whom it took "nine to make a man." [44]

So far so good, but the names are not merely technical terms. They have that quality of association which goes with poetry, and the associations bear with them not merely the

mechanical history of "things artificial" which Bacon com-
mends, but also that other history, of "things natural."
"Snout" has obvious animal connections, and was used in
Shakespeare's time for fish and bird as well as beast. The
name "Starveling" by its image of thinness brings in the
body and food, and the word was used not only for human
beings but also for animals or plants. "Snug" suggests a
bodily, almost animal, warmth, as do the words "snuggle"
or "nestle." "Quince" is fruit and tree. Flute the bellows-
mender suggests by that combination of woodwind and bel-
lows the moving breath which is life itself (lungs and bellows
make as obvious a pair as do heart and pump), a life which
is also capable of translation into music. His own quality
of voice is drawn to our attention in his choice for Thisbe
and his remonstrance, "Nay faith, let me not play a woman,
I have a beard coming," and in Bottom's desire to out-flute
Flute, "I'll speak in a monstrous little voice." Last and best,
there is Bottom himself. He calls attention to his own
name: "It shall be called Bottom's Dream because it hath
no bottom." It carries its obvious bodily reference and also
the trade meaning which I shall come back to before long.
But meantime we can take stock of what the names so far
have done for us. They imply the great unity of natural his-
tory, plants and trees, animals, man as body and mind, the
arts. The mechanicals are dove-tailed into the whole uni-
verse of nature which is the subject matter of the *Dream;*
but they have their own proper distinction in it. They are
not bestialized, nor are they oafs or boors. They have strug-
gled up out of the vegetable and animal into the human
condition and they hold to their human status and, one
might almost say, dignity, as Theseus recognizes, "If we
imagine no worse of them than they of themselves, they may
pass for excellent men." Because they are human, they form
a society, depicted here as the play's cast, close-knit and
friendly; and they speak.

Speech, the acting and speaking of their play (notice the constant reference throughout the *Dream* to cues) is their whole endeavor here, and to speech everything is referred. "Have you the Lion's part written? pray you if it be, give it me, for I am slow of study," says Snug in their first scene. Moon, Wall, Lion, all are somehow assimilated to the human condition and made to talk, not as in fairy tales with their own voices, but with those of Snug and Snout. Nature is acted upon by words, but not tortured into speech. Because of the simplicity of those who act her or act upon her, these virgin minds, Shakespeare comes as near as is possible to lending nature speech in them and their play. He can then observe the results.

In the very first exchanges between Quince and Bottom, something begins to happen. Bottom says, "You were best to call them generally," where he means "severally"; and Peter Quince announces the play as "the most lamentable comedy." Strange juxtapositions, exchanges, substitutions, occur in the mechanicals' use of words. This pattern set up in their conversation is continued and intensified in their play.

> A tedious brief scene of young Pyramus
> And his love Thisby; very tragical mirth

their playbill reads, and Theseus comments, "That is, hot ice, and wondrous strange snow." Sun and moon run together in one of Pyramus' speeches, "Sweet Moon, I thank thee for thy sunny Beams." The senses are exchanged for one another—"he goes but to see a noise that he heard and is to come again." "I see a voice, now will I to the chink / To spy an I can hear my Thisby's face"; "Tongue, lose thy light." The animals undergo a series of verbal substitutions, begun in Bottom's "I will roar you as gently as any sucking dove; I will roar you an 'twere any nightingale," and taken up by the verbal quibbling of the court occasioned by the play's performance: "This lion is a very fox for his valour." "True, and a goose for his discretion." "Well moused, Lion." These are of course only verbal play, but they shadow something else, as does Quince's Prologue, where grammar and syntax are all upset, i.e. the forms and structures of language are changed, and the sense is contradicted by the form. This occasions the following remarks,

LYSANDER:	He hath rid his Prologue, like a rough colt: he knows not the stop. A good moral my Lord. It is not enough to speak, but to speak true.
HIPPOLYTA:	Indeed he hath played on his Prologue, like a child on a recorder, a sound, but not in government.
THESEUS:	His speech was like a tangled chain: nothing impaired but all disordered.

They cannot manage their instrument, but their very mistakes draw attention to the nature of that instrument and show the language situation for what it is, a dynamic and not a static one. Mistakes are nearly always dynamic or working situations. Language is presented as a net of working forms, and even though the mechanicals cannot manage its poetry (for that is what its dynamism is) they point toward it, as Shakespeare's perfected poetry could not do.

It is here that Bottom has his particular significance. If we turn back a moment to the question of his name, we find that this technical term in weaving has other connections. The *Oxford English Dictionary* says: "BOTTOM: A clew or nucleus on which to wind thread; also a skein or ball of thread." The first example given is 1490, from Caxton's *Eneydos:* "He must take wyth hym a bottome of threade." Later among the examples comes this, from Ralegh's *History of the World,* "He received from her [Ariadne] a bottome of threde." It is interesting that the word "bottom" should apparently have a peculiar right of entry into the story of Theseus and Ariadne and the labyrinth, the combination of names reappearing in the *Dream* where Theseus is a character and Ariadne is mentioned. Is Bottom the weaver the "clew" to this play and what it says about postlogic?

So far we have been looking at natural history, which in Bacon's and Shakespeare's hands gives the range of postlogic (the natural universe considered as alive throughout) and its terms of reference (process as a whole, seen as fertility and generation and as operation of all kinds, through nature and up to and including man). Man is language; and here Bottom is to the fore. Others of the mechanicals show a tendency toward poetry or rhetoric, as in Quince's confusion of "paragon" and "paramour" for instance. Only a noble feeling for rhetoric would induce so risky an extension of vocabulary; it is easy for anyone to be correct in Basic English. But it is Bottom, regarded by his peers as the fine flower of their society, the best wit in all Athens, the *sine qua non* of their play, who carries this tendency furthest. Their play with its mythological subject from the *Metamorphoses* is a communal effort, but it is Bottom who is on familiar terms with myths outside the play, who speaks of Ercles and Phibbus with a breezy and inaccurate familiarity. They play in verse, but it is Bottom who quotes verse outside the play, and who when put to it has a rude vein of poetry in his own imagination. Bottom is the mind working with language; he is also dynamics, for he alone moves out of the framework of the little play into that of the larger one, by his "dream" which gives him, even if only briefly, the entry to another universe. With him we shall move on now to the Baconian forms which have been shadowing us for some time, and to the transformations in the *Dream* itself.

7

A Collection of all varieties of Natural Bodies . . . where an Inquirer . . . might peruse, and turn over, and spell, and read the Book of Nature, and observe the *Orthography, Etymologia, Syntaxis,* and *Prosodia* of Nature's Grammar, and by which as with a *Dictionary,* he might readily turn to and find the true Figures, Composition, Derivation, and Use of the Characters, Words, Phrases and Sentences of Nature written with indelible, and most exact, and most expressive Letters, without which Books it will be very difficult to be thoroughly a *Literatus* in the Language and Sense of Nature

INCOMPLETE as it is, Bacon's doctrine of forms has given rise to accusations of slovenliness and imprecision. It is certainly not easy, but we must remember that Bacon is, after all, trying to say something new. Forms are touched on in *Valerius Terminus,* chapter 11, where he calls the discovery of a form "the freeing of a direction"; they are outlined in the *Advancement* and *De Augmentis,* and are eventually treated more fully, though not definitively, in *Novum Organum,* Book II, which deals with forms and induction, "being," as he says of this work in the *De Augmentis* (Bk. v, chap. 2), "the most important thing of all."

This is how that second book begins:

> On a given body to generate and superinduce a new nature or new natures, is the work and aim of Human Power. Of a given nature to discover the form, or true specific difference, or nature-engendering nature, [the Latin is *natura naturans,* a phrase with a wonderful tradition of its own through Saint Augustine and Saint Thomas] or source of emanation (for these are the terms which come nearest to a description of the thing), is the work and aim of Human Knowledge. Subordinate to these primary works are two others that are secondary and of inferior mark; to the former, the transformation of concrete bodies, so far as this is possible; to the latter, the discovery, in every case of generation of motion, of the *latent process* carried on from the manifest efficient and the manifest material to the form which is engendered; and in like manner the discovery of the *latent configuration* of bodies at rest and not in motion.

From this Aphorism till the 9th, Bacon explains and adds to the opening statement. Part of the uncertainty of his doctrine lies in the question whether his forms are in matter or in the mind. Bacon realized this, and comments on it in Aphorism 2:

> Nor have I forgotten that in a former passage I noted and corrected as an error of the human mind the opinion that Forms give existence. For though in nature

nothing really exists besides individual bodies, performing pure individual acts according to a fixed law, yet in philosophy this very law, and the investigation, discovery and explanation of it, is the foundation as well of knowledge as of operation. And it is this law, with its clauses, that I mean when I speak of *Forms;* a name which I the rather adopt because it has grown into use and become familiar.

By "forms" Bacon means the inner laws of working of natural phenomena as they may be perceived, expressed, or translated by the mind. (As a professional lawyer, he must have had a dynamic and living concept of law itself which one would do well to remember, the lay mind tending to think of the law in this sense as a fixed codex rather than as its practitioners think of it: "an indubitable structure, organic and living.") [45] These are the "laws of motion and alteration" mentioned in *Valerius Terminus,* the "laws of action" in matter in *Novum Organum,* Book I, Aphorism 51, the "laws of pure act" of 85. To them there must correspond a mental method which shall register and control these working laws of phenomena. For Bacon knowledge is the primary form of operation:

> From the discovery of Forms therefore results truth in speculation and freedom in operation. [Aphorism 3]

> Now these two directions, the one active the other contemplative, are one and the same thing; and what in operation is most useful, that in knowledge is most true. [Aphorism 4]

Action in matter becomes, through forms and mind, action upon it. In Aphorism 9 he says that the investigation of these forms is the task of metaphysics; and then to physics he assigns the more operative part by which "latent process" and "latent configuration" are to be examined, although here too the mind remains the fundamental instrument for all operation upon matter.

What Bacon seems to have in mind is that all matter is in a constant state of hidden motion and change which is to be investigated. "For what I understand by it is not certain measures or signs or successive steps of process in bodies which can be seen; but a process perfectly continuous, which for the most part escapes the sense" (6). He relates this part of the investigation to individual natures rather than to nature as a whole, adding that it will almost certainly be easier in operation, because less general and fundamental, than the inquiry into forms themselves. "Latent process" is touched on in Aphorisms 5 and 6. It is related to generation, growth, and development, but also to other motions and operations of nature. In Aphorism 7 he speaks of "latent configuration" as also "a new thing," discussing anatomy and similar disciplines in connection with this process yet finding them insufficient so far, since this investigation needs not merely material analysis (whether physical or chemical or mechanical) but also the right type of mental analysis and method. "We must pass from Vulcan to Minerva," says Bacon, "if we intend to bring to light the true textures of bodies; on which all the occult, and, as they are called, specific properties and virtues in things depend; and from which too the rule of every powerful alteration and transformation is derived." So we are brought back to the need for method, and it becomes clearer why in Bacon's mind the natural history, the forms and the induction could not be separated the one from the other.

No apology is needed for so dynamic and modern a vision, of matter in particular and of nature in general as forms, inner and outer, which are the products of laws of motion discoverable by the mind if it has the right way of working. Its greatness and interest have been seen by Ba-

con's more perceptive commentators, Orphic minds such
as Shelley, Coleridge, or—perhaps supremely—Robert
Hooke, one of the first members of the Royal Society and
an Orphic scientist of the first order. (His Orphic title
includes—besides his estimation of the "incomparable
Verulam," as he calls Bacon in his posthumous work on
natural philosophy, and a mention of Orpheus as an early
conveyor of scientific knowledge—a remarkable interpre-
tation of the myths in Ovid's *Metamorphoses* as figured
descriptions of early geological eras of the world.) This is
what Hooke has to say about that area of postlogical activ-
ity where the Baconian forms operate:

> To observe the Transitions of Nature in the Forms
> and Proprieties of Creatures, how it passes from one to
> the other. . . . Another way of discovering Nature, is
> by taking more especial notice of such of her Works,
> wherein she seems to act yet more secretly and farther
> remov'd from the Detection of our Senses, such as in
> the Formation and Configuration of Bodies. . . . An-
> other way of discovering Nature, is by taking notice of
> the Transitions of Nature, by what degrees and steps
> it passes from one thing to another in the Formation of
> Species. . . . But as for the Discovery of the more
> internal Texture and Constitution, as also of the Mo-
> tion, Energy, and operating Principle of Concrete
> Bodies, together with the Method and Course of Na-
> ture's proceeding in them: these will require much
> deeper Researches and Ratiocinations.[46]

This is the Baconian vision of experiment and thought to-
gether aiming at the discovery of the motion, energy, and
operating principles of the forms of nature. Coleridge picks
up this point in his essay on Bacon in *The Friend*,[47] talk-
ing of the relationship between laws and ideas in Bacon's
concept of nature; and some of Bacon's most modern com-

mentators have at length come to appreciate (perhaps because we are only now, scientifically speaking, in a position to do so) the potentialities of Bacon's concept of form as a working principle of nature and mind both, of his vision of things as patterns and laws of motion, and of matter as essentially alive with an inherent law of motion, to which the mind must apply a kind of logic or method which also moves in time.[48] D'Arcy Thompson sets out something remarkably close to this in the first chapter of *On Growth and Form*. "Now the state, including the shape or form, of a portion of matter is the resultant of a number of forces, which represent or symbolise the manifestations of energy," he says, and it is particularly interesting to find this beautifully exact mind sorting out in this field from the start what is matter and what is mind, so to speak, and—in my terms if not in his—characterizing the terms "form" and "force" as poetry: "It [force] is a term as subjective and symbolic as form itself, and so is used appropriately in connection therewith." This is the point of working where mind and matter cannot separate themselves, as Bacon saw, and where the operation necessarily becomes myth, the operative point for each man's art or science or interpretation of nature, whether that man be Bacon or D'Arcy Thompson—or Shakespeare, for he is at work here too.

Forms in transformation—forms in nature and in the mind—are part of the *Midsummer Night's Dream*. Shakespeare as dramatist cannot discuss his forms; he has to present them. So the forms of nature become forms indeed, the forms of Titania and Oberon, spirits visible to the audience admitted to the mythological situation or the dream, but invisible to the mortals in the play ("I am invisible," Oberon says to make things quite clear, when Demetrius and Helena enter, Act II, Scene 1). In mortal form but not of mortal kind, as Titania explains when she says to Bottom:

And I will purge thy mortal grossness so
That thou shalt like an airy spirit go,

these are spirits which can nonetheless partake of mortal
shape, and their motions, of love or jealousy and dishar-
mony, are joined with the general course of nature, so that
disturbance in the one breeds a like disturbance in the
other. These are shadows of what will happen in the storm
scene in *Lear,* where not spirit-in-human-shape and nature
but man and nature are set in this same relationship of
analogy and unity. Again when Shakespeare comes to forms
as the working of the mind he can only present us with a
character, and what we are given is Bottom. The two meet
in Bottom's interlude with Titania: forms as operative
powers in natural phenomena, and forms as instruments
of the thinking mind. Behind these, however, the whole
of nature is seen to be in movement. Everything is chang-
ing. The seasons change; the lovers exchange partners;
myth itself may alter: "Apollo flies, and Daphne holds the
chase." (ii.1). The word "change" comes round over and
over again.

The spring, the summer,
The chiding autumn, angry winter change
Their wonted liveries. [ii.1]

Run when you will, the story shall be changed. [ii.1]

O Bottom, thou art chang'd; what do I see on thee? [iii.1]

What change is this, sweet love? [iii.2]

And there is a marvelous refrain throughout the play of
words for inner and outer changings, of natural and mental
forms. "The rest I'ld give to be to you translated" we begin
with, Helena wishing to be Hermia and Demetrius' be-

loved. This word occurs twice more: "Bless thee Bottom, bless thee; thou art translated," says Peter Quince, a phrase caught up later by Puck, "And left sweet Pyramus translated there." But there are others too. "Things base and vile, holding no quantity, / Love can transpose to form and dignity," Helena says. At the end of Bottom's idyll, Puck is bidden by Oberon to take "This transformed scalp / From off the head of this Athenian swain." Later it is said of Bottom, "He cannot be heard of. Out of doubt he is transported." And lastly Hippolyta says of the lovers and the whole dream they have undergone, "all their minds transfigur'd so together."

The forms in this play are in movement as they were in that dark Orpheus scene with which we began, and Bottom's metamorphosis and translation are part of this (he moves in his double capacity—as Bottom translated and as "sweet Pyramus translated"). This is the nature of mythological thinking made manifest, and because Shakespeare is wholly committed to it he can afford to make it as funny as it is, our animal affinities somehow drawn up among the powers of nature which we as yet neither understand nor control, but to which we are united. Bottom is the human condition, the newly thinking mind subjected to natural forms and trying to make forms of its own by which to understand them.

We have arrived now at the point where, in both these great Orphic inquirers, forms in natural history converge on the method to be employed. It is a crucial point, for with it comes the question, in Bacon and in general: what is that interpretation of nature which Bacon aimed at?

There is one remark of Bacon's, set in a place of honor as the opening word of the *Novum Organum,* which comes close to a brief definition of it. "Homo naturae minister et interpres" it runs: man the interpreter of nature and its servant (perhaps one needs to think of the English "servant"

and "minister" to get its meaning more fully). Bacon insists
continually that "the work of the Interpreter" is the heart
of the matter. There is a general statement on it in the "Plan
of the Work": "For the matter in hand is no mere felicity
of speculation, but the real business and fortunes of the
human race, and all power of operation. For man is but
the servant and interpreter of nature; what he does and
what he knows is only what he has observed of nature's
order in fact or in thought; beyond this he knows nothing
and can do nothing. For the chain of causes cannot by any
force be loosed or broken, neither can nature be com-
manded except by being obeyed. And so those twin objects,
human knowledge and human Power, do really meet in
one." The same points are repeated more formally in
Aphorisms 3 and 4 of Book 1 of the *Organum.*

Shakespeare does not claim such functions for himself.
It is not consonant with his role as dramatist. It is therefore
the more interesting to find them claimed for him, ex-
plicitly, in Bacon's terms, by one of his later Orphic com-
mentators, Herder. In the essay on Shakespeare in *Von
deutscher Art und Kunst,* Herder calls him "Dollmetscher
der Natur in all' ihren Zungen," interpreter of nature in
all her tongues; a little later he says, "Da ist nun Shake-
speare der grösste Meister, eben weil er nur und immer
Diener der Natur ist"; this poet is the greatest master be-
cause he is always and only the servant of nature. *Homo
naturae minister et interpres.*

Interpretation involves language. At this point the
method of each has to fit itself to that point at which nature
may be made to speak. Each method, and each of these
two minds, has to declare its vision of language at the meet-
ing-place of mind and nature. Orpheus has to be revealed
in his dark powers as a re-former of the natural order.

Bacon's Orpheus, we remember, stood for philosophy.

He might well be a very modern one, for in and through him Bacon wrestles with method as logic and language.

He conceives of his whole task in the first place as logic. In the *De Augmentis*, Book v, chapter 1, we find the phrase twice repeated, "the Interpretation of Nature, or the New Organon," an echo of that entry at the beginning of the "Plan of the Work" where the *Novum Organum* is given the subtitle "Directions Concerning the Interpretation of Nature." For Bacon, the interpretation is the logic. That same "Plan of the Work" sets the theme plainly:

> The art which I introduce with this view (which I call *Interpretation of Nature*) is a kind of logic; though the difference between it and the ordinary logic is great; indeed immense. For the ordinary logic professes to contrive and prepare helps and guards for the understanding, as mine does; and in this one point they agree. But mine differs from it in three points especially; viz. in the end aimed at; in the order of demonstration; and in the starting point of the inquiry.

"A kind of logic"—the phrase stirs the mind, and we need to acknowledge at once the extraordinary nature of this endeavor, this recognition by a great mind that something new is to be attempted with the very workings of mind itself. It is not a new field for thought that is proposed, but a new instrument of thinking. (This indeed is the theme of Bacon's great "Proœmium" to the whole work.) He calls it, in that first quotation, an art. In the next paragraph he refers to it as a science; and to science he directs it. What we might call it is an attempt to discover a new myth for thought.

There is an admirable statement of it in the *De Augmentis:* "And this is the very thing which I am preparing and labouring at with all my might,—to make the mind of

men by help of art a match for the nature of things." The
nature of things consisted in those forms which were laws
of action and motion. To this the mind must offer a match,
not in the sense of opposition but in that of a wedding.
What is needed, as Bacon indicates, is a mental process more
dynamic, subtle and precise than the logic then in use (see
his reference to "living axioms" in the *Organum*, 1.104; to
the need for greater subtlety in his preface to the *Instaura-
tion;* and to a process "just and methodical" in the *Or-
ganum*, 1.26). It is an Orphic vision, the matching of two
moving processes, one in nature, one in the mind and lan-
guage, whereby reality may be altered and controlled. Could
this be achieved, there might result what Bacon sets out
in a very beautiful passage of the "Plan," the match or mar-
riage indeed:

> The explanation of which things, and of the true re-
> lation between the nature of things and the nature
> of the mind, is as the strewing and decoration of the
> bridal chamber of the Mind and the Universe, the
> Divine Goodness assisting; out of which marriage let
> us hope (and be this the prayer of the bridal song) there
> may spring helps to man, and a line and race of in-
> ventions that may in some degree subdue and over-
> come the miseries and necessities of humanity.

If a man means to make a new myth to replace old ones,
he must show why he thinks this necessary, and so Bacon
attacks the Aristotelian method, as he conceived it, of rea-
soning from first principles to particulars, and proposes in-
stead his notion of induction, or reasoning which starts
with observation of a number of particular cases and from
these moves on to infer general principles. The current
logic seemed to Bacon too far removed from the nature of
things, the syllogism "acting too confusedly and letting
nature slip out of its hands." Induction, for him, "upholds

the sense and closes with nature, and comes to the very brink of operation, if it does not actually deal with it."

This abstractness in formal logic which in his view rendered it useless in operation has for him something to do with words.

> The syllogism consists of propositions; propositions of words; and words are the tokens and signs of notions. Now if the very notions of the mind (which are as the soul of words and the basis of the whole structure) be improperly and over-hastily abstracted from facts, vague, not sufficiently definite, faulty in short in many ways, the whole edifice tumbles.

Bacon clearly saw the tendency of formal logic toward those extremes of formalism to which it has since been taken. He is too sweeping in his condemnation, for of course formal logic is useful, and beautiful, precisely because it can abstract and formalize so completely. But the important thing is that Bacon sees another possibility, a logic holding to things, a logic of content as well as form; postlogic in fact. And words for him are in a highly ambivalent position between these two logics or myths, the old one and the new one he is proposing.

He thinks of Aristotelian logic as tending to disputation rather than reality, to dialectic or one of the three subdivisions of the trivium, only one-third of the total task of language. In *De Principiis*, for example, he praises the pre-Socratic philosophers for their concept of their task, saying of them, "Therefore all these submitted their minds to the nature of things. Whereas Plato made over the world to thoughts; and Aristotle made over thoughts to words; men's studies even then tending to dispute and discourse, and forsaking the stricter enquiry of truth." The answer to this, for Bacon's logic, would be to develop as far as possible the countertendency in words, their content and closeness to things, their mythical and poetic quality. There is a hint of such a possibility in the *De Augmentis,* where in Books v and vi Bacon extends logic to cover the whole domain of intellectual activity, apart from that covered by ethics. In Book vi the working of the mind with language, i.e. logic, is freed entirely from that assimilation with dialectic for which he condemns the current logic. The other two divisions of the trivium, grammar and rhetoric, are given their meed of attention. There are interesting passages on philosophical grammar, and on rhetoric as a form of demonstration directed toward the imagination and of a more flexible nature than the demonstrations of logic—subjects which he discusses more fully in the *Advancement* and *Valerius Terminus.*

Language does not enter only here in Bacon's system. A great language metaphor runs right through his work of inquiry into the point where nature may be made to speak in and through forms which are also method. In passages in the *Advancement* and *De Augmentis,* the forms are expressly compared with the letters of the alphabet. Nature in this figure appears in her elements at the level of letters, in her higher organizations or organisms as words and sense, in her totality as a corpus of language or a book. Bacon is known to have written an *Abecedarium Naturae* which is lost. The metaphor appears most clearly in all its levels in his introduction to the "Natural and Experimental History," Part iii of the *Magna Instauratio:*

> we must exhort men again and again . . . to approach with humility and veneration to unroll the volume of Creation, to linger and meditate therein, and with minds washed clean from opinions to study it in purity and integrity. For this is that sound and language which went forth into all lands, and did not incur the

confusion of Babel; this should men study to be per-
fect in, and becoming again as little children conde-
scend to take the alphabet of it into their hands, and
spare no pains to search and unravel the interpretation
thereof.

Yet this is the same Bacon who seems so often opposed to
words, which he includes among the "Idols of the Market
Place" as insufficiently subtle for the investigation of na-
ture, and leading men away from facts. The same division
appears also in his commentator, Hooke, who likewise in-
veighs against language, but who yet saw the properties of
bodies as "the first elements of Letters of Information,"
gave to crystals the marvelous name of "the Elemental
Figures, or the ABC of Nature's working," and who wrote
the beautiful extended version of this metaphor with which
this section is headed (above, p. 134). For both these Orphic
thinkers language and the mind's operations with it lie at
the living center of natural structures where forms also may
be supposed to be. This is what Bacon has in his hand—
and he does with it exactly what we saw him do in his
preface to the *De Sapientia Veterum*.

Spedding, in his interesting preface to the *Parasceve*,[49]
written in dialogue form, where he is trying to find out for
himself what the real nature of Bacon's innovation and
importance might be, puts forward a metaphor of his own,
closely akin to Bacon's: nature as "a manuscript in a char-
acter unknown." It is an image for the task of interpreta-
tion, and Spedding imagines two men at work on it by
different methods, by whom he means to represent Galileo
and Bacon. This opposition is, I think, mistaken to some
extent, but the image is a good one. Spedding phrases the
two possibilities as "expert maker-out of puzzles," and
"work on the laws of language." If we translate this back

into Baconian terms, we see the same dilemma that confronted Bacon when thinking about myths. Is nature's book or language a code or a hieroglyphic?

Bacon makes the same answer he made then, and chooses the code, despite the fact that such a choice runs counter to the whole nature of his vision. To this his method of induction, such as we have it, is directed. It is because of this that it can be, he claims, exercised by any mind irrespective of ability. Decoding, as a system of operation, can be taught to anyone if they will obey the rules. So he tries to have it both ways, to construct postlogic out of formal logic, because he will not trust himself to poetry.

He describes in the *Organum* (1.105) the induction of which his logic or interpretation consists: "the induction which is to be available for the discovery and demonstration of sciences and arts, must analyse nature by proper rejections and exclusions; and then, after a sufficient number of negatives, come to a conclusion on the affirmative instances." Priority is given to analysis and negation, and the only detailed exposition we have of it, Book II, Aphorisms 15 to the end, is in those terms. No room is to be left, as one commentator after another has pointed out, for that imaginative unity, call it hypothesis or hunch or what you will, which from the beginning must hold this kind of work together.[50] What Bacon proposes is a rigorous analytic intellectual formalism for a situation whose essential nature he himself saw in his poetic moments as living and creative. No wonder the method never has worked and, as such, never will.

It is Hooke, Bacon's Orphic commentator, who expresses the meaning of what happened: "Some other kind of Art for Inquiry than what hath been hitherto made use of must be discovered; of this Engine, no Man except the incomparable Verulam, hath had any thoughts, but there is yet somewhat more to be added, which he seem'd to want time to compleat . . . And indeed it may not improperly be call'd a Philosophical Algebra." [51] These letters which Bacon spoke of as the forms of nature and which ought to have made up a living language or book are turned by the mind in an opposite direction, and become not words and poetry but meaningless symbols for formal operation in a pattern system of analytics. We are back to formal logic after all, with only the orphaned postlogical titles in Bacon's method, those wonderful imaginatively named "Instances," to point us to the postlogic we might have had from his mind. Yet Hooke is right in this: he *was* the incomparable Verulam, who saw the possibility of postlogical thinking over and over again even if he was defeated in his realization of it, and who left everything open, with the plea that later ages should complete what he left undone. Spedding, one of his most devoted exponents, says, "I must think that the Baconian philosophy has yet to come." I think so too; and we may remember that the Baconian philosophy is Orpheus himself. At least in New Atlantis, on the authority of its first pioneer, "they have excellent poesy."

The last word here is not with Bacon, but with one who is in his own foolish way wiser. It is Bottom, in that admirable speech of his when he wakes, at the end of Act IV, Scene 1, who gives the clue to the method Shakespeare proposes for his interpretation of forms in nature—the answer Bacon was afraid to give. "I have had a most rare vision," he says in one of the loveliest phrases in the play. At first he despairs of expressing this in any form at all, saying it was a dream. But after a time he says "I will get Peter Quince to write a ballad of this dream . . . and I will sing it in the latter end of a play." It is poetry, allied with a play and a dream, which is put forward as the method we need.

8

It has been said, that in the constructing of Shakespeare's Dramas there is, apart from all other "faculties" as they are called, an understanding manifested, equal to that in Bacon's *Novum Organum*

Now, to hark back a moment, what was it that Bacon asked of his new logic or instrument or method or interpretation? That it be more subtle than the old, more exact, generative, analogous to the natural process it figures, universal, close to things and to reality. "Subtil, minutieux, fin, microscopique comme elle [la nature], immense . . . la virilité toujours, l'inspiration partout, autant de métaphores que la prairie, autant d'antithèses que le chêne, autant de contrastes et de profondeurs que l'univers, sans cesse la génération, l'éclosion, l'hymen, l'enfantement, l'ensemble vaste, le détail exquis et robuste, la communication vivante . . ." That is another of our Orphic line, speaking of poetry in general and of one poet in particular. It is from Victor Hugo's great essay on Shakespeare.[52]

The later Orphic voices speak now. They are Vico, Herder, Goethe, Coleridge, and Hugo. They corroborate the Baconian postlogic in gross and in detail, in the vision of nature as a language to be interpreted, and in the threefold scheme for the work, natural history, forms, and *organon*. Only when Bacon betrays his own vision do these commentators propose Shakespeare in his place, as another and greater interpreter of nature, who is to venture further into poetry, and so effect the transformation of man's mind in its relation to nature which Bacon saw and could not carry through.

Nature as language appears in Vico as the central concept of ancient mythological thought: "All of nature was the language of Jupiter. Every pagan nation believed that it knew this language through divination, which the Greeks called *theology*, which is to say, knowledge of the speech of the Gods." [53] Goethe in his turn thinks of nature sometimes as a sibylline language,[54] and makes the wonderful statement, "Man is the first speech that Nature holds with God." This language is not language-as-science; nor is it a code. It is here given its full complement of metaphor and figure and myth: if nature is language, it is language-as-poetry. This is the speech which the human mind, gifted as it is with powers of speech of its own, has to apprehend and interpret. Insofar as man's own language is poetic, it conforms to the workings of nature considered under this figure of language. The poet therefore resembles what he is trying to discover. So the Orphic voices say:

> Le poète, nous l'avons dit, c'est la nature. [Hugo]

> Nature, the greatest of poets. [Coleridge]

> I had come to the point of thinking of my in-dwelling poetic talent as Nature pure and simple, all the more because I was disposed to view outward nature as its proper subject matter. [Goethe] [55]

This is not unlike Bacon's position when he includes arts as part of his natural history. If we include poetry and

myth among the arts he was considering, what he says holds
good: that the arts are a part of nature, and that they are
not passive analogies but active points of operation, the
very points at which Nature can be made to speak. So in
the phrase *Homo naturae minister et interpres* the "serv-
ing" becomes an active conforming to nature, and the inter-
pretation becomes not a detached decoding but something
much more like the "interpretation" of an actor, who in-
terprets a character by uniting himself with it. Coleridge
describes such an inclusive thinking process:

> The groundwork, therefore, of all true philosophy is
> the full appreciation of the difference between the
> contemplation of reason, namely, that intuition of
> things which arises when we possess ourselves as one
> with the whole, which is substantial knowledge, and
> that which presents itself when transferring reality to
> the negation of reality . . . we think of ourselves as
> separated beings, and place nature in antithesis to the
> mind, as object to subject, thing to thought, death to
> life. This is abstract knowledge, or the science of the
> mere understanding. By the former we know that
> existence is its own predicate, self-affirmation . . . It
> is an eternal and infinite self-rejoicing, self-loving, with
> a joy unfathomable, with a love all-comprehensive. It
> is absolute; and the absolute is neither that which
> affirms or that which is affirmed, but the identity and
> living copula of both. On the other hand, the abstract
> knowledge which belongs to us as finite beings, and
> which leads to a science of delusion then only when it
> would exist for itself instead of being the instrument of
> the former—instead of being, as it were, a translation of
> a living into a dead language, for the purposes of
> memory, arrangement and general communication,—
> it is by this abstract knowledge that the understanding

distinguishes the affirmed from the affirming. Well if
it distinguish without dividing! [56]

What might seem to be mere rhapsodizing by a poet turns
out to be a sober and reliable exposition of the working
of the mind in postlogical thought. This is in itself im-
portant, for if we fall back now into thinking of figura-
tive language as merely figurative—ornamentation or word
play or whimsy—we shall lose everything. Figures in post-
logic and in Orphic minds are instruments of discovery, and
we have to realize this now when we come to what the
Orphic commentators say about Shakespeare himself. For
he too is set in a figure: he is identified with nature.

Herder says of Shakespeare, in *Von deutscher Art und
Kunst,* "The whole world is a body for this great spirit;
all the phenomena of nature are limbs for this body." He
speaks, too, of Greek drama and Shakespearean drama as
products of nature, and Novalis says the same thing of
Shakespeare, "those dramas of his are products of nature
too, deep as nature herself." [57] And in a remarkable passage
from *Shakespeare und kein Ende* (1815), Goethe relates
Shakespeare to the world-soul or *Weltgeist,* saying that
whereas the latter has the task of keeping the secrets of
nature, it is the poet's task to discover them and speak them
out. Goethe claims that in Shakespeare the whole of nature
becomes articulate, inanimate things, the elements, the
wild beasts, all the phenomena of the world. In effect he
presents Shakespeare as Orpheus, and warns us against
thinking that all this is merely figure and not a true part of
the action.

What the Orphic voices are saying is that the poet and his
work, particularly the supreme poet of all, is a part of natu-
ral history, that first Baconian category in postlogic. We
are to think that in Shakespeare we see a process of nature
experimenting, an individual process yet not wholly differ-

ent from other such processes observable in the natural world. This idea of natural process operating in Shakespeare is developed more fully by Coleridge. He relates it to the second Baconian category, those forms which were also part of the work of interpretation and which Bacon thought of as the laws of action in matter and mind.

> Nature, the prime genial artist, inexhaustible in diverse powers, is equally inexhaustible in forms . . . and even such is the appropriate excellence of her chosen poet, of our own Shakespeare,—himself a nature humanized, a genial understanding directing self-consciously a power and an implicit wisdom deeper even than our consciousness.

And going beyond this, he sketches in a time sequence in which these forms can develop, identifying this process with the progression of the human species in its temporal biological evolution.

> O! few have there been among critics who have followed with the eye of the imagination the imperishable yet ever wandering spirit of poetry through its various metempsychoses, and consequent metamorphoses;—or who have rejoiced in the light of clear perception at beholding with each new birth . . . the human race frame to itself a new body, by assimilating materials of nourishment out of its new circumstances, and work for itself new organs of power appropriate to the new sphere of its motion and activity! [58]

Here is poetry or postlogic seen as Bacon saw his new *organon*, an instrument of power perpetually renewed.

The three divisions of Bacon's instrument begin now to draw together into a closer unity than even their author proposed for them. If, as we claimed at the very beginning of this Part, something happened to thought in the first ten years of the seventeenth century in England, this is the point of that happening: the work of Shakespeare. In this work we are to witness as a part of natural process the metamorphosis of one of the forms in human thought. So we come to the third Baconian category, the way to the new method of mind and language. The *Organum* itself is here a form inside the natural history.

It is encouraging that certain Shakespearean critics have recognized that Shakespeare in his drama accomplishes the Baconian work. The claim is made for one play specifically, *King Lear:* "Shakespeare's own creation, the real Novum Organum of human thought" (Danby).[59] We have looked at postlogic in *A Midsummer Night's Dream,* and beyond *King Lear* lies *The Tempest* with which we shall not have space to deal but which belongs in this trilogy of especially mythological plays in which Shakespeare is working intensively at the instrument of thought.

That earlier Shakespearean mythological *Dream* included mental order within the natural order, but *Lear* includes the moral order as well. In this play the great questions are asked, of love, justice, evil, suffering, the Godhead. We said, at the beginning of this Part, that we were going to leave human nature, as love and morals, out of our investigation for the present, holding only to Orpheus' power over nature. To deal with *King Lear* on these terms may seem crazy if not almost sacrilegious. But it can and must be done for our limited scope. I believe the play will bear it. Great works, like great people, are patient of small approaches.

That this play deals with the nature of Nature is common knowledge; indeed, it has come to be regarded as a kind of essay on this subject.[60] But we shall consider it not as an essay but as an experiment, in Baconian terms, as the *Dream* was also in lesser fashion. It is a field of operation. In *Lear* the Orphic mind will order, in a cosmic darkness, according to its own poetic forms, those forms of nature, fierce, intransigent or merely inert, human and inhuman, which move in that darkness also. Orpheus confronts here nature in her most inexorable and inclusive forms; not only the fearful powers of wind and weather, sea or fire or beasts of prey, though the play includes all these, but also every form nature can take in man. The unity of nature is so held that Orpheus' moving of stones and trees and beasts must here be corresponded to by humanity also, where eyes are crystals, naked men are worms, limbs of families and limbs of men are one with limbs of trees, a man mad as the sea crowns himself with weeds, and the evil bring with them all the bestial terrors of the wilderness, vultures, kites, tigers, boars, while lesser men are dogs and rats and geese. Yet it is not upon any of these in the first place but upon the mind of man, the thinking instrument, that a change is to be worked. That is why it is a play to be afraid of.

This has long been recognized.[61] Keats speaks of it in his sonnet *On Sitting Down to Read King Lear Once Again.* These are its last ten lines:

> Adieu! for once again the fierce dispute
> Betwixt damnation and impassion'd clay
> Must I burn through; once more humbly assay
> The bitter-sweet of this Shakespearean fruit.
> Chief poet! and ye clouds of Albion,
> Begetters of our deep eternal theme,
> When through the old oak forest I am gone,
> Let me not wander in a barren dream;
> But when I am consumed in the fire,
> Give me new Phoenix wings to fly at my desire.

The image of fire, of the trying of metal in it which accompanies the chemical or alchemical word "assay," the prayer for a purification into a new life after a phoenix-like destruction—these mean what they say. The last thing this transformation (if it be possible at all) must do for us is deliver us to a barren dream. That would be the false poetry which Bacon set up when he called poetry "a dream of learning" and separated it from logic and science. In *King Lear* poetry is to be not an empty dream of learning but a dream of logic in which we as well as the characters in the play are the subject of the experiment. Postlogic in its most intense drive will go through logic itself and establish itself if it can on the far side. So it is to logic that Lear is delivered, not in abstraction but in terms of flesh and blood,[62] and accompanied by the whole natural universe. This logic, as Bacon wished his new logic to be, is indeed close to things. Nature accompanies the mind in its vivisection by the logic it has itself set up. The more the analysis of the King proceeds, the mind into incoherence, the heart "into a hundred thousand flaws," the more is the closeness with the natural universe emphasized. Logic is here not merely a form of the mind but, in and through the mind, a form of nature itself, part of the operation of a natural law. As such, it is allowed to analyze into nothingness both mind and nature in the person of the King:

> O ruined piece of nature, this great world
> Shall so wear out to naught. Dost thou know me? [63]

This cannot fail to remind us of Prospero whose great globe too will dissolve, leaving no wrack behind; but it is useless to long for the beauty of that postlogical affirmation of dream, for we are a long way from it yet. We are committed at present to logic. On rigorously logical terms, and on these alone, must the Orphic power begin its operations if it is not to deny the mind its rightful instruments but transform them for new purposes and discoveries. Shakespeare accepts the terms, and on these elements he is ready to work for us.

9

The word *sun,* or the figures *s, u, n,* are purely arbitrary modes of recalling the object, and for visual mere objects they are not only sufficient, but have infinite advantages from their very nothingness *per se*. But the language of nature is a subordinate Logos, that was in the beginning, and was with the thing it represented, and was the thing it represented. Now the language of Shakespeare, in his *Lear* for instance, is a something intermediate between these two; or rather it is the former blended with the latter

SO MANY THINGS have been said about tragedy and about *King Lear* that we need to be as simple as possible, and to keep our eyes on Lear himself: for Lear, the King, the image and embodiment of natural power (and kingship is here, I believe, seen as a natural phenomenon, as it is in fairy tales [64] and dreams)—the King *learns*. This is the myth of the play, its working figure; and as myth it bears a reflexive relation to itself and to us. *King Lear* is at once an account of imaginary happenings and an instrument for understanding them, a means of learning and a treatise upon learning. Myth is also inclusive. It is never a mere narrative, a detached report to be detachedly received. It is always an invitation or command to mind and body to identify with it in order to attain a power of interpretation. Because of the nature of the dramatic situation between play, players, and audience, the theater is one of the greatest means yet discovered by which this function of myth can work upon us, its experimental epistemological side. In the *Midsummer Night's Dream* myth entered as fairy world and as play-within-play, and the complexity protected characters and audience alike from the demand of myth that we unite with it in its function of change. In *Lear,* however, the narrative or fable of the play does not comment upon or include myth, it is myth itself. Bottom's contact with myth changes him only temporarily in a metamorphosis which is passing and painless; the change required of Lear is such that body and mind alike are broken by it.

Two great forms or systems are presented in the play to the King and to ourselves. Each is a power of change; thus Bacon saw his forms, inside and outside the mind. The first figure I shall call analytic logic; it has inevitability for its characteristic; the image associated with it in the play is a machine, engine, or wheel; its term is nothingness, the logical end of analysis. The second figure I am calling postlogic; its characteristic is recurrent transformation or metamorphosis; its image in the play is the human being itself, in its living polarity of life and death, youth and age, fertility and decay; its term seems to be the endless iteration of itself. The sphere of operation of both is the universe, but very particularly the human organism, where figures natural and mental meet. The play is not to be seen as a dialectic between two opposing systems; rather, each offers man a means of interpretation of nature, including his own. The touchstone of each system is death. (The repetition of the word "nothing," as of the word "nature" in this play, is too well known to need emphasis.) Yet Gloucester utters the curious phrase "the quality of nothing" as if that might vary, and death as nothingness may vary too, appearing as annihilation or as the point of metamorphosis in a system which has power to recreate form out of so total and inclusive a transformation. By their deaths you shall know them. The characters align themselves partially or wholly with one or other of these forms of change, and undergo and exemplify them. Only Lear embodies both.

The first figure of logic as operation, engine, or machine in nature and human nature might be law or chance or blind fortune with her wheel or the stars. But as the play's action and the process of learning advance, it becomes clear to the characters and to us that "chance," and this whole system, is in fact iron necessity, operating upon us all but imposed not from without, by circumstances, but from within, self-induced and consciously willed, and hence not an external tyranny but a true logic.

The two characters in the play who are wholly committed to analytic logic are Goneril and Regan. That it leads them to their destruction is not here to be taken as an indictment of the method of operation; it is merely the following through of the analysis to its logical conclusion. These two characters logic themselves into nothingness; in the end they seem almost to disappear. In the great scene where Lear begins to speak his transfigured speech, Act v, Scene 3, he answers Cordelia's question, "Shall we not see these daughters and these sisters?" with "No, no, no, no," as if he recognizes that they are already vanishing. Their deaths are logical conclusions to their system of operation and yet irrelevant to what is going on in the later reaches of the play. After their bodies are brought in, Albany's brief, "Even so. Cover their faces," expresses this, and it comes out yet more plainly in the exchange between Lear and Kent a little later:

KENT Your eldest daughters have fordone themselves,
And desperately are dead.
LEAR Aye, so I think.

This is not mere wandering. It is the poetic statement of the nothingness inherent in these deaths. Lear's mind, and the mind of the play, are busied elsewhere. Edmund is the third character who adopts the figure of analytic logic as his own. Like the two women, he is reduced to nothingness and irrelevance ("That's but a trifle here" is how the news of his death is greeted), but he is more interesting than either of them, because of his identification of himself with "Nature," and because, at his death, while he recognizes the logic of his own progression, he seems to try to transfer himself into the other system, the metamorphic rather than logical. "Some good I mean to do, Despite of mine own nature," he says when he tries to undo the command he and Goneril have given for the death of Lear and Cordelia. It is characteristic of the logic of the play that he is unsuccessful.

The other figure, of youth and age, birth and death, threads through the play in the same way. The two terms of the image are not seen, however, as beginning and end of a logical progression, but rather as implying possible substitution, transformation, and affinity. Sometimes the two poles of the image are inverted, in contempt feigned or real. Edmund puts into Edgar's mouth the theory that old fathers should become their sons' wards (1.2); Goneril speaks out for herself, "Old fools are babes again." Later the Fool in his own vein of bitterness takes up the theme,

"ever since thou madest thy daughters thy mothers," talk-
ing of the hedge-sparrow with the cuckoo nestling, that
"had its head bit off by its young." Sometimes there is a
kind of counterpoint between them. (Since we are think-
ing of *pre-* into *post-* logic it is interesting that the prefixes
in the play would, under a living figure, move toward one
another.) In the scene between the mad Lear and the
blinded Gloucester, the one old man says this to the other:

LEAR   Thou must be patient; we came crying hither:
       Thou knowst, the first time that we smell the air
       We wawl and cry.—I will preach to thee: mark.

It is a strange sermon but it bears out this figure, and later
a younger man, Edgar, speaks it more directly still.

                    Men must endure
       Their going hence, even as their coming hither.
       Ripeness is all.

The relationship between these extremities, youth and
age, birth and death, is deep and subtle in this play. Hu-
manity or postlogic is figured by both, not alone by death
but by life too, not a logical progression into nothingness
but a transformational operation.

   The transformation is to be seen at the point where the
two systems encounter one another in human beings.
Change is the lot meted out by logic to those whose work-
ing system is not analytic logic. Cordelia is the first to meet
it, with a suddenness which is highly dramatic; then Kent;
then Edgar; lastly, and with a difference, Lear himself.
This nothingness or analysis or move toward death tends
to take the same pattern. It affects those two special instru-
ments of postlogic, language and the body. The first is
reduced to silence, namelessness or incoherence, according
to the particular case; the second to nakedness, or mutila-
tion, at worst death. Edgar loses his name—"Edgar I noth-

ing am"—and adopts a disguise of nakedness. Kent is stripped by Lear's sentence of banishment to a "trunk"; we learn at the end of the play that after banishment he had called himself Caius, but when he first appears in the guise of a servant he answers simply "A man" to Lear's question "What art thou?" Cordelia herself renounces the use of speech which has been so profaned by her sisters' misuse of it, and is then stripped of position and dowry, lastly of her life. Lear when he begins to realize the workings of his own logic, in which he is caught, says "Does any here know me? This is not Lear . . . Who is it that can tell me who I am?" and a moment later asks his daughter's name; as the process goes forward he too moves toward nakedness, up to the cry "Off, off, you lendings: come, unbutton here."

Thus Lear follows the general pattern of the other postlogical characters when their system crosses with that of analytic logic. Yet his essential role is infinitely larger than this. He alone in the play embodies the two systems, logic and postlogic. He has to transfigure the one into the other, in his own body and mind. He stands where Bacon's Interpreter of Nature was to stand, between man as body and mind, and nature, with speech at the meeting point, and is questioned on the relationship of all three. It is his inadequacy in this role which brings about all the disasters of the play. He mistakes the relationship of nature and man doubly in himself, by misunderstanding his own figure as King, and his bond with his daughters. The two come together in the test he has imagined in this connection—the kingdom is to be divided according to his children's power to put their love for him into words in public. The importance of language in the right and due relationship between nature and men is implied all the way through this scene, though not by Lear. His emphasis is wrong—"Which of you shall we *say* doth love us most?"

"Our eldest-born, *speak* first," and such false emphasis
wins the answer it deserves, "I love you more than words
can wield the matter." In the kingship he delivers himself
over to analysis, dividing the kingdom "with reservation
of a hundred knights," and, as he fondly supposes possi-
ble, "the name and all the additions to a king." Language
here cannot be split from its proper contact with natural
reality, upon which all poetry and truth depend. So Kent
who sees what is at issue says "Reserve thy state." But Lear
chooses logic in place of postlogic, and is then analyzed
by those skilled in this instrument, on his and its own
terms—"What need you five-and-twenty, ten, or five?" Just
as he accepts the unnatural division of the kingdom, so
too he accepts the hyperbole of Goneril and Regan as po-
etry, conforming to their true nature, whereas for them
language is a manipulative tool for particular ends. Lear
sides with logic here also, aligning himself with those who
are to operate on this system. His own speech takes on the
mechanical and inflexible qualities of analytic logic, and
is turned upon Cordelia and Kent, in the "vows" and
"sentences" which are never to be altered or subverted.
Misunderstanding nature and man as he does, he causes
the death of language in its four great functions of poetry,
naming, truth-telling, and prayer.[65] Cordelia's "Nothing,"
the renunciation of the poetry that is rightly hers, is the
first death of the play. Thus the end is prefigured in the
beginning.

Lear emerges from this first scene having made his
choice: thereafter he is left to be ground by the engine
of his choice. Gradually he begins to learn that the choice
was wrong. He cannot annul logic—that would in any
case be impermissible, for it has its own rights in the uni-
verse. All he can achieve is to embody within himself a
transformation of logic into postlogic, of engine back into
organism, of the old man into something like a child again.

He will not see Cordelia again until this metamorphosis is almost completed.

At the heart of the play the reduction of the King, through logic which is not merely an external tyranny but a system to which he has deliberately committed himself, is completed. This is the second death of the play. The reduction is total, the hovelling with swine and rogues forlorn as Cordelia says, the stripping of the bodily dignity, and the abasement of the mind, "past speaking of in a king." Yet it is not just destruction. It is a total reassessment, by inclusion and not exclusion, of the relation between man and nature. Man is Poor Tom, nature is the storm, and in the end Lear unites himself with both. For background or chorus to this change, Shakespeare has set the voice of the storm, the inarticulate language of nature without man. Nature can speak no language of her own. For this she depends upon man. Lear has to learn to speak the universe. He does so gradually, even in the midst of madness, by regaining a kingship "Every inch a king!" which is yet still a man, "I am not ague-proof." His speech in these acts too, particularly when directed toward the pitiful Gloucester, shows gleams of what is to come.

By the time Lear is reunited with Cordelia, in a sense his death is past. His awakening from sleep there is presented as a resurrection, and it is at this point that for Lear the figure of the engine finishes. He had sent himself to torture and death through his own choice of logic as interpretation. He sees himself as bound to a flaming wheel, made one bodily with a mechanism which has become an engine of torture, and from this, as from the misunderstood logic, he is here freed. The difference can be seen in what he says, his own use of language. Love, humility, uncertainty in this scene wander around blindfold still in his speech. "I am old and foolish." "Pray you forget and forgive." They are childish utterances, and rightly so, for here the counterpoint between age and youth is working. Age moves into renewal through the simple love of its own child.

Cordelia, the simple embodiment of naturalness and of language as truth, and Lear in his new childlike yet regal universe as befits a man, delivered from his false interpretations, appear before us in their last two scenes; yet neither of them is delivered from the workings of that analysis which keeps its power right to the end. It was because it cheated on this point that the "happy ending" version of the play was such a travesty. Cordelia, at the close of the play as at the opening, speaks by silence, by what she is. It is a masterstroke that she does not die on the stage, that it is her dead and dumb body which is carried in at the end—that last terrible inversion of the age and youth figure, where the young lie dead in their parent's arms, for this is a Pietà and speaks that same language. "Never, never, never, never, never"—the absoluteness of logic is not for an instant evaded. Cordelia is speechless as nature is, and it is Lear who interprets in his speech, for man and nature, for Bacon, for us all.

Postlogic or myth is reflexive and inclusive. We can now remember also its other great characteristic, the one Bacon so particularly required of it: that it should be close to things. For it is this which begins to appear in the last speeches of Lear, in "No, no, no, no: come, let's away to prison," and what follows after "Howl, howl, howl," at the end; the very repetition is extraordinary, seeming to image the endless iteration of nature, that stubborn self-affirmation which we suggested as the term of postlogic as opposed to analytic logic's final nothingness.

No, no, no, no: come, let's away to prison.
We two alone will sing like birds i' th' cage:

When thou dost ask me blessing, I'll kneel down
And ask of thee forgiveness: so we'll live,
And pray, and sing, and tell old tales, and laugh
At gilded butterflies: and hear poor rogues
Talk of court news, and we'll talk with them too,
Who loses and who wins; who's in, who's out;
And take upon's the mystery of things
As if we were God's spies: and we'll wear out
In a wall'd prison, packs and sects of great ones,
That ebb and flow the moon.

This is fatidic or Orphic speech. It begins to gather up the universe—birds and butterflies (in the next speech the beasts come in too, with fire and food and flesh and fell); here is language as fairytale or prelogic, and as prayer, and in union with music. There is an astonishing sense of space, the heavens, the tides with humanity flowing with them, the vision of the world as a seat of mysterious royalty of which scattered and conflicting news may be got by language and from various messengers, of vast secrets yet to be discovered, and all this from a prison as small and enclosed as any one single human organism which is yet in relation with the whole of creation, in its metamorphic death as well as in life. The same theme will be taken up at the very end, when Lear rises to new vision and sorrow after Cordelia's death. She is there the earth itself, dead as earth; and again the creatures of earth, inanimate and animate, are summoned, men or beasts to howl, the stones, a feather, a looking-glass which is itself a stone, and these two to be stirred or misted by Cordelia's breath (as if an atmosphere of air and clouds) or by an imagined word, "What is't thou sayest?" So it is that with "Look on her lips," the bodily organ of speech and life, that Lear dies.

Language and the human mind and body are here raised to a new power, an instrument in their own right, set in a dynamic reciprocally interpretative relationship to nature. "Man = Metaphor," Novalis says, and again, "We are looking for the blue-print of the world—that is what we are ourselves." [66] This is postlogic as King Lear expounds it. The play affirms that logic is not the sole or even the right instrument for the interpretation of nature. The method, the lute strung with poets' sinews, consists in the use of the self, body, and mind, heart as well as intelligence, as an instrument of wider interpretation, with language assisting in the process. It will be for later Orphic voices to develop this vision further.

PART III

Erasmus Darwin and Goethe: Linnaean and Ovidian Taxonomy

1

For we poets have our lineal descents and clans as well as other families

ORPHIC GENIUS, each time it occurs, is more than just the appearance of one particular mind, active in thinking and writing. It constitutes itself a point of transformation or metamorphosis, a living instance of postlogic in the context of its own historical period. In this tradition, each such mind is itself an example of the process it seeks to discover and perfect. There is the closest possible connection between the nature of genius of this sort and its theme.

Its occurrences are not necessarily frequent. In terms of history—civil, literary, or scientific—the 200 years from Bacon and Shakespeare to Erasmus Darwin and Goethe, from early seventeenth to late eighteenth and early nineteenth centuries, may seem a long time. In terms of a natural history, however, the perspective would be different; and some such natural history, of the mind or of poetry, is our concern. It is also the concern of the Orphic minds themselves. Renan envisages something of the sort in 1848, seeing it as part of the transformation of scholarship from the static to the evolutionary; and in Emerson, the first American Orphic mind which I have come upon (he mentions Orpheus in the essays, published in 1848

also, "History" and "Nature"—what could be more appro-
priate?), we find the actual phrase "a natural history of
the intellect." Among Orphic minds we seem to have a
genuine family descent. Having identified our species,
earlier and later, we shall think about temporal relation-
ships between them and trace the other specimens, during
those 200 years, of the Orphic line, for it never dies out.
It is identified by the appearance of Orpheus, varied and
adapted according to the particular historical circum-
stances to which genius of this kind is highly sensitive.
It seems possible that it is to be found operating always
at the point of its century's particular need.

I am using, to describe the task before us in this Part,
the terminology of natural history, not through affecta-
tion but because it is to the point. The two centuries be-
tween Shakespeare and Goethe are valuable because they
make us take history into account and think about tem-
poral descent and a kind of evolution. This means that
our own thinking will fall in with the general preoccupa-
tions of natural historians during these same two centuries.
Classification and description of living beings, accom-
panied by the inquiries, which are bound to follow, into
relationships in time as well as space—these are the classic
achievements of the seventeenth and eighteenth centuries
in natural science, culminating in Linnaeus, who is of the
Orphic line himself.

It is not surprising, then, that at this point in the con-
text of taxonomy—which is the science of the classification
of living beings—and morphology—which is the study of
the characteristic shapes of such beings—the respective
Orpheus figures of Erasmus Darwin and Goethe appear,
at the point of the recognition and appraisal of natural
forms and the application of words to them. We might
have expected that the presiding deity of these two sci-
ences would still be that Orpheus of Bacon and Shake-

speare who reorders creation by his power. There is, however, a change in Orpheus at this point.

Erasmus Darwin's Orpheus occurs in his second long poem, *The Temple of Nature,* published in 1803, one year after its author's death (he was born in 1732). The first appeared in 1791.[1] This was *The Botanic Garden,* with its two parts, "The Economy of Vegetation" and "The Loves of the Plants," by which Erasmus Darwin is remembered nowadays, if he be remembered at all; but though we may know vaguely that he wrote such a work and it was parodied in *The Loves of the Triangles,*[2] we should be hard put to it to say what the poem was really about. The author in his preface will tell us: "In the first poem the physiology of Plants is delivered, and the operation of the elements, as far as they may be supposed to affect the growth of vegetables. In the second poem . . . the Sexual System of Linnaeus is explained." The second long poem, *The Temple of Nature,* though almost entirely forgotten now, is the better production. Here, too, in a preface the writer tells us what he is about: "to bring distinctly to the imagination the beautiful and sublime images of the operations of Nature, in the order, as the Author believes, in which the progressive course of time presented them." We are going to talk about both poems later on, but already something interesting suggests itself, for what we seem to have is one poem on morphology and classification and one on evolution. I could say "the progress of Nature in time" or some such noncommittal phrase; but I hope to show that the term "evolution" is justified, fifty years before Erasmus Darwin's grandson dealt with that matter.

His Orpheus makes a gradual appearance, revealing himself as he goes. It is as if this figure too, in its relation to the poem, has to work in an evolutionary or genetic way. The first hint of him is in the preface where Darwin (as I shall call him from now on, and if ever I mean Charles Darwin, I will say so) informs his reader that he has chosen the Eleusinian Mysteries for the fundamental image system of the poem. In other words, Darwin is choosing to image the progress of nature by means of a mystery religion; Orpheus was connected with such rites, but does not appear explicitly yet. The next hint of his coming is early in Canto 1, where there appears the creation myth of Orphism, as expressed in the Orphic hymns and fragments come down to us from classical times. A little later we come to Orpheus himself:

> So when ill-fated Orpheus tuned to woe
> His potent lyre, and sought the realms below,
> Charm'd into life unreal forms respir'd
> And listening shades the dulcet notes admir'd . . .
> His trembling bride the bard triumphant led
> From the pale mansions of the astonish'd dead,
> Gave the fair phantom to admiring light,—
> Ah, soon again to tread irremeable night.

It is the second of our Orpheus figures which Erasmus Darwin recommends to us for this stage in our thinking, once again an image of power and poetry in conjunction, but now with the closest, most loving, human connections in Eurydice. Darwin's Orpheus is in a sense double, for in connection with myth and mystery he appears as the historical and not merely the mythological Orpheus, the founder of a cult and associated with Orphism in the literary tradition. This, however, is no concern of ours. We shall stick to our own Orphic line; here Darwin has two Orphic predecessors in his own country not long before him. He knew the work of the first and may have known that of the second.

The first is Bishop Warburton. In Book ii of *The Divine*

Legation of Moses, published in 1738, he embarks on a
discussion of the classical Mysteries, and shows himself,
if only by glints and flashes, a true Orphic man. After
coming upon a "ritual composed in hieroglyphics" we
meet "the SPECTACLES in the ELEUSINIAN MYSTERIES, where
everything was done in show and machinery." There are
the Mysteries and the machinery set ready as if for Darwin's
hand, and before long we come, after a passing reference
to Ovid, to Orpheus himself—"Orpheus, the most re-
nowned of the European Lawgivers; but better known
under the character of Poet: for the first laws being written
in measure . . . the fable would have it, that by the force
of harmony, he softened the savage inhabitants of Thrace."
It reminds one of Vico. Finally of the Mysteries he says,
"Their MAGIC was of three sorts." This is Pico's or Bacon's
magic; and the second of the three sorts is, according to
Warburton, "the Magic of Transformation or METAMOR-
PHOSIS."

Darwin's second Orphic precursor is Thomas Taylor
whose translation of the Orphic hymns appeared in 1787,
under the title of *The Mystical Initiations; or, Hymns of
Orpheus, Translated from the Original Greek, with a Pre-
liminary Dissertation on the Life and Theology of Or-
pheus*. Here is another Orphic voice, who celebrates Or-
pheus in high and fitting words:

> the founder of theology among the Greeks; the in-
> stitutor of their life and morals; the first of prophets
> and the prince of poets; himself the offspring of a
> Muse; who taught the Greeks their sacred rites and
> mysteries and from whose wisdom, as from a perpetual
> and abundant fountain, the divine Must of Homer,
> and the philosophy of Pythagoras and Plato flowed;
> and, lastly, who by the melody of his lyre, drew rocks,

woods, and wild beasts, stopt rivers in their course,
and even moved the inexorable king of hell, as every
page, and all the writings of antiquity sufficiently
evince.

So far so good—a recognition of the link between Orpheus
and poetry and scientific philosophy, and a shift of the
reader from the first Orpheus figure to the second, to-
gether with the mention of classical literature. But there
is more in this classicist's preface and dissertation, for he
saw something of what might happen to the science of his
day (that science which Sprat so distortedly commended)
should it lose touch with mythological thinking in the
fullest and best sense. He characterizes that science as "ex-
perimental enquiries, increased without end, and accumu-
lated without order," the split Baconian vision with the
loss of the true method or interpretation. He uses the word
"philosopher" in its Orphic Baconian sense: "This opin-
ion a modern philosopher . . . will doubtless consider as
too ridiculous to need a serious refutation . . . because
he believes the phenomena may be solved by mechanical
means"; and then he goes on to speak of a "philosophical
mythology, as an accurate conception of its nature will
throw a general light on the Hymns, and, I hope, con-
tribute to the dispersion of that gloom in which this sub-
lime subject has been hitherto involved, through the
barbarous systems of modern mythologists." What has been
happening to Bacon in 200 years is plain.

  Goethe's Orpheus appears in 1817, among the later
poems (Goethe's own dates, to set the chronology, are
1749–1832). With Erasmus Darwin's clear-cut Orpheus be-
fore our eyes, Goethe's at first seems much more shadowy.
Five stanzas, of eight lines each, with Greek names: Dai-
mon, or individual life-force; Tyche, or fortune; Ananke,

or necessity; Eros, or love; and Elpis, hope, are given the title *Urworte: Orphisch.*

Orphic words out of the beginnings of things—this is something of what that prefix *Ur* conveys. It has to do with distance in time, as in its use in *Urgrossvater* where we should say "great-grandfather," or *uralt*, meaning "very old indeed." There is no English equivalent. It turns up fairly constantly in Goethe. He has an *Urpflanze* or *Ur*-plant, an *Urtier* or *Ur*-beast; *Ur*-phenomena of various sorts, including, delightfully, the "Urschildkröte im Welt-sumpf," an *Ur*-tortoise in the primeval world-bog. It is like Kipling's All-the-Camel-there-was; he would have been the *Ur*-camel when the world was so-new-and-all. These *Urworte* with which Orpheus is associated keep company by their prefix with some of Goethe's deepest biological questioning into the forces which govern form in the organic world. Here the questioning includes man as well, for the forces in the *Urworte* apply to him.

Herder, Goethe's mentor and associate from an early age, speaks in his *Aelteste Urkunde des Menschengeschlechts* of the Orpheus story as the "Urgesang aller Wesen," the original song of all created beings. It is fitting that Herder should come in here, for he was part of Goethe's Orphic education. In a letter written in 1774 Goethe likens this essay of Herder's to an Orphic song: "He has descended into the depths of his feeling, has stirred up from there all the holy might of simple Nature and now brings it up and sends it over the wide earth in half-conscious, summer-lightning-lit, sometimes morning-friendly-smiling, Orphic song." That translation is Mr. Humphry Trevel-yan's, and he suggests, in *Goethe and the Greeks*,[3] that the style of this letter may be modeled on that of the Orphic hymns, of which a new edition, with Latin trans-lation, appeared in 1765 in Germany and was reviewed by Herder that same year; Herder may have introduced Goethe to these works or have furthered his interest in them. What is more interesting from our point of view is, however, the metaphor in the letter: Herder is tacitly identified with Orpheus in this second figure of our myth, as if Herder's writing and thinking took him down to the underworld, to the roots of things. He was a developmental or evolutionary thinker in his whole concept of nature and history.[4] He saw things primarily from the historian's standpoint, and we find him dealing with the origin of language in his essay *Über der Ursprung der Sprache* in 1772, an interest he shares with a later Orphic thinker, Renan, who published his *De l'Origine du langage* in 1848. There is a reference in *Dichtung und Wahrheit* [5] to this question of the origins of language, dating from the time of Goethe's connection with Herder, but Goethe takes the origin, divine or natural, of languages for granted —which is to say he is not particularly interested in it. His *Urworte* are of another kind.

These Orphic *Urworte* represent first of all an oracular voice out of a dim past, reminding us, as Darwin's Orpheus did, of the Orpheus of cult and classical literature. But they do more than this, for they do indeed belong with the *Urpflanze* and the *Urtier,* by their subject matter as well as by their name. Goethe, realizing as all of us have done since, that these are very dark sayings, wrote a series of notes on the poems in 1820. He tells us there that these five stanzas were published in the second volume of his *Morphologie.* This gives them part of their setting, and of their significance, on which Goethe himself insists.[6] This Orphic pronouncement has to do with the great forces which mold and control human forms as well as those in nature. Orpheus in Goethe is a dark poetic oracle upon the meeting-point of living things and language in the processes of time and change.

2

The slightest adumbration of a dynamical morphology

OUR LINE of descent stems from Bacon and Shakespeare; but of the two, it is the Baconian line which is easiest to follow. The Shakespearean one seems to go underground after Milton, not to reappear until that wonderful burst of Orphic recognition and celebration of Shakespeare at the end of the eighteenth century and through the nineteenth, in Germany and England for the most part, though it moves into France later with Hugo and Renan. Erasmus Darwin is involved in this slightly, Goethe profoundly, though it is Coleridge who sorts out most clearly the respective claims of Bacon and Shakespeare upon Orphic minds.[7]

Great visions such as Bacon's perpetuate themselves according to their own powers but also according to the powers of those who receive and transmit them. Greatness can transmit its own integrity, though always with modification, because this is no mechanical process. But any vision has, besides its greatness, peculiar failings, and Bacon's has these in full measure. The result upon lesser minds may be that they receive only a part, take it to be the whole, and distort the whole activity of the vision thereby. Orphic minds are a danger in this way to non-Orphic ones.

Sprat is a classic example of what happens. Demythologizer of science as he thought he was, he was busy removing the so-called "facts" further and further from the operation upon them of the constructive mind, from myth in its true sense, working with figures and language. If Bacon half-heartedly began the divorce proceedings between science and poetry, his disciples carried them on with gusto.

Where Sprat provides evidence on what was happening to lesser scientists in these circumstances, Cowley provides it for the poets, at the same time as Sprat, on almost identical grounds and in close collaboration with him. He contributed an Ode, in guarded praise of Bacon and in celebration of what was already then coming to be thought of as scientific method, to Sprat's history of the Royal Society, and he was himself one of the original members of that Society. It is a pity that it has since given up the habit of admitting poets to its numbers,[8] but perhaps the poets are partly themselves to blame for this. Cowley, writing in 1661, four years before Sprat, puts forward *A Proposition for the Advancement of Experimental Philosophy*. In this he proposes a "Colledge" for those chosen for this work. He recalls Bacon's *New Atlantis*, but regards this as altogether too visionary: "We do not design this after the Model of *Salomon's* House in my Lord *Bacon* (which is a Project for experiments that can never be experimented)." But when he comes to consider what his own foundation is to study, the program is this: "briefly, all things contained in the Catalogue of Natural Histories annexed to My Lord *Bacon's Organon*." He too succumbs to this fascination, though as befits a poet he has glimmerings of something else: "and because the truth is we want good Poets (I mean we have but few) who have properly treated of solid and learned, that is, Natural Matters, (the most part indulging to the weakness of the world, and feeding it either with the follies of Love, or with the Fables of gods and Heroes) we conceive that one Book ought to be compiled of all the scattered little parcels among the ancient Poets that might serve for the advancement of Natural Science." Cowley is not going to let poetry and science be completely separated; but it is instructive that all he can propose to hold them together is another compilation or collection or catalogue, not a living union of the two in a discipline of thought, which is what is needed. Hooke in his turn caught the vision, but again only partially.

There are degrees of authority and confidence in Orphic voices. The least, those who get into this line by accident or almost by misadventure, can only reflect the dualism, the broken vision which unfortunately they approve of and foster. Greater ones struggle to reassert a unity but fall short for various reasons. The greatest Orphic voices of all stand, as their minor fellows do, against their period's wrong-headedness and disharmony; but it must not be thought that they are themselves split, as the first group is, or that they struggle to heal the divergencies in the thought of their age. They know of no such split, and they are right, for it is a chimera, a nonbeing. They do not argue against dualism, they utter and exemplify unity. Only the lesser figures are attainted; the greater ones go their own way, living by the life of their own Orphic tradition, unaffected by the sicknesses of philosophy and scientific methodology. They have their own tradition, and the rest is irrelevance. It is by this kind of simplicity that they minister to our distractions. Their method is not dialectic but poetry.

There arise now three great scattered Orphic figures, which carry us on to the Orpheus of Darwin and Goethe. These are Giambattista Vico (1668–1744), Emanuel Swedenborg (1688–1772), and Carolus Linnaeus (1707–1778).

The first of our three is Vico. I wish it were possible to take this man's greatness for granted, needing here only corroboration and gratitude, but this is not possible at all. He is scarcely known. A true prophet, as Orphic voices must be, he lies ahead of us still; by his own contemporaries he could not be heard at all. He has his own Orphic genealogy, though he has a habit of bursting upon us utterly unexpectedly, as he burst upon Michelet.[9] He draws his descent direct from Orpheus, who is mentioned several times in his works as the founder of what Vico calls "poetic theology"; and after Orpheus, from Bacon. Vico came upon him in 1707 and found in him "incomparable wisdom."[10] Vico is the truest and greatest Orphic progeny Bacon and the Baconian vision of postlogic have yet had, answering fittingly his master's *Novum Organum* with the *Scienza nuova,* the new made new again a hundred years afterward. From these two a direct line runs to Coleridge. In 1825 Coleridge was lent a set of Vico's works, and he writes of them as follows: "I am more and more delighted with G. B. Vico, and if I had (which thank God's good grace I have not) the least drop of *Author's* blood in my veins, I should twenty times successively in the perusal of the first volume (I have not yet begun the second) have exclaimed: 'Pereant qui ante nos nostra dixere.'" Coleridge, we are told, planned a translation of the *Novum Organum* to be illustrated with Vichian parallels.[11] Other lines of descent from Vico run to Germany, through Hamann to Herder and thence to Schelling and Goethe, who during his Italian Journey was lent Vico's works while he was staying at Naples and writes a paragraph on them in his journal, calling them sibylline premonitions of something good and true that was still to come. Another runs to France, through Michelet and then Renan's *L'Avenir de la science.* Vico enters *Das Kapital* in an interesting footnote, in the company of Charles Darwin. And in modern scholarship we can count Croce, Collingwood, and Cassirer among Vico's devotees.[12] All in all, it is little enough.

What Vico meant to write was an account of the development of social man, a synthesis of all other sciences. This is what he says about it, in the French of Michelet's edition (Vol. 2, Bk. v):

> A travers la diversité des formes extérieures, nous saisirons *l'identité de substance* de cette histoire. Ainsi ne pouvons-nous refuser à cet ouvrage le titre orgueilleux peut-être de *Science nouvelle.* Il y a droit par son sujet: *la nature commune des nations;* sujet vraiment universel, dont l'idée embrasse toute science digne de ce nom.

This has the same sweep of undertaking as Bacon's pronouncements had. Elsewhere Vico says he means the *Scienza* to be "une histoire des idées humaines"; he ties these absolutely to language, admitting that in the first version of the *Scienza* (there are several versions) "he erred . . . because he treated the origins of ideas apart from the origins of languages, whereas they were by nature united." Back to language, then, he goes, to assert that poetry comes up out of nature and is the first natural speech; nature is seen as language and myth, "la nature passionnée, cette image prodigieuse"; while from what he calls poetic knowledge or wisdom come theology, logic, jurisprudence, economics, politics, in fact all the structures of human society and scholarship. He is the first to give myth its full status as a subject of historical study (Cassirer traces out the results this had upon much later scholars such as Schelling and Strauss).[13] Vico has been called the founder of the philosophy of history, of the modern philosophy of language, of the philosophy of mythology.

This sounds very academic, put in those conventional terms. But on our own terms, here is a new specimen of our Orphic species who suddenly appears out of nowhere, like an idea itself, or as Collingwood says,[14] like Vico's idea about how ideas appear. Orphic scholar or scientist (the fact that the *Scienza nuova* has been called a great poem [15] will not contradict but confirm that title) of unmatched originality and fertility, his importance for us here is threefold. First, in a period when Bacon's "natural history" was in danger of attenuation into mere cataloguing, here is a historian who sees history as part of nature and never loses sight of the method, which for him resides in the very nature of speech itself. The *Scienza nuova* works upon what Novalis would call an organology of language and thinking. Second, he confirms the nature of the full Baconian postlogic, in its poetry, its closeness to language, its mythological method, its powers of synthesis, the inclusive nature of its thinking—"celui qui médite cette science s'en crée à lui-même le sujet. Quelle histoire plus certaine que celle où la même personne est à la fois l'acteur et l'historien?"—and the recognition of myth as a means of research—"ces germes féconds nous ont laissé voir dans l'imperfection de sa forme primitive la *Science* de réflexion, la science de recherches . . . On peut dire en effet que dans les *fables, l'instinct* de l'humanité avait marqué d'avance les principes de la science moderne." [16] Third, he sends our minds forward into the future, by the strange history of his own thought, by what he says, and by what has been said about him. Croce says of him, for instance, that his whole thought was "dynamic and evolutionary," Adams that he designed "the beginning of a morphology of human culture." [17]

Our next Orphic voice is Swedenborg. This may seem surprising. Is he not a religious visionary, and what would he have to do with the Orphic inquiry? He did not, however, begin his career of visionary till he was over fifty. In 1745, he says, heaven was opened to him. Up till then he had been an active scholar and scientist, and here his Orphic credentials occur. During his early pursuit of literature and science over a very wide field he published in

1715 *Camena Borea: cum Heroum et Heroidum Factis Ludens: sive Fabellae Ovidianis Similes,* of which the twelfth deals with "Orpheus redivivus et relapsus in Tartara." In addition we have Orphic commentary on this figure: Emerson, with Coleridge to second him.

Swedenborg appears first before us as simply a brilliant young Swede with a passion for study, pursuing science and letters. After the publication of *Camena Borea* his literary interests wane, and we find him in the following year undertaking the editorship of periodic collections of essays devoted to scientific subjects and discoveries. They bear the not uninteresting title of *Daedalus Hyperboreus.* Then come years of scientific and technological activity, and a rise to eminence in these fields. In 1734 he publishes his *Principia Rerum Naturalium,* written mainly from the point of view of physics. He knew and combated Bacon in this work, which is dull, the only interesting thing in it from our point of view being that the author more than once quotes the *Metamorphoses* in serious illustration of scientific discussion, as if Ovid had not been left entirely behind. In 1740–41 he publishes the *Oeconomia Regni Animalis,* a work on human physiology and man as a rational animal. The range of his scientific interests is considerable and he seems to have been in certain respects in advance of his times. What matters to us, however, is something which appears already in this last work, and which will carry through into his later life. This is his doctrine of correspondences.

He puts it as follows in the *Oeconomia:* "In our Doctrine of Representations and Correspondences we shall treat of these Symbolical and Typical Representations, and of the astonishing things which occur, I will not say in the living Body only, but throughout Nature, and which correspond so entirely to Supreme and Spiritual things, that one would swear, that the Physical World was purely

Symbolical of the Spiritual World." This passage is not altogether clear; it could suggest merely Platonic Ideas, or allegory, with neither of which, nor with "symbolism" as such, is postlogic concerned. But it could suggest something else, however vaguely: a relationship between created things and mental forms, a correspondence between natural orders and systems of the mind. Upon this depends a living science of classification and taxonomy. Swedenborg gives us a hint about the nature of this science. By it he becomes a precursor of Linnaeus' efforts, and confirms his Orphic status and that seemingly accidental Orphic and Ovidian beginning which he had. And by it he exercises his later influence: on Coleridge, who calls him a philosophic genius, anticipating much of what is most valuable in the work of Schelling and others; [18] and on Emerson, who returns to him again and again with a kind of admiring exasperation, in the two series of *Essays,* and at greater length in the judicious study of Swedenborg in *Representative Men,* 1850.

Emerson's interest in Swedenborg is itself taxonomic in character. He sees in this vision of correspondences the distinguishing mark which admits Swedenborg to the company of the poets. The poet "stands one step nearer to things, and sees the flowing and metamorphosis; perceives that thought is multiform; that within the form of every creature is a force impelling it to ascend into a higher form; and following with his eyes the life, uses the forms which express that life, and so his speech flows with the flowing of nature." A moment later Emerson adds, "This is true science," and applies it boldly to astronomy, chemistry, and biology.[19] He puts it more compactly elsewhere, "The whole of nature is a metaphor of the human mind." This is in the chapter on language in the long essay on "Nature" in the first series, where language and nature together form the "grand cipher, the standing problem which has exercised the wonder and study of every fine genius since the world began; from the era of the Egyptians and the Brahmins, to that of Pythagoras, of Plato, of Leibniz, of Swedenborg." In another essay Emerson places Swedenborg squarely at the point of interpretation: "Swedenborg of all men in the recent ages, stands eminently for the translator of nature into thought. I do not know the man in history to whom things stood so uniformly for words. Before him the metamorphosis continually plays." [20] (The metamorphosis here is the interchange of nature and thought through the medium of language; what we are calling myth.)

Already we have one of Emerson's attempts to give his specimen, once identified, a due genealogy. He tries this over and over again, and the connections he suggests are most helpful. One of them goes back to Orpheus himself. "But the highest minds of the world have never ceased to explore the double meaning, or, shall I say, the quadruple, or the centuple, or much more manifold meaning, of every sensuous fact: Orpheus, Empedocles, Heraclitus, Plato, Plutarch, Dante, Swedenborg." Here is another: "Pythagoras, Paracelsus, Cornelius Agrippa, Cardan, Kepler, Swedenborg, Schelling, Oken." Here is a third: "A colossal soul, he lies vast abroad on his times, uncomprehended by them, and requires a long focal distance to be seen; suggests as Aristotle, Bacon, Selden, Humboldt, that a certain vastness of the human soul in nature is possible." [21] The Baconian connection is re-emphasized in the *Representative Men* essay, whence that last quotation comes. Emerson refers to the passage from Swedenborg's *Oeconomia* which we quoted earlier, and says, "The fact, thus explicitly stated, is implied in all poetry, in allegory, in fable, in the use of emblems, and in the structure of language . . . Lord Bacon had found that truth and nature differed only as seal and print . . . The poets, in as far as they are poets, use it . . . Swedenborg first put the fact into a detached and scientific statement . . . It required an insight that could rank things in order and series." Not content with Bacon, he gives us in this essay Shakespeare as well, "I have sometimes thought that he would render the greatest service to modern criticism, who shall draw the line of relation that subsists between Shakespeare and Swedenborg"; and a little later he makes a connection between Swedenborg and Linnaeus.

Emerson calls Swedenborg a man with the insight that could rank things in order and series, i.e. a taxonomer. Emerson sees that task, the translation of nature into thought, as a language job, to be effected by the poet. Here he indicts Swedenborg for failure, in a remarkable sentence: "Strange, scholastic, didactic, passionless, bloodless man, who denotes classes of souls as a botanist . . . the warm, many-weathered, passionate-peopled world is to him a grammar of hieroglyphs." What Swedenborg turns into, for this refers to his theological works, is, instead of a living taxonomer, a botanist in the driest sense, a dusty grammarian. Neither botanical classification nor grammar are dull in themselves, but the life in each depends on myth and poetry. Without this, they fossilize rapidly. It is as a true taxonomer (which is to say, a scientist and poet) that Swedenborg fails. It is not that he is wholly astray but that he is so nearly right, "wrong but in consequence of being in the right, but imperfectly," as Coleridge said of him.[22]

He was called to a living relationship with myth by his vision of Correspondences. This was his first vision, taking precedence over all the later visions and more truly theological than any of them. He fails in his calling on two counts: he mishears the language and misconstrues his function as interpreter. The work, as Emerson puts it, "was narrowed and defeated by the exclusively theologic direction which his inquiries took." That is carefully and well said. What happens to Swedenborg is not that he misdirects himself into theology, but that he misunderstands the nature of the Word, in the full Christian sense, and hence of the language he is to work with. So he fuses the language of nature and the language of the Bible in a rigid and congealed hypostasis, and then mistakes the role of interpreter, opting not for hieroglyphic but for cipher. The correspondence, that manifold meaning Emerson was talking about, petrifies immediately into a lifeless one-to-one code, as Emerson sees,[23] and Swedenborg becomes the only man who can read it, *The* Interpreter. His letter to the Academy of Sciences in Stockholm, written in 1770 long after he had turned away from the directly Orphic vision, and usually published as an appendix to his treatise *On the White Horse Mentioned in the Apocalypse*, 1758, is an example of this. In it he suggests that the Academy might aid and support him in a study of Egyptian hieroglyphics, which, he claims, signify the correspondences between natural and spiritual things. In the *White Horse* he had opined:

> That the Science of correspondences and representations was pre-eminently THE SCIENCE among the ancients.
> Especially among the people of the east.
> And was cultivated in Egypt more than in other countries.
> Also among the Gentiles, as in Greece, and in other places.
> But that at this day the science of correspondences and representations is lost, especially in Europe.
> That, nevertheless, this science is more excellent than all other sciences, inasmuch as without it the Word cannot be understood.

In the letter he adds a few details, and then proposes himself as interpreter of the hieroglyphics.[24] "They deserve that someone among you should look into them," he says; "I am ready, if so desired, to develop and publish the hieroglyphics, a task which can be accomplished *by no-one else.*" The emphasis is his own, and is melancholy.

Swedenborg is an extraordinary case, perhaps unique, of a mind with the Orphic vision but with the power of poetry denied it. Emerson saw it: "It is remarkable that this man, who, by his perception of symbols, saw the poetic construction of things, and of the primary relation of mind to matter, remained entirely devoid of the whole apparatus of poetic expression, which that perception creates. He knew the grammar and rudiments of the Mother-Tongue —how could he not read off one strain into music? . . . The entire want of poetry in so transcendent a mind betokens the disease." And so, Emerson concludes, we still lack "this design of exhibiting such correspondences which, if adequately executed, would be the poem of the world, in which all history and science would play an essential part . . . The dictionary of symbols is yet to be written. But the interpreter, whom mankind must still expect, will find no predecessor who has approached so near to the true problem." Let that be Swedenborg's epitaph.

3

not as the inventory but as the programme of nature

"THE STUDY of natural history, simple, beautiful, and instructive, consists in the collection, arrangement, and exhibition of the various productions of the earth." That is Linnaeus in his introduction to the *Systema Naturae*.

In the eyes of contemporaries and of posterity, Linnaeus is the taxonomer par excellence. He is not the first in the European field, for apart from classical and medieval attempts the first great taxonomer is the Englishman John Ray (1627–1705). But Linnaeus took the work further than any other, devoting his whole life to inventing and recasting systems of tabulation for the orders of living creatures. His activity culminated in the *Systema Naturae* and the later botanical works and neither familiarity nor inattention should blind us to the due grandiloquence of that title. An English title page of a translation of it, published in 1800, will show the scope: "A General System of Nature, through the three Grand Kingdoms of Animals, Vegetables and Minerals: systematically divided into their several Classes, Orders, Genera, Species, and Varieties, with their Habitations, Manners, Economy, Structure and Peculiarities. In 5 Volumes." D'Arcy Thompson sees the whole work of classification as a response to the master's command: "This secular labour," he says in *Growth and Form*, "is pursued in direct obedience to the precept of the *Systema Naturae—'ut sic in summa confusione rerum apparenti, summus conspiciatur Naturae ordo.'* " [25] But another mind sees it reciprocally, not just as the mind ordering nature but nature bending the mind itself to her purposes: "Nature hastens to render account of herself to the mind. Classification begins . . . But what is classification but the perceiving that these objects are not chaotic, and are not foreign, but have a law, which is also a law of the human mind?" That is Emerson in "Man Thinking" in the first series of *Essays*. In "Nature" he goes farther:

> For the problems to be solved are precisely those which physiologist and naturalist omit to state. It is not so pertinent to man to know all the individuals of the animal kingdom as it is to know whence and whereto is this tyrannizing unity in his constitution, which evermore separates and classifies things, endeavouring to reduce the most diverse to one form . . . I cannot greatly honour minuteness in details, so long as there is no hint to explain the relation between things and thoughts; no ray upon the *metaphysics* of conchology, of botany, of the arts, to show the relation of the forms of flowers, shells, animals, architecture, to the mind, and build science upon ideas.

Are we, with these voices, what they speak of and whom they speak of, in science or in poetry? In cataloguing, which Bacon as well as Emerson deplores, or in something else?

It is only to be expected that in our present climate of opinion, with centuries of the split Baconian system behind us, the main emphasis should fall upon Linnaeus as cataloguer, either with approval as a systematic logician or with disapproval as a mere codifier.[26] Taxonomy, too, may be seen as a working logic, and attempts have been made to connect it with symbolic logic. There are difficulties, however, in fitting Linnaeus into such a view. Was logic the principle on which Linnaeus operated, or something more akin to intuition? Was he a scientist or an artist, or a queer mixture of both? His biographers insist on his pronounced artistic side.[27] Taxonomy itself, wherever it is pursued by a mind above that of a filing-clerk, raises the same questions. It has been said to be based on intuition, with the logic developing later out of this; and scientists such as Agnes Arber and Michael Polanyi insist upon the kinship of taxonomy and morphology to aesthetic and artistic pursuits. Linnaeus and his essential characteristic are a taxonomer's problem; how is he, or his activity, to be classified? Since this becomes a question of method, a methodological voice shall speak to the point:

> Un jour viendra, que je crois avoir entrevu dans le cours de mes observations, un jour où la science sera constituée, où les grandes familles d'esprits et leurs principales divisions seront déterminées et connues . . . Pour l'homme, sans doute, on ne pourra jamais faire exactement comme pour les animaux ou pour les plantes; l'homme moral est plus complexe; il a ce qu'on nomme *liberté* et qui, dans tous les cas, suppose une grande mobilité de combinaisons possibles. Quoi qu'il en soit, on arrivera avec le temps, j'imagine, à constituer plus largement la science du moraliste; elle en est aujourd'hui au point où la botanique en était avant Jussieu, et l'anatomie comparée avant Cuvier, à l'état, pour ainsi dire, anecdotique . . . Je suppose donc quelqu'un . . . de propre à être un bon naturaliste dans ce champ si vaste des esprits.

This is Sainte-Beuve, in the long two-part essay on Cha-
teaubriand, Vol. 3 of the *Nouveaux Lundis*, 1870, in which
he examines his own method, literary criticism. The terms
he uses seem so significant that one wonders whether this
man may not turn out to be one of the central figures of
literary development in the last 150 years, and his method
an instrument with immense possibilities as yet scarcely
even recognized. Jussieu and Cuvier belong, of course, in
the great line of systematic biologists to which we shall
come in a moment. Here they attest Sainte-Beuve's aware-
ness of what he was after—a new flexible taxonomy of
minds. He goes on to set up some of the categories need-
ing investigation: heredity, family relationships, the group,
the environment; in other words, a genetic and ecological
approach. Elsewhere he talks of "la critique physiolo-
gique," while his method of investigating the individual
in a dynamic context of time suggests a morphology of or-
ganism and behavior.

We have always been led to suppose that Sainte-Beuve's
method was historical-biographical and petered out in
manuals of literary anecdote. It seems we were wrong.
What this suggests is that literary criticism is capable of
being an instrument akin to the best scientific methodolo-
gies, engaged on a common task, a wide natural history.
Sainte-Beuve himself says this: "Être en histoire littéraire
et en critique un disciple de Bacon, me paraît le besoin du
temps et une excellente condition première pour juger et
goûter ensuite avec plus de sûreté." This reinterpretation
of biology as a fit instrument by which to explore the nat-
ural history of the world of ideas and words is peculiarly
French, and is often consciously derived from Bacon him-
self. Lamarck has it in 1809; [28] the *Philosophie zoologique*
has friendly references to Bacon, and incidentally to po-
etry. De Maistre has it, by inversion, in his great attack
on Bacon of 1836. Renan has it in *L'Avenir de la science;*

so in his own way does Comte; both of them mention Bacon. The latest to affirm it is Teilhard de Chardin. This is the interpretation fully understood, not mere cataloguing but the patient observation and collecting held together and caught up and transformed by activity of the mind, in the making of dynamic systems, the making of myth. This is postlogic, and upon it the life of taxonomy depends. So what we have is a provisional classification for Linnaeus, a postlogician (which, it must always be remembered, is not antilogician). Only one person can confirm or deny this—Linnaeus himself; and Linnaeus appeals to Orpheus.

It is peculiarly delightful that, with Linnaeus, Orpheus turns up in a catalogue. In the *Deliciae Naturae*,[29] Linnaeus runs through a list of "the artful and the curious." It begins reasonably soberly with hippopotamuses and peacocks and crocodiles; at least in this part of the list, if one were to indict anyone for lack of sobriety, it would have to be the Creator and not Linnaeus. But then the list seems to get out of hand, and we come to Dragons, and Pegasuses (in the plural, as if there might be herds of them), and eventually to Orpheus and his heavenly singing. The zoological and the mythological run straight into one another.

To the Sprats of this world, the semi-Baconians, this must be either scandal or playfulness which is irrelevant to serious science. Orpheus has no business alongside *ordines naturales*. Playful this catalogue certainly is, and charmingly so; but that does not mean it is irrelevant. It is an Orphic microcosm of taxonomy, a catalogue of living things into which Orpheus and myth have been admitted by the greatest taxonomer of them all.

Our minds, grown stiff in an ill tradition, are unaccustomed to science keeping mythological company. But nearer to Linnaeus' own time no such nice feelings prevailed. An Orphic mind like Erasmus Darwin's recognizes, even if only half-consciously, Linnaeus' affinity to myth, and apostrophizes it thus in Canto 1 of *The Loves of the Plants:*

> BOTANIC MUSE! who in this latter age
> Led by your airy hand the Swedish sage,
> Bade his keen eye your secret haunts explore
> On dewy dell, high wood, and winding shore;
> Say on each leaf how tiny Graces dwell;
> How laugh the Pleasures in a blossom's bell;
> How insect loves arise on cobweb wings,
> Aim their light shafts, and point their little stings.

Even the poet and scientist who are not specifically Orphic may do the same thing. We find in France two such collaborating, in Jacques Delille's *Les Trois Règnes de la nature,* which was published in 1808, with notes by Cuvier, whose *Le Règne Animal distribué d'après son organisation* appears in 1817. Cuvier's systematics depend on comparative anatomy. For the first time inner structure and morphology were used as the directing principle of a taxonomic system. It is as if we come eventually to that "latent configuration" which was to be part of Bacon's study of forms. This is the man to whom, we remember, Sainte-Beuve appeals.[30]

In Delille's volume Cuvier discusses his method. He sees it as logic, as is to be expected; but then he calls it an art, and suggests a scope for it far wider than any set of zoological pigeon holes—a method of ordering not facts but ideas:

> Cette habitude que l'on prend nécessairement en étudiant l'histoire naturelle, de classer dans son esprit un très-grand nombre d'idées, est l'un des avantages de cette science dont on a le moins parlé, et qui deviendra peut-être le principal, lorsqu'elle aura été généralement introduite dans l'éducation commune; on

s'exerce par là dans cette partie de la logique qui se nomme la méthode . . . Or cet art de la méthode, une fois qu'on le possède bien, s'applique avec un avantage infini aux études les plus étranges à l'histoire naturelle.

In his notes to Canto 6 of Delille's long scientific poem, Cuvier discusses method in relation to Linnaeus and Buffon:

Le premier, effrayé du chaos où l'incurie de ses prédécesseurs avait laissé l'histoire de la nature, sut, par des méthodes simples et par des définitions courtes et claires, mettre de l'ordre dans cet immense labyrinthe, et rendre facile la connaissance des êtres particuliers; le second, rebuté de la sécheresse d'écrivains, qui pour la plupart s'étaient contentés d'être exacts, sut nous intéresser à des êtres particuliers, par les prestiges de son langage harmonieux et poétique.

To find a professional scientist of the highest order complaining of writers overvaluing exactitude is as encouraging as it is rare. It is the poet in this team, however, even a poet as thin as Delille, who puts things a little more clearly. For him, too, Linnaeus is the orderer, and rightly so:

Et Linné sur la terre, et Newton dans les cieux,
D'une pareille audace étonnèrent les dieux.

This is in Canto 6, but a little earlier in that same Canto, where the poet is dealing at greater length with Linnaeus, he gives him a full mythological setting:

Linné surtout, Linné dévoila ces mystères,
Leurs haines, leurs amours, leurs divers caractères,
Leurs tubes infinis, leurs ressorts délicats.
Flore même en naissant le reçut dans ses bras.

This could be mere classical reference and ornament. De-
lille goes on at once, however:

> Flore sourit d'espoir à sa première aurore;
> Non point cette éternelle et ridicule Flore
> Qui pour les vieux amours compose les bouquets,
> Mais celle qui du monde enseigne les secrets.

Myth is at the heart of the living world, explaining or un-
winding its mysteries; and here Linnaeus also belongs.
Even a minor poet has glimpses of this; and it is good for
us to glimpse also that we need not be so scornful of didac-
tic poetry as an inferior deviation from the true stock.
Didactic poetry might even teach us something, if only
that poetry has many other functions than simply to win
the approval of critics. It has its own taxonomic functions,
and it may be the poets who can tell us most about the
nature of taxonomy.

4

The constructive intellect produces thoughts, sentences, poems, plans, designs, systems. It is the generation of the mind, the marriage of thought with nature

THERE have been frequent meetings between the traditions of morphology and taxonomy on the one hand, and poetry and word studies on the other. Erasmus Darwin and Goethe are not the only examples of their kind. Taxonomers spill over into something closely akin to poetry, as John Ray does in *The Wisdom of God Manifested in the Works of Creation,* published in 1691 when Ray was a member of the Royal Society, and containing that wonderful phrase "plastick Nature." Poets move into taxonomy, as did the poet Gray; his studies not only in the classics, in music, the plastic arts, and history, but also in many branches of natural history earned for him the reputation of being "perhaps the most learned man in Europe." One of Gray's visitors says, "He had Linnaeus's Works, interleaved, always before him, when I have accidentally called upon him," [31] while another, the Swiss de Bonstetten, adds a delightful comment on his host: "After breakfast appear Shakespeare and old Lineus [sic] struggling together as two ghosts would do for a damned soul. Sometimes the one gets the better, sometimes the other." [32] And small genealogies spring up, based on non-scientific preoccupations among the professional scientists. H. K. Airy Shaw, discussing the post-Darwinian development of botanic taxonomy, mentions one such, a groping toward a "dynamic" taxonomy which he traces back to Michel Adanson (1727–1806), through Hans Hallier, whose scientific work appears from about 1890 to 1920, to Hayata, a contemporary Japanese botanist. Of these men he says: "Adanson's . . . interest in reformed spelling and in languages in general constitutes a remarkable parallel with Hallier's absorption in comparative philology." Hallier, we are told, also wrote "whimsical little botanical poems," while Hayata had a profound admiration for Goethe and, the author says, produced his dynamic system largely under the influence of the *Metamorphose der Pflanzen*.[33] We shall meet Adanson again, as one of Linnaeus' critics; but he comes in here also as the founder of another small line of descent, those scientists who have written about plants as if they were sentient beings. A. J. Wilmott says, "Adanson . . . considered plants from all angles, even to a paragraph on their souls!" [34] The exclamation mark indicates at least the conventional sense of shock; but Adanson is not the only one to take this line. Erasmus Darwin in a delightful passage in *Zoonomia* (1794) says, "This leads us to a curious enquiry, whether vegetables have ideas of external things." He then discusses for a page or two the capacity of vegetables for ideas and sentiments, including love, and ends, "I think we may truly conclude, that they are furnished with a common sensorium belonging to each bud, and that they must occasionally repeat those perceptions either in their dreams or waking hours, and consequently possess ideas of so many of the properties of the external world, and of their own existence." The classic case of this is Fechner's *Nanna, oder Über das Seelenleben der Pflanzen,* of 1848. I am not assessing these ideas as working methods, good or bad; what I want to do is to draw attention to the nature of the method these scientists are using. It is evidence, and it points to the likelihood of our conjecture that morphology and taxonomy are postlogical and consequently nearly related to poetry, which in its turn is morphological and taxonomic in character. The groping toward a dynamic systematics which accompanies an interest in poetry and words, the anthropomorphic botanical thinking (which is an experiment in mythological methods, as Fechner certainly knew) [35] are part of postlogic.

Science, myth, and poetry are never far apart. It is instructive to see how readily great scientists drop into poetry, especially when deeply moved by some idea which they have had—that is to say, by a great new field of unexplored relations to which they for the first time see an entry. One recalls Kepler in astronomy and his great outburst; [36] Sir Ronald Ross in medicine; Alfred Russell Wallace, who appends a poem to the end of his chapter "Colours and Ornaments Characteristic of Sex" in *Darwinism,*[37] a poem peculiarly interesting because it treats its subject, the marvelous adaptation and structure of a peacock's feather, as a word in Nature's poem—a poem on Nature as poetry, in fact. That the poems are not great poems does not matter in the slightest; the impulse is right and is immensely valuable evidence that science and poetry are potentially convertible disciplines, evidence which is supported by the lives and activities of so many of the men we are thinking about. The scientists speak to the point, but on the whole by, not of, their systems and methods. It is to the poets we must turn, and here there is an Orphic voice waiting. "Naturforscher und Dichter haben durch *eine* Sprache sich immer wie *ein Volk* gezeigt," it says—researchers into nature, and poets, have always shown themselves to be one race of men through their one language. This is Novalis in 1798.

This young German who lived barely twenty-nine years, from 1772 to 1801, the ardent and holy Novalis as Emerson calls him, was a poet, lawyer, administrator, and something of an expert on mining, besides being a passionate student of mathematics, physics, chemistry, and philosophy. Novalis knew Bacon's work, but it seems almost as if by divine accident that he completes it, as far as Orpheus is concerned. He perfects the great figure Bacon shadowed forth but could not fulfill, Orpheus as the fusion of poetry and philosophy. In Novalis, Orpheus stands explicitly for both. "Only then when the philosopher takes it upon himself to be Orpheus will the whole enterprise fall into order, into clearly-formed, regular, significant fields, hierarchically disposed,—into true branches of science." But Orpheus is also poetry: "They [the poets] do not yet realize what powers they hold in sway, what worlds are bidden to obey them. Is it not indeed true that rocks and woods fall in with the music and, tamed by the poets, do their will as our tame animals do ours?" And what appears here in mythological form is repeated elsewhere as more sober theory. "The perfected form of every branch of knowledge must be poetic"; "poetry is the key to philosophy, its aim and its meaning." [38]

The saying about scientists and poets having the same language comes from a narrative fragment called *Die Lehrlinge zu Sais*, the apprentices or novices at Sais. Sais is a place at which are gathered a number of apprentices, under the guidance of a remarkable teacher, learning to understand nature by collecting natural objects such as shells and birds' feathers and pebbles, making patterns with them, and observing the inner workings of their minds, the whole thing set in a great metaphor of a hidden language to be found out.

This work is one of the great prophetic utterances of the eighteenth century, which bides its time. It is a myth upon taxonomy. Appropriately, we receive our chart or map to this science in poetic form. Because the work is little known here and because it is one of the links in the Orphic chain, I shall spend some time on it. It is in any case very beautiful.

It exhibits in itself the doubling and yet the unity of the Baconian Orpheus, for it has two parts, the one corresponding to philosophy and the other to poetry; there are also a few short notes added at the end which suggest what the completion of the work would have been. The bulk of *Die Lehrlinge* consists of Part II, which is called "Nature." This is philosophy, a commentary on the nature of postlogical activity, sometimes in the form of simple exposition, sometimes in dialogue; beautiful in itself, but a commentary only—in short, philosophy. Part I, only about three pages long and entitled "The Apprentice," is poetry, and to that we shall come after we have summarized what Part II has to say.

Language, Novalis says in the *Fragmente*,[39] is itself a product of the historical processes of organic development. (So Herder had seen it also, fourteen years previously; so Vico too, earlier in the century; and to remind ourselves of this is not to attack anyone's originality but merely to recall that it is the nature and the task of Orphic voices to say the same thing over and over again, each in his own way.) It is upon this profoundly evolutionary and scientific point of view that Part II is based. The poet first considers language as myth, seeing mythological thinking as an early, highly developed, and specialized instrument of inquiry and knowledge, concerned with the most important questions of all in man's relationship to nature; he calls this *Gestaltenerklärung*, the explanation or interpretation of *Gestalten* (Goethe's word) or forms (Bacon's word) in nature. Poetry and folk tales tell of this, as Novalis says in one of his poems:

> Und man in Märchen und Gedichten
> Erkennt die wahren Weltgeschichten
>
> (And recognize in tale and verse
> True histories of the universe).

These show us gods, men and animals at work upon a world in process of being made, with analogy to human life as the best method of interpretation. There is a correspondence between man and nature, and this is seen most clearly in poetry, which is why that art holds a special position among those who want to understand nature. A discussion follows of the differing methods and functions of the natural scientist and poet, with emphasis on the varied ways in which nature can be approached and understood, of which technology is not the least. (Once again we find an Orphic poet asserting poetry and technology as kindred disciplines.) The true postlogician then, as we would call him, will be interested in everything and will go round observing the unconscious poetry that exists in all operations and occupations.

The qualities necessary for this kind of operative understanding of nature are described next: "Long and tireless practicing, a way of looking at things that is both untrammeled and ingenious, sharp eyes for slight indications and marks of significance, an inner poetic life, well-trained senses, a simple and god-fearing spirit." Then comes a fairy story inserted into the philosophical discussion, a young man who sets off to find the veiled virgin who is the mother of all things, and when he lifts the veil discovers that the goddess is his beloved whom he had left behind, so that the story ends with a marriage and children, or with sex and fertility seen as a means of comprehension. The na-

ture of attention is next examined, an absolute giving of
the self to the subject matter and the watching of oneself
thinking at the same time as thinking about something
else, a marvelous definition which Coleridge would sup-
port.[40] Out of this come systems, the raw material for all
system-makers still to come, a line which has had a few
great, indeed divine, voices but which has now lapsed so
that we think of nature merely as a machine, a mechanical
uniformity. What is needed is a reinstatement of the his-
torical approach, and a realization that it is not only an-
swers to questions that we are seeking, but the questions
to which the knowledge we possess is the answer. Only
the poets, it is suggested at this point, may have the neces-
sary power. This is where Orpheus is mentioned, and then
comes a passage about nature and the mind as the inter-
pretation of each other which looks straight forward to
Wordsworth and *The Prelude,* so we will not stop with it
now. Life and living are put forward as the basis of the
whole art of interpretation; this is once again expressed in
sexual terms, as mating with nature and bringing forth the
forms for understanding. And the whole ends with a state-
ment by the Teacher of the Apprentices about what it
means to be a true inquirer into, and a teacher of, the ways
of nature.

This is the philosophy, and it is remarkable enough;
but the brief First Part is better still, for it translates all
the discussion into image and action. Here is the begin-
ning:

> Men go their several ways, each different from other.
> Whoever traces these ways out and compares them
> will find that marvelous figures rise to meet his gaze,
> figures which seem to belong to that grand cipher and
> script which is to be found all over the place,—on
> wings, on the shells of birds' eggs, in clouds, in snow,

in crystals and rock formations, on water freezing, in the inward and outward structuring of mountains, of plants, animals, human beings, in the lights of heaven, in the markings on smooth surfaces of pitchblende or glass, in the patterns of iron filings round a magnet, and in strange conjunctions of chance. In all of these the mind gropes after the key to that marvelous text, its essential grammar and syntax; but the groping will not take firm and reliable shape, and the key is not forthcoming.

We are admitted at once to the great Orphic and Baconian vision of nature as a language. (I have in the above passage borrowed the phrase "the grand cipher" from Emerson, who uses it in just this sense in his essay "Nature.") The holy text needs no interpretation, a voice says; it is self-subsistent, and can only be interpreted by a living and speaking organism which analogizes it or chimes in with what is being said:

> That must certainly have been the voice of our Teacher, for he knows how to gather up the hints which are scattered abroad everywhere. His glance kindles with a peculiar fire when the great runes lie spread out before us and he looks into our eyes to see if in us that star has yet risen which shall make the figures visible and comprehensible. If he finds us sad because there is no illumination in our darkness, he comforts us and promises better things to come for the true and persevering watcher. He has often told us how as a child his passion to exercise and employ and fulfill all his senses left him no rest. He looked at the stars and copied their courses and conjunctions in the sand. He was forever looking up into the sky, never weary of watching its airy expanse and the things that moved there, the clouds and lights. He collected

for himself stones, flowers, beetles of all kinds, and laid them in rows, trying one pattern and then another. He paid close attention to animals and to men; he used to sit at the sea's edge or look for shells. He kept himself always aware of his own feelings and thoughts. He did not know the end to which all this longing was driving him. When he grew older . . . he began to see connections everywhere, to notice meeting-points and coincidences. From now on he saw nothing in isolation. The lore he drew from his senses began to concentrate itself into immense coloured images: he heard, saw, touched, and thought all in one and the same action.

The same characteristics, though in a lesser degree, have brought the apprentices to Sais. Some are then described, particularly a child with a miraculous power of divination in these matters, and then another, an apparent failure.

This one always looked sad; he had been here for many years, but nothing went right for him; he was bad at finding things when we went out looking for crystals or flowers; he could not see far into the distance, had no gift for making striking patterns and rows of specimens. Everything fell to pieces in his hands. But none of us had so strong an impulse to the task, or so much passion for seeing and hearing. . . . One day he had gone off sadly, and then night began to fall and there was no sign of him. We were greatly troubled about him; then all at once, as morning began to dawn, we heard his voice in the glade of trees nearby. He was singing a high and happy song; we were all astonished, and the Teacher looked toward the sunrise, such a look as probably I shall never see again. He came among us before long, bringing with him, with a face full of unspeakable happi-

ness, a little stone strangely shaped, nothing much
to look at. The Teacher took it in his hand, kissed
the boy dearly, looked at us with tears in his eyes and
laid that stone in an empty space among the other
stones laid out there, at the exact point where radius
after radius of the pattern met and intersected.

Finally the apprentice-spokesman describes himself, one
of the unskillful ones, whose especial vision it yet is to
see the whole quest in terms of love between man and
woman. This, too, is approved by the Teacher as one of
the many approaches to the supreme task, the reason why
all are gathered at Sais, the unveiling of the hidden god-
dess. Part 1 ends thus: "So I too shall describe my own
figures, and if it is true, as that inscription up yonder says,
that no mortal can lift the veil, then we must strive to be-
come immortal. He who does not wish to lift the veil is
no true apprentice of Sais." As if for a postscript to this, the
first of the fragmentary notes at the very end of the work
runs as follows: "Someone succeeded in the attempt—he
lifted the veil of the goddess of Sais—but what did he see?
—He saw—wonder of wonders—himself."

Novalis provides one other major imaginative clue to
his Orphic kinsman Linnaeus. He left an unfinished novel,
Heinrich von Ofterdingen, whose subject matter, among
all the imaginary happenings, is the vocation of the poet.[41]
One of the main themes of the book, a famous one, is the
quest for the *blaue Blume,* the blue flower which is also
the face of a girl and which has clear and conscious sexual
meanings. This is not merely an image of so-called "Ro-
mantic" *Sehnsucht* and emotionalism. To understand it
better we have to range beside it Linnaeus' systematics.
He based his botanical classification upon the sexual
characteristics of the flowers, their "vegetable loves" as
Erasmus Darwin says in Canto 1 of *The Loves of the*

Plants, line 10, to which he adds this footnote: "Linnaeus, the celebrated Swedish naturalist, has demonstrated, that all flowers contain families of males or females, or both; and on their marriages has constructed his invaluable system of Botany." It is this in Linnaeus which Darwin primarily celebrates, moving on from there to celebrate sex itself in *Phytologia* as "the chef d'oeuvre, the masterpiece of nature."

The Orphic mind is active at this point, and we begin to see what lies behind the shift in our prevailing Orpheus figure from that of the ordering of nature to that of the search for Eurydice. This Novalis gives us in the *blaue Blume:* Orpheus seeking Eurydice, trying to master the universe, life and death, by the power of poetry and in the name of love, which appears here as marriage and fertility. The idea runs all through the second part of *Die Lehrlinge zu Sais.* In such a form of thinking, sex becomes not merely an object of thought but in some sense an imaginative method of comprehension; one of the great answers, as Novalis says, which nature offers us, and to which we have to try to formulate the question: "die Frage zu dieser unendlichen Antwort" ("Natur," in *Die Lehrlinge zu Sais*)—"The organs of thought are the world's reproductive system, the sexual parts of nature as a whole." Elsewhere, as if to complete the circle, he says, "Poetry is generation," a full and perfect use of all our organs, and thinking is probably very much the same.[42]

It is difficult for us in this day and age to think freely about sex. In the last fifty years we have exchanged one bondage for another, emancipated from prudery only to be caught in dogmatism. Much of Freudianism in particular has claimed, like Swedenborg, to be *the* Interpreter, which is disastrous. But if we keep to our own terms of postlogic, we shall realize that what Novalis and Linnaeus have to say is something we have come upon already. They emphasize it newly, but we have already found sex and fertility as part of the working method of postlogic, in our discussion of the *Midsummer Night's Dream* and of Bacon's "generations." And although we could not deal with this aspect of *King Lear*, the immense struggle in that work to formulate and free the operation of postlogic may have a great deal to do with the part played there by fertility and sex.

When Linnaeus chose sex as the basis for his taxonomic system, he was moving directly along the Orphic line. He came, like Swedenborg, upon one of the great hieroglyphic keys to the natural universe, and like Swedenborg he has to struggle to make use of it, for to wield an Orphic instrument is no small matter. It is always—and sex is no exception—a method of operation, a myth inseparable from the working mind; not a logic but a postlogic.

5

The poet is not only the man made to solve
the riddle of the universe, but he is also
the man who feels where it is not solved

LINNAEUS at Adam's task of naming the living creatures
is an endearing figure. He tells us in flashes, as he sees it
himself, what he is about; his language has a certain
splendor and pride of its own; and he does not consider
the task as accomplished once and for all.

One might almost say that he has a *mystique* of naming.
"To give true and proper names to plants belongs to the
genuine systematic botanists, and to them only," he says
in the *Philosophia Botanica,* "for such only are able to
distinguish the *genera,* and to know the names which were
formerly in use." Later in the same work he says, "If
botanists had once arrived so far, that they could deter-
mine every species by an essential name, they could pro-
ceed no farther towards perfection in the art." [43] What did
Linnaeus see in the name that was so essential? He tells
us in the introduction to the *Systema Naturae:*

> Man, the last and best of created works, formed
> after the image of his Maker, endowed with a por-
> tion of intellectual divinity, the governor and sub-
> jugator of all other beings, is, by his wisdom alone,

able to form just conclusions from such things as present themselves to his senses, which can only consist of bodies merely natural. Hence the first step of wisdom is to know these bodies; and to be able, by those marks imprinted on them by nature, to distinguish them from each other, and to affix to every object its proper name.

These are the elements of all science; this is the great alphabet: for if the name be lost, the knowledge of the object is lost also; and without these, the student will seek in vain for the means to investigate the hidden treasures of nature.

METHOD, the soul of Science, indicates that every natural body may, by inspection, be known by its own peculiar name, and this name points out whatever the industry of man has been able to discover concerning it: so that amidst the greatest apparent confusion, the greatest order is visible.

This is a noble statement, and an echo of earlier ones. For Linnaeus "the great alphabet" is classification, whose proper use will lead to the interpretation of nature itself. What is to be found out and interpreted he tells us in the *Philosophia Botanica:* "Besides all the above-mentioned systems . . . which may . . . be called artificial, there is a natural method, or nature's system, which we ought diligently to endeavour to find out . . . And that this system of nature is no *chimaera* . . . will appear . . . from hence, that all plants, of what order soever, show an affinity to others to which they are nearly allied." This natural system was the hidden model for all systematics invented by man, and it had not yet been found.

Linnaeus, looking for the "natural system," was trying to improve upon Ray,[44] and Linnaeus' successors in their turn try to improve his method. If taxonomy were logic and scientists worked on principles of analytic exactitude alone, we might expect post-Linnaean scientists to try to perfect the system in that direction, urging Linnaeus, as it were, toward greater precision, into language-as-science or pseudo-mathematics. In fact the contrary happens. Scientists complain from the beginning that Linnaeus is too mathematical and rigid. They push him not into logic but into postlogic.

Buffon as early as 1745 says in a letter to Jalabert: "On pèche en physique en attribuant à la nature trop d'uniformité; c'est aussi par là que pèchent toutes les méthodes de botanique; et celle de Linnaeus me satisfait moins encore que toutes les autres." This by way of general introduction; now come three proposals for improving the system. The first is Adanson with his *Familles des plantes* in 1763, calling Linnaeus a "name-changer" and contemplating a new and more dynamic form of classification for plants. Then in 1789 comes Jussieu's *Genera Plantarum*. His descendant Adrien de Jussieu describes the methods of both as follows:

> Adanson . . . found out that in order to group the genera into families, attention ought to be paid to the whole of their characteristics and not to a single one . . . Each point of their organisation, considered separately, would give us a separate system, which would present all of them in a certain order. If, in all these partial systems thus obtained, the two same genera happen to be constantly brought into juxtaposition, it is evident that they resemble one another in all the points of their organisation, that they form part of the same natural group . . . [Jussieu adopted] the employment of a principle which had escaped the notice of Adanson: that of the *subordination of the characteristics*, which in Jussieu's system are, ac-

cording to his own expression, weighed and not counted. They are considered as having unequal values: so that a characteristic of the first order is equivalent to several of the second, and so on.[45]

In Adanson there is a move away from analysis to a more synthetic approach, in Jussieu a move toward a more qualitative or evaluative method; and in both we begin to see what scientists may mean when they speak of a "dynamic" classification. The dynamics are in the mind inventing or using the system, acknowledged and accepted as part of the system's workings. Plants do not move themselves around in alternative arrangements; the mind does it for them. So a system of this kind is a myth in our original terms, a working interpretation of world plus mind, an inclusive and not an exclusive mythology. The third would-be reformer is Erasmus Darwin. Much as he admires Linnaeus, he also makes a suggestion that will move Linnaeus away from mathematics toward perception or bodily thinking, which is also a part of postlogic. In the *Phytologia*, 1800, he says,

> Often as I have admired the classification of vegetables by the great Linneus deduced from their sexual organs of reproduction, some of the classes have appeared to me to be more excellent than others, as they seemed to approach nearer to natural ones. On further attention to this subject, I perceived that those classes which were deduced from the proportions or situations of the stamina . . . were more natural classes than those, which were distinguished simply by the number of them.[46]

The Frenchmen appeal to abstract thought, the Englishman to the senses, as if to illustrate their respective traditional approaches to natural history; but each is postlogical in his own way, and they complement one another.

It is another Englishman, Darwin's grandson, who will next attempt a Linnaean reform, in the *Origin of Species*. He has his own interpreter who appointed himself to the "humbler, though perhaps as useful, office of an interpreter between the 'Origin of Species' and the public": [47] Thomas Henry Huxley. The encounter between Charles Darwin and Huxley is one of the most interesting in the whole Baconian tradition. I use the word "encounter" advisedly. Huxley is generally thought of as battling with all comers on behalf of Darwin and the theory of natural selection, and this is part of the story but not the whole. His work suggests that he has another battle on his hands, a more secret one with Darwin and with himself. For Huxley resembles Bacon with his vision and his inconsistencies. Darwin is half a Bacon, that half which was hypnotized by facts and mechanisms (and for which in an 1887 essay Huxley takes Bacon to task). [48]

To Darwin his own position was clear: he was to take Bacon's dictum, that the seeker must go to the facts for everything, as comprehensive, final, and the one path of scientific rectitude. Huxley reports him as saying that on reading his grandfather's *Zoonomia* he was much disappointed, the proportion of speculation to facts being so large. [49] Even Huxley has difficulty with the factuality of the *Origin of Species*, calling it "a sort of intellectual pemmican—a mass of facts crushed and pounded into shape, rather than held together by the ordinary medium of an obvious logical bond." He adds a little later, "Due attention will, without doubt, discover this bond, but it is often hard to find." [50] But it may be a postlogical bond which Huxley is really missing. The determination to reduce everything to facts can be seen perhaps most clearly in *The Descent of Man*. Thus, for instance, chapter 3: "My object in this chapter is to show that there is no fundamental difference between man and the higher mammals in their mental faculties." (Wallace [51] strongly objected to this, as contrary to the available evidence.) Determination to reduce everything to material fact can be a powerful working prejudice. It nearly succeeds in turning *The Descent of Man* from a scientific inquiry into special pleading. Upon this Huxley's interpretation had to work.

Huxley's cast of mind is much less simple. He says of himself: "my great desire was to be a mechanical engineer . . . and though the Institute of Mechanical Engineers would certainly not own me, I am not sure that I have not all along been a sort of mechanical engineer *in partibus infidelium* . . . notwithstanding that natural science has been my proper business, I am afraid there is very little of the genuine naturalist in me . . . what I cared for was the architectural and engineering part of the business." That might be Bacon himself—the appeal to the mechanical arts; yet this is the same Huxley who could say in 1856, "Nature is not a mechanism, she is a poem," [52] and so exhibit Bacon's own dilemma, the split between engines and postlogic which Shakespeare set out to bridge by poetry in *King Lear*.

Huxley has glimpses of postlogic, and they unsettle him. He will search the *Origin of Species* for logic, yet applaud Kepler as "the wildest of guessers." [53] When he comes to interpret Darwin, Huxley tries to redraw his picture on more flexible, imaginative, and, in the long run, explicitly Baconian lines. He does what Bacon did: affirms two contraries simultaneously. From this springs his curiously ambivalent attitude toward Darwin and his book, so different from uncomplicated agreement and disagreement such as Wallace's. Darwin was for him "the incorporated ideal of a man of science," but Huxley's interpretation is always toward something more like postlogic —"It was this rarest and greatest of endowments [honesty] which kept his vivid imagination and great speculative powers within due bounds," [54] he says of Darwin. And when he comes to official encomium, in his memorandum on the proposed Darwin Memorial, 1885, the words in which he describes Darwin's work are Bacon's own. He calls Darwin "one of those rare ministers and interpreters of Nature," while the *Origin of Species* is described as the source of "a great renewal, a true 'instauratio magna' of the zoological and botanical sciences." [55]

The identification, for Huxley, is completed. But calling Darwin a Bacon does not make him one, and it is not from the postlogical Baconian standpoint that Darwin deals with Linnean taxonomy, but from his own. In the chapter on classification in the *Origin* he says this:

> From the most remote period in the history of the world organic beings have been found to resemble each other in descending degrees, so that they can be classed in groups under groups. This classification is not arbitrary like the grouping of the stars in constellations . . . Naturalists, as we have seen, try to arrange the species, genera and families in each class, on what is called the Natural System. But what is meant by this system? . . . Expressions such as that famous one by Linnaeus, which we often meet with in a more or less concealed form, namely, that the characters do not make the genus, but that the genus gives the characters, seem to imply that some deeper bond is included in our classifications than mere resemblance. I believe that this is the case, and that community of descent—the one known cause of close similarity in organic beings—is the bond which, though observed [*sic; obscured?*] by various degrees of modification, is partially revealed to us by our classification . . . All the foregoing rules and aids and difficulties may be explained, if I do not

greatly deceive myself, on the view that the Natural
System is founded on descent with modification . . .
all true classification being genealogical; that com-
munity of descent is the hidden bond which natural-
ists have been unconsciously seeking, and not some
unknown plan of creation, or the enunciation of gen-
eral principles, and the mere putting together and
separating objects more or less alike.

Darwin is claiming that he has found once for all the
natural system which Linnaeus set up as a goal before the
eyes of taxonomers. There is no more unknown plan to
be read. The dynamics will no longer be those of mind
and natural objects but simply those of actual time or his-
tory as incorporated in the biological specimens themselves,
which can then be reduced to full logical order, with no
further need for imaginative speculation. True to his long
endeavor, Huxley tries to interpret this very statement of
Darwin's more flexibly: "No doubt Mr. Darwin believes
that these resemblances and differences upon which our
natural systems or classifications are based, are resem-
blances and differences which have been produced genet-
ically, but we can discover no reason for supposing that
he denies the existence of natural classifications of other
kinds." [56] But that passage from the *Origin* belies him.
Darwin presents his system as the consummation of the
Linnaean taxonomy, its un-postlogical logical conclusion.
The partial Baconian view was reasserted with all the
weight of a great name behind it, and the consequences,
for the good estate of science and poetry in their mutual
relationship, have been melancholy and prolonged.

We shall assume that this was not in fact the end of the
matter. What we have to do now is to retrieve the line
of postlogical taxonomy where we can find it still unbroken
in Erasmus Darwin and Goethe.

6

Nature has dearly at heart the formation
of the speculative man, or scholar . . .
He is no permissive or accidental appear-
ance, but an organic agent, one of the es-
tates of the realm, provided and prepared,
from of old and from everlasting, in the
knitting and contexture of things

IT WAS IN 1775 that Goethe accepted the young prince's
invitation to go to Weimar, and went on a visit which was
to last for the rest of his life. Already a poet and writer of
repute, he moves now into the intensive microcosm of
culture, government, and intellectual activity which that
little duchy could offer him. He himself dates the begin-
nings of his scientific interests from this point,[57] ascribing
them to the practical knowledge he needed, in forestry
or mining for instance, in order to fulfill the official duties
which he increasingly assumed until his death almost sixty
years later. In 1786 he makes his Italian Journey, that
strange secret flight to the Rome he had so ardently de-
sired to see, followed by two years spent in Italy where
he broods on ancient art and natural science and his own
vocation and sets it out in the *Italienische Reise* and, salted

with classical reference and sensual passion, in the beauti-
ful *Römische Elegien*. After his return to Weimar the
Metamorphose der Pflanzen appears in 1790, and there-
after till his death in 1832 the steady stream of literary
and scientific works continues, along with autobiography,
letters, journals, notes, and conversation of which records
were kept.

Erasmus Darwin's life is packed into a shorter span.
By 1775 he was already a successful doctor in the Mid-
lands, apparently as speculative and experimental in his
practice as he was in his thinking.[58] Here too was a small
provincial world that was not without claims to literary
and scientific culture, and Dr. Darwin seems to have taken
full advantage of local society, consorting with literary
figures such as Anna Seward, the Swan of Lichfield, avoid-
ing Dr. Johnson at all costs as a juggernaut of a conversa-
tional rival, and belonging to that remarkable society the
"Lunatics," which included four Fellows of the Royal
Society—Erasmus Darwin, James Watt, Samuel Galton,
and Joseph Priestley, besides Edgeworth and Thomas Day,
the author of *Sandford and Merton*.[59] The Doctor's written
works fall in the last twelve years of his life: *The Botanic
Garden*, 1791; his first scientific work, *Zoonomia, or, The
Laws of Organic Life*, 1794; his second, *Phytologia, or,
The Philosophy of Agriculture and Gardening with the
Theory of Draining Morasses and an Improved Construc-
tion of the Drill Plough*, 1800; and the second, post-
humous, poem, *The Temple of Nature*, 1803.

Darwin's fellow countrymen have agreed to dismiss
him, unread, as a figure of fun. In science it is not until
the 1870's that he is given recognition, and then by a
German, Ernst Krause, who compares Darwin with Goe-
the,[60] gives the former his due in the development of
evolutionary thought, and maintains that he was bound
to be misunderstood by his contemporaries because he

was a hundred years ahead of them. This recognition of Darwin is taken further by Samuel Butler in *Evolution Old and New,* which appeared in 1882, and by Shaw in the preface to *Back to Methuselah.* In literary criticism, Erasmus Darwin has had no recognition at all. This is partly the result of what Coleridge said about him: a man who was generally if comprehensibly unjust to Darwin and whose critical reputation now stands so high that it may tacitly prevent a true assessment of Darwin's contribution to our tradition.[61]

With Goethe something else happens. I can speak only for Anglo-Saxon minds, but here he is generally little known and little liked. At best he will be accorded an aloof recognition as one of the great but not as a patron and friend; at worst he will meet with an odd puritanical rejection, of the man and his work both, on the grounds of his arrogance and unapproachability. If he was right when he said to Eckermann, May 12, 1825, that always and everywhere one learns only from those one loves, we have put ourselves in a position where we can learn nothing from him at all. Only the Orphic minds turn to him, as did Novalis, Carlyle, Emerson, and, eventually, Rilke after a long reluctant capitulation. In the history of scientific thought, Goethe's position has been the subject of prolonged controversy which is still going on.[62] I shall not enter into this; but it is noticeable that among contemporary scientists only those with a postlogical turn of mind, such as Agnes Arber, Michael Polanyi and Lance Whyte, have a real understanding for what Goethe may have been trying to do.

The clearest Orphic commentator on Goethe is Emerson. When he writes about Goethe in *Representative Men,* he casts him for a particular part: "I find a provision in the constitution of the world," Emerson says, "for the writer or secretary who is to report the doings of the mi-

raculous spirit of life that everywhere throbs and works."
To the noble metaphor of nature as a language is added
a hint that the interpreter of that language belongs to a
kind of celestial Civil Service, the "secretary" and the "re-
port" bending themselves that way, a fitting way of think-
ing about Goethe and his allegorical life. Then Emerson
goes on:

> Nature will be reported. All things are engaged in
> writing their history . . . The air is full of sounds;
> the sky, of tokens; the ground is all memoranda and
> signatures; and every object covered over with hints,
> which speak to the intelligent . . . Nature conspires.
> Whatever can be thought can be spoken, and still rises
> for utterance, though to rude and stammering organs.
> If they cannot compass it, it waits and works, until,
> at last, it moulds them to its perfect will, and is artic-
> ulated.

The task of Nature's secretary, however, is never just that
of taking dictation, "mere stenography" as Emerson calls
it. The speculative mind of the poet comes in also. So
Emerson adds the wonderful sentences which head this
section, above, where the Orphic mentality is seen in its
fullness, part of the evolutionary processes of nature which
it is to interpret under the joint forms of poetry and nat-
ural science.

We have to think of the Orphic mind as a natural
phenomenon. This is certainly how Goethe thought of
himself. He was in his own eyes the "organic agent" Emer-
son speaks of, and it is this that he records so carefully and
at such length in all his work. He is secretary to the uni-
verse and to himself, the two being indivisible. To think
of him in this way will at first make matters not easier but
harder. A natural living phenomenon on which we possess
a multitude of data is one of the most difficult things to

think about in the world; worse still when it is conscious of its matrix in nature and thinks about this, these thoughts being then also part of the data we have to work with. Goethe is bedded down into nature like a huge thinking tree, and to come to terms with this will need some other method than dislodging or dismembering. Here Erasmus Darwin is going to be helpful. He is a like phenomenon but a less gigantic one, and he does not complicate his state or ours by thinking about it himself. Clear, straightforward, detached, not much interested in himself but much interested in almost everything else, he has nonetheless an Orphic mind, as Goethe has. Silent about himself on the whole, he yet does not go unrecorded, for fate allotted him a remarkable biographer, Anna Seward the poetess (the feminine gender is wholly appropriate in her case). Her *Memoirs of the Life of Dr. Darwin* is a minor classic in its own right, fascinatingly florid in style, frequently irrelevant, but never dull, exhibiting from time to time unmistakable and enjoyable feminine malice, unreliable in its facts, but containing shrewd critical judgments on Darwin's literary work. Where Goethe is vast, general, and profound, Darwin will be, in the same direction, much more specific, and will tell us what to look for in the operations both he and Goethe are engaged on.

In a well-known passage in the *Geschichte meines botanischen Studiums* appended to the *Metamorphose der Pflanzen,* Goethe says that after Spinoza, whom we shall not be concerned with here, and Shakespeare, the greatest single influence upon him had been Linnaeus, "precisely because he aroused so much antagonism in me." Goethe maintained a life-long relationship with Shakespeare. Bacon appears too in Goethe's work, but in a minor capacity. "Einen bewundernswürdigen Geist," Goethe calls him, and gives a quiet and judicious assessment of him as a scientist in the historical section of the *Farbenlehre.* For

Darwin, too, Linnaeus is central. *The Loves of the Plants*
is one long celebration of the work of "the Swedish sage,"
and he appears frequently elsewhere in Darwin's work,
never without reverent and enthusiastic comment. For
his Orphic ancestry, however, in the light of which the
work upon Linnaeus is to be done, Darwin turns back
not so much to Shakespeare (though he mentions him often
and with affectionate admiration, singling out for special
mention two of the mythological plays, *A Midsummer
Night's Dream* and *The Tempest*, in the Interludes be-
tween the Cantos in *The Loves of the Plants*) as to Bacon.
It is not Bacon the scientist whom he invokes, however,
but the mythologist and postlogician. In the "Apology"
preceding *The Economy of Vegetation* Darwin says: "many
of the important operations of Nature were shadowed
or allegorized in the heathen mythology, as the first Cupid
springing from the Egg of Night, the marriage of Cupid
and Psyche . . . etc, many of which are ingeniously ex-
plained in the works of Bacon." He returns to these
mythological interpretations of Bacon in the notes to
these poems. In that same Apology he talks about hiero-
glyphics and then the Eleusinian Mysteries. These are
dealt with at some length in note XXII to the *Economy*,
in connection with the Portland Vase, where Darwin men-
tions Warburton, that more immediate Orphic ancestor
of his; and eventually they become the "machinery" for
The Temple of Nature.

It seems right that Goethe should hold particularly to
Shakespeare, for the latter's Orpheus, the lute strung with
poets' sinews, expresses Goethe's position too, the poet his
own instrument and an agent of the power which controls
and directs nature itself. That Darwin should opt for
Bacon and postlogic is more surprising. By doing so he
lands at one bound right into the middle of myth as a

methodology. More than this, he places himself full in
that long steady tradition which in England goes back
to the beginning of the sixteenth century, and elsewhere
goes back further still.

Darwin is not yet done, however. He shows an Orphic
insight when it comes to Linnaeus himself and to the in-
adequacy which both he and Goethe sense in the Linnaean
taxonomy. What did this sense of inadequacy spring from,
and what could be done about it? Goethe makes a number
of direct attempts at self-examination on the subject. We
find him making the cryptic remark that he had learned
infinitely much from Linnaeus with the sole exception of
botany.[63] He takes his Linnaeus with him, touchingly, on
his mad dash into Italy, an essential piece of luggage ap-
parently; but he is not happy with him: "True, I have
my Linnaeus with me, and his terminology dutifully in
my head; but will the time and the quietude of mind neces-
sary for analysis be forthcoming?—and in any case, if I
know my own nature, analysis is never going to be my
strong point" (*Italienische Reise*, entry for September 7,
1786). Later he is haunted by Linnaeus again, no less un-
comfortably:

> Confronted with so many new and renewed plant-
> forms, I found that old obsession of mine turning
> up again: whether amongst all this crowd I could dis-
> cover the *Urpflanze*. There must be such a thing!
> How otherwise should we recognize that such and
> such a form was a plant at all unless they were all
> built on the same model? I made an effort to find out
> in what ways the many differing forms were really
> distinct from one another. And all the time I kept
> seeing them as more alike than unlike, and when I
> called up the reinforcements of my botanical termi-

nology, that was well and good but it facilitated noth-
ing; it merely made me uneasy without helping me
forward.   [Ibid., April 17, 1787]

In the *Geschichte meines botanischen Studiums*, immedi-
ately after the mention of the trinity of Spinoza, Shake-
speare, and Linnaeus, Goethe goes on to discuss the latter's
system and his reaction to it:

> Through sheer repetition the names imprinted
> themselves on my memory; in analysis too I acquired
> rather more skill, but the success was more apparent
> than real . . . Were I to try consciously to clear up
> my situation, I should say: think of me as a born
> poet, whose aim was to shape his words and forms of
> expression directly to fit his subject-matter, whatever
> that might be, in order to do it justice as far as pos-
> sible. Such a one was now called upon to memorize
> a ready-made terminology, to have a squad of terms
> and sub-terms at the ready, so that when a specimen
> came his way he would be able, after some quick se-
> lective thinking, to line it up in its due order accord-
> ing to its particular characteristics. This way of going
> to work always reminded me of a sort of mosaic, where
> ready-made pieces are put together one by one so as
> ultimately to produce out of hundreds of petty de-
> tails some semblance of a picture. The demands made
> by this method always went against my judgment.
>
> Although I have come to see the necessity for this
> kind of thing, aiming as it does at enabling the stu-
> dent, by means of a general body of information, to
> come to terms with certain external characteristics of
> plants, and to do away with uncertainty about plant-
> forms, yet I found that this would-be precise use of

terms created the worst difficulty of all, plant organs being so versatile.

There is a suggestion of the same sort of difficulty in a conversation reported by Falk, "This is this and that is that! But what good does it do me to have all this nomenclature in my head? . . . What use are bits and pieces, and the names of bits and pieces? What I want to know is what it is that so breathes through each part of the universe that each seeks its fellow, serving it or commanding it according to that intellectual law, innate in all in greater or lesser degree, which fits out one for one role, another for another. But it is just at this very point that complete and universal silence reigns." [64]

Goethe demands greater dynamics and flexibility in Linnaean taxonomy. So did Darwin in the passage in *Phytologia* quoted above, p. 214; he then adds, "I profess myself incapable to execute the plan, which I have suggested here, as it would . . . demand a genius which few possess, capable of reducing the complex and intricate to the simple and explicit." It is as if he left the actual task to Goethe, but he tells us more clearly than Goethe and in the purest Orphic and postlogical terms the nature of the change Goethe must work on Linnaeus. He tells us this in his poetry, not in his scientific prose. Miss Seward describes, inimitably, the birth of the idea in his mind.

"The Linnaean System is unexplored poetic ground, and an happy subject for the muse. It affords fine scope for poetic landscape; it suggests metamorphoses of the Ovidian kind, though reversed. Ovid made men and women into flowers, plants, and trees. You should make flowers, plants and trees into men and women. I," continued he, "will write the notes, which must be scientific; and you shall write the verse."

Miss Seward observed that, besides her want of
botanic knowledge, the subject was not strictly proper
for a female pen; that she felt how eminently it was
adapted to the efflorescence of his own fancy.[65]

Darwin himself, in the "Proem" to the work in question,
The Loves of the Plants, takes up the tale: "Whereas
P. OVIDIUS NASO, a great necromancer in the famous
Court of AUGUSTUS CAESAR, did by art poetic transmute
Men, Women, and even Gods and Goddesses, into Trees
and Flowers; I have undertaken by similar art to restore
some of them to their original animality, after having re-
mained prisoners so long in their respective vegetable man-
sions; and have here exhibited them before thee."

The clue Darwin offers, for himself and for Goethe, is
an attempt to turn Linnaeus into Ovid. Darwin and
Goethe are to transform systematics into metamorphoses.
Darwin is explicit about his own intentions. How will
Goethe's work respond to such an interpretation of it?

A connection between Goethe and Ovid exists already,
established by Goethe himself. We come across Ovid in
the middle of Goethe's scientific thinking, just as we do
in Darwin's; Goethe mentions him in connection with
comparative anatomy, animal and human, Darwin in con-
nection with hybrid plants.[66] But the Goethe-Ovid rela-
tionship is a matter not simply of classical or scientific
reference, but of love. Ovid, so Goethe tells us in *Dichtung
und Wahrheit,* entered his life early. "I early became ac-
quainted with the Ovidian transformations, and so my
young head was filled soon enough with a mass of images
and events, forms and happenings full of significance and
wonder" (Vol. 1, Bk. 1). Later he mentions that he formed
in childhood the rather strange habit of learning by heart
opening passages of books, and says that he did this with

the Pentateuch, the *Aeneid,* and the *Metamorphoses.* And
what an opening that last is!

> In nova fert animus mutatas dicere formas
> corpora; di, coeptis (nam vos mutastis et illas)
> adspirate meis primaque ab origine mundi
> ad mea perpetuum deducite tempora carmen!

If that young growing mind of Goethe's had needed a de-
vice for its present and future activity, it could scarcely
have found a better.

Metamorphosis is for Goethe one of the great underly-
ing principles of all natural phenomena. "Everything in
life is metamorphosis," he says to Sulpiz Boisserée in 1815
(*Goethe im Gespräch,* p. 185), "in plants, and in animals,
up to and including mankind as well." It is to this last
and crucial kind of metamorphosis that the *Urworte* have
been held to refer.[67] Agnes Arber records that in his life-
time his use of the word *Metamorphose* in his scientific
treatises produced Ovidian misconceptions:

> The word *Metamorphose,* in the title of Goethe's
> book, was not altogether a happy one for his purpose.
> From classical times it had had poetical associations,
> which might well lead the reader to expect a work
> of fancy rather than of science, especially when the
> author was already famous for imaginative writing.
> Goethe himself complains that, on telling one of his
> friends that he had published a little volume upon
> the metamorphoses of plants, the friend expressed his
> delight in the prospect of enjoying Goethe's charm-
> ing description in the Ovidian manner of narcissus,
> hyacinth and daphne.   [*Goethe's Botany,* p. 74]

It is possible, however, that this was a "good" error. A
man as steeped in Ovid as Goethe was cannot have failed

to realize the associations of the word "metamorphosis" which he chose to use for scientific purposes. The fault may have lain with that particular friend's notion of Ovid, the conventional one perhaps, which Herder also held. In his autobiography (Vol. 1, Bk. x) Goethe describes the battle he had with Herder about Ovid. Herder took what is still the general critical view of the Latin poet: "No real and direct truths were to be found in these poems; this was neither Greece nor Rome, neither a primeval nor a civilized world, merely imitation of what was already in existence, presented with the kind of affectation one might expect from a hypersophisticate." Goethe counters this judgment with one of his own, remarkable in itself and for its conformity with what we have seen already of Orphic ways of thinking about poets and their relation to natural history: "I tried to maintain that the productions of an outstanding individual are themselves products of nature." That is to say that nature interprets herself through the figuring mind, in taxonomy and in myth alike, at that dynamic point where the mind thinks with language.

Coleridge implies this when he says, "As for the study of the ancients, so of the works of nature, an accidence and a dictionary are the first and indispensable requisites." The metaphor once again is of nature as a language, and the study of the classics is set on a par with natural history, excellent for our purpose for we need an approach to Ovid, unequipped as we are through our system of education in the Latin classics, which teaches them, if they are taught at all, as exercises in translating or in pedantic footnotage, never as poetry or ideas. After this opening Coleridge comes directly to Linnaeus, for it is thither that he is proceeding. He says that for the dictionary and accidence [68] of the works of nature we are indebted to "the illustrious Swede." But, he goes on, "neither was the central idea of vegetation itself, by the light of which we might have seen the collateral relations of the vegetable to the inorganic and to the animal world; nor the constitutive and inner necessity of sex itself, revealed to Linnaeus." Here is a remarkable diagnosis of the Linnaean case. Do Orphic minds call in Ovid to the rescue in hopes of finding in him a central idea of vegetation, collateral relations between the orders of nature, and the constitutive necessity of sex? It is possible at least. A little later Coleridge goes on, "What is botany at this present hour? Little more than an enormous nomenclature; a huge catalogue . . . The terms, system, method, science, are mere improprieties of courtesy, when applied to a mass enlarging by endless appositions but without a nerve that oscillates, or a pulse that throbs in sign of growth and inward sympathy." [69] It is at this point that we are referred by Darwin and Goethe to Ovid's poem.

In the meager critical literature available, Ovid tends to be set down as a witty but only half-serious compiler of traditional myths, whose ingenuity, great as it is, is insufficient to give unity to this compendium of stories he strung together on the single thread that each of them contains a change of form of some kind. He becomes a high-class hack cataloguer. Yet there is evidence that this view of him is inadequate, simply because of his central position among Orphic minds. [70] Did Shakespeare, Milton, Goethe, Wordsworth find in Ovid merely a useful dictionary of mythology?

The *Metamorphoses* are of epic length; there are fifteen books of them. The poet in his own person speaks the first peerless four lines as prologue, and the last nine lines as epilogue. In the first four he claims the whole of time for his poetic province, explicitly, from the beginning of the world to his own day, with all the changes there may be between. Then at the end he moves almost casually into

eternity, partly as immortal soul and immortal poet, partly
on the strength of the civilization to which he belongs,
though the claim is made with what looks like a slight lift
of the eyebrow:

> Parte tamen meliore mei super alta perennis
> Astra ferar: nomenque erit indelibile nostrum.
> Quaque patet domitis Romana potentia terris,
> Ore legar populi: perque omnia saecula fama
> (Si quid habent veri vatum praesagia) vivam.

If the divinations of poets are to be trusted—it is a nice
point; but at least life has the last word in the poem, just
as novelty had the first, and between the two runs a long
span of about a hundred stories, beginning with the crea-
tion of the world out of chaos and ending with the deifica-
tion of Julius Caesar. Most of the stories contain a trans-
formation, some more than one. Those involved may be
gods, demigods, heroes, mortals, living creatures of all
kinds, plants and trees, rocks, earth, water, the elements.

Book I, after the poet has spoken in his own voice, starts
with the creation of the world out of chaos, first the ele-
ments of the world itself, then the living creatures, then
the creation of man. After a description of the Four Ages,
Gold, Silver, Bronze and Iron, a decline from beauty and
innocence into human crime and rebellion, comes the first
metamorphosis, the retrogression of man into wolf; then
comes the Flood and the second metamorphosis, the stones
thrown by Deucalion and Pyrrha which turn into men
and women. So in 450 lines the world is settled and ready
to proceed, and we come to what is the first type-metamor-
phosis of the vast majority that are to follow: Apollo con-
strained by Cupid to love Daphne, daughter of a river god,
who eludes him by turning into a laurel tree. Now we are
fairly launched, and from here until the end of Book IX

story succeeds story in a series that might well be infinite. There seems to be a gradual progression from preoccupation with the gods, who are powers in human shape, and with half-gods such as nymphs and local geniuses, the embodiments of natural objects, to more purely human stories; but the gods and godlings do not vanish, they continue to weave in and out of the stories of men all the time. So the first nine books go.

With Book x comes Orpheus, to whom Ovid gives greater prominence than to any other single figure in the work. He enters with the Eurydice story. The whole of Book x is his song, which falls in with the serial pattern of the earlier books, though framed now by the consciousness we have of the singer singing it. Book xi opens with the account of his power over natural things; then his death. In the very next story, that of Midas, he is kept in our minds by a reference as we go along, and then immediately we find ourselves watching the building of the walls of a city,[71] Troy, which here as in the *Aeneid* is held to be the ancestor of Rome; and the cities continue to grow and change and struggle throughout the remaining books of the poem. In xiii and xiv the myths continue, but prehistory and history grow up with them now; the invasion of Troy; the pilgrimage of Aeneas which, divided into three parts, weaves through the two books in between the mythological themes; the deification of Aeneas; the founding of Rome. In Book xv the summing up begins, with a long speech by Pythagoras on Orphic cultic lore.[72] Pythagoras also recapitulates the main theme. "Cuncta fluunt: omnisque vagans formatur imago," he says, and then a little later:

> coelum et quodcunque sub illo est,
> Immutat formas, tellusque, et quicquid in illa est.
> Nos quoque, pars mundi . . .

and in between, all the changes are mentioned, the slow revolutions of time on the earth's surface, the workings of natural history, the growing and decaying of the cities and societies of no less mutable man. We end with the deification of Julius Caesar and the apostrophe to Augustus. The final passage is not merely a self-interested diversion. This is not to deny the aim of self-commendation, but a great poet can achieve such functional ends, if they can be called so, as he goes along, inside the texture of the poem itself. What this passage says is that politics are themselves part of the process the poem has been concerned with—an immense addition to the theme which we can only notice here and pass by.

This poem is one superb vision of growth and process taking form first in the purely natural world and then in the world of man, the changing figures of the one moving on continuously into those of the second. The work divides in the proportion of 3:2. Books I–IX form the first part, story following upon story. The profusion of connection and disconnection is not due to accident or failure of skill; it is a marvelous correspondence with the poet's subject matter. This is exactly what, from one point of view, the world is—a seemingly endless series of stories, of powers and phenomena, birth, transformation, death, soon related and soon over, making way for other stories, connected or unconnected. What Ovid is doing is adopting the narrative approach to natural history—"as a tale that is told." He gives three-fifths of his span of time to the workings of the natural world, and leaves the remaining two-fifths for the more human developments which grow directly up and out of it. Here cities begin to rise and civilizations to develop, seen in their turn as part of the great natural round of growth and change which time visits upon us all:

> Cities and Thrones and Powers
> Stand in Time's eye
> Almost as long as flowers,
> Which daily die . . .

It is a vision that stands any poet worthy the name in good stead. So the forms of man's thinking and society grow up, at one with the processes of the elemental powers and inanimate things and living bodies, but transcending them as part of the same process.

At the hinge of the work, mediating that shift from inorganic and organic to consciously human, is Orpheus. With his arrival the pattern of development (of universe and poem) begins to complicate itself and to move in new directions. In Orpheus' position in this poem are implicit all the claims made for his civilizing influence in sphere after sphere. But Orpheus is not merely an individual mythological figure; he is the figure of poetry as power. So poetry, as myth and language, and as the instrument of human consciousness (it is with Book x that the song of the poem becomes, as it were, conscious of itself) becomes also the instrument of progress into society and culture, the development from organismic into organizational activity.

Far from being a collection of imaginary if pretty stories, the poem begins now to assume such proportions that it is hard to speak of it adequately. The *Metamorphoses* is a vast postlogic in its own right: in the reciprocal dynamics of its subject matter and method; in its affirmation of the central position of language and poetry in the person of Orpheus; in its preoccupation with sex as one of the working principles in matter and method; in its use of myth as the instrument by which the whole span of natural process is to be understood and interpreted; in the reflexive use

of that instrument to hold the universe and the mind to-
gether, the forms under consideration being always partly
phenomenal and partly mental and imaginative. By all
of this it takes its primal place in the direct tradition, as
"a portion of that wider Science of Form which deals with
the forms assumed by matter under all aspects and condi-
tions, and, in a still wider sense, with forms which are the-
oretically imaginable." So D'Arcy Thompson in chapter
17 of *On Growth and Form* characterizes the activity of
morphology. It is here that Ovid belongs; as much a part
of this, the Orphic tradition, as is D'Arcy Thompson him-
self, or Erasmus Darwin and Goethe and the Linnaeus they
set out to metamorphose.

7

POET:	And yet the very improbable monsters in Ovid's *Metamorphoses* have entertained the world for many centuries.
BOOKSELLER:	The monsters in your *Botanic Garden,* I hope, are of the latter kind.
POET:	The candid reader must determine.

WE ARE doubly in a difficulty when we come to consider *The Botanic Garden*. We know it only as work which has been most successfully ridiculed; and we are hampered by the prevailing critical fashion, which is to read a poet not so much for matter or method as for style and attitude, and then to pass judgments of literary value. We shall never do justice to Erasmus Darwin in this way, and I want to propose two things to help us. First, since he is so little known, we will look at him at his best. Second, we will turn for assistance to his contemporary critic, Miss Anna Seward, part of the purpose of whose book on Dr.

Darwin is, she says, "an investigation of the constituent excellencies and defects of his magnificent poem, the *Botanic Garden*." (She does not deal with *The Temple of Nature*, which she had not seen at the time of writing her biography.)

To see Darwin at his best as a poet, we have to go, rather surprisingly, to *Phytologia*. Anyone reading that work, which is interesting in its own right, will be rewarded by coming upon a set of verses concealed in Part III, translated in part, so the author says, "from an elegant Latin poem of Edward Tighe Esq." and bearing the title "The Cultivation of Brocoli." It is a little too long to quote in full, but a selection follows:

> There are of learned taste, who still prefer
> Cos-lettuce, tarragon and cucumber;
> There are, who still with equal praises yoke
> Young peas, asparagus and artichoke;
> Beaux there are still with lamb and spinach nurs'd,
> And clowns eat beans and bacon till they burst.
>
> This boon I ask of Fate, whene'er I dine,
> O, be the Proteus-form of cabbage mine!—
> Cale, colewort, cauliflower, or soft and clear
> If BROCOLI delight thy nicer ear,
> Give, rural Muse! the culture and the name
> In verse immortal to the rolls of Fame.
>
> When the bright Bull ascending first adorns
> The Spring's fair forehead with his golden horns,
> Italian seed with parsimonious hand
> The watchful gardener scatters o'er his land;
> Quick moves the rake, with iron teeth divides
> The yielding glebe, the living treasure hides;
> O'er the smooth soil, with horrent horns beset,
> Swells in the breeze the undulating net;

Bright shells and feathers dance on twisting strings,
And the scar'd Finch retreats on rapid wings . . .

Pants thy young heart to grasp the laurel'd prize,
And swell thy Brocoli to gigantic size?
Soon as each head with youthful grace receives
The verdant curls of six unfolding leaves:
O, still transplant them, on each drizzly morn,
Oft as the moon relights her waning horn;
Till her bright vest the star-clad Virgin trails,
Or corn-crown'd Autumn lifts his golden scales.
Then ply the shining hoe with artful toil,
E'er the grey night-frost binds the stiffen'd soil;
And as o'er heaven the rising Scorpion crawls,
Surround the shuddering stems with earthen walls.
So shall each plant erect its leafy form
Unshook by Autumn's equinoxial storm;
And round and smooth, with silvery veins emboss'd,
Repel the dew-drops, and evade the frost.
Thus on the Stoic's round and polish'd brows,
Her venom'd shafts in vain misfortune throws;
By virtue arm'd, he braves the tented field,
The innocuous arrows tinkling on his shield. . . .

Oft in each month, poetic Tighe! be thine
To dish green Brocoli with savory chine;
Oft down thy tuneful throat be thine to cram
The snow-white cauliflower with fowl and ham!
Nor envy thou, with such rich viands blest,
The pye of Perigord, or swallow's nest.

This needs no commending: it commends itself, and if all
of Darwin were of this kind we should have no difficulties.
But this is not so, as even the two short passages of his verse
already quoted will have shown. In the first, the Orpheus
passage on page 174, he is competent and flat. In the sec-

ond, the invocation to the Botanic Muse on page 196, he is competent and elegant. Both passages illustrate well enough the mean of his style, what one might call his middle register. The problem does not lie here, however, but in the extremes of his style. He is capable of considerable magnanimity of vision; he is also capable, and in the same breath, of fearful lapses into unconscious humour or bathos. His characters are all too apt to "titter" at solemn moments; his readers also. Let me give an example; it is from Canto 1 of *The Temple of Nature* and describes the Muse beginning the pilgrimage which the whole poem relates:

> Charm'd at her touch the opening wall divides,
> And rocks of crystal form the polish'd sides;
> Through the bright arch the Loves and Graces tread,
> Innocuous thunders murmuring o'er their heads;
> Pair after pair, and tittering as they pass,
> View their fair features in the walls of glass.

The opening has its points; indeed the whole passage has, and as it advances it becomes curiously reminiscent of *Kubla Khan*. All very well for Coleridge to object to the "palaces of ice" of Darwin's verse; perhaps those who live in stately pleasure domes of the same stuff should not throw stones. The lapse at the end, however, is Darwin's very own, and all of a piece with many other such, with the ladies "in slight undress" who sit about on the lawns, the poetized pump, the simperings, the "compliments to ingenious professors" (which Miss Seward reprobates, consigning them "more properly to the Notes"), the Homeric simile beginning "So the lone Truffle . . ." These are the features with which *The Loves of the Triangles* made merciless play. Yet if we are going to take too high-minded a view of poetry here, we shall not merely undervalue Darwin in every way but lose half the enjoyment he has to offer. For his verse is enjoyable precisely because of its extraordinary capacity to give the reader a sustained aesthetic pleasure punctuated with constant occasions of laughter. We gain in fact from Darwin what we should gain from a first-rate comic poet, but in alternating and not direct current. Darwin's lapses are not weaknesses. They are examples of misdirected or miscalculated energy, and the energy is the delight.

It is here that Miss Seward comes in. She is trenchant in her criticism of Darwin yet never loses her enthusiasm for him whom she calls "this extraordinary man." She diagnoses his case: his lack of simplicity which led him into "a meretricious rage for ornament"; his capacity to be seduced by his own poetic imagination; the fundamental division in this Orphic mind: "He wished to keep prose too plain, and his warmest admirers will surely acknowledge that he insists upon poetry being dressed with too elaborate magnificence." She accords him experimental status: "Adapting the past and recent discoveries in natural and scientific philosophy to the purposes of heroic verse, the *Botanic Garden* forms a new class in poetry, and by so doing, gives to the British Parnassus a wider extent than it possessed in Greece, or in ancient, or modern Rome." She gives a résumé of the subject matter as she advances, in which we need not follow her, but her interest lies in interpreting Darwin's interpretation of that subject matter; not in pursuing the Nymph of Botany in *The Economy of Vegetation* through her "astronomic, electric, aerial and mineralogic properties" as well as her vegetable ones, or through the transformations in *The Loves of the Plants,* but in assessing Darwin's method and his success or failure as a postlogician. It is in no small part her perceptive commentary which encourages us to look at *The Botanic Garden* less as an exposé of science than as a kind of Darwinian *Discours de la méthode.*

Darwin chose for his mythological machinery in the first part of this poem what he calls the myths of Rosicrucianism, which he mixes with occasional classical figures. It was a poor choice. The gnomes and sylphs who pervade the work are unfamiliar, superficial, and imaginatively quite inadequate to the breadth of Darwin's conception. All they did was to provide material for parodists. This has obscured what is positive in Darwin here—his tremendous emphasis on, and enthusiasm for, myth, and his glimpses into its possibilities as an interpretative instrument. Wherever these insights occur, Miss Seward follows them up. She confirms Darwin's general proceedings while criticizing him acutely at just his most vulnerable points, as for instance when she objects to the narrow frame of his mythology in *The Economy of Vegetation,* claiming that he should have taken Nature for his central figure; or when she complains that in his treatment of the Orphic creation myth, "the noble fable of Eros, or Divine Love, issuing from the great egg of night, floating in chaos," he makes the "image of this celestial love too gay . . . the cyprian but not the hieroglyphic Cupid," a remarkable phrase. Personification, Darwin's second great mythological instrument in the *Economy,* also attracts her attention. "The deadly and salubrious winds; the volcanic and pestilential airs; the Tornado, dreadful to mariners, etc; every thing here has animal life and consciousness," she says. (There are fine illustrations of these very things by Fuseli and Blake in early editions of *The Botanic Garden.*) "Universal personification was the order of the Muse in this work, not to be infringed; else, when circumstances are in themselves sublime . . . they are more likely to be of diminished than increased force, by the addition of *fabled* endowment." Personification may take the form of ascribing life to the inanimate, which is what mostly goes on in the *Economy,* or of interchanging types of life as in the

Loves, where, according to Miss Seward, "the floral ladies, and their harems, rise to the amused eye in all the glow of poetic colouring."

Now to ascribe life to everything is not mere fabling. It comes straight from Bacon's trio of pretergenerations, generations, and arts as methods of natural history and embodies two mythological working principles. It is an experiment in flexibility inside that Baconian range of metaphor for natural subjects, the range running from organisms through "monsters" to mechanical arts. Orphic minds must be friendly to that whole range, including the machines, just as they are friendly to logic as well as postlogic. Darwin possesses this friendliness, as his work shows; but the personifications in this poem indicate his final choice of myth: the organism envisaged as in itself an interpretative instrument for a wide range of structures and happenings in nature. This leads on to the second stage of mythological operation in personification, for it is also an experiment in inclusive mythology, the use of figures inclusive of the body and of the thinker's mind as part of the interpretative situation.

Darwin proves, as working mythologizer or poet, inadequate on each count, as Miss Seward realizes: "the passions are generally asleep, and seldom are the nerves thrilled by his imagery, impressive and beauteous as it is, or by his landscapes, with all their vividness." Yet she recognizes in him something else, no less postlogical: "the lavish magnificence of the imagery in this work, genius alone, bold, original, creative and fertile in the extreme, could have produced." However inadequate the execution, she seizes upon the operational principle, the fertility of genius bodying forth the figures by which to interpret no less fertile nature (she quotes Shakespeare's Theseus at this point, and applies his words to Darwin). We can hardly expect the lady to discuss fertility and sex as part of the Doctor's matter or method, but it is interesting to find her vindicating him from charges of sensuality, on grounds not of poetic license but of scientific realism. "As to the amours of the Plants and Flowers . . . the floral harems do not form an imaginary but a real system, which philosophy has discovered, and with which poetry sports. The impurity is in the imagination of the reader, not on the pages of the poet, when the *Botanic Garden* is considered, on the whole, as an immodest composition." So the principle of sex, in Darwin's method and in postlogic, is upheld. And last of all Miss Seward for all her criticism of him compares her "daring Bard" with Ovid, and on more than one occasion; thus, for instance: "He is surely not inferior to Ovid; and if poetic taste is not much degenerated, or shall not hereafter degenerate, the *Botanic Garden* will live as long as the Metamorphoses."

It is a pleasingly preposterous claim. Respective merit and expectation of life apart, however, Ovid and Darwin are of the same family. These are in themselves the admirable transformations of the Orphic tradition, and we may realize that from Darwin we have already drawn at least a shadow of all those characteristics which we made out in Ovid a little while back. What is lacking is Orpheus, and to him we now come.

The Botanic Garden has been buried under one hundred and fifty years of ridicule and dust; perhaps with reason, perhaps not. But that Darwin's second poem should have vanished into complete oblivion shows how incapable we are as yet of profiting from our own Orphic tradition. As characteristically Darwinian as the first in its ups and downs, this is nevertheless a noble poem.

Its full title is *The Temple of Nature, or, The Origin of Society*. It has four cantos, dealing with the origins of life, reproduction, the progress of the mind, and good and evil. The impulse that moves the cantos forward is the natural one of time, starting with the creation, rising through inorganic to organic life and its forms of reproduction and of advance, then to the emergence of mind, to man with his language and his arts, and finally to social man with all his complexities and responsibilities. We begin with the creation of the world and come down to the poet's own day. This also is a poem in celebration of time and transformation in the figures of nature, and, far more deeply than *The Loves of the Plants,* an Ovidian poem of full scope. Darwin is at his best when there is inherent sublimity in his subject, as there is here, that vision of an immense fertile series or network (Darwin calls nature a kindling net) of figures running through time and developing into complexities which disguise but do not falsify the unity of the whole. The poem has a perceptible and pleasing form: a dialogue, varied by descriptive pieces. One would say that the poet has profited from the exercises and ineptitudes of *The Botanic Garden* were it not that this, like his sense of humour, is obscure. Take, for instance, the opening line of the poem, "By firm, immutable, immortal laws"; when we come almost to the very end, the last words spoken in the dialogue, before the closing passage, are "With hand unseen directs the general cause / By firm, immutable, immortal laws." One's pleasure at the circling movement of the whole is in no way spoiled by the strong suspicion that this felicity may be the result of accident and the doctor's tendency to repeat himself, the rhyme-word "cause," the same in each case, perhaps accounting for it. The verdict has to be an open one, however, for Darwin has improved in other directions too, in the mythological framework, for example. This time he appreciates that he needs something capable of representing nature as a whole. He uses first of all the image of a pilgrimage into that temple of nature which gives the poem its name and which is half a shrine and half a labyrinth, those two great Baconian and post-Baconian metaphors for Nature. The double nature of the edifice is implied in the description of it in Canto I, but later in Canto III it is stated outright, where the pilgrim is encouraged to

> Eye Nature's lofty and her lowly seats,
> Her gorgeous palaces and green retreats,
> Pervade her labyrinths with unerring tread,
> And leave for future guests a guiding thread.

The guiding thread which Darwin himself provides is supplied by the two figures who speak the dialogue (or perhaps alternate monologues would be a better phrase) of which much of the poem consists, and who move on the pilgrimage attended by troops of at times slightly over-elaborated Loves and Graces who yet offer opportunities for incidental delight, as in such passages as this,

> Next with illumined hand, through prisms bright,
> Pleas'd they untwist the sevenfold threads of light;
> Or, bent in pencils by the lens, convey
> To one bright point the silver hairs of Day.

It is the two main figures, however, to whom our attention is drawn. The first is the hierophant, or priestess of one of the mystery religions (the description of her is wonderful, resembling those eighteenth-century prints of classical theater costumes for women, all purple ostrich feathers, gold fillets on amber hair, draperies, and a long train). In the preface to the poem Darwin says, "In the Eleusinian Mysteries the philosophy of the works of Nature, with the origin and progress of society, are believed to have been taught by allegoric scenery explained by the Hierophant to the initiated, which gave rise to the machinery of the following Poem." The second figure is the muse, Urania. With an invocation to her the whole poem begins:

> By firm, immutable, immortal laws,
> Impressed on Nature by the great First Cause,
> Say, Muse! how rose from elemental strife
> Organic forms, and kindled into life.

As in the *Metamorphoses,* we must first get the world created before we can consider what is going on there. Darwin begins with the great Orphic and Baconian creation myth:

> Immortal Love! who ere the morn of Time,
> On wings outstretch'd, o'er Chaos hung sublime,
> Warmed into life the bursting egg of night,
> And gave young Nature to admiring light.

He proceeds then to fill in creation in astronomical, physical, and chemical terms, interspersed with description of the Temple, the beginning of the pilgrimage, and the entry of the hierophant. Nature herself sits, a veiled figure, at the center:

> Shrined in the midst majestic Nature stands,
> Extends o'er earth and sea her hundred hands,
> Tower upon tower her beamy forehead crests,
> And births unnumber'd milk her hundred breasts;
> Drawn round her brows a lucid veil depends,
> O'er her fine waist the purfled woof descends . . .

Prayer is made to her, the journey to be undertaken is likened to Orpheus' journey to the Underworld, and then the muse puts this question:

> First, if you can, celestial guide! disclose
> From what fair fountain mortal life arose,
> Whence the fine nerve to move and feel assign'd,
> Contractile fibre, and ethereal mind;
> How Love and Sympathy the bosom warm,
> Allure with pleasure and with pain alarm,

With soft affections weave the social plan,
And charm the listening savage into man.

It is a large question, and it takes time to answer, for the hierophant goes back to the very beginnings of organic existence and brings the line up from there; admirable in two ways, for it means that we neither lose sight of the continuity of natural process nor forget that evolution does not terminate in body but in mind. This is how the coming of life is described:

Organic life beneath the shoreless waves
Was born and nurs'd in Ocean's pearly caves.
First forms minute, unseen by spheric glass,
Move on the mud, or pierce the watery mass . . .
These as successive generations bloom,
New powers acquire, and larger limbs assume;
Whence countless groups of vegetation spring
And breathing realms of fin and feet and wing.

She ends her discourse thus:

So erst, ere rose the science to record
In letter'd syllables the volant word;
Whence chemic arts, disclos'd in pictured lines,
Lived to mankind by hieroglyphic signs;
And clustering stars, portrayed on mimic spheres,
Assumed the forms of lions, bulls and bears;—
—So erst, as Egypt's rude designs explain,
Rose young Dione from the shoreless main;
Type of organic nature! source of bliss!
Emerging beauty from the vast abyss!

This is admirable, and with it we leave Canto I for Canto II, where the doubling and redoubling of this emergent beauty is to be considered. Here the poet first rejects mechanical explanation and analogy:

> Self-moving engines by unbending springs
> May walk on earth, or flap their mimic wings;
> In tubes of glass mercurial columns rise,
> Or sink, obedient to the incumbent skies;
> Or, as they touch the figured scale, repeat
> The nice gradations of circumfluent heat.
> But Reproduction, when the perfect Elf
> Forms from fine glands another like itself,
> Gives the true character of life and sense,
> And parts the organic from the chemic Ens.

He then discusses "the goddess Form" in her various transformations through asexual and sexual reproduction, and calls upon all nature to "hail the deities of sexual love." These are given a triumphal progress through this canto, embodied in the figures of Cupid and Psyche—body and mind, never body alone. In Canto III we come to the progress of the mind, moving in the terms of Darwin's psychology, which is always a dynamic one, from the importance of the hand as an instrument of human consciousness up to the mind itself.

> As the pure language of the Sight commands
> The clear ideas furnish'd by the hands,
> Beauty's fine forms attract our wondering eyes,
> And soft alarms the pausing heart surprise . . .
> Hence to clear images of form belong
> The sculptor's statue and the poet's song,
> The painter's landscape and the builder's plan,
> And Imitation marks the mind of Man.

But here too we do not lose sight of nature working and transforming, so that such passages will have amongst them couplets like this:

> Time, motion, number, sunshine or the storm
> But mark varieties in Nature's form,

and when we arrive at language and its achievements in
the whole process we are watching, there follows another
such reminder:

> The Giant Form on Nature's centre stands,
> And waves in ether his unnumber'd hands;
> Whirls the bright planets in their silver spheres,
> And the vast sun round other systems steers,
> Till the last trump amid the thunder's roar
> Sound the dread sentence, "Time shall be no more!"

The kinship of the human mind with the animal's is
pointed out, and the scope of the whole process, in which,
for Orphic minds, art rises out of nature, is stated once
again:

> All human science worth the name imparts
> And builds on Nature's base the works of Arts.

In Canto iv the struggle for existence is dealt with, as part
of the whole metamorphic process:

> While Nature sinks in Time's destructive storms,
> The wrecks of death are but a change of forms.

Man's rise through social achievements is here celebrated,
and the change of forms, individual or social, is finally
imaged as the phoenix rising starry and renewed from its
own ashes. So the exposition of the whole range of forms
and figures circles back to its starting point, and the poem
closes with a picture:

> By hands unseen are struck aerial wires,
> And Angel-tongues are heard amid the quires;
> From aisle to aisle the trembling concord floats,
> And the wide roof returns the mingled notes.
> Through each fine nerve the keen vibrations dart,
> Pierce the charm'd ear and thrill the echoing heart.

—Mute the sweet voice, and still the quivering strings,
Now Silence hovers on unmoving wings.—
Slow to the altar fair Urania bends
Her graceful march, the sacred steps ascends,
High in the midst with blazing censer stands,
And scatters incense with illumined hands:
Thrice to the Goddess bows with solemn pause,
With trembling awe the mystic veil withdraws,
And, meekly kneeling on the gorgeous shrine,
Lifts her ecstatic eyes to Truth Divine.

It seems we have come to Sais after all.

So Ovid and the *Metamorphoses* are retold. Orpheus is
for Darwin the type figure of this journey through nature
and time, an evolutionary study of natural forms in the
grand manner. The Orpheus-Eurydice figure which Dar-
win gives us ends in failure, but it ties love and life and
death and poetry and power in one, as the motive force
behind that journey of exploration. In *The Temple of Na-
ture,* however, Orpheus does not appear simply inciden-
tally, in the four lines of the Orphic creation myth, or the
twenty lines of the Eurydice episode. He is implied in the
whole framework of the poem, not merely in the journey
but also in each of the two main figures and speakers. We
have already noticed the connection between the Eleusin-
ian Mysteries and Orpheus, so that the hierophant is
connected with him. But so is Urania, the muse whom
Darwin invokes, the second person of his dialogue. This
is the muse Milton addresses in *Paradise Lost,* Book VII,
where Orpheus, her son, dies; [73] and Wordsworth is to
pick up this very invocation to Urania in his fragment of
The Recluse where he speaks of the task attempted in *The
Prelude,* that poem in which Orpheus and Eurydice occur
again and which Coleridge called "an Orphic song in-
deed." It is right that we should look forward to Words-

worth in this way. Darwin here and now is leading us on to Goethe and Linnaeus; he could reaffirm the Ovidian transformation, but could not achieve it. But he leads on to Wordsworth too. They seem worlds apart only because a false and un-Orphic tradition has taught us to divide them so. But after all only two years separate the publication of *The Temple of Nature* from the first version of *The Prelude:* 1803 and 1805.

8

This is the difference between the mere botanist's knowledge of plants, and the great painter's or poet's knowledge of them . . . The one counts the stamens, and affixes a name, and is content; the other observes every character of the plant's colour and form; considering each of its attributes as an element of expression, he seizes on its lines of grace or energy, rigidity or repose . . . he associates it in his mind with all the features of the situation it inhabits, and the ministering agencies necessary to its support. Thenceforward the flower is to him a living creature, with histories written on its leaves, and passions breathing in its motion

WE LEFT GOETHE meditating on the nature of his instinctive dissatisfaction with Linnaean classification as a method of understanding the plant realm. It might seem as if botany were after all only a small corner of scientific research and little to do with wider issues; but for Orphic minds plants or any other natural phenomena are always part of the whole range of natural figures, including those of the mind. To and fro within this range moves the interpreter at his task. The greater the interpreter the wider the scale of movement, so that in Goethe's case there is no single work or even limited group of works which presents itself as suitable for isolated attention. There are hints in Goethe's life of something that might have served such a purpose. We are told, for example, that he planned a sizable philosophical nature poem in collaboration with Schelling.[74] A project something like this occurs in his journal for 1799. He had just acquired a telescope and watched an eclipse of the moon through it. "And so at last," he comments, "I became better acquainted with this near neighbor, so long beloved and marveled at. All the while there was constantly in the background the thought of a long nature poem which was hovering dimly in my mind." It is a lovely picture; but the poem was never written, and we have to look elsewhere for our material.

Maybe this is just as well. Goethe himself was always hostile to those who, he felt, split his work up and forgot what he calls its genetic relationship, as in his opinion Madame de Staël had done.[75] We shall take as texts here the *Metamorphose der Pflanzen,* and that only in general, and a handful of poems from the group Goethe entitled *Gott und Welt;* but with these we will keep some of the self-descriptive and autobiographical fragments, from the journals and elsewhere, so that the self is always there, integrally belonging.

For this, we must recognize, is part of Goethe's Orphic contribution. It is to the inclusiveness of postlogic, the methodology which includes the working self, that Goethe directs his attention, whose scope is the universe, and whose instrument of interpretation is the Orphic self. It is essential that we understand this, lest once again the hoary accusations of arrogance be brought up. All poets know the dangers of the method, bordering as it does on lunacy and Lucifer; Goethe knew them better than anyone,[76] but they are part of the poet's professional hazards. It is here that he will work, as Erasmus Darwin did, at a shift of taxonomy to a dynamic morphology or metamorphology, from Linnaeus to Ovid. Goethe worked all his life at observing and classifying nature and himself, according to taxonomic principles insofar as he found these appropriate, then according to morphology as he conceives of it. This is his Orphic interpretation of the forms of universal nature. Once we have grasped this we shall not be tempted to separate the poetry from the science in this man's working. We shall see that the most lyrical and self-absorbed poem is always systematic in character, belonging to natural history, and the most detached scientific work is always self-interpretation.

Goethe has all the Orphic mind's native delight in classification as such. In the *Gott und Welt* poems, for instance, there is a cycle of three, *Atmosphäre, Howards Ehrengedächtnis* and *Wohl zu Merken,* which were published in 1820 in the first collection of Goethe's writings on natural science. Howard is the man who invented a form of classification for cloud shapes, cirrus and cumulus and so on, and in the three poems Goethe celebrates this taxonomic achievement of giving form to that which previously was, for the mind, unstructured. The first poem is short (the translations are going to be rather light-hearted), but it expresses the predicament of approach, and the possible answer:

"Die Welt, sie ist so gross und breit,
Der Himmel auch so hehr und weit;

Ich muss das alles mit Augen fassen,
Will sich aber nicht recht denken lassen.''

Dich im Unendlichen zu finden,
Musst unterscheiden und dann verbinden;
Drum danket mein beflügelt Lied
Dem Manne, der Wolken unterschied.

("The world is vast, the world is wide,
The heavens reach out on every side;
I take it in with my two eyes,
But how to grasp and realize?"

To cope with boundless breadth and height,
You first divide and then unite.
So wing, my song, in praises vowed
Of him who classified the cloud.)

The second, longer, poem, with an Indian mythological
setting, describes the cloud forms and celebrates Howard's
work in these terms, surely the perfect answer to those who
think of poetry as a dim and vague business:

Was sich nicht halten, nicht erreichen lässt,
Er fasst es an, er hält zuerst es fest;
Bestimmt das Unbestimmte, schränkt es ein,
Benennt es treffend!—Sei die Ehre dein!

(What had no grip or substance for the mind,
He, first of any, holds it well-defined,
Limits the illimitable in a frame,
And names it duly!—Honour to *thy* name!)

Characteristically, Goethe in the third poem says that
when once the systematic divisions are made, we must lend
them our own living gifts if they are not to die themselves;
so painter and poet, familiar with Howard's classification,
will move on from there into further worlds of airy and

yet human interpretation. It is a perfect statement, in a microcosm, of how he works; and it is how he will work with himself.

It is interesting that in this little poem about method Goethe commends that transmigration, from systematic to postlogical thinking, to poet and painter, just as Ruskin did in the passage about botanical systematics with which the present section is headed. Not just poet, but painter too. This is the first and the most fundamental of Goethe's attempts at self-classification, and one which, in my experience, is not sufficiently emphasized. We hear a lot about the supposed scientist-poet dilemma, as if this were a real parting of the ways, whereas for an Orphic mind it need and should not be so at all. But we hear far less about the choice Goethe had to make between devoting himself principally to painting or poetry, although it gave him, I think, more concern and went very deep. This makes sense, for these are genuinely separate ways of handling figures and nature, much more so than poetry and science, and Goethe rightly felt that he had to make up his mind between them, not as to which was the better form of interpretation, but which suited his own nature. In the end this was something his Italian Journey accomplished for him. Toward the end of his journal on that occasion he says (Rome, February 22, 1788): "It is daily becoming plainer to me that really and truly I am born to be a poet, and that I must spend the next ten years—the most I can count on for active work—in cultivating this talent and making something solid out of it; in the past my success had been largely due to youth and its fire, without much trouble having been taken. I shall draw this advantage from my long stay in Rome—that I renounce any further activity as a working painter." I think one can hear the note of regret there, the more so since it turns up elsewhere. Nine years later (August 30, 1797), in his journal of his travels

in Switzerland, we find him saying it is sheer folly of paint-
ers to make themselves out as rivals of poets, since they,
the former, have at their command that which could drive
a poet to despair. And there are recurring instances of
Goethe speaking in dispraise of language and, occasionally,
of poetry itself. The plastic artist's method seemed to him
perhaps more direct, less dependent on an ambiguous
medium. If he could have had such a direct method, or the
even more direct one by which the figuring is done with no
medium at all but one's own life raised to the power of
an interpretative art and methodology, he would have been
glad; but the latter form of interpretation is reserved for
heroes and saints, neither of which callings forms part of
the poet's professional vocation, and Goethe was too good
a self-taxonomer not to recognize in the end that he was a
poet born.

He says as much in an interesting autobiographical
fragment, *Selbstschilderung,* written in the third person,
of the year 1797, one of the clearest of his attempts at self-
definition:

> The central point and the very basis of his existence
> was poetry as a kind of life-force, increasingly active
> and developing inwardly and outwardly. Once this
> is grasped, all the apparent contradictions can be re-
> solved. The drive of this force is unceasing, and if it
> is not to devour itself for lack of material it has to
> be directed outwards; once this is done, since it is ac-
> tive and not contemplative by nature, it is bound to
> begin to work on what it comes upon. This accounts
> for the numerous wrong turnings taken here: toward
> painting and art, for which he was not fitted by na-
> ture; toward active public life for which he had in-
> sufficient adaptability; toward the sciences, for which
> he lacked the necessary staying power. But because

his approach to all three was based on self-adaptation and development, and he tried in each case to come at the true nature of what they had to offer and at the unity and elegance of form that would fit them, even these mistaken endeavors were fruitful, in outer life and in the life of the mind.

This is the point where, as if in a Linnaean taxonomy, a name can be affixed. Goethe is a poet: well and good. But this is only the beginning. For the name is in this method of thought merely the starting point for the development of a system of morphological figures designed to express the nature and activity of this living being so named. This Goethe has already begun to describe in the passage above. The first activity is ruled out; to have "no organ," as it stands in the German, cannot be got over. But the second and third wrong turnings, toward public and political life and science, are interesting and are almost certainly, for a powerful enough Orphic mind, not wrong turnings at all. Goethe himself says in *Geschichte meines botanischen Studiums* that every energetic talent is universal. (There is a whole field of relations between the Orphic tradition and political thinking which we cannot go into here but which is part of the picture, for these too are structures within the Ovidian scope of speculation, metamorphosis, and myth.) Poetry and science in the Orphic mind spring from the same fundamental activity, and it is this which Goethe is concerned to identify and interpret in himself.

Poetry as life-force, as living activity, is what he is interested in, the interest that makes him say in the first of the *Episteln* that it is the life that forms the man and words count for little; that made Faust alter the opening of Saint John's Gospel to "In the beginning was the Deed"; that made Goethe call his autobiography *Dichtung und Wahrheit*, implying not merely an ambiguity between

truth and fiction but a triple unity between truth, poetry
and the life that lay behind them. It is characterization
of life under this form that Goethe is after, not a private
introspective venture nor a limited professional inquest.
We find him saying to Eckermann, January 31, 1827, "I
realize more and more that poetry is common property
among men, and that it has appeared in hundreds and
hundreds of people, and in all ages . . . We must each
say to ourselves that poetic gifts are nothing out of the
way, and no-one has any call to be puffed up about them."
It is the commonness of poetry that gives it its morpho-
logical value. For Goethe, the poet's morphology will be
a way of understanding man himself, and out of the self-
characterization Goethe gives us there emerges a more
remarkable and fundamental image still, of the poet as
in some way the sheer archetype of the living organism
as such, self-regardant it is true, but only in that way dif-
fering from all the other living creatures of which it can
be the type and, because of its consciousness, the inter-
pretative key.

There are four things which Goethe says about the
poetic genius and its being and working.

(1) Goethe's works are evidence of a talent which
does not develop step by step, any more than it gropes
around at random and aimlessly; on the contrary,
working from one particular central point it tries
out its strength in every direction at one and the
same time, striving to act upon things that are close
at hand no less than upon those that are further away.
[1816]
Nobody has a right to prescribe to the gifted indi-
vidual the areas in which he should be active. The
mind from its center shoots out its radii toward the
periphery; as soon as it comes up against something

it comes to rest there and sends out fresh lines of experiment from the center. The aim is, if not to reach beyond its own limits, which it is not given it to do, at least to know those limits as far as possible, and fill them to the full. [1807]

(2) I was possessed of the developing, growing, unfolding method, and absolutely not of the method that sets things side by side and orders and arranges them. [1794]

(3) I let objects produce their effects on me, in all patience and quietness, then I observe these effects and take pains with myself to give them back or reproduce them, true and undistorted. This is the whole secret of what people are pleased to call genius. [Between 1812 and 1832]

(4) The very greatest genius would not get very far if it had to bring forth everything out of itself. What is genius if it is not the capacity to make use of everything that it meets with? . . . Everything I have ever seen, heard or taken notice of, I have stored up and turned to good account. [1832] [77]

Outlining a behavioral morphology of poetic genius, Goethe seems to be outlining life itself: the central phenomenon of the individual as a discrete living center working outward from its central vitality to grope and extend its own given boundaries of form; the nature of growth in any organic being, and the kinship of this with the methods of the mind; living and thinking considered as the establishment of a favorable relationship, an equilibrium between action and passivity, between the organism and its ecological surroundings; the ability of the living creature to nourish itself with, and adapt itself to, external material, to be flexible and resourceful.

That is, in part at least, what genius, and the poet, is for—to provide in itself a working system by which to interpret other systems in nature, animate and perhaps even inanimate as well. It is of course anthropomorphism, in its most highly specialized and beautiful form. Goethe was quite clear about this; good postlogician that he is, he adds that all thinking, no matter how apparently "scientific" or detached, is going to be anthropomorphic, and we shall do well to recognize this. "The mind of man," he says, "when it is really at one with itself, shares this oneness with everything that is not itself, draws it into its own unity, until mind and object are one." [78] This is like Coleridge and is the great postlogical interpretative process. It is not merely one way, but reciprocal. For a mind so attuned there is not subject and object but two dynamic systems interpreting each other. So in the *Wahlverwandschaften* the workings of chemical elements interpret human relations, since, as Goethe says in this connection, there is but one nature.[79] So it is too with the scientific treatise on botany which Goethe published in 1780 and which he called *An Attempt to Explain the Metamorphosis of Plants.*

It is upon this one small work at present that Goethe's status as a scientist mainly rests. (We have made little yet of the *Farbenlehre,* Goethe's anti-Newtonian foray into the world of physics, but that too may follow the same method as the *Metamorphose* though in a different field, akin to Poe's *Eureka* as a speculative treatise on the cooperation of phenomena and the postlogical imagination.) [80] The *Metamorphose,* Goethe himself thought, would be unreadable to any except experts. An exercise in the morphology of plant development, it was not, we are told by Agnes Arber, even a wholly new idea; she also points out the vagueness of the concept of metamorphosis as Goethe used it, and his inadequate knowledge of the relevant literature and of the practical research which had been done in the field. Yet she compares him, in nature and stature, to Bacon, and another critic says that Linnaean thought and Goethean thought in botany bear the same relation to each other as alchemy to chemistry.[81]

It would have been helpful from the start if, from the purely scientific point of view, this work had never been unnaturally isolated from its fellow works and commentaries, the two poems *Metamorphose der Pflanzen* and the *Metamorphose der Tiere* where Goethe moves over to the animals; or, no less important, the passage in the autobiographical writings where he describes, in an unused introduction to the third volume of his autobiography, how he conceived and wrote the first three volumes according to the laws demonstrated by the plant-metamorphosis of his more scientific preoccupations. In an extended metaphor of great beauty Goethe says that the child was to resemble the first seedling with its root-making activity and cotyledons; then the boy was to come, more full-fledged with leaves; and in the third volume the young man would appear, in the flower of youth and full of promise. Then Goethe goes on sadly, "In the next period I was to come to, the flowers fall; the fruit does not set in all of them, and even where it does it seems insignificant, swells only very slowly, and ripeness seems as if it will never come . . . Thus it is with the works of nature, and thus it was with myself and with my works." If it could be accepted that this is not fancy but postlogical method, we could avoid much uncertainty about this work and Goethe's work in general.

Goethe's theme in this treatise is that a plant consists fundamentally of one single organ, from which all its other organs, however varied and seemingly different from one another, can be deduced and are in fact developed. He takes the leaf as the type-organ, the one basic plastic unit of identity. This is what the plant, a highly flexible system within its own due limits, reworks and transforms into its other parts. Each part is the metamorphic manifestation of a single adaptable unity.

In this lies the whole of Goethe's systematics. Just as Goethe attempts to classify his own nature from within, so here taxonomy as a working principle is applied first within the organism, not to a group of organisms. The ordering starts with the single living being, but when it is extended it does not lose its nature. It is, as again Goethe shows in his consideration of himself, based upon a morphology of form and behavior, which can also apply to the wider forms or figures of a group. When Goethe moves on to consider organisms collectively, as genera and species, he works in exactly the same fashion. Within each group he will postulate a single basic plastic unity, the equivalent of that Protean leaf in the plant. With plants this is the *Urpflanze*, the plastic original plant form and plant stuff from which all plants of any shape or form might be derived, which he sought so earnestly in the profusion and beauty of the gardens at Padua, on September 27, 1786: "In these manifold forms, which are new to me and here present themselves, it is borne in upon me more and more that perhaps one could elaborate all plant forms out of One Form. Only so would it be possible to draw the genuine limits of genera and species, which, so it seems to me, has only been done very arbitrarily so far" (*Italienische Reise*). With animals, the *Urtier* appears when Goethe turns his attention to zoology. In his comparative anatomy and osteology the same principle holds. "An inner, original, fundamental community (*Gemeinschaft*) lies at the base of all organization," he says in *Die Skelette der Nagethiere* (1823–24). The most general expression of the principle, showing the whole range Goethe envisaged for it, appears in his journal for 1790: "I was absolutely convinced that one common type, progressing through metamorphosis, ran through the whole of organic life, every feature of which could be observed without undue difficulty in certain intermediate stages, and which must and should be recognized even where it reached its highest level in mankind and there discreetly withdrew into invisibility." [82]

A taxonomic formulation providing the framework and principle for, and shading over into, a behavioral morphology, the whole system to include the thinker's mind: here are Linnaeus, Ovid, and Goethe in conjunction. Goethe uses it cumulatively; to discover plants and himself, in the prose *Metamorphose der Pflanzen;* to explain the human love-relationship by the plant kingdom, in the poem of that name, of 1798; to inquire into the animal kingdom and thence into man's social activities and relationships in the *Metamorphose der Tiere* poem of 1806; lastly into the whole shape and significance of human life in the *Urworte* of 1817.

9

But Life is in every movement and in every form; for every movement reveals a force in the act of expressing itself, and every form reveals a force which has taken expression . . . Our spirit, recognizing itself under another guise in both, contemplates itself in the plant, which is a power, just as it contemplated itself in the animal which is a thought

THE TWO LONG *Metamorphose* poems provide a kind of progression toward the *Urworte* that are eventually going to take shape in the mouth of Orpheus. They reaffirm Linnaeus and Ovid, but give only hints as yet of their relation to language-as-poetry. In his arrangement of them in the *Gott und Welt* poems (they were first published in the scientific volumes) Goethe puts them in a group, introduced, divided, and concluded by much smaller, lyric poems on nature and ways of thinking about her. To this group he applies the names *Parabase, Epirrhema,* and *Antepirrhema,* the names for sections or figures of the chorus in a Greek play. It is as if he were putting forward these two poems, with lyrical accompaniment, as part of a great nature-play.

The poem *Metamorphose der Pflanzen* is addressed to Goethe's wife, Christiane. It begins with her in the garden, in a prospect of flowers as it were, bewildered by the profusion and confusion of it all and her ear besieged by the barbaric sounds of its nomenclature. Linnaeus and language appear together, in all their seeming stiffness. Goethe suggests that plant forms and words together make up a riddle and he desires if he can to give her the answer, the password, the resolution, "das lösende Wort," to this. Then immediately, with the injunction "Werdend betrachte sie nun"—look at them as in a state of "becoming"—we shift to Ovid. First the metamorphoses of the individual plant are described, up to the final transformation into the flower where sex and fertility appear and the circle is at once closed and reopened. But, the poem says, this process applies more widely than just in the individual plant; not just the individual but the whole of nature is to be thought of as *belebt*, alive or enlivened, according to the same laws. These laws the plant forms speak, so that here we come back to language again:

Jede Pflanze verkündet dir nun die ewgen Gesetze,
    Jede Blume, sie spricht lauter und lauter mit dir.
Aber entzifferst du hier der Göttin heilige Lettern,
    Überall siehst du sie dann, auch in verändertem Zug.

Once that language is deciphered, it will apply in wider and wider figures, and Goethe moves into the figures of the love between man and woman, tracing the growth and development of the relationship between Christiane and himself up to its fulfillment in sexual love and fertility. These figures are one with the processes of nature, a marriage of true minds their consummation, the shared method of contemplating nature which is to be the final bond be-

tween the lovers.[83] This is one of the great themes of Ovid's
Metamorphoses, the reciprocal interpretation of the *Ur-*
forms and metamorphoses of nature as sex, and nature as
mind, the poet holding, by virtue of his power of language,
the communication point between them.

After the brief *Epirrhema*, the *Metamorphose der Tiere*
follows. Where the first of these two longer poems began
with a *du*, a "thou," this begins with an *ihr*, a "you";
but a loving friendliness prevails nonetheless in the open-
ing: "If, thus far prepared, you will venture to climb the
last step of this summit, then give me your hand, and
turn your frank gaze toward the broad field of Nature."
So we are reminded that this is a continuation of the earlier
poem, building its own unity. Nature is here seen as some-
thing unlimited which yet limits itself, according to flexible
but firm laws, in each of its manifestations. An *Urbild* ap-
pears behind all the varied organization of the animal
kingdom, hidden and secret but present even in the strang-
est forms, "Und die seltenste Form bewahrt im geheimen
das Urbild." Here is taxonomy again, yet with emphasis
on plasticity and variability in the adaptation of the ani-
mal to its environment and the interdependence of form
and living habits. In the middle of the poem Goethe de-
velops this further under the concept of a balance held
between novelty and heredity, where each new advantage
an animal gains may have to be compensated for by a cor-
responding lack elsewhere in its organization. Then in
the last twelve lines he sums up in terms of poetry, as pos-
sessing the characteristic note of "power and limits, caprice
and law, freedom and control, order in movement, ad-
vantage and lack" which the opening of the poem pointed
to. This balance or synthesis inherent in the sacred muse
is applied far beyond the limits of zoology; it is the prin-
ciple of the ethical philosopher, the man of action, the

artist and poet, the ruler worthy the name. So the figures rising up out of the animal world permeate and interpret man and society up to the highest levels of art, ethics, and politics. And in Goethe the truth comes through poetry, "vom Munde der Muse," as, in Ovid, Orpheus mediated the transition between the natural figures and those of human society.

Gradually with these poems we have been moving closer to the classical world, and to poetry as the language of nature. Now in 1817 we find Goethe writing to a correspondent [84] that he has been reading works upon Greek mythology, and has been initiated into what he calls the Orphic darkness; he adds that it is an extraordinary world which there opens before the eyes, but one which is not much illuminated by the learned men who deal with it, since what one casts light on, the next obscures again. It is at this time, under this influence, that the *Urworte: Orphisch* are written. Goethe says of them, in the 1820 notes to these verses in *Kunst und Altertum,* that they originally appeared in his second Morphology volume but have a significance beyond this; also, that they present in concentrated form, "poetisch-kompendios, lakonisch," what has been handed down "in older or more recent lore." They do not merely do this; they synthesize also Goethe's own Orphic approach to postlogic.

URWORTE. ORPHISCH

DAIMON, Dämon

Wie an dem Tag, der dich der Welt verliehen,
Die Sonne stand zum Grusse der Planeten,
Bist alsobald und fort und fort gediehen
Nach dem Gesetz, wonach du angetreten.
So musst du sein, dir kannst du nicht entfliehen,

So sagten schon Sibyllen, so Propheten;
Und keine Zeit und keine Macht zerstückelt
Geprägte Form, die lebend sich entwickelt.

(The Daimon, individual Life-Force

Planets and sun in high conjunction o'er us,
The day that first advanced us to creation,
Sealed us ourselves at once, and all before us
Follows the law of that initiation.
Sibyls and Prophets uttered it in chorus:
Will we or nill we, we must hold our station.
No power on earth, no time-scale can disfeature
Impress of form that grows, a living creature.)

TYCHE, das Zufällige

Die strenge Grenze doch umgeht gefällig
Ein Wandelndes, das mit und um uns wandelt;
Nicht einsam bleibst du, bildest dich gesellig,
Und handelst wohl so, wie ein andrer handelt:
Im Leben ists bald hin-, bald widerfällig,
Es ist ein Tand und wird so durchgetändelt.
Schon hat sich still der Jahre Kreis geründet,
Die Lampe harrt der Flamme, die entzündet.

(Chance

Yet round these rigid limits seems to waver
A shifting force whose breath and play enfolds us.
Our actions come to have a social flavor:
Not loneliness, our fellows' presence molds us.
Sometimes we're in, sometimes we're out of favor;
It's all a game—as such, it scarcely holds us.
But silent seasons have fulfilled their turning;
The lamp awaits a light, to set it burning.)

Eros, Liebe

Die bleibt nicht aus!—Er stürzt vom Himmel nieder,
Wohin er sich aus alter Öde schwang,
Er schwebt heran auf luftigem Gefieder
Um Stirn und Brust den Frühlingstag entlang,
Scheint jetzt zu fliehn, vom Fliehen kehrt er wieder:
Da wird ein Wohl im Weh, so süss und bang.
Gar manches Herz verschwebt im Allgemeinen,
Doch widmet sich das edelste dem Einen.

 (Love

  And then it comes!—One comes, from Heaven
   darting,
  Who rose from ancient void to that high seat,
  Hovering, a springtime breeze of feathers startling
  Forehead and breast that feel that airy beat;
  Always upon the wing, but not departing—
  O whence these pangs, so strangely bitter-sweet?
  Most loves are held in common and commotion;
  Great hearts alone pursue the one devotion.)

Ananke, Nötigung

Da ists denn wieder, wie die Sterne wollten:
Bedingung und Gesetz; und aller Wille
Ist nur ein Wollen, weil wir eben sollten,
Und vor dem Willen schweigt die Willkür stille;
Das Liebste wird vom Herzen weggescholten,
Dem harten Muss bequemt sich Will und Grille,
So sind wir scheinfrei denn, nach manchen Jahren
Nur enger dran, als wir am Anfang waren.

 (Necessity

  Now, back to what the stars' designs predicted,
  We feel the law's compulsion and constriction;

Wish is but will, duty-bound and restricted,
Whim's will-o'-wisp exorcised by conviction;
Out of the heart the dearest is evicted;
"I want," "I would," are bent by Must's infliction.
Thus, after years, to freedom's semblance winning,
We're but more straitened than at our beginning.)

ELPIS, Hoffnung

Doch solcher Grenze, solcher ehrnen Mauer
Höchst widerwärtge Pforte wird entriegelt,
Sie stehe nur mit alter Felsendauer!
Ein Wesen regt sich leicht und ungezügelt:
Aus Wolkendecke, Nebel, Regenschauer,
Erhebt sie uns, mit ihr, durch sie beflügelt,
Ihr kennt sie wohl, sie schwärmt durch alle Zonen—
Ein Flügelschlag—und hinter uns Äonen!

(Hope

Yet these bronze walls, these boundaries unbend-
  ing,
Though they stand rock-like, centuries together,
They and the soul's despair at last have ending;
There's one who rises free of any tether;
Lent wings by her, we're airborne and ascending,
With her, through ceiling-fog and rainy weather.
Known everywhere, all tracts of the globe remind
  us.
One pinion-stroke—and aeons lie behind us!)

These five poems hold all the operating principles of
Goethe's method. In the first verse appears the Linnaean
Ur-form within the individual's own development, that
taxonomic character which is fixed and yet capable of

growth, seen here in its human form and taken as the type of all organic life. In the second is the theme of change, the Ovidian metamorphoses induced in this and the following verses, that union of obdurate selfhood and adaptability to surroundings, fixity and freedom, which is characteristic of living figures; here the figures of human life and thought and action take their partly conditioned shape, rising up out of inanimate nature and remaining at one with it. In the central place held by the third verse comes Eros, reminding us of the *Metamorphoses* and sex and love as interpretative instruments in mythology, this being the one stanza graced by the lovely touch of alternating masculine and feminine rhymes. In the fourth stanza the progression of the figures up to and including those of social and moral patterns in society—also an Ovidian touch—is shown; there is another feature of this stanza also, in that it circles back to the beginning in its first and last lines, as if it were closing the cycle of time opened by the individual's birth. Yet the last stanza is not an end but a beginning, as if the five poems had not merely to narrate but to figure the kind of organic time-cycle Goethe described in the plant poem. The fifth verse relates us once again to the comparative timelessness of earth and nature (here seen as weather and rocks), endows us with a future to which the virtue or power of hope is necessarily directed, but also with an immemorial past.

(I believe there is implicit in these verses and in Goethe's whole systematics a concept of the organism as its own independent time-universe, where time is not serial but a cumulative simultaneous present, individual and ancestral,[85] operating not by "past" and "future" tenses but by living powers of memory and prophecy, and observable only within a living organism itself which is subject to change but changes always into itself, as Mallarmé says the poet does—"Tel qu'en Lui-même enfin l'Éternité le change," as he says of Poe.)

But if the *Urworte* are a synthesis of subject matter, they are also a synthesis of method, or more properly both at once, reflexively. Here a mind passionately interested in the dynamics of life, in the individual organism, in nature at large, in human beings and in his own thinking and feeling and acting self, having tried to evolve a dynamic of nonmathematical thought as a means of interpreting life, brings this home, centrally and finally, to words, poetry and myth. The postlogic which has been visible throughout Goethe's activity here receives its final seal, its ultimate connection with language. These are not just any words; they are *Urworte,* working taxonomic concepts as *Urpflanze* and *Urtier* were, from which to develop a morphology of metamorphoses, applicable to mind and nature alike.

Each of the *Urworte,* the primordial words, is a poem; and each is identified with a myth, Daimon and Eros and so on. These myths are five great powers which Goethe sees as operative in, and definitive of, organic life, including that of the thinking mind. The words are a working discipline of human metamorphosis according to powers presented as myths. Man is subject to these; by these he must interpret the universe and himself. Metamorphosis was for Goethe not just a phenomenon; it was a working discipline. It is Spengler who points this out, telling us to look for its principles in the *Orphische Urworte;* quoting Goethe as saying, "The methodology of forms (*Gestalten*) is the methodology of transformations. The working discipline of metamorphosis is the key to all the signs in nature"; and attempting himself to produce with it an organic and morphological world-history.[86] It is here that Goethe stands, he and his Orpheus with him. What they offer is a method—a biology moving into language, or a poetry—highly generalized and potentially capable of adaptation to any field of thinking about organic life. This Goethe saw, embodying it in his own existence as well as in what he wrote. The European Orphic tradition moves on now from here.

PART IV

Wordsworth and Rilke: Toward a Biology of Thinking

1

> and rapt Poesy,
> And arts, though unimagined, yet to be,
> The wandering voices and the shadows these
> Of all that man becomes

IT IS Orpheus' function to mark out the essential poetic tradition in any period by indicating those who are at work on the peculiar question and task of poetry in their time; also, to make plain the nature of that questioning endeavor. In this new period of the nineteenth and twentieth centuries we begin once more with indications. They come from various sources, for once again the Orphic line cuts across borderlines of nationality, discipline, or those restricted "movements" into which literary critics and historians tend to divide the Orphic unity.

At the beginning of the period there is a double manifestation of Orpheus, a great poet conceiving of his own task as Orphic, while his credentials are confirmed by another great poet, in Orphic terms again. This is the springboard of our own inquiry here. Wordsworth in Book 1 of the 1805 version of *The Prelude* (the later revised version was published in 1850) describes his vocation in Orphic terms:

> Then, last wish,
> My last and favourite aspiration! then
> I yearn towards some philosophic Song
> Of Truth that cherishes our daily life,
> With meditations passionate from deep
> Recesses in man's heart, immortal verse
> Thoughtfully fitted to the Orphean lyre.

This is the first great Orphic voice of our modern period. The last is Rilke and his fifty-five *Sonette an Orpheus* of 1923. Between these two the inquiry moves, with the help of other Orphic voices. What is its nature?

The voices themselves are clear and explicit about the unity of the task upon which they are engaged. Four of them, widely varied, speak it out:

> episodes to that great poem, which all poets, like the co-operating thoughts of one great mind, have built up since the beginning of the world.
>
> [Shelley, *A Defence of Poetry*]

> Un génie finit l'autre. Mais pas dans la même région. L'astronome s'ajoute au philosophe; le législateur est l'exécuteur des volontés du poète . . . le poète corrobore l'homme d'état . . . L'oeuvre est mystérieux pour ceux mêmes qui la font. Les uns en ont conscience, les autres point.
>
> [Hugo, *Shakespeare*]

> J'irais plus loin, je dirais Le Livre, persuadé qu'au fond il n'y en a qu'un, tenté à son insu par quiconque a écrit, même les génies : l'explication orphique de la terre, qui est le seul devoir du poète et le jeu littéraire par excellence.
>
> [Mallarmé, *Autobiographie*]

> *The poet,* there's where the great names . . . no
> longer matter,—it's the same thing, it's the poet; for,
> in the ultimate sense, there is only one, that infinite
> one who, here and there through the ages, asserts him-
> self in some spirit that has been subjected to him.
> [Rilke, letter of 1920] [1]

Rilke in the Orpheus sonnets puts it more specifically,
"Ein für alle Male, ists Orpheus wenn es singt,"—once
and for all, where singing is, Orpheus is. Of these Orphic
voices, Shelley's Orphic password, a very beautiful one,
occurs in the fourth act of *Prometheus Unbound:*

> Language is a perpetual Orphic song
> Which rules with Daedal harmony a throng
> Of thoughts and forms which else senseless and shapeless
> were.

The Hugo of the 1864–65 essay on Shakespeare we have
met already. Orpheus enters first in Book IV in connec-
tion with a lost play of Aeschylus, then in a wider context
in Book V, where Hugo broadens his theme to a considera-
tion of the nature of genius in general; Orpheus figures
twice in the roll call Hugo makes of genius from the be-
ginnings of time and in every field of human endeavor.
Mallarmé's pronouncement is here patent, giving us, ob-
scure and difficult poet as he is held to be, one of the clear-
est statements we possess of what the poet is engaged in.
Rilke's Orphic badge is clear. One more name remains
to be added, again a familiar one: that of Renan, who in
L'Avenir de la science, written 1848–49 and published
only forty years later, sees Orpheus as one of the founders
of civilization and as the very type of that union of sci-
entific and poetic thinking to which this great essay of his
is devoted. This, then, is the Orphic line with which we

shall span the period from 1800 to the present day—Words-
worth, Coleridge, Shelley, Hugo, Renan, Mallarmé, Rilke;
English first, German last, French in between, to whom
we shall turn first.

The French contingent is admirably varied, the sup-
posed arch-Romantic who refused to use the terms "Ro-
manticism" and "Romantic" at all, he found them so
misleading; [2] a philosophic historian and man of letters
and science; and one of the purest of Pure Poets who ever
had the label "Symbolist" pinned on to him.

Hugo's and Renan's respective Orphic essays are little
known. Hugo's is buried in the section "Philosophie" of
his *Oeuvres complètes* and under the general prejudice
which hides this great mind from us. Renan's is simply
neglected. I shall therefore give something of their con-
tents.

Hugo, in true Orphic fashion, takes one of the supreme
minds in the poetic genealogy for his starting point. His
inquiry moves beyond the individual, however, into the
history and natural history of genius. But it is not just
the incidence and format of genius which interests Hugo.
His standpoint is genetic. It is the making and emergence
of mind that he is concerned with, in individual man or
in the race. "Dieu n'a pas fait ce merveilleux alambic de
l'idée, le cerveau de l'homme, pour ne point s'en servir,"
he says in Part I, Book II. "Le génie a tout ce qu'il faut
dans son cerveau. La pensée est la résultante de l'homme."
The point of view here is conceived almost in terms of
body chemistry in the processes of evolution. Later Hugo
will contemplate the equal mystery of the making of the
individual mind, in particular that of the genius. "La pro-
duction des âmes, c'est le secret de l'abîme. L'inné, quelle
ombre! Qu'est-ce que c'est que cette condensation d'in-
connu qui se fait dans les ténèbres, et d'où jaillit brusque-
ment cette lumière, un génie? Quelle est la règle de ces

événements-là? O amour! Le coeur humain fait son oeuvre sur la terre, celà émeut les profondeurs . . . Deux urnes, les sexes, puisent la vie dans l'infini, et le renversement de l'une dans l'autre produit l'être. Ceci est le norme pour tous, pour l'animal comme pour l'homme. Mais l'homme qui est plus qu'homme, d'où vient-il?" (Book v). So love and sex are brought in, as in the *Metamorphoses,* alongside those scientific "condensations" and "rules."

Hugo first considers genius as synthesis within itself— thus Dante is a visionary and an exact grammarian, Newton a physicist and an expounder of the Apocalypse. Then he summarizes what has been gained so far: humanity develops from within—this is civilization properly speaking; radiating outward from itself, the human mind wins, masters, and humanizes matter; this work has particular phases, and each phase is introduced or concluded by one of those beings whom we call by the name of genius. Now follow the lists of them, with Orpheus at the head and Shakespeare in his due place in time to follow.

Genius, now being considered as poetry, is no narrow calling. "Poet," Hugo says, implies historian and philosopher, and the history is both fact and fiction, or history and fairy tale. He sees poetry now as an instrument of research, into such things as the enigmas of the mind, and of nature, which is also a mind, vague premonitions of the future, amalgams of thinking and events—all of which can be translated by the mind into delicate figurations. For Hugo this is the task of the poetic imagination, as in Shakespeare, who is at once genius, poet, and scientist.

> Shakespeare est, avant tout, une imagination . . . Aucune faculté de l'esprit ne s'enfonce et ne creuse plus que l'imagination; c'est la grande plongeuse. La science, arrivée aux derniers abîmes, la rencontre. Dans les sections coniques, dans les logarithmes, dans

le calcul différentiel et intégral, dans le calcul des
probabilités, dans le calcul infinitésimal, dans le calcul
des ondes sonores, dans l'application de l'algèbre à
la géometrie, l'imagination est le coefficient du calcul,
et les mathématiques deviennent poésie.

This passage stands with Puttenham's Enginers and Cap-
taines Stratagematique as one of the great statements on
the relations between postlogic and the exact sciences,
akin to Poe's *Eureka* and Mallarmé's *Un Coup de dés,*
and predating Poincaré by a considerable period.

Hugo is not hypnotized by the exact sciences, however,
despite his friendliness toward them. His real concern is
nature, in itself and in the mind and art of genius which
he identifies with nature. In the workings of these, nature
may be observed, and that observation is the task of the
poet. Yet, he maintains, instead of comprehending nature
and her ways by conforming to them, we have, in poetry
as in thinking, fallen away into exaggerated sobriety, steril-
ity, hypercriticism. He draws a wonderful picture of the
Garden of the Muses, all a-growing and a-blowing, fertil-
ity of mind and nature being of the same kind: "partout
l'image idée, partout la pensée fleur, partout les fruits,
les figures . . . ne touchez à rien, soyez discret. C'est
à ne rien cueillir que se reconnaît le poète." A little later
he adds the passage of this work we quoted above, page
150; it ends thus, "la fécondation, la plénitude, la produc-
tion, c'est trop; celà viole le droit des neutres." This is
Ovid; it is also postlogic, and Hugo goes on to tell us that
postlogic is postcritical.[3] In Book iv it runs, "Quoi donc? pas
de critique? Non. Pas de blâme? Non. Vous expliquez
tout? Oui. Le génie est une entité comme la nature, et
veut, comme elle, être accepté purement et simplement
. . . Quant à moi, qui parle ici, j'admire tout, comme une
brute. C'est pourquoi j'ai écrit ce livre. Admirer. Être

enthousiaste. Il m'a paru que dans notre siècle cet exemple était bon à donner." It is no less good in the following century also.

Hugo directs us from science into poetry. Renan does the same in *L'Avenir de la science*. After a preface written in 1890 in which he says that his youthful self was "évolutionniste décidé en tout ce qui concerne les produits de l'humanité, langues, écritures, littératures, législations, formes sociales," Renan in section 1 of the essay proper considers the intervalidity of the mind's disciplines, poetry among them: "Un système de philosophie vaut un poème, un poème vaut une découverte scientifique . . . L'homme parfait serait celui qui serait à la fois poète, philosophe, savant, homme vertueux, et cela non par intervalles et à des moments distincts . . . mais par une intime compénétration à tous les moments de la vie . . . La faiblesse de notre âge d'analyse ne permet pas cette haute unité; la vie devient un métier, il faut afficher le titre de poète, d'artiste ou de savant, se créer un petit monde où l'on vit à part, sans comprendre tout le reste et souvent en le niant." Poetry as Renan sees it is not a calling restricted to those who manipulate words; it is a general vocation, and minds abdicate from it, as also from religion or science, at their peril. In section 3 Renan embarks on a nostalgic celebration of myth as a noble form of thought; he holds it now no longer possible, but still envisages a new form of thought to come, less analytical, less critical, which would closely resemble it. "Le passé n'a été qu'une introduction nécessaire à la grande ère de la raison. La réflexion ne s'est point encore montrée créatrice. Attendez! Attendez!" In section 8 there is a wonderful discussion of grammar and the part played by that study and by philology in the understanding of language and the human mind. Philology and natural science are parallel ways of making nature comprehensible, and Renan postulates accordingly a science of the human mind (it is significant that Vico enters the essay at this point), a science not just of the cogwheels of the mind, Renan says, but its very history. He sees the possibility of this in the great advance of modern thought: the shift of attention from static to dynamic, each phenomenon seen as in process of making itself (section 10). In section 15 he discusses the relation of sex and divinity, and affirms that in order to understand myth it is necessary in some sense to believe in it and live with it on its own terms, this being the truly scientific approach. Goethe and Hugo are brought in, with Lamartine, as examples of great modern nature poets whose work is subtended by all the resources of modern learning and scholarship. Then in section 16 he puts forward a last plea for a synthesis of disciplines again, "Une science . . . qui, en devenant complète, deviendrait religieux et poétique." He sees this as the task of the future, when Orpheus will arise once more.

In each of these men, the middle-aged Hugo and the young Renan, there is wide confirmation of the Orphic tradition, and a hint of the particular form the Orphic research is to take in the modern period. Renan in his later work makes the modern task clearer. He does not again make a general statement on the nature of postlogic, as he does in *L'Avenir de la science,* but his own evolution carries him forward on postlogical lines, into writing on the origins of language; into history; into the relations between myth, science, and religion which he considers in the *Vie de Jésus;* into the "drames philosophiques" (he believed that only in dramatic form could philosophy be adequately communicated), the two sequels he wrote to *The Tempest*—*Caliban* and *L'Eau de Jouvence* of 1878 and 1880—nonetheless interesting for being very bad plays indeed. But wherever he goes, he shows the same preoccupation Hugo manifested in his essay on Shakespeare:

the interest in mind in the making. Renan interprets *The Tempest* in this very way,[4] saying in the preliminary notice "Au Lecteur," "Prospéro, duc de Milan, inconnu à tous les historiens;—Caliban, être informe, à peine dégrossi, en voie de devenir homme;—Ariel, fils de l'air, symbole de l'idéalisme, sont les trois créations les plus profondes de Shakespeare." The same note is heard in the preface to the *Vie de Jésus:* "Notre planète, croyez-moi, travaille à quelque oeuvre profonde . . . La nature, qui a doué l'animal d'un instinct infaillible, n'a mis dans l'humanité rien de trompeur." Perhaps the clearest indication of all comes in *De l'Origine du langage,* 1848. Here Renan gives us outright a wonderful phrase for what Orphic minds are now to pursue: "Il y aurait à créer une *embryogénie* de l'esprit humain" (italics in the original). To this he adds a few pages later, "Mais il y a un monument sur lequel sont écrites toutes les phases de cette Genèse merveilleuse . . . poème merveilleux qui est né et s'est développé avec l'homme . . . Ce monument, ce poème, c'est le langage." [5]

Renan and Hugo give two points of emphasis for the Orphic research. Renan directs us to the postlogical unity of science with language, poetry and myth. Hugo agrees with this, and directs us to the history and natural history of Orphic genius. The titles of those two essays are very significant in themselves. Together they pick up that challenging vision of a biology extended into study of the human mind, with language and poetry as part of its essential methodology. We noticed already, in Pt. 1, how in the last century plea after plea was made to biology for just this extension; but the pleas were not met, and have still not been met today.[6] This was to be the form taken by that "explication orphique de la terre" of which Mallarmé spoke. Yet he himself did not pursue it on those terms, and his case is significant. He went another way, toward the exact sciences and a kind of verbal algebra—"Enfin du moi et du langage mathématique." So to some extent did Valéry, who is also an Orphic poet, and both of them in so doing missed the main theme of their time. Our literary fashions obscure such a possibility from us, ranking as they do Mallarmé and Valéry considerably above Hugo and Renan. But the Orphic line suggests otherwise—that on grounds of depth and fertility, exact and up-to-date intuition of what poetry has to accomplish in our day and the prophetic strength which comes from such insight, Hugo and Renan are incomparably more important. The Orphic tradition, which is the mainstream of poetry, lies with life and words, not with pure forms; misunderstanding this, Mallarmé and Valéry lead into an impasse into which a great deal of contemporary literature has followed them. Science has taken a rather similar road, for attempts at extending biology into the realm of mind met with the same fate in the second half of the nineteenth century as did Orphic poetry—a substitution of mathematics for poetry as the gauge of exactitude and reliability in research. The two comparatively new disciplines which bear the magnificent names of "psyche" and "anthropos" bear the mark of this from their beginnings. It is the poets who have to begin the task of extending the range of biology so that it shall include thinking man, and to see how poetry can function as methodology in such a study. This is the specific task of Orphic minds in the nineteenth and twentieth centuries.

2

Suddenly around Milton on my Path the
   Starry Seven
Burn'd terrible; my Path became a solid
   fire, as bright
As the clear Sun, and Milton silent came
   down on my Path

THE ORPHIC QUESTION and methodology are given their shape early in the nineteenth century in England by Coleridge, Wordsworth, and Shelley. Each of these voices agrees in its own way with the endeavor to be set out at greater length by Renan and Hugo: the need to keep science and poetry together, the reaffirmation of the great Orphic tradition in which particular minds will be selected for special love and attention, the research into the natural history of thinking.

The clearest prose statement about the relations between poetry and science is to be found in the Preface to the 1802 edition of *Lyrical Ballads*, which Coleridge said was almost a child of his own brain but in which he also noted "considerable additions" by Wordsworth, "one on the Dignity and character of a Poet, that is very grand, and of a sort of Verulamian Power and Majesty." [7] The exposition in the Preface begins quietly, with a comparison of the ways in which poet and man of science—chemist and mathematician—go to work. Gradually as the comparison advances the writing takes fire:

> The Man of science seeks truth as a remote and unknown benefactor; he cherishes and loves it in his solitude: the Poet, singing a song in which all human beings join with him, rejoices in the presence of truth as our visible friend and hourly companion. Poetry is the breath and finer spirit of all knowledge; it is the impassioned expression which is in the countenance of all Science. Emphatically it may be said of the Poet, as Shakespeare hath said of man, 'that he looks before and after.' He is the rock of defence for human nature; an upholder and preserver, carrying everywhere with him relationship and love . . . Poetry is the first and last of all knowledge—it is as immortal as the heart of man. If the labours of Men of science should ever create any material revolution, direct or indirect, in our condition, and in the impressions which we habitually receive, the Poet will sleep then no more than at present; he will be ready to follow the steps of the Man of science, not only in those general indirect effects, but he will be at his side, carrying sensation into the midst of the objects of science itself. The remotest discoveries of the Chemist, the Botanist, or Mineralogist, will be as proper objects of the Poet's art as any upon which it can be employed, if the time should ever come when these things shall be familiar to us, and the relations under which they are contemplated by the followers of these respective sciences shall be manifestly and palpably material to us as enjoying and suffering beings. If the time should ever come when what is now called science, thus familiarised to men, shall be ready

> to put on, as it were, a form of flesh and blood, the
> Poet will lend his divine spirit to aid the transfigura-
> tion, and will welcome the Being thus produced, as a
> dear and genuine inmate of the household of man.

I know of no finer statement anywhere on the human func-
tions of postlogic in the interpretation of the natural
world. But far more important than any prose statement,
however much to the point, is what is happening in poetry,
for it is only there that Orphic question and method can
really be worked on.

There hovered before both Coleridge and Wordsworth
a vision of a great poem on man's place in nature. Cole-
ridge in 1797 describes his aspirations thus:

> I should not think of devoting less than 20 years to
> an Epic Poem. Ten years to collect materials and
> warm my mind with universal science. I would be a
> tolerable Mathematician—I would thoroughly know
> Mechanics, Hydrostatics, Optics, and Astronomy, Bot-
> any, Metallurgy, Fossilism, Chemistry, Geology, Ana-
> tomy, Medicine—then the *mind of man*—then the
> *minds of men*—in all Travels, Voyages and Histories.
> So I would spend 10 years—the next 5 to the com-
> position of the poem—and the last 5 to the correc-
> tion of it. So would I write, haply not unhearing of
> that divine and rightly-whispering voice, which speaks
> to mighty minds of predestinated garlands, starry and
> unwithering.[8]

The burden of such a task was in the end to fall to
Wordsworth, not to Coleridge; yet it is Coleridge who
recognizes immediately, authoritatively, and with a mov-
ing generosity and gratitude the significance and greatness
of Wordsworth's accomplishment of the task, in *The Prel-
ude*. This is the theme of his poem *To William Words-*

worth, from which we have already drawn that testimony to *The Prelude* as "an Orphic song indeed." In the poem he laments his own infertility but comes nonetheless "a welcomer in herald's guise," as he says, "Singing of glory and futurity." Two passages are especially significant:

> Friend of the wise! and teacher of the good!
> Into my heart have I received that lay
> More than historic, that prophetic lay
> Wherein (high theme by thee first sung aright)
> Of the foundations and the building up
> Of a Human Spirit thou hast dared to tell
> What may be told, to the understanding mind
> Revealable; and what within the mind
> By vital breathings secret as the soul
> Of vernal growth, oft quickens in the heart
> Thoughts all too deep for words!—
>   Theme hard as high . . .

Coleridge recognizes at once the central Orphic intent of Wordsworth's poem, that investigation into the growth of the mind, and sees it as partly history and partly prophecy, as if here a discipline were being founded for future as much as for present use. Later he develops this note further, relating Wordsworth's task to the great genealogy of minds of genius, and to truth, twice repeated.

> O great Bard!
> Ere yet that last strain dying awed the air,
> With steadfast eye I viewed thee in the choir
> Of ever-enduring men. The truly great
> Have all one age, and from one visible space
> Shed influence! They, both in power and act,
> Are permanent, and Time is not with them,
> Save as it worketh for them, they in it.

> Nor less a sacred roll, than those of old,
> And to be placed, as they, with gradual fame,
> Among the archives of mankind, thy work
> Makes audible a linked lay of Truth,
> Of Truth profound a sweet continuous lay,
> Not learnt, but native, her own natural notes!

Almost every word here is significant if we are to draw full advantage from the comment of one great Orphic mind on another: the diagnosis of the theme of *The Prelude;* the recognition of the historical importance of this poem as a document of knowledge, science, and truth whose full meaning for mankind will only gradually emerge; of the timelessness and unity of the central poetic task in which there is neither supersession nor emulation; the originality of the enterprise; the likening of the poet's subject matter and method to organic growth. Yet there is one strange note here—"theme *hard* as high"—"thou hast *dared* to tell." What does this mean?

Only Wordsworth can answer this question, and it has to do with Orphic question, method, and genealogy all at once.

In the 107 lines of blank verse prefixed to the 1814 edition of *The Excursion* but possibly written much earlier (Mary Moorman's biography suggests 1798), Wordsworth sets out his own aims. They do not relate only to *The Excursion,* but were intended as an introduction to that life work of his which he had always in his eye but never completed. "The following passage," he says, "taken from the conclusion of the first book of 'The Recluse,' may be acceptable as a kind of *Prospectus* of the design and scope of the whole Poem." It begins:

> On Man, on Nature, and on Human Life,
> Musing in solitude,

the great universal themes of natural history and history itself, individual and social. After a few lines of introduction Wordsworth expands his theme and aim:

> Of Truth, of Grandeur, Beauty, Love and Hope,
> And melancholy Fear subdued by Faith;
> Of blessèd consolations in distress;
> Of moral strength and intellectual Power;
> Of joy in widest commonalty spread;
>   Of the individual Mind that keeps her own
> Inviolate retirement, subject there
> To Conscience only, and the law supreme
> Of that Intelligence which governs all—
> I sing:—"fit audience let me find though few!"

So we are led to the mind in its full complement of correspondence with and responsibility to the Mind of the universe, and then at once, by the *Paradise Lost* quotation, to Milton. This is no accident, and Wordsworth at once fills out the reference.

> So prayed, more gaining than he asked, the Bard—
> In holiest mood. Urania, I shall need
> Thy guidance, or a greater Muse, if such
> Descend to earth or dwell in highest heaven!
> For I must tread on shadowy ground, must sink
> Deep—and, aloft ascending, breathe in worlds
> To which the heaven of heavens is but a veil.
> All strength—all terror, single or in bands,
> That ever was put forth in personal form—
> Jehovah—with his thunder, and the choir
> Of shouting angels, and the empyreal thrones—
> I pass them unalarmed. Not Chaos, not
> The darkest pit of lowest Erebus,
> Nor aught of blinder vacancy, scooped out

By help of dreams—can breed such fear and awe
As fall upon us often when we look
Into our Minds, into the Mind of Man—
My haunt, and the main region of my song.

This is, however you look at it, an astonishing passage, but
for the moment we will carry on with the poem itself be-
fore looking at it a second time. In the next ten lines he
speaks of a Paradise perhaps realizable on earth, springing
from

the discerning intellect of Man
When wedded to this goodly universe
In love and holy passion,

which he clinches with a phrase of pure Baconian vintage,
speaking of his own hope to chant, prophetically, long
before such a time could come, "the spousal verse Of this
great consummation." This is Bacon's vision of his *Or-
ganum;* Wordsworth describes his own:

while my voice proclaims
How exquisitely the individual Mind
(And the progressive powers perhaps no less
Of the whole species) to the external World
Is fitted:—and how exquisitely, too—
Theme this but little heard of among men—
The external World is fitted to the Mind;
And the creation (by no lower name
Can it be called) which they with blended might
Accomplish: this is our high argument.

He describes next where and how this is to be done; not
in the haunts of nature alone, but in cities and in social
life, as the Ovidian progress moved also. Then comes an
invocation to the power by which this must be accom-
plished:

Descend, prophetic Spirit! that inspir'st
The human Soul of universal earth,
Dreaming on things to come; and dost possess
A metropolitan temple in the hearts
Of mighty Poets: upon me bestow
A gift of genuine insight.

So Shakespeare too is summoned up. The method is to be, in part at least, autobiography:

And if with this
I mix more lowly matter; with the thing
Contemplated, describe the Mind and Man
Contemplating; and who, and what he was—
The transitory Being that beheld
This Vision; when and where and how he lived;—
Be not this labour useless.

And with a final invocation of the "dread Power" and "un-failing Love" sustaining all things, the statement or plan of research—for it is no less—comes to an end.

Research into the nature and development of the mind, its genetics and evolution, in the individual autobiograph-ically, more generally in the species—this is what Words-worth proposes for himself. It is a self-imposed vocation which is to add to the sum of human knowledge, and no academic blindness or would-be scientific prejudice must come between us and the realization, so badly needed in our present state of learning and literature, that this is poetry's function, as it is that of science. Yet even so, why the particular excitement? After all, others before Words-worth had written about the mind, and autobiography had been attempted before. To describe and account for one-self is admittedly no easy matter, but it need not seem so alarming. How explain this note, in these lines, in Coleridge's poetic commentary, and intermittently all through *The Prelude* too?

The explanation is to be found in the very lines which express the excitement most clearly, the lines about Milton and *Paradise Lost*. What Wordsworth is saying is that he means to take on where Milton left off, on a task as cosmic in scope and even more difficult. When one thinks of the grandeur of Milton's work and of his stature, this becomes audacious indeed; but we must confront the audacity. Wordsworth is claiming the direct succession; not so much, as it has been called, a "by-passing" [9] of the thunderous and angel-beclouded Jehovah of Milton's theology as a carrying forward, in new and yet related terms, of the selfsame task, the explanation of the universe, the Baconian Work of the Interpreter.

Hazlitt and Lamb each came up against this claim in Wordsworth, for he makes or implies it in other places as well as here.[10] They were roused by it as presumption; but they are lesser voices speaking out of turn, for poetry, like wisdom, is justified of all her children, and Wordsworth's insight is vindicated by greater minds than these. Keats' letters and his poem to Milton and Blake's *Milton* suggest something similar going on in other great minds of this time, corroborating Wordsworth's perhaps supreme attempt in the same direction. The clearest Orphic evidence here lies in Shelley's *Prometheus Unbound*, and we will glance at this before returning to Wordsworth's central task.

The vision in *Prometheus Unbound*, which is cast in dramatic form with lyrics and chorus (Shaw claims it is a forerunner of Wagnerian libretto and engaged on the same task), is of an all-embracing renewal of nature in and through the human mind. Shelley's insight takes him to the central Orphic question of his time, and to Greek myth in which to embody the theme, the Titan Prometheus, at first chained to the precipice under the ban of the tyrant Jupiter till the latter is overthrown by Demogorgon, who is Eternity, the Spirit of the Hour, and Prometheus' own progression into deeper love and understanding, after which a new era dawns in which Prometheus is reunited to his beloved, Asia, and "the world's great age begins anew."

It is possible to take this as allegory, to say that Prometheus is, as Shelley says in the preface, "the type of the highest perfection of moral and intellectual nature, impelled by the purest and the truest motives to the best and noblest ends," that Jupiter is the conventional concept of God, that Asia is Nature. But myth, if properly used, always goes beyond allegory, and Shelley's use of myth is postlogical in that it is at once an exposition of subject matter and a comment upon method. The latter becomes explicit from time to time in the poem, as for instance in passages where science and poetry are given equal rights in the new awakening of the mind:

> He gave man speech, and speech created thought,
> Which is the measure of the universe;
> And Science struck the thrones of earth and heaven
> Which shook, but fell not; and the harmonious mind
> Poured itself forth in all-prophetic song.

Later, in Act iv, the Chorus of Spirits sing, after the great liberation has taken place:

> We come from the mind
> Of human kind
> Which was late so dusk, and obscene, and blind,
> Now 'tis an ocean
> Of clear emotion,
> A heaven of serene and mighty motion . . .

> From the temples high
> Of Man's ear and eye,
> Roofed over Sculpture and Poesy;
> From the murmurings
> Of the unsealed springs
> Where Science bedews her Daedal wings.

Poetry and myth are being used as the figures by which mind and nature are to interpret each other, and this play is truly mythological in that one is not certain whether the action takes place inside or outside the mind, a good reflexive ambivalence which mythological theater fosters. Shelley in his preface explains that the imagery he uses in the play "will be found, in many instances, to have been drawn from the operations of the human mind, or from those external actions by which they are expressed." He then adds, "This is unusual in modern poetry, although Dante and Shakespeare are full of instances of the same kind: Dante indeed more than any other poet, and with greater success." So he begins the tale of his own Orphic ancestors, Dante, whom Goethe claims as a forerunner of "metamorphosis in the higher sense," Shakespeare, of whom Goethe says that he is "more epic and philosophic than dramatic," as if that great corpus of plays could be looked on as one immense philosophical epic.[11] (Bacon appears in Shelley's preface also, as in that to *The Revolt of Islam*, where there is another list of ancestors, and in *The Defence of Poetry:* "Lord Bacon was a poet." Shelley is as fervent a Baconian as Coleridge.) But Shelley's most interesting reference of all is this:

> The only being resembling in any degree Prometheus, is Satan; and Prometheus is, in my judgment, a more poetical character than Satan, because, in addition to courage, and majesty, and firm and patient opposition to omnipotent force, he is susceptible of being de-

scribed as exempt from the taints of ambition, re-
venge, envy, and a desire for personal aggrandizement,
which, in the Hero of *Paradise Lost,* interfere with the
interest.

This is a misinterpretation of Milton's intent, similar to
that shown by Blake in *The Marriage of Heaven and Hell;*
but this does not affect Shelley's heartfelt piety toward him
whom he calls the sacred Milton, nor does it annul the
rightness of the comparison Shelley makes between his
poem and that of Milton.

We glanced at Milton as we came by in Part II, Section
2, noticing then his obsession with the final Orpheus fig-
ure, the tearing asunder and the resolving into water and
stars and song, at which neither we nor the Orphic research
have yet arrived. It is not only his choice of figure which
is prophetic. His great work may be so also, capable of
anticipating the Orphic research of the present time and
giving it direction. Milton in these terms is not a great
poet bound down by theology. He is a free spirit inquiring
into the nature and status of the human spirit in the uni-
verse, natural and supernatural, writing an epic upon
Genesis; the generation of the universe in Raphael's nar-
ration in Book VII, to which Urania and her son Orpheus
act as prologue; the genesis of man in Adam's recapitula-
tion in Book VIII of his calling into life; and conscience or
genesis in the spirit, the beginnings of moral obligation,
choice and failure. To this the modern Orphic voices, in-
tent with their own kindred questionings, turn as if by
compelling and common instinct.

The tradition, before and after Wordsworth, gives us
sanction to take Wordsworth at his word: to assume that
he is indeed the successor to the Milton of *Paradise Lost,*
that he is to assimilate all Milton's resources of subject
matter and instrument in their reciprocal relationship,

and to take them forward. The subject matter is a genetic inquiry into the human mind, set in the universe natural and moral. The instrument is epic, and this means not just one single example but the whole epic tradition. So we come to *The Prelude* as epic, and epic as postlogic.

3

where that immortal garland is to be run
for, not without dust and heat

THAT *The Prelude* is an epic has been said before, and
beautifully said, by Lascelles Abercrombie, himself a poet.
He compares the poem with the *Iliad,* the *Aeneid,* the
Divine Comedy and *Paradise Lost,* on equal terms, and
says of *The Prelude* and its theme of the correspondence
of universe and mind, "This is the modern epic; this is
the heroic strain today, the grand theme of man's latter
experience." [12] Wordsworth himself had epic in mind as
his goal. In 1805 he is saying of *The Prelude,* "This work
may be considered as a sort of *portico* to 'The Recluse,'
part of the same building, which I hope to be able, ere
long, to begin with in earnest; and if I am permitted to
bring it to a conclusion, and to write, further, a narrative
poem of the Epic kind, I shall consider the *task* of my life
as over." [13] He sees *The Recluse,* and the projected epic,
as lying ahead of him. In fact he never wrote either, and
I think the reason is, in part, that the task was already
done. You cannot, after all, write something you have al-
ready written. *The Prelude* is the great poem "On Man,
on Nature and on Human Life," and is itself epic.

What is epic? We may well ask. It is a form of poetry
which has suffered a strange fate at the hands of critics.

It has been supposedly embalmed and buried, and now falls under the heading of literary archaeology. It has been classified as "oral" or "authentic" epic, arising in primitive heroic society, and as "literary"; also as "primary" and "secondary." But even literary and secondary epic is now considered to be gone for good. We are told that *Paradise Lost* is the last, that epic found there "a finality which forbade any extension of its scope." [14]

What then of Wordsworth's proposal, in those pre-*Excursion* lines, to take over from Milton? Either the poet is unaware that epic is dead, and, misled himself, misleads us, or epic is not dead at all. Funeral services for it may be well enough as an occupation for critics, but they are no concern of the poet, intoned as they are over an empty grave. For the poet epic is no more dead than lyric, or poetic drama, or any other of those tough, infinitely adaptable, and lively organs of his. It is eternally available, with its own special resources, as a method of postlogical research. Poets cannot afford to be bereft of their working instruments in this way, and neither can human thinking in general. That is why it matters so much that we should let Wordsworth reassure us, in his poetic practice if not in his theorizing, that epic is as alive and prophetic as ever it was, moving forward in our name and changing and developing as it goes.

Epic is one of the greatest of the postlogical disciplines. Just how postlogical it is we can begin to see when we look at some of its characteristics, its preoccupation with the structure of the universe and the place and course of man's life and death within it, its essential activity, its attachment to mythology. This is supremely the point where poetry espouses time, in the form of narrative, on the grand scale. It is therefore peculiarly adapted for thinking, on that scale, about any human relationships and activities in the universe which are susceptible of development or process, up to and including history and natural history, individual or general.

But it does not merely deal with developing subject matter; it develops itself in its progress through time, in that reflexive interaction and identification of subject, instrument, and agent which is part of postlogic. When an Orphic mind selects a poetic instrument as appropriate for a special work of discovery in that day and age, that instrument will and should be changed; but the change is never a perversion, a forcible wrenching of an old tool to untried uses. Each poet who sets himself in the epic tradition is going to reinterpret that tradition. The process of reinterpretation, however, resembles a process in nature and organic growth, the drawing-out of latent possibilities, the discovery of a *Novum Organum*. These are the metamorphoses of the poetic spirit of which Coleridge spoke, by which the human race forms for itself new instruments of power according to its new needs and activities. This is the nature of living tradition.

It is beyond my competence to say much about the experiments which are made before Wordsworth's, though it seems that as early as the *Aeneid* epic is beginning to take on a more explicitly genetic character,[15] confirmed by Milton; he too conceives of epic activity as in the spiritual rather than the military field, as Dante does, who also begins to illuminate the inclusiveness of the methodology by involving the poet in his own subject matter. Now in *The Prelude* it is the reflexiveness of postlogic which comes to the forefront. The mind becomes its own subject matter.

Epic, seen from the point of view of the working poet, is a dynamic instrument concerned with heroic achievement, advance, exploration. The significance of these, in terms of man moving between earth and heaven, is inquired into in the person of the epic hero. Here, too, our critical and historical sense has not helped us. To represent epic as the high doings of one solitary figure of however superhuman proportions, a great cult of individualism, is to strike it dead, just as to represent the heroic age of such deeds and discoveries as primitive and left far behind is to strike us all dead. Unprecedented deeds and explorations, with which epic deals, are lonely courses, and necessarily so. But the important thing from the beginning has been that the hero is identified with his people. He *is* his people in some sense. What are Gilgamesh or Beowulf or Dante or Adam doing if they are not carrying us forward with them, exploring and struggling and suffering, out in advance of us but one with us still? [16] It is as if the deeds were consolidated only later, by after-comers, and find their ultimate justification in that; for achievement and discovery that relate solely to one individual are useless. Only the transmissible in some terms, tradition or heredity which are so closely linked together, is of value. This is, so far as we know (and we do not know much about it yet) how nature and human nature make progress into newness of any kind. With this, epic is of right concerned. It is Wordsworth's vocation to apply it to the contemporary Orphic question, the relation of the mind to nature, its origin and development. He will explore the question, in the main, within himself.

Can this be in any sense regarded as fit circumstance for heroic epic? Wordsworth turns the question over in his mind more than once. By the time he could begin seriously on his "inquisition," his more bustling days were already over. "The Recluse, At Home in Grasmere" (as the title runs of the only fragment of that central work which exists),[17] the poet in domestic retirement surrounded by those quiet hills—is this a setting for deeds of intrepid adventure? In that same fragment Wordsworth asks himself this question, and seems almost to an-

swer it in the negative. From line 703 onward he describes
how his temperament since childhood was passionate for
adventure; it is good for us to be reminded of this lest
we make him into a pastoral softy in our minds. Then
he says,

> Yea to this hour I cannot read a tale
> Of two brave Vessels matched in deadly fight,
> And fighting to the death, but I am pleased
> More than a wise man ought to be. I wish,
> Fret, burn, and struggle, and in soul am there.
>
> [720–24]

Later, he seems to relinquish hope of an epic strain, and
to resign himself to something different.

> Then farewell to the Warrior's schemes, farewell
> The forwardness of Soul which looks that way
> Upon a less incitement than the cause
> Of Liberty endangered, and farewell
> That other hope, long mine, the hope to fill
> The heroic trumpet with the Muse's breath! [744–49]

Yet this is not a farewell to utterance, for there follows the
line, "A voice shall speak, and what will be the theme?"
and then immediately begins that passage we have already
looked at, which Wordsworth used later to introduce *The
Excursion,* the great Miltonic statement "On Man, on Na-
ture and on Human Life." That in itself suggests that
epic has not really been renounced; the real aim emerges
from a slightly earlier passage in *The Recluse* fragment
which we will now look at, and from the parallel discussion
in Book 1 of *The Prelude.* To turn to the exploration of
the mind is not to renounce epic, but to reinterpret it. At
line 732 of *The Recluse* the poet has this to say:

> That which in stealth by Nature was performed
> Hath Reason sanctioned. Her deliberate voice

Hath said, "Be mild and cleave to gentle things,
Thy glory and thy happiness be there.
Nor fear, though thou confide in me, a want
Of aspirations that *have* been, of foes
To wrestle with, and victory to complete,
Bounds to be leapt, darkness to be explored,
All that inflamed thy infant heart, the love,
The longing, the contempt, the undaunted quest,
All shall survive—though changed their office, all
Shall live,—it is not in their power to die."

Wordsworth saw in his poetry, if not so clearly in his prose or letter-writing mind, what was at issue. There is no farewell to epic as such, only to earlier forms of it which need now to be changed and renewed, a vision closely linked to that which Milton expressed in Book IX of his epic, where he speaks of his subject as

Not less but more heroic than the wrath
Of stern *Achilles* in his foe pursu'd
Thrice Fugitive about *Troy* Wall; or rage
Of *Turnus* for *Lavinia* disespous'd . . .
Not sedulous by Nature to indite
Wars, hitherto the only Argument
Heroic deem'd, chief Maistrie to dissect
With long and tedious havoc fabl'd Knights
In Battles feign'd; the better fortitude
Of Patience and Heroic Martyrdom
Unsung; or to describe Races and Games,
Or tilting Furniture, emblazon'd Shields . . .
Not that which justly gives Heroic name
To Person or to Poem. Me of these
Nor skill'd nor studious, higher Argument
Remains, sufficient of itself to raise
That name . . .   [14–18, 27–34, 40–44]

Heroism and epic must be taken forward, as Milton and Wordsworth both saw. The references in each to predecessors are to be interpreted not as rejections but as recognition of the ground, now no longer adequate, from which advance is to be attempted—but advance in the same terms. To work a change upon heroism is not to lose it, nor epic either. It is as Wordsworth so finely says, a change of office, no more; it is not in their power to die. And he sees his task in marvelous, almost Malory-ish terms of high prowess, "the dauntless quest," "darkness to be explored." It fits with the passage to come later where he declares the nature of his quest, "into our minds, into the Mind of Man," that brief phrase expressing in itself the personal heroic quest and its universal significance for universal humanity; now he says

> For I must tread on shadowy ground, must sink
> Deep,—and aloft ascending, breathe in worlds
> To which the heaven of heavens is but a veil.

It is a *geste,* this exploration of the mind, and because the poet is to pursue it in his own mind he is at once the hero and the setting of his own epic, though always in relation to, interpreted by and interpreting, the natural universe. That is why there is that sense of bracing oneself for momentous enterprise in Wordsworth's poetic statements of program. Mary Moorman says, very finely, that he was about to embark upon "the loneliest adventure ever undertaken by the human mind" (*William Wordsworth,* chap. 11).

Already in the figures which Wordsworth has been using to describe his research there appears the image of a dark and hazardous journey, downward and upward. When, in Book 1 of *The Prelude,* he is considering possible epic subjects, the sequence culminates in a hint of the form such a journey might take and the means by which it could be accomplished. This is that "last and favourite aspiration," the philosophic Song of Truth, which we have mentioned already. Now we need to look at these lines rather more attentively:

> With meditations passionate from deep
> Recesses in man's heart, immortal verse
> Thoughtfully fitted to the Orphean lyre.

The deep recesses of the heart, the workings of the heart, one might say, as if they were mine-workings—into them the journey is to take place and out of them are the meditations to come. And the instrument is the Orphic power of poetry. Milton had used the same image in Book III of *Paradise Lost* to describe his own poetic experience in that poem:

> Through utter and through middle darkness borne,
> With other notes then to th' *Orphean* Lyre
> I sung of *Chaos* and *Eternal Night,*
> Taught by the heavenly Muse to venture down
> The dark descent, and up to reascend,
> Though hard and rare.   [16–21]

We see now what we have come to. This is the second figure of the Orpheus myth, the descent into hell in search of Eurydice and the return, baffled yet not perhaps wholly so. Wordsworth takes from Milton the hint that this is the means by which to interpret this journey he has to make into the mind.

The figure does not move from Milton to Wordsworth in order to stop there, however. The Orphic voice goes on, as the Orphic research does. A hundred years after Wordsworth, in 1907, the next Orphic voice is saying in a letter, "but if I go on writing now, I must go up to the stars and down to the bottom of the sea." [18] There is adventure and exploration of the universe in that image, but this poet has moved the Orphic journey one stage further on. For if the second Orpheus figure, the Eurydice one, is a journey, so is the third, in a sense—only a posthumous one, for after Orpheus had been torn to pieces by the women, his head and lyre make a journey down river to the sea, and the lyre goes up among the stars. Wordsworth in one of his shorter poems picks up the first Orpheus image, as we shall see, but moves on in another to the Eurydice figure, which he abides under. His successor makes an early and significant halt at Eurydice also, in a lyric, moving on to all three figures in his major Orphic work. But it is the last figure, I believe, which is his real working instrument of interpretation, therefore also the one by which he is most nearly interpreted, and that is why his vision of the journey entailed by the modern Orphic research takes the form it does. This poet is Rilke.

Rilke is as well-known and as little-known as is usual with a German-speaking poet who has been widely and rather variously translated into English and whose name moves in and out of discussions of modern literature, with, in most minds, only a rather vague image following. I want therefore to say a little about him, now, at this point of his introduction into our inquiry. For although a century separates him from Wordsworth, the pattern he follows and the research he pursues are close to Wordsworth's, and we shall need Rilke with us from now on.

Biographies, commentaries, and critical works on Rilke there are in plenty. All I mean to do here is to give a minimum of indications about him as an Orphic voice, making no pretense at any kind of more general summing-up. Born in Prague in 1875 and dying in Switzerland in 1926, he was from the beginning a hypersensitive being and apparently without the robust stamina a poet needs. His childhood was enclosed and unhappy, although later he looks back to it as a singular source of inspiration for poetry.[19] His adolescence in a military academy was un-happier still, accounting in part at least for his convulsive determination to get himself exempted from military con-scription in the first World War.[20] His lyric output, from the first collection in 1895 to his death, is immense; there is also a certain amount of prose, and Rilke is one of the world's classic and voluminous letter writers. He married in 1901, but left his wife and daughter before long for the self-realization in solitude which he sought. Where Wordsworth became, of his own choice, the Recluse at home in Grasmere, Rilke became a recluse at home no-where, wandering over Europe more or less incessantly, from Spain to Sweden, from Denmark to Italy, going as far afield as Russia and North Africa and Egypt, and so-journing for longer or shorter periods in various cities, Rome, Munich, Paris, where he was for some time Rodin's secretary until they quarreled, or else in isolated chateaux lent him by aristocratic friends. One of these abodes, Schloss Duino, gives the name to the *Duineser Elegien*. All this while he is a being bent long and lovingly over things, "things that impart themselves so uninterruptedly and sublimely," "I really can't use any human models at all yet . . . and shall be occupied with flowers, animals and landscapes for years to come"; [21] and he is equally bent in anguish over his own self, bodily and spiritual, over his poor health, his incapacity to work at his poetry, his pro-longed periods of inner drought and frost. The latter is largely the theme of his letters, the former that of his poems, with, also, a continual circling around religious or more specifically Catholic themes, springing from an uneasy relation to the religiosity of his mother, never wholly resolved.

This is a poet who has all the Orphic characteristics, in embryo. We find him with a passionate interest in things inorganic and organic, and a desire to become acquainted with the sciences that deal with them. In 1903 and 1904 he is complaining that he knows so little about stars, about flowers and animals, and about all the processes of life, and resolves "to read books on natural science and biology and to attend lectures." Later the plan becomes more explicit: "Then, in the summer semester, I shall go to a University and study: History, natural science, physiology, biology, experimental psychology, some anatomy etc." He adds, in a footnote, "Not to forget Grimm's dictionary." [22] He had a deep interest and belief in life, its workings, and the human being as part of its working, harmonious and not at variance with the natural universe in which he has come to be over a millennium of time.[23] He understands growth and metamorphosis—"if only we are on the track of the law of our own growth"—"Self-transformation is precisely what life is." [24] He says most beautifully that we have to reverence our own fertility, for whether it is of the body or the spirit it is all one.[25] He knows about myth. The great Orphic names of the past are scattered through his letters, Shakespeare, Goethe, Ovid, Hölderlin, even Linnaeus. Yet it is only by hints and brushes; there is no study, no passionate cleaving to these as food for the growing spirit. Rilke denied himself steadily, through devotion to his poetic vocation as he saw it, the nourishment the Orphic mind needs, if we are to judge by what has gone before: the company of the Orphic ancestors, the great body of science and learning, the full involvement in life itself.

This is the man who stands alongside Wordsworth, and he makes, even biographically, an interesting comparison with him, for Wordsworth's decision to withdraw into Lakeland seclusion in the company of first one and then two devoted women is not unlike Rilke's pursuit of solitude and disengagement. This is how each man assessed his own poetic and physical needs and obligations. Wordsworth's decision caused him heart-searching. There is an echo of it still in the *At Home in Grasmere* fragment, and a note of self-justification. (Earlier, just after his return from France, he had said, in a letter, something rather different: "Cataracts and Mountains are good occasional society, but they will not do for constant companions"; we know also how much Wordsworth's move worried Coleridge, anxiety which was perhaps justified in the sequel.) [26] There is anguish in Rilke also: "I tell you, Princess, some change has got to come about in me, all and all, all and all, otherwise all the miracles in the world are useless." This is in a letter of December 17, 1912, to the Princess von Thurn und Taxis. Although he suffered in the régime he chose, however, he does not question fundamentally its rightness for him; he simply saw any other possible way of life in terms of greater suffering still, and a betrayal of his poetic gifts.

There need be no question here of passing judgment. The course of action taken in each of these cases was certainly decided upon in good faith and may have been inevitable. But equally, no good can come of upholding or considering as indifferent a course of action which, to judge by precedents and results, looks as if it may be dangerous. In particular, no good can come of setting it up as a model for younger poets to follow. The Orphic line matters too much for this. We shall be lost if we let ourselves be persuaded by such examples that poetry is unconcerned about what is going on in the world and in ordinary life, or that the poet's life is wholly separated from what he has to say. Poetry is a discipline of full involvement in life, not of withdrawal from it. The opposite danger is obvious and I am not denying it—the danger that involvement in the cares of this world will choke a poetic gift through sheer dissipation of energy and time on nonpoetic matters. Goethe is the great example to the contrary here. Perhaps there are no nonpoetic matters in the universe. At any rate, the dangers of withdrawal are very real, for what the Orphic poet does with himself will be bound to affect what he has to say to us, in its completeness and perfection, and those dangers are shadowily presented in each of these last two poets of our Orphic line.

On the whole it told less upon Wordsworth. He had that in him which could contribute to an epic vocation in any circumstances—courage, toughness, the masculinity of mind which Coleridge remarks upon (at one point in his life Wordsworth thought of becoming a soldier),[27] his early championing of the revolutionary cause in France, his abiding interest in politics and social questions. He has, too, the advantage that he wrote *The Prelude* early, carried forward by the élan of his adventurous childhood and youth which is also his subject matter, giving him a double interest from his epic capital, though with it a foreboding that he might outrun it:

> I see by glimpses now; when age comes on
> May scarcely see at all.
>
> [1805 *Prelude,* XI, 338]

Rilke did not have these advantages. He had to struggle forward toward his Orphic achievement, which he did not reach until the end of his life. This achievement is represented by the twin works of the Duino Elegies and the Sonnets to Orpheus. When its time at length came, it was with a suddenness startling to everybody, including their author. Two Elegies had been written in 1911–12, a third in 1913, a fourth two years later. Then in February 1922, in what Leishman and Spender call a tempest of creative activity, all the remaining Elegies were either completed if they had been fragmentarily begun or written in their entirety, and in addition the whole of the fifty-five Orpheus sonnets, all within three weeks.[28]

When I say that Rilke was unlucky in having to struggle to his Orphic work at the end of his life, I do not mean simply that his effort and suffering were much prolonged: that is an ordinary human lot. He was unlucky because by the time he reached his mythological endeavor, scarcely anything but fragments was possible. He had been self-isolated too long, and in his isolation he had grown or in-grown into preoccupation with peculiar themes which in the Elegies are put forward as public revelation: the angels, the dolls, the acrobats, the newly dead, the great lovers, the urge to make the visible invisible. These are not public oracles, as Orphic myth and statement must be. They are private toys which Rilke mistook for public revelation. The Elegies are very broken indeed. There are hints of Orphic statement and seeking in them, but no more. But in the *Sonette an Orpheus* something else happens, and it happens because Orpheus is there. At long last Rilke's poetic instincts led him to that marvelous myth, which offers him a narrative framework and a classic ancestral mythological instrument. By its strength many of his own private instruments, inadequate on their own, fall into place; and grounded on the myth itself, something approaching an "Orphean insight" here too becomes visible. I believe for this reason that the Sonnets are much more important than the Elegies, although Rilke valued them less.

Now we have two poets, and two works, ranged before us; we will see first what each poet has to say about the nature of his research, in the shorter poems each wrote under Orpheus' name and sign.

4

that scientific imagination which precedes
the purely poetic and is nothing more nor
less than the faculty of true observation of
nature. This is the maternal well-spring of
all mythology, full of mastery and power
still in this present age which is urged to-
ward, and led back to, mythology by the
dynamics of science

WORDSWORTH gives us two minor poems in which Or-
pheus appears, and they have interestingly parallel titles.
The first is *Power of Music*, written in 1806 and the sec-
ond, *On the Power of Sound*, written in 1828. Both are
included in the section of his works called "Poems of the
Imagination," as if both were related, as expression or
questioning, to that Imagination which is the height and
depth of the poetic faculty and which plays such a part
in *The Prelude* itself. Neither of these poems is among
the greatest, by common consent, nor among the most
familiar of this poet's works, but each is a revelation of
Wordsworth's own Orphic nature, and that repeated em-
phasis on power is interesting in this connection. The first
is the Orphic power in its first figure, the control and re-
ordering of the things of creation; the second is the power

needed in the second Orphic figure for the journey to the underworld and the unloosing of the bands of death.

Power of Music follows immediately *The Reverie of Poor Susan* in the Poems of the Imagination, and has the same unpretentious street-ballad-like meter sorting with the subject matter. Like so many of Wordsworth's poems, its complete apparent simplicity and naiveté make it the kind of thing we find utterly unacceptable when young, when we are looking for stronger stuff—sacred underground rivers, perhaps, or skeleton barks ribbed black against the sunset; and that is well enough. But later on, the more one looks into this type of Wordsworthian poem, the more one comes to see in it, and I believe this would be true of almost any poem of this kind he wrote. They show a profound subtlety, infinitely removed from sophistication, a subtlety whose precondition is the simplicity of the approach and of the subject.

The poem begins in this fashion:

An Orpheus! an Orpheus! yes, Faith may grow bold,
And take to herself all the wonders of old;

the Orpheus turns out to be a fiddler in Oxford Street who gathers a crowd round him and holds them spellbound by his music. At first it seems so pedestrian and commonplace as to be almost insulting to the high myth the poet invokes: a street-player—"He fills with his power all their hearts to the brim"—this seems no adequate Orpheus, with his chance audience, lamplighter, apprentice, newsman, lass with a barrow. Only slowly do we notice, or notice backward after we have passed the stanza in question, that the language has a touch of Gospels or Beatitudes,

The weary have life, and the hungry have bliss;
The mourner is cheered, and the anxious have rest.

Then comes the first of the two beautiful nature similes
of the poem, also keeping very common company:

As the Moon brightens round her the clouds of the night,
So He, where he stands, is a centre of light;
It gleams on the face, there, of dusky-browed Jack,
And the pale-visaged Baker's, with basket on back.

Sooty sweep and floury baker's boy are made one with
the gentle light and dark of moon, clouds and night sky;
a celestial image, and is it too, as we thought Orpheus was,
out of keeping? But now we begin to see what is happen-
ing. They are compared not as like to unlike but as like
to secret like. The people of this city are part of nature,
at least the humble and simple people such as these, and
the Orphic power runs right through nature from celestial
bodies into human bodies and souls, recognizable in the
response made, as here, to manifestations of the Orphic
power. Suggestions of this unity of nature, up to and in-
cluding man, under Orpheus' singing are to be found in
earlier interpretations of the myth, when Orpheus is said
to tame not only brute nature and wild beasts, but savage
men also, "stony and beastly people" as Sir Philip Sidney
says. But Wordsworth has another vision, of an immense
relationship through the whole of nature including man,
manifested in a mutual interchange of gifts, as the pennies
drop into the hat of the violin player,—"The one-pennied
Boy has his penny to spare."

Then Wordsworth brings us up short. Casually, as if
it were pure accident or were to be taken for granted, he
says that the player is blind. It is impossible not to be
reminded of that other blind figure in Wordsworth's po-
etry, that strange and wonderful image in *The Prelude,*
set among his experiences in London (I give the 1850
version, which is slightly the better):

And once, far-travelled in such mood, beyond
The reach of common indication, lost
Amid the moving pageant, I was smitten
Abruptly, with the view (a sight not rare)
Of a blind Beggar, who, with upright face,
Stood, propped against a wall, upon his chest
Wearing a written paper, to explain
His story, whence he came and who he was.
Caught by the spectacle my mind turned round
As with the might of waters; an apt type
This label seemed of the utmost we can know,
Both of ourselves and of the universe;
And, on the shape of that unmoving man,
His steadfast face and sightless eyes, I gazed
As if admonished from another world.

In that visionary and mysterious passage the Orphic power speaks to, and in, Wordsworth about the universe. In the lesser poem the image and center of the power, the Orpheus, is also blind. Does this nullify the unity of nature, set him among the deformed and unnatural? The next stanza, however, goes on unperturbed to a living creature of splendid physique, "a giant in bulk and in height," an image of strength and plenitude, not weakness and deprivation, and gives us the second of the nature similes, drawing him in to that blindly executed power:

Not an inch of his body is free from delight . . .
Can he keep himself still, if he would? oh, not he!
The music stirs in him like wind through a tree.

Nothing is lost, the maimed and the halt and the blind are simply added in as part of the total, which is beautiful as nature itself. Now in the next verse come the Cripple, who has by sheer immobility taken on the character of an immemorial landscape:

Mark that Cripple who leans on his crutch; like a tower
That long has leaned forward, leans hour after hour,

followed by a recurring figure in Wordsworth's thoughts
and poetry, the mother whose mind is astray; she is here
with her baby and together they make their own answer
to the music's joy. Only in the last verse do we see a world
where there is no response, the world of the busy and the
rich which has nothing to do with the world of the simple
or with that of nature.

Now, coaches and chariots! roar on like a stream;
Here are twenty souls happy as souls in a dream:
They are deaf to your murmurs—they care not for you.

Only here is there no power and no relatedness between
the natural universe and human beings. The rich and
careless are rejected not as immoral but as irrelevant, and
the poor and meek do indeed here inherit the earth, the
earth of nature. So in Wordsworth's first Orpheus poem,
Orpheus is a musician, and in and through his music a
power is traced running through and binding together the
whole of nature, apart from those mortals who have chosen
to harden their hearts and to fall out of the natural unity
of things.

   The second poem, *On the Power of Sound,* is substantial,
consisting of fourteen long stanzas, and possessing at its
best a sober sublimity. It is not well-known, and it is the
more interesting to find that Wordsworth set particular
store by this poem, and at one point put it at the end of
the "Poems of the Imagination" to show what it meant
to him.[29] The range of subject now is wider: this is not
Power of Music, but Power of Sound. (Its development
is not very easy to follow, as Wordsworth himself must
have sensed, for he put at the beginning of the poem a
brief *Argument* or synopsis.) Sound will here include all

the voices of earth, from the lions roaring after their prey
to the music of the spheres. With Orpheus at the heart
of the poem, however—he occurs in stanza 8—we may find
that he lends us a shape for the whole. Besides the middle
stanza we will look at the first and the last, with Orpheus
to link them; the intervening verses, though with inter-
esting hints in them, are mostly illustrations and images
of sounds "acting casually and severally," as the Argument
says, the "wandering Utterances" of stanza 11. But the
first, middle, and last verses give a kind of framework for
this, with a development of their own:

1

Thy functions are ethereal,
As if within thee dwelt a glancing mind,
Organ of vision! And a Spirit aërial
Informs the cell of hearing, dark and blind;
Intricate labyrinth, more dread for thought
To enter than oracular cave;
Strict passage, through which sighs are brought,
And whispers for the heart, their slave;
And shrieks, that revel in abuse
Of shivering flesh; and warbled air,
Whose piercing sweetness can unloose
The chains of frenzy, or entice a smile
Into the ambush of despair;
Hosannas pealing down the long-drawn aisle,
And requiems answered by the pulse that beats
Devoutly, in life's last retreats!

8

Oblivion may not cover
All treasures hoarded by the miser, Time.
Orphean Insight! truth's undaunted lover,
To the first leagues of tutored passion climb,

When Music deigned within this grosser sphere
Her subtle essence to enfold,
And voice and shell drew forth a tear
Softer than Nature's self could mould.
Yet *strenuous* was the infant Age:
Art, daring because souls could feel,
Stirred nowhere but an urgent equipage
Of rapt imagination sped her march
Through the realms of woe and weal:
Hell to the lyre bowed low; the upper arch
Rejoiced that clamorous spell and magic verse
Her wan disasters could disperse.

14

A Voice to Light gave Being;
To Time, and Man his earth-born chronicler;
A Voice shall finish doubt and dim foreseeing,
And sweep away life's visionary stir;
The trumpet (we, intoxicate with pride,
Arm at its blast for deadly wars)
To archangelic lips applied,
The grave shall open, quench the stars.
O Silence! are Man's noisy years
No more than moments of thy life?
Is Harmony, blest queen of smiles and tears,
With her smooth tones and discords just,
Tempered into rapturous strife,
Thy destined bond-slave? No! though earth be dust
And vanish, though the heavens dissolve, her stay
Is in the WORD, that shall not pass away.

The stanzas are relatively independent, so that one can begin in the middle without being too much out of context. The seventh does not lead particularly closely into the eighth, while the ninth seems to make a fresh start again, although only someone who had forgotten the *Metamorphoses* and Wordsworth's love of it would ignore the way in which here also the Orpheus story leads straight into the building of a city wall. On the whole, however, in this poem as in Ovid's, Orpheus seems just to appear, at the heart of things.

In stanza 8 Orpheus comes in twice, at beginning and end. First there is the adjective "Orphean," qualifying "insight," so that we have a power or method before we have anything else. The actual mythological narrative does not come till the end of the verse, and then it proves to be the second figure, the search for Eurydice. The two are not really separated, however. From the very beginning we have a suggestion of a journey backward into time to rediscover or recover something. The Orphean insight (the phrase reminds us of the *Prelude-Recluse* epic, in whose prefacing lines Wordsworth begs "the gift of genuine insight") is to accomplish two things. First, it is to restore to us an ancient treasure, partially but not wholly lost; but because that journey of recovery also is couched in Orphic terms at the end of the verse, the Orphean exploration is to take the form of a recapitulation of the Orphic journey, and by its own power to discover and interpret its own nature. The goal is not merely self-discovery, however. The Orphean insight is called "truth's undaunted lover," and so by a lovely shift of figure Eurydice and truth become one and the same, to be sought by the power of love and poetry in an endeavor perpetually renewed, never wholly completed, and depending the whole time on a necessarily blind faith.

In the middle of the verse the Orphic power is introduced at first as music, as it was in the earlier poem *Power of Music*. Then, with the lines beginning "Yet *strenuous* was the infant Age," carrying Wordsworth's own emphasis, the poet broadens out the Orphic quest. We now see art

as that quest, a daring and difficult feat of discovery sped
by the forms of imagination. At last the exploration be-
comes explicitly Orphic: "Hell to the lyre bowed low."
But the last lines take us further still. We have gathered
up the powers of music, art, and mythology in this stanza;
now we come to a direct mention of poetry, the "magic
verse" of the penultimate line.

So the progression from the first poem to the second,
and within this second poem itself, becomes clearer. The
chorus of nature rises up in unity to humanity, passes
through human music, and reaches its consummation in
articulate speech and poetry. This is profoundly impor-
tant, not merely for this poem or for Wordsworth, but
for the whole Orphic line, forward and backward. (One
cannot help remembering Milton's *At a Solemn Music*,
with its "sphere-born harmonious sisters, Voice and
Verse," [30] where also music is given the due complement
of words.) In Wordsworth's poem, music and words appear
together again in stanza 13:

> Unite, to magnify the Ever-living,
> Your inarticulate notes with the voice of words.

But the progress goes on, and stanza 14 seals man and lan-
guage home in the most exalted level possible to thought,
for finally Wordsworth invokes the Logos, in Whom a
poet may indeed see, if he be so minded, his most absolute
and amazing letters of credence. That is the term of the
harmony which Wordsworth sees, as universal nature,
throughout the poem, rising up to, and contained in, the
Eternal Word.[31] Not merely does the poet give language
the supremacy over music; he gives sound as language
the supremacy over silence. The ninth and tenth lines of
the last stanza are closely akin to the lines in the Immortal-
ity Ode about our noisy years being moments in the eternal
silence, but the resolution is different. Wordsworth speaks

up for harmony, language, and mankind, and this is ex-
tremely important in view of what was to happen later
with the Orphic line in Mallarmé and Valéry. Each of
them would have preferred, absolutely, either music or
silence above the "impurity" of human language. It is
most interesting to see Wordsworth in this poem rule that
out long beforehand as reaction and *impietas*, poetically,
humanly, and theologically.

So far we have worked through the poem by means of
the thought in it, but there is still the starting point to
consider, to which that central Orphic verse can lead us
back, as it led us forward to the main theme. We saw how
in *The Prelude* the culminating vision of the possible epic
took the form of a journey where something was to be
brought to light from "the deep recesses of man's heart."
Now in the first stanza of this poem the place or map of
that journey is indicated, for it has a place, it is not solely
in the imagination, though it is there too. We start with
the two most articulate of the organs of sense, eye and
ear. The first is given almost a mind of its own, so close
is it to the operation of thinking; but it is to the second
that we are more nearly directed. (The first of the *Sonette
an Orpheus* will begin in the same way.) Now an extraordi-
nary thing happens. We come once again to that labyrinth
which has followed us all through this investigation, as
an image or hieroglyphic, only to find that it has now
become literally embodied, anatomically, in the most pre-
cise terms, for the labyrinth here is part of the mechanism
of the human ear. This becomes now the starting point
of the journey of exploration. The epic which is to in-
quire into the biology of thinking begins as a journey in
and through the body.

The whole stanza confirms this, the labyrinth of sense
as the strict passage into a dark world which is the body
but is mind as well, for did not Wordsworth say of that,

"I must tread on shadowy ground"? This is Orpheus'
journey, accredited even in the Miltonic echo in lines
10–12 in this stanza, the piercing sweetness of music un-
loosing chains; this is *L'Allegro* and the linked sweetness
long drawn out which there too unwinds chains and then
leads straight on in Milton's mind to Orpheus and "his
half-regained Eurydice," so that one feels they must have
been in Wordsworth's mind also from the beginning. But
this is not all. The shadowy ground of body and mind is
shadowy in a double sense, as the end of this first verse
tells us: it is dark in itself, but it is also haunted by the
shades of the dead. The exploration lies between the two
kingdoms, of life and death, which Wordsworth, in the
beautiful image which closes this stanza, sees as correspond-
ing to and answering each other:

> And requiems answered by the pulse that beats,
> Devoutly, in life's last retreats.

This is not fancy; this is imagination with a profound
bearing on the epic biology of thought and its origins
which we are trying to trace out. The origins of all our
bodily and mental powers are in an exact sense with the
dead, in heredity and tradition; thus the dead are not
wholly dead here within the living body. The heart and
center of the kingdom of the dead to which Orpheus goes
in search of Eurydice is also the penetralia of the indi-
vidual human life which pulsates and thinks (with the
"beating mind" which Shakespeare and Wordsworth speak
of).

An exploration of the labyrinth of body-and-mind, a
field between living and dead with the poetic self as the
instrument of investigation, as Orpheus' lyre had the power
to bring him through those dark passages—this is the maze
we human beings run, in comparison with the rats of our
experiments. It may have been run, on exactly these terms,

since the beginning of human time. Anthropology suggests that the labyrinths of primitive man, the maze emblems and the real mazes of the caves, were capable also of being the body, and the site of a journey between the two worlds of living and dead.[32] The Orphic search here goes past Orpheus back into immemorial antiquity. The search, or research, is as old as the hills or the caves in the hills, and the figures of its workings are changeless.

With Rilke we have something else. At first sight it seems as if we are on the same territory as Wordsworth; for the shorter Orpheus poem of Rilke's which we are going to look at, the *Orpheus. Eurydike. Hermes*[33] of 1904, published in the *Neue Gedichte* in 1907, is apparently a straightforward and beautiful re-telling of this same second figure. At least it begins by picking up, in its wonderful opening lines, the image of the Orphic vision and task as we have so far found them in Wordsworth, the journey into and through the body which is at once the kingdom of the dead and of the living. (We badly need, one begins to see, a new vision in science and poetry that might elucidate these relations between dead and living.) It is good that there should be this reconfirmation, almost a hundred years later, of the nature of the Orphic research, for no matter how different the modes, the task is one. These are the first six lines of the poem (and as with Goethe's poems, I will give a rough translation):

Das war der Seelen wunderliches Bergwerk.
Wie stille Silbererze gingen sie
als Adern durch sein Dunkel. Zwischen Wurzeln
entsprang das Blut, das fortgeht zu den Menschen,
und schwer wie Porphyr sah es aus im Dunkel.
Sonst war nichts Rotes.

(That was the wondrous mine-workings of souls.
Like unobtrusive silver-ore they travelled

as veins across its darkness. Between roots
sprang up the blood that issues in the living;
it looked as deep as porphyry in the darkness.
No other crimson.)

Yet as the poem advances, something begins to happen,
something not entirely clear which calls up our close at-
tention and a strange sense of reserve, for all the beauty.
After this great opening there is a certain respite. Eight
lines follow of description of the landscape into which
those mine-workings open out, and then we are introduced
to the characters. Orpheus comes first, as he must do, ahead
of the other two. He has 26 lines, and he is beautiful, and
ordinary, dowered with two or three lovely images which
yet, as can often happen with this poet's almost unrivaled
gift for simile and metaphor, become pure ornament in-
stead of inherent body in the poem. (This does not mean
that they are not to be enjoyed, as ornament, for their own
sake; no need to be puritanical in these things.) After him
comes Hermes; then the being whom the god leads by
his left hand. "*Sie*" it stands in the poem, in italics, and
in the next line, "Die So-geliebte," she, the so dearly be-
loved, making her entrance softly but emphatically at
what is almost exactly the mathematical center of the
poem, at the turn of the 46th to 47th line in a poem of
95. The numbers are relevant, for at first we may be al-
most more aware of the exquisite shape of the poem than
of what is happening in it. For after that introduction
there is a second landscape passage answering the first
one, only here the landscape is called into being by Or-
pheus' lamentation, a world and then a universe of mourn-
ing, "a sky of mourning with contorted stars." And then
Eurydice too, like Orpheus, is given 26 lines. But what
a difference! "Sie aber" as that passage begins, but she,
is something quite other. What does Rilke make of her

when he has detached her from that world of Orpheus'
grief? This is part of how he presents her:

Sie aber ging an jenes Gottes Hand,
den Schritt beschränkt von langen Leichenbändern,
unsicher, sanft und ohne Ungeduld.
Sie war in sich wie Eine hoher Hoffnung,
und dachte nicht des Mannes, der voranging,
und nicht des Weges, der ins Leben aufstieg.
Sie war in sich. Und ihr Gestorbensein
erfüllte sie wie Fülle.
Wie eine Frucht von Süssigkeit und Dunkel,
So war sie voll von ihrem grossen Tode,
der also neu war, dass sie nichts begriff.

Sie war in einem neuen Mädchentum
und unberührbar; ihr Geschlecht war zu
wie eine junge Blume gegen Abend . . .

Sie war schon nicht mehr diese blonde Frau,
die in des Dichters Liedern manchmal anklang,
nicht mehr des breiten Bettes Duft und Eiland
und jenes Mannes Eigentum nicht mehr . . .

Sie war schon Wurzel.

(But she went forward at that god's left hand,
her steps constrained by the long winding-bands,
hesitant, gentle, and without impatience.
She was self-folded, like one long expectant,
had no thought for the man that went before them,
none for the road ascending to the living.
She was self-folded. And her Being-dead
Fulfilled her into plenitude.
Like fruit filled out with sombre sweetness, she
was full of her own death, a thing so great
and still so new she comprehended nothing.

She was enclosed in new virginity,
inviolable; sex in her was closed
like a young flower towards evening . . .
No longer now was she that golden woman
who in the poet's songs often resounded,
no longer the broad bed's fragrance and island
and that man's property not any longer . . .

Made root already.)

This is, unlike Wordsworth, no simple matter. It is
full of ambivalences, and only when we have glimpsed
the nature of these shall we be in a position to trust Rilke,
in his turn, and to understand his kind of science. Let
us see first of all the evidence given us by these lines.

First (though each point leads into the others), the iden-
tification of the poet not with the male, Orpheus, the
likely self-image in the circumstances, but with the woman.
There is no mistaking the sudden leap in power, intensity,
sympathy, at the point at which she enters the poem. Be-
side her, Hermes and Orpheus are almost lay figures. Sec-
ond, what I might call the long, loving, cherishing, utter
rejection of sex and fertility. The language in which
Eurydice is described suggests pregnancy; *guter Hoffnung
sein* means to be expecting a child, and the "Fülle" of
four lines later implies a rounding of the body as well as
the idea of abundance. But the fruit within her is not life
but death. Next she is moved back one stage, into an earlier
order of creation, the plants, and their cycle of reproduc-
tion, and here too the poet inverts the normal sequence,
for he makes her first fruit, then flower, finally, as cul-
mination, root, as if to take her back, away from fruition
into the earth, into the grave. Then comes the rejection
of sex between man and woman in marriage, beginning
quietly, rising to an unmistakable note of triumph in that
third repetition of "nicht mehr"—"Und jenes Mannes

Eigentum nicht mehr." Rejection in favor of what? First, in favor of restored, insulated self-hood for the woman; for marriage is rejected not only as sex but also as relationship between one individual and another, of which it is the highest and closest type. Rilke almost abolishes her partner, for a little later in the poem when Hermes turns to her exclaiming, "He has looked round," she is so self- and death-absorbed that she does not understand and asks "Who?"—*Wer?*, the one other italicized word in the poem besides the *Sie*, the only partner she is to have in the perfection of her isolation. Lastly, and closely connected with what has gone before, there is the apotheosis of death in this poem. Death is preferred to fertility, to relationship between people, to life; and the poem ends with Eurydice already started back, of her own accord, to the world of the dead from which she was being wooed away.

At first sight this seems to be a contradiction, point by point, of every note of postlogic, puzzling in any true poet, doubly so when it appears, as it does here, in direct connection with Orpheus himself. It is, moreover, no accident in Rilke's work, but something essential to it. The figures of this poem—the identification with the woman rather than the man, the rejection of sex and fertility, of love and relationship, the apotheosis of death—are ratified time and again in Rilke's poetry, including the *Sonette an Orpheus*, and not only there but in his letters and life as well.[34] How are we to interpret this? Looking at those figures again, considering them in their relationship to the writer's life, and living as we do in the mid-twentieth century, we are likely to make one answer to that question: Freud. The whole situation seems to direct us that way, and this is all to the good, provided we go carefully.

Over the last thirty years or so there has been so much appropriation of Freudian psychology by literary critics that it has come to seem almost a matter of course that that discipline has some prescriptive right over the interpretation of minds, including poetic ones. This shows how far our concept of poetry has fallen away from its true direction and purpose as an instrument of research into the natural world, including the mind. Abdicating from its responsibilities, criticism (which is at best and worst inseparable from poetry) went a-begging, asking to borrow from Freud and to a lesser extent from Jung the means of interpreting those structures which were poetry's own province first and foremost, namely, myth and the working forms of the mind, for the investigation of which poetry is peculiarly adapted by virtue of its postlogical reflexiveness of method and subject matter, and its singular appropriation and development of one of the greatest of all human instruments of research, language. Only the Orphic poets have pressed on with poetry's specific modern task, the development of a biology of thinking. Wordsworth was well launched on it by 1805—not even then as a novelty but as a conscious extension of the epic tradition, which means that it is practically immemorial.[35] Rilke takes this up in allied yet rather different terms. In the Orpheus figure of each lies the clue to what is going on.

Wordsworth in his working figure gives us Orpheus at the beginning of his quest for Eurydice, entering upon the dark labyrinth. Rilke in this lyric of his which we are considering presents that same figure as already drawing to its close. Eurydice is here doubly lost, twice dead as it were by the time the poem finishes; and it is in her that the poet embodies the turn he is giving to the Orphic myth—the shift from life to death, the abdication from human relationships into a kind of scattered organic unity with nature at large (so Eurydice has become a root already and is compared elsewhere in the poem to fallen

rain, "hingegeben wie gefallener Regen"), the with-
drawal from marriage into a negation emphasized by the
poet's identification of himself with the woman and not
with the man in the poem. In postlogic something else
can be done with the notes of this Orphic poem than to
regard them as clinical neurotic symptoms. They are marks
of a metamorphosis taking place in the myth itself—that
is, in the method of thinking. For all these notes belong
not in the second Orphic figure, the quest for Eurydice,
but in the third, where Orpheus meets his fearful death.

In the last figure of the Orpheus story, the poet is at-
tacked and torn to pieces by the Thracian women or
Maenads, "the rout that made the hideous roar," who
overwhelmed the song of Orpheus and thereby his power.
One version of the story says that the reason for the attack
was that he had been preaching the cult of Apollo against
that of Dionysus; another says that he had been advocating
love between man and man and not between man and
woman. The broken body was scattered over the soil, the
head and lyre thrown into the river, only to float down
to the sea, singing as they went. The head comes to rest
in an island cave, to prophesy and eventually to be buried.
The lyre goes up to heaven to become one of the constella-
tions.

What Rilke does is to offer us this third Orphic figure
as the new figure of interpretation for the current work
in the biology of thinking. (We have suggested above in
Section 3, from other evidence, that it was in terms of
this, the third Orphic figure, and not the second, that Rilke
envisaged the Orphic journey and research.) The instru-
ment is a shift of attention within the myth itself, moving
us on to this difficult and dark stage of the story. We have
not lost Freud and psychoanalysis in this metamorphosis,
for the emphasis on, and the ambivalent attitude to, sex
and death are right inside the story itself. What we seem

to have done is gained a second name and discipline to accompany us. Dark rites, a bloody sacrifice which is to water the fields and to restore fertility in human beings —these suggest Frazer, *The Golden Bough,* and anthropology. We have met psychology and anthropology in conjunction already, as the two disciplines to which the professional study of myth has, in our modern period of mythological exhaustion, been consigned.

We found this Orpheus figure haunting Milton. Now it haunts Rilke, and it is interesting that Milton should in this way be as direct a forerunner of Rilke as he is, in another way, of Wordsworth. It looks almost as if preoccupation with this death figure of Orpheus betokens a period when the body of learning is torn apart. This is what has happened in the modern age. What might have been a common front of advance in the natural history of thinking, with biology, poetry, psychology, and anthropology all contributing, fell to pieces under the influence of a narrow and outmoded concept of the nature of science, inherent in Charles Darwin's work but going back to Sprat and ultimately to the false side of Bacon. The result was the isolation of each of these disciplines from the others. We have just glanced at what happened to poetry; what happened to biology was in our minds as early as Part I. Freud, a true mythological thinker who had to work at inventing his myths of interpretation for his subject matter, was hampered by not recognizing that this was the nature of his task, myth and poetry being unacceptable in this era as scientific method.

(It takes a poet to recognize what Freud was doing. So W. H. Auden in his admirable poem in memory of Sigmund Freud includes Eros and Aphrodite among the household mourners for that great mind; in addition he speaks of Freud going down like Dante among the lost, so giving him epic as well as mythological status, and indicating the unity of the task.) [36]

Frazer in his turn adopted an equally rigid exclusive detached method of thought (like Lévy-Bruhl but without the latter's honorable uneasiness at what he saw himself as compelled to do), and therefore neither conforms to nor respects his subject matter.[37] However grand *The Golden Bough* may be as a collection of material, it insulates itself from poetry and renders its author, in the terms of Salomon's House in the New Atlantis, a Depredator rather than an Interpreter.

Nothing is to be gained by the isolation of these disciplines from one another. Once they are thought of as reunited in a common search for knowledge about man, mind, and nature, there need be no question of psychology or anthropology, who are latecomers in this field, explaining poetry or myth, though there is everything to be said for an interchange of interpretative methods and material between all these sciences or arts. Orpheus, who is poetry and myth and postlogic thinking about itself, is not subject to interpretation by other disciplines; he is himself interpretation, the specific instrument of the poet's researches. Wordsworth moves into and through Orpheus to offer himself as subject matter. Rilke identifies himself more directly with Orpheus, commenting thus on the methodology. Each has the natural historian's motive: clarity, and generality. To relegate these works to poetry, in isolation, is to miss their point. Wordsworth was at pains to emphasize it in the Preface to the *Lyrical Ballads,* "Among the qualities there enumerated as principally conducing to form a Poet, nothing is implied different in kind from other men, but only in degree." Similarly, Holthusen, a writer on Rilke, has said that the Sonnets to Orpheus are not "I-Lyric but We-Lyric" (*Rilkes Sonette an Orpheus,* Munich, 1937, p. 36). The aim is general, as befits a discipline of investigation into the biology of thinking, a study of the development of the mind-body in the world of nature alive and dead. Of this *The Prelude* and the *Sonette an Orpheus* are textbooks, and in their thinking and validity akin to, and co-equal with, every branch of biology, in the widest possible sense including psychology and anthropology, having a similar aim and field.

5

what is a Thought but another word for "I thinking"?

IT IS GOOD and appropriate that we should possess two versions of *The Prelude,* of 1805 and 1850, with half a lifetime between them. The 1805 version is still embedded in that marvelous period at the start of the nineteenth century when European thought underwent one of its greatest revivifications, still to be fully profited from. The second, in 1850, is in English poetry a last note of the trumpet, the Orphic confidence and prophecy in it contrasting markedly with the other long poem published in that same year, *In Memoriam,* which exhibits the weakness resulting from the loss of Orpheus from our tradition for the time being, the timorous and negative relationship to the natural universe, science and religion, the paralysis of poetic and heuristic power. In this study we shall use in general the 1805 text of *The Prelude,* and quotations will be from that unless otherwise indicated.[38] We need not, however, get involved in the strictures of editors and critics upon the second version, for its tampering with the integrity of the original record, the toning down of certain exuberant passages, the introduction of a more specifically Christian note into the later version. A genetic relation between two forms of one work dealing with the

337

genetic development of a mind is part of the evidence, although we shall not be concerned directly with this.

Our introduction to Wordsworth's major Orphic work has so far been the poet's own questioning of his aims, in the verse preface to *The Excursion* and in Book I of *The Prelude,* where epic and Orpheus appear in company. Here we have found three main points: first, an intention to look into the mind, and the ways in which that mind, of individual and species, is fitted to the universe and the universe to the mind; second, a vision of this inquiry as a journey to be made, an epic quest in search of some new insight into truth, figured by Orpheus' descent into the underworld; third, a realization that the field of inquiry is both body and mind in its relation to nature, and that this field can be considered as one of mutual making or creation between the outward and the inward forms, to be explored by Orphean insight, memory, self-observation, and recording. We find now that these three points are taken up right at the beginning of *The Prelude,* and will provide us with clues with which to go forward through the poem.

The work begins so quietly that we may almost be in danger of missing what is going on. (It is part of Wordsworth's power that under his apparent simplicity lies a wealth of ordered complication.) Where is one to begin with a growing, a history of a growing as this is, the Growth of a Poet's Mind? The question of method as well as of matter is with us from the start. Wordsworth is to speak of this in a little while, in Book II, but the beginning of the poem speaks implicitly too. It turns out to be as natural, exact, and multiform as the subject demands, as the mind itself is. The poem begins with a figure, in a double sense; the figure of the poet in a landscape, and the great over-all poetic figure or trope of a journey which he is about to undertake. Here Orpheus sets out:

> Oh there is blessing in this gentle breeze
> That blows from the green fields and from the clouds
> And from the sky; it beats against my cheek,
> And seems half-conscious of the joy it gives.

So the Orphic song opens, with the poet in a prospect of wide landscape and open sky. A quiet beginning for epic; but nothing here is passive. Something is stirring; not just the air, not just the body receiving that sensation; the mind is active too as part of the whole situation, tentatively endowing the breeze with feelings akin to its own, while the word "beats" suggests a pulse of life outside as well as inside the human being. From the very start, inward and outward nature, mind and world, are set in a to-and-fro moving network of relatedness and interchange. Forty lines later the breeze is answered from within, where a wind that is spirit moves across a landscape of its own:

> For I, methought, while the sweet breath of Heaven
> Was blowing on my body, felt within
> A corresponding mild creative breeze,
> A vital breeze which travell'd gently on
> O'er things which it had made, and is become
> A tempest, a redundant energy
> Vexing its own creation.

[41–47]

So the first of the three great themes of this inquiry as we are envisaging it is fully introduced: the active interpenetration of nature and human nature, the forms of the universe and the forms of the mind. Yet this, too, is not passive. The ecological relationship of the organism to its environment is active and in movement; and in the mind the two sets of forms interpret each other. So the first theme is at once subject matter and methodology, the first stage of Wordsworth's myth.

The next figure is that of the journey. The intricacy
and accuracy of the pattern the poet has chosen for his
inquiry begin now to be discernible. The dynamic is not
simply that of interchange between two sets of relations,
those in mind and in nature. The ecological dynamic is
combined with a forward movement in time, as the organ-
ism, fully alive to its ever-present interplay with its en-
vironment, sustains also its progress in time as growth
and development, exhibiting that beautiful fusion of
simultaneous and successive relations with which poetry
seems always to be deeply occupied, whether its preoccupa-
tions are mathematical or biological. So in this poem the
self stands ready to begin its journey, and myth already
blossoms into its double function of dynamic inclusive
framework for thought and of narrative in time.

The journey is first of all a real one, a piece of auto-
biography.

> Now I am free, enfranchis'd and at large,
> May fix my habitation where I will.
>
> [10–11]

This moment of liberation into a sense of power, con-
fidence, and promise was experienced by Wordsworth at
a particular point in time. It is a real happening and it
is important to bear this in mind; but that is only the
start of what follows. Already there is considerable subtlety
here, simply in the time relations [39] which are dealt with
in these first sixty-seven lines. Wordsworth says that he
composed the opening fifty-four lines at the very time of
the experience; now he is recording and remembering
that moment, now past, and reconsidering what it prom-
ised for the future.

> Thus far, O Friend! did I, not used to make
> A present joy the matter of my Song,
> Pour out, that day, my soul in measur'd strains

Even in the very words which I have here
Recorded: to the open fields I told
A prophecy . . .
My own voice chear'd me, and, far more, the mind's
Internal echo of the imperfect sound;
To both I listen'd, drawing from them both
A chearful confidence in things to come.

[55–60, 64–67]

There is an echo here of something we glimpsed in Goethe's way of thinking about living beings: past and future time in the organism are transmuted into the living functions of memory and prophecy. These are not merely time-scales, they are methodology also, the making of a mythological structure to accord with perceived (which is to say, created) truth. Here again the question of method in Wordsworth's endeavor comes to our attention.

This is the first unfolding of the figure of the journey, but there is more to come. The sense of exaltation in these opening passages, the absolute freedom matched with equally absolute confidence,

I look about, and should the guide I chuse
Be nothing better than a wandering cloud,
I cannot miss my way,

[17–19]

suggest much behind the actual event, and the clue to this comes when Wordsworth chooses (the word "choose" is important for this first Book, opening and closing it) to epitomize his sense of freedom by saying "The earth is all before me." The first of the many Miltonic echoes in the poem, says Selincourt's note; [40] and what a beginning! With it we are sent back, as we were in the *Excursion* preface, to *Paradise Lost*, not this time to the poem as a whole but to one particular part of it. The original line, "The world was all before them, where to chuse," comes

from the very end of the last book, and it is as if Words-
worth meant to dovetail his epic directly into the very
place where the Miltonic epic ends. This is not the only
epic remembrance these opening lines of *The Prelude* con-
tain. The poet goes on to say that in his new freedom he

> May quit the tiresome sea and dwell on shore,
> If not a Settler on the soil, at least
> To drink wild water and to pluck green herbs,
> And gather fruits fresh from their native bough.
>
> [35–38]

Here is a hint of the *Odyssey*, a hint taken up by a passage
much later in the work:

> What avail'd,
> When spells forbade the Voyager to land,
> The fragrance which did ever and anon
> Give notice of the Shore, from arbours breathed
> Of blessed sentiment and fearless love?
> What did such sweet remembrances avail,
> Perfidious then, as seem'd, what serv'd they then?
> My business was upon the barren sea,
> My errand was to sail to other coasts.
>
> [XI. 48–56]

This journey in the poem, then, is the epic journey still,
if remade to modern needs, and there are reasons for be-
lieving that Wordsworth's statement in *The Recluse* was
right and that none of epic's ancient glories are lost in the
process of transformation. There are hints of a kind of
martial and heroic glory in this quiet poem, woven so
closely into the substance of Wordsworth's themes that one
scarcely notices them at first. Phrases come to mind such
as this one at the end of Book I:

> even then I felt
> Gleams like the flashing of a shield.[41]

They come at crucial points, when the poet is considering the field of action between the beauty of outward forms and the mind. Here is another from Book XI:

> lights and shades
> That march'd and countermarch'd about the hills
> In glorious apparition.

[141–43]

What Wordsworth calls the impressive discipline of fear may be a part of this, in this poet's marvelously positive attitude to experiences that we should be liable to think of as fearful and traumatic, especially for a child (for example, seeing the body of a drowned man brought to the surface, described in Book V). In Book I, line 440, Wordsworth speaks again of the discipline of "both pain and fear," as if the very wounds the mind inevitably receives could be themselves a glory; and the words the poet uses of himself take a color almost of warlike endeavor,

> Of prowess in an honourable field,
> Pure passions, virtue, knowledge, and delight,
> The holy life of music and of verse,

a theme expanded in Book III in the retrospective passage (line 168) which begins, "And here, O Friend! have I retrac'd my life," which speaks of glory, of Genius, Power, Creation, and Divinity, of the awful might of Souls:

> This is, in truth, heroic argument,
> And genuine prowess,

the rest of the passage claiming, for poet as for all men, godlike hours and a majestic sway "As natural beings in the strength of nature." Epic is with us from the start of this journey, epic in its varied forms.[42] To this the Miltonic inscription leads, just as it is to lead into the great list of possible epic subjects which occupies lines 177–238 in Book I, culminating in the image of Orpheus' dark journey which we have already singled out and fitted to Wordsworth's inquiry. But the *Paradise Lost* reference does more than simply affirm the poem's status and genealogy. In it Wordsworth identifies himself not only with Milton and the epic tradition but with the hero of *Paradise Lost,* with those of whom it was first said "The world was all before them." These are Adam and Eve, which is to say, all humanity, seen here at the point of being driven from Eden following the Fall and making their way, sadly yet hopefully too, into and through the natural universe. Wordsworth does not merely take over from Milton; he takes over from Adam in Milton's poem, the poet now being his own subject matter and hero, to continue the narration of the next chapter in that epic journey which is the poem of mankind.

The working myth for this inquiry is now displayed. It is to be the poet's own life as memory presents it to him. This is also to be the journey he undertakes, as he makes clear at the end of Book I:

> I will forthwith bring down,
> Through later years, the story of my life.
> The road lies plain before me; 'tis a theme
> Single and of determined bound; and hence
> I chuse it rather at this time, than work
> Of ampler or more varied argument.

So the choice is made, and the image of the journey continues throughout the work, here for instance in Book III:

> Enough: for now into a populous Plain
> We must descend.—A Traveller I am,
> And all my Tale is of myself;

> [195–97]

where again the site of the journey is both inward and outward; or in Book xɪ:

> Thou wilt not languish here, O Friend, for whom
> I travel in these dim uncertain ways,
> Thou wilt assist me as a pilgrim gone
> In quest of highest truth.

[390–93]

The figure of the journey which is the individual life is given its other name from time to time—that of history—in phrase after phrase: "a poet's history," "my own history," "this history . . . of intellectual power," the history that is "the discipline and consummation of the Poet's mind," "the history of a Poet's mind," "this meditative history." [43] This is the second great theme, autobiography as natural history of the mind.

The scope of the Wordsworthian endeavor begins to be apparent. Coleridge is the one who recognized this from the beginning, celebrating the singer and his Orphic song, the high and passionate thoughts *to their own music chanted,* song that was substance and structure to itself, and had to be so by the nature of the inquiry. The great dilemma of psychology has been that only by mind can mind be investigated and that we have direct access only to one such, our own. In terms of a narrow analytic detached methodology this inevitably falsifies the mind's evidence upon itself. Wordsworth suggests that we allow that evidence confidently,

> the mind is to herself
> Witness and judge,

[xɪɪ.367]

not as special pleading but as part of a different, no less valid methodology, appropriate here because it conforms

to the nature of what is being inquired into. Wordsworth
is working for an extension of scientific method in this
branch of biology, and against the view that a totally de-
tached observation, recording and arranging of facts are
the sole acceptable method in science. Perception and
thought, for Wordsworth, are not of this nature. They are
a making from the start, and the fact that Wordsworth sees
this puts him in close touch with modern thought, for we
are coming to realize that mind and body are not a camera
and tape-recorder, but makers and organizers from the
start.[44] This may be what Wordsworth meant by that "cre-
ation" he speaks of in the verse preface to *The Excursion,*
which mind and nature "with blended might accomplish."
It recurs in the great passage on the dawn of the life of
body and mind in the baby, in Book II. Here, too, there is
no passivity; under the dispensation of maternal love by
which the child is first united with the external world of
nature to which he too belongs,

> his mind spreads,
> Tenacious of the forms which it receives,
>
> [253]

but it is no passive reception:

> Emphatically such a Being lives,
> An inmate of this *active* universe;
> From nature largely he receives; nor so
> Is satisfied, but largely gives again,
> For feeling has to him imparted strength,
> And powerful in all sentiments of grief,
> Of exultation, fear, and joy, his mind . . .
> Creates, creator and receiver both,
> Working but in alliance with the works
> Which it beholds.
>
> [265–75]

In this way of looking at the world you cannot avoid "making" and "creation." It is all action and power, those two words that occur so often throughout *The Prelude*.

In addition to admitting self and creation, Wordsworth admits the testimony of memory, another area where the mind may make and remake the evidence upon itself. He proposes a historic or genetic approach from the beginning, but with memory as the appropriate instrument for the uncovering of this. "Each man is a memory to himself" it runs in Book III, line 189, and the famous injunction of emotion recollected in tranquillity may have a bearing on the investigation of the mind as well as the writing of *Lyrical Ballads*. This is the postlogical method proposed for the "natural history"; and the "forms" are here also, as methods of interpretation. We are formed by our environment, and so it becomes part of our natural history as organisms bodily and mental. This is a constant theme of *The Prelude,* a very clear example of it occurring at the end of Book VII. But the intercourse and interpretation work both ways. We are not to think of it

> as if the mind
> Itself were nothing, a mean pensioner
> On outward forms.
>
> [VI.666–68]

Each set of forms is a key to the other.

This is the extension of postlogic which Wordsworth sees, and it goes with a concept of the organism not as a fixed entity or pattern but as a "making" and a "being-made." Psychologically it affords a glimpse, in its union of form and memory, of a method still to be attained which might combine Gestalt and analytic psychologies in a more flexible discipline, not unlike what Goethe aimed at, an observation "beweglich und bildsam." [45]

This is little more than a hint of the contribution this

poem can make to the biology of thinking. It is, as Coleridge says, laid up in the archives of mankind, for gradual unfolding. A true poem, its whole structure is itself commentary upon methodology and matter: the explication and replication of the narrative, the interweaving of image and meditation that recalls Bacon's great definition of the faculty of memory as pre-notion and emblem.

We shall trace two aspects of the development of postlogic in *The Prelude,* using methodological passages in the poem to direct us into the emblems in which each reaches its climax. The first theme is the relation in thinking between logic and postlogic, the Baconian and even more the Shakespearean work which in Wordsworth culminates in the dream of the Arab in Book v. The second theme is that of form as metamorphosis and method of interpretation, the continuity of forms up through nature and into man as thinking and social being, and the function of language and the poet in this progression. This is the Ovidian theme, and it culminates in the emblem of mountains, sky, and water as the power of mind in the poem's last book.

6

No matter how far or how high science explores, it adopts the method of the universe as fast as it appears; and this discloses that the mind as it opens, the mind as it shall be, comprehends and works thus

IN BOOK II of *The Prelude* Wordsworth, as if for the first time, confronts consciously the difficulty of what he has set out to do, the inquiry into the origins and progress of his own mind. The 1850 version is the more telling here, and I give the passage in that form:

> But who shall parcel out
> His intellect by geometric rules,
> Split like a province into round and square?
> Who knows the individual hour in which
> His habits were first sown, even as a seed?
> Who that shall point as with a wand and say
> "This portion of the river of my mind
> Came from yon fountain?"
>
> [203–10]

The series of images is interesting in itself, the rounds and squares, the organic image for the mind's faculty, the river for that mind's continuum, an image which is to re-

appear in the last book with imagination as a river above
and below ground whose course the whole inquiry has
been tracing. The main point, however, is that from the
beginning a mathematical, analytic type of method is
ruled out as useless. It should be understood that this is
not a general dislike for mathematics or for geometry;
quite the contrary. In Book VI (1805) Wordsworth cele-
brates geometry as a natural taste of poets, and shows real
delight in it.

> So was it with me then, and so will be
> With Poets ever. Mighty is the charm
> Of those abstractions to a mind beset
> With images, and haunted by itself.
>
> [177–80]

And he goes on to speak of its constructions as an inde-
pendent world, "created out of pure Intelligence." There
is no lack of understanding of what is going on, and it is
important to remember this in view of what is to happen
in the great dream. It is simply that Wordsworth recog-
nizes the need for some other instrument for the subject
matter he is dealing with. He turns next to Coleridge, as
if to discuss with him the nature of science and this limited
analytic methodology [46] which is regarded as obligatory
only by those who have not paid attention to how their
own minds work. The following lines are reminiscent of
some of Coleridge's best pronouncements about the na-
ture of thinking, in *The Friend, Aids to Reflection,* and
elsewhere: [47]

> Thou, my Friend! are one
> More deeply read in thy own thoughts; to thee
> Science appears but what in truth she is,
> Not as our glory and our absolute boast,
> But as a succedaneum and a prop

To our infirmity. No officious slave
Art thou of that false secondary power
By which we multiply distinctions, then
Deem that our puny boundaries are things
That we perceive, and not that we have made.

It is a plea for a method of thinking which shall deal with wholes and be adequate to that task. There follow the lines:

To thee, unblinded by these formal arts,
The unity of all hath been revealed;

and after saying that neither of them would be prepared to classify and label their mental faculties in analytic fashion (which is interesting in view of the currency of the word "analysis" in contemporary psychological vocabulary) Wordsworth says:

Hard task, vain hope, to analyse the mind,
If each most obvious and particular thought,
Not in a mystical and idle sense,
But in the words of Reason deeply weighed,
Hath no beginning.

The dismissal of analysis is not to mean a retreat into some vague poetasting (mystical *and* idle—the conjunction has always seemed to me admirable as far as a poet is concerned, whose task is to "deal boldly with substantial things").[48] The appeal is to Reason, working in another mode. This, too, it is important to remember in view of the final image of mind which this poem puts forward.

This negative clarity about unsuitable method leads a little later to another statement on methodology which shows Wordsworth's gathering grasp of how he is to go about his work. This is in Book III. He proposes here his own formal method; "formal" in its true, living Baconian sense and not those dead forms of the "formal arts" to be eschewed which he mentioned in the last passage.

> A track pursuing not untrod before,
> From deep analogies by thought supplied,
> Or consciousnesses not to be subdued,
> To every natural form, rock, fruit or flower,
> Even the loose stones that cover the high-way,
> I gave a moral life, I saw them feel,
> Or link'd them to some feeling;
>
> [121–27]

If we see in this merely "anthropomorphism" or "pathetic fallacy" we shall miss the point completely. To start with, Wordsworth is right in appealing to tradition in what he is doing here. The track is indeed not untrod, for the Orphic tradition insists all the way through that the mind, in order to think and to interpret nature, must lend itself to what it is thinking about; that thinking is not manipulation but marriage, and in the end between like forms, the mind and body and "this great frame of breathing elements," as Wordsworth elsewhere describes the universe.[49] This is that correspondence of inner and outer landscape which we saw a while ago, working sometimes one way:

> An auxiliar light
> Came from my mind which on the setting sun
> Bestow'd new splendour,
>
> [II.387–89]

and sometimes the other,

> Hush'd, meanwhile,
> Was the under soul, lock'd up in such a calm
> That not a leaf of the great nature stirr'd
>
> [III.539–41]

but always working, for this is again action and power, and a vision of all the kindred works of creation working at one another,[50] a dynamic concept of a universe working in the sense in which yeast or new wine or, in country parlance, storm-brewing weather "works." This is why the poet's mind from childhood had seen

> The surface of the universal earth
> With triumph and delight, and hope, and fear,
> Work like a sea,
>
> [I.499–501]

a passage which has just spoken of "forms" and "characters," suggesting that this traffic is a language, which we shall think about a little later on. Meantime we may notice how in the present passage the analogies are supplied by thought and by consciousnesses, mind and body working together.[51] Of the nature and sensitivity of that instrument Wordsworth speaks next:

> whatsoe'er of Terror or of Love,
> Or Beauty, Nature's daily face put on
> From transitory passion, unto this
> I was as wakeful, even, as waters are
> To the sky's motion; in a kindred sense
> Of passion was obedient as a lute
> That waits upon the touches of the wind.
>
> [132–38]

This is a Wordsworthian elaboration upon the Shakespearean Orphic figure, the lute strung with poets' sinews, the exquisitely attuned instrument which Goethe saw as scientific as well as musical instrument. Then, after reaffirming the making of its own world by the mind in the next line or two, Wordsworth again questions the rationality or irrationality of this methodology he has sketched out.

Some call'd it madness: such, indeed, it was,
If child-like fruitfulness in passing joy,
If steady moods of thoughtfulness, matur'd
To inspiration, sort with such a name;
If prophecy be madness; if things view'd
By Poets in old time, and higher up
By the first men, earth's first inhabitants,
May in these tutor'd days no more be seen
With undisorder'd sight.

[147–55]

He appeals first to tradition, the poets who immemorially
have worked according to this measure, and behind them
the very Ancients whom Bacon and Vico thought about,
the earliest of men with their mythological thinking; sec-
ond, he claims their thinking *as* thinking and not feeling
or delirium, steady thought with that capacity to think
forward in time which is one of poetry's most mysterious
and undeniable attributes. Is this unreason? And Words-
worth faces out his pseudo-scientific era and its opinions,
and answers thus:

It was no madness, for I had an eye
Which in my strongest workings, evermore
Was looking for the shades of difference
As they lie hid in all exterior forms,
Near or remote, minute or vast, an eye
Which from a stone, a tree, a wither'd leaf,
To the broad ocean and the azure heavens,
Spangled with kindred multitude of stars,
Could find no surface where its power might sleep,
Which spake perpetual logic to my soul,
And by an unrelenting agency
Did bind my feelings, even as with a chain.

[156–67]

The appeal is in the end to true science itself, to passion-
ate powers of observation, penetration,[52] discrimination,
and exactitude. Postlogic is here the wide morphological
and taxonomic discipline we have glimpsed it to be. This
is the perpetual logic, as Wordsworth says, with which
postlogic mates and works in an unceasing activity.

The greatest statement, however, upon logic and post-
logic is made not in an expository passage but in a figure.
This is the dream of the Arab in Book v. Its timing is to
be noticed; for this is the section of the poem dealing with
books and their part in the growth of the mind. It is as if,
having reached this point, the poet can settle this first
theme and then proceed, through a consummate dream-
transition which has both themes in it, to the second stage
of methodological thinking, the function of language and
poetry in the great continuity of forms in nature and hu-
man nature.

In the 1805 version Wordsworth ascribes the dream to a
friend, though even here the narrative drops into the first
person half way through. In the 1850 *Prelude* Wordsworth
drops the fiction and gives it simply as his own. It is an-
other example of his lending his own life as interpretative
material and instrument. We should in any case deduce
the dream as his from its very power. De Quincey calls it
"a dream which reaches the very *ne plus ultra* of sub-
limity." [53] It shows what dreams may do for us in post-
logical thinking when they are removed from their present
over-narrow interpretative framework and better under-
stood, not as objects of interpretation but as instruments
of it.

Dreams occur frequently in *The Prelude;* not re-
counted as this one is, but mentioned as part of the power
and action by which the outer forms are translated into
the inner. Wordsworth says that landscape and sky "held
me like a dream," or appeared "like something in myself,

a dream, A prospect in my mind." They are admitted by
him to full membership of the faculty of thought: "what
my dreams / And what my waking thoughts supplied." [54]
Dream, we remember, came up in the respective work
upon postlogic of Bacon and Shakespeare. Bacon rejected
it; Shakespeare restored it in the *Dream* itself, united with
myth and poetry, and then moved on to a higher stage of
methodological discussion in *King Lear,* denying logic at
no point but showing how postlogic might absorb logic
and have powers beyond it. Yet although it is Shakespeare
and not Bacon whom Wordsworth follows, there could
scarcely be a more perfect fulfillment of Bacon's would-be
derogatory phrase, "Poetry is a dream of learning," than
the dream in *The Prelude.* It is poetry, it is a dream and
something more, "speaking no dream but things oracu-
lar" [55] as Wordsworth meant his poetry to do, and it is a
dream of learning in its profoundest sense. So the Orphic
voice, despite the shortcomings of its human instruments,
works out its own perfection.

I cannot quote the whole dream, nor do I want to frag-
ment it. It has to be read. The best thing I can do is to
single out a point here and there.

The dream is first of all a shift, into the sleeping mind
and its organizing powers, of the perfectly natural outer
forms in which the poet found himself. He was sitting in
a cave by the shore, reading a book—*Don Quixote*—and
meditating about poetry and geometry as two forms of
"the knowledge that endures." On this the dream begins
its construction.

The man with the lance who rides into the center of
the dream is an Arab of the desert, and as the dream pro-
ceeds he gradually becomes also Don Quixote—both at one
and the same time. Thus epic enters the dream and the
poem in yet another form; this time it is not Homer or
Milton but Cervantes, while the Arab figures in his per-

son those tales of imagination from the East which Wordsworth is to celebrate explicitly four hundred lines later. Indeed it is hard not to see in this double figure a cunning dream pun on the name "Arabian Nights." [56] He carries a stone and a shell; inanimate and animate nature, and yet also quite simple properties of any seashore. The Arab tells the questioning "I" that "in the language of the Dream" both stone and shell are books. The former is (not "symbolizes" but *"is"*) Euclid's elements. The inanimate structure embodies the book or language of mathematics, of which it is said that it

> held acquaintance with the stars
> And wedded man to man by purest bond
> Of nature, undisturbed by space and time;
>
> [104–6]

a voice of nature binding man to the stars and to his fellow man. We are not told what the shell is. It appears "of a surpassing brightness." After the Arab has said that the first object is geometry he says only of the second as he points to it, "This . . . this other . . . this Book is something of more worth." Then, when held to the questioner's ear on the Arab's invitation, the shell, as shells do, gives out sound,

> in an unknown tongue,
> Which yet I understood, articulate sounds,
> A loud prophetic blast of harmony,
> An Ode, in passion utter'd, which foretold
> Destruction to the Children of the Earth,
> By deluge now at hand.

The organic structure, a product of the earth no less than the stone is, begins to speak a language unknown to man and yet capable of interpretation. This is once again the Baconian point at which nature may be made to speak,

or Shelley's figure of Earth crying that language is a per-
petual song. And we feel the mind progress, as if by evo-
lution, through these six lines, growing in power of com-
prehension, advancing from an unknown tongue to artic-
ulation, then prophecy, then poetry itself in the form of
ode; and its subject is an epic one, Noah, Deucalion, or
Utnapishtim. But we are not told that the shell is poetry
or language or myth. It is bright, it is precious, it utters;
the comment on it is:

> Th' other that was a God, yea many Gods,
> Had voices more than all the winds, and was
> A joy, a consolation and a hope.

There is power and myth, a language which like the first
is embedded in nature, and in human nature no less. The
1850 version makes this even clearer by saying, instead of
that last line, that it had power

> To exhilarate the spirit, and to soothe
> Through every clime, the heart of human kind.

The two languages, logic and postlogic or mathematics
and poetry, are languages of nature; and they are also lan-
guages between man and nature and between man and
man. There is no question of their being opposed to one
another. Both, the poet says, are treasures, and the Arab
is on his way to bury both to save them from the apoc-
alyptic menace with which the dream closes as dreams so
often do, the authentic touch of nightmare in that "bed
of glittering light" (as 1850 has it) along the horizon, the
waters of all the world advancing to destroy dream and
dreamer who wakes in terror only to find the quiet wak-
ing world as he had left it a moment before.

This is the first provisional conclusion on method in
the poem: that each language is a treasure of the earth
but that poetry is the more valuable (as if our word, *post-*

logic, might here receive additional justification). The re-
mainder of the poem is a further investigation of this.

Faithful to its purpose, the poem accomplishes this in
the first place by the continuation of the autobiography.
Book v ends, more or less, Wordsworth's account of his
formal education (he discusses the education of children
in a long passage in this book, from line 223 onward).
Now come other shaping forces and fields of action: travel
in Europe and a glimpse of France in 1790, in the first
flush of revolutionary fervor; then London, "preceptress
stern" who instructs on the quality and nature of man in
cities and society; then further experience in France, with
the poet now deeply involved in personal and political
responsibility. This development demands an extension
and deepening of the methods of postlogical thought and
interpretation. To this Wordsworth proceeds through the
"forms." He gives much care to describing in the early
books how in his childhood the roots were laid of that ac-
tive community of outer and inner forms which was to
be his great method of interpretation.[57] This is, in Words-
worth's scheme, the fundamental dynamic or myth of the
mind, but it too has to grow as the mind and the life grow.
It proves to be capable of this development. The inter-
change of forms moves forward as the living mind does,
the mind of individual or of the whole species, from the
fields of inanimate and animate nature to those of social
life, politics, and history.

> By slow gradations towards human kind
> And to the good and ill of human life;
> Nature had led me on.
>
> [VIII.861–63]

The logic and postlogic theme engaged Wordsworth
upon one of the great methodological endeavors of the
Orphic line. This is another. It is to be seen in Erasmus

Darwin's *Temple of Nature* as in Goethe's *Urworte*, the attempt to shape a metamorphic morphology of human life in its due place in the cosmos. Above all, however, this line goes back to Ovid, whom, we may remember, Wordsworth loved. In the *Metamorphoses* is the classic vision of the continuity of forms in nature from rock and tree and beast and bird up to contemporary politics, with metamorphosis as the dynamic of the process and myth as the instrument capable of conforming to and hence interpreting this immense range of Protean subject matter. And for Ovid, Orpheus, the poet, is at the crucial point of transformation between natural and social forms.

Wordsworth works to develop this vision. First, he alters the proportion or emphasis. Ovid's work, we saw, divided in a proportion of 3:2, the larger proportion devoted to natural history, the smaller to human doings. Wordsworth gives this quite another turn. In his poem the pre-occupation with nature as against human nature is 5:8 in 1805 (Books I–V, VI–XIII), and 5:9 in 1850 because of the rearranging and numbering of the later books (Books I–V, VI–XIV). It is an indication of the growing need for the development and investigation of the thought in these fields. The subject is discussed at length in Book VIII, which has the title "Retrospect: Love of Nature leading to Love of Mankind." Further, he draws out Ovid's concept of the poet as the mediator between the forms, natural and social, and shows something of what that concept implies.

The two themes come together in a late passage on methodology, Book XII in 1805, XIII in 1850 which is the more interesting version and from which I quote.

> Nature for all conditions wants not power
> To consecrate, if we have eyes to see,
> The outside of her creatures, and to breathe

Grandeur upon the very humblest face
Of human life. I felt that the array
Of act and circumstance and visible form
Is mainly to the pleasure of the mind
What passion makes them; that meanwhile the forms
Of Nature have a passion in themselves,
That intermingles with those works of man
To which she summons him; although the works
Be mean, have nothing lofty of their own;
And that the Genius of the Poet hence
May boldly take his way among mankind
Wherever Nature leads; that he hath stood
By Nature's side among the men of old,
And so shall stand for ever.

[283-99]

At the working point of the forms the poet is to be found, and has always been found there from the time of the Ancients onwards. So the poet is knit up with this work of nature, but that is not all. Wordsworth goes on:

Dearest Friend!
If thou partake the animating faith
That Poets, even as Prophets, each with each
Connected in a mighty scheme of truth,
Have each his own peculiar faculty,
Heaven's gift, a sense that fits him to perceive
Objects unseen before, thou wilt not blame
The humblest of this band who dares to hope
That unto him hath also been vouchsafed
An insight that in some sort he possesses,
A privilege whereby a work of his,
Proceeding from a source of untaught things,
Creative and enduring, may become
A power like one of Nature's.

[299-312]

This is both a statement of the Orphic tradition and an example of its continuity. That poets and poetry are a work of nature has been said by Orphic voices many times; by the Romantics about Shakespeare; by Goethe about Ovid and about himself; by Emerson. Here it is Wordsworth's turn to say so. He does so first in connection with books in his own Book v, where books are said to be

> only less
> For what we may become, and what we need,
> Than Nature's self, which is the breath of God.
>
> [220–22]

Earlier he gives examples, Homer whom he calls the Thunderer, linking him thus with myth and with the greatest of all nature's inarticulate voices; then "the voice / That roars along the bed of Jewish song"; the "low and wren-like warblings" of folk song. Each is a different voice of nature.

The voice is the clue. Not merely the poet and the thinking mind but language itself comes up out of the earth, as it were, bearing its own continuity with the natural forms and at the very point of translation of those forms into the social ones. This was already part of the shell's revelation in the dream, uttering as it did there a sound, voice, or language, at first unknown, then, as the ear grew attuned to it, revealing itself as poetry, which is what language, as a natural form, must be. One phrase should be remembered—that the shell "had voices more than all the winds." This idea of a continuity not only of forms but of voices or language in nature is present in the poem *Power of Sound* which we looked at earlier, where Orpheus appears. Here, besides the shell in the dream, it is taken up in two other passages which carry forward not only the image of voices and winds in nature but also the

whole tradition at this Ovidian and Orphic point. This
is the first:

> for I would walk alone,
> In storm, in tempest, or in starlight nights
> Beneath the quiet Heavens; and at that time
> Have felt whate'er there is of power in sound
> To breathe an elevated mood, by form
> Or image unprofaned; and I would stand,
> Beneath some rock, listening to sounds that are
> The ghostly language of the ancient earth,
> Or make their dim abode in distant winds.
> Thence did I drink the visionary power.
> I deem not profitless these fleeting moods
> Of shadowy exultation: not for this,
> That they are kindred to our purer mind
> And intellectual life; but that the soul,
> Remembering how she felt, but what she felt
> Remembering not, retains an obscure sense
> Of possible sublimity, to which
> With growing faculties she doth aspire,
> With faculties still growing, feeling still
> That whatsoever point they gain, they still
> Have something to pursue.

[II.321–41]

This is by no means an easy passage, but we can catch
glimpses: the language of the earth, akin to spirit as the
word "ghostly" suggests, stretching back to age beyond
all human Ancients, the mind stirred by it stretching
forward, in evolution, to growing powers and achieve-
ments; power residing in the effect of the earth-voice upon
the mind, arousing there a corresponding power which,
visionary and exulting, does not lose its kinship with the
reason but is part of that too. The central passage, how-

ever, for our purposes here is that where language, winds, power, and shadows hover together. These are taken forward in the closely connected lines in Book v:

>   he who, in his youth,
> A wanderer among the woods and fields,
> With living Nature hath been intimate,
> Not only in that raw unpractis'd time
> Is stirr'd to ecstasy, as others are,
> By glittering verse; but, he doth furthermore,
> In measure only dealt out to himself,
> Receive enduring touches of deep joy
> From the great Nature that exists in works
> Of mighty Poets. Visionary Power
> Attends upon the motions of the winds
> Embodied in the mystery of words.
> There darkness makes abode, and all the host
> Of shadowy things do work their changes there,
> As in a mansion like their proper home;
> Even forms and substances are circumfused
> By that transparent veil with light divine;
> And through the turnings intricate of Verse,
> Present themselves as objects recognis'd,
> In flashes, and with a glory scarce their own.

>   [v.610–29]

Here power is abroad like the winds in that deep and shadowy gulf of the mind, but now the breathing abyss and the intellectual power and the words are one. Wordsworth, as Orphic voices have done so often before, brings postlogic home to words and language, and sets in the mysterious workings of the mind and language all the action of the Baconian forms and the Ovidian metamorphoses, the Shakespearean transformations and mutations. But this remarkable passage is interesting in another way. Portraying the mind as a working abyss of creation and change, it forms part of the development of Wordsworth's epic vision described in the *Excursion* preface, where the Orphic task becomes the exploration of that mind, seen as a chasm of more-than-Miltonic chaos. This image also leads forward to the final emblem of *The Prelude,* which takes this form.

Here is for Wordsworth the heart of postlogic, its central operative field of power. He seems to need a concept or name for it, akin to poetry yet not professionally tied to it. It is part of the greatness of this work that although for its author words were "a passion and a power" [58] he does not make the working of the mind a technical poetic business, but maintains the breadth of his inquiry into genius itself as a more generalized power. Now in Book VI the name and vision of this power rise before him, with a dramatic suddenness, and out of the abyss itself. Wordsworth has just crossed the Alps and is confronting (once again actually, not just in a daydream) those mighty heights and depths.

> Imagination! lifting up itself
> Before the eye and progress of my Song
> Like an unfather'd vapour; here that Power,
> In all the might of its endowments, came
> Athwart me.
>
> [525–29]

There, all at once, is the name. But the 1850 wording is even more significant:

> Imagination—here the Power so called
> Through sad incompetence of human speech,
> That awful Power rose from the mind's abyss
> Like an unfathered vapour that enwraps,
> At once, some lonely traveller.
>
> [592–96]

The name is there; so is the dissatisfaction with it, as if
the power he conceives is more than this term generally
implies. To this he will return at the end of the poem.
The term meanwhile appears fairly frequently in the text
from now on, while "Imagination, How Impaired and
Restored" will title two of the books themselves. Then
in the last book it receives its ultimate embodiment and
commentary.

The opening lines describe the quintessential Words-
worthian landscape, mountains, mist, water, sky, ocean,
with a few figures—the poet, his friend, a shepherd and
his dog. The final emblem is again autobiography, and
takes the form of a journey in outer and inner landscape.
(The formal beauty of the construction of the poem as a
whole should not be overlooked.) The company sets out
on a misty summer night to climb Snowdon. After a long
ascent they suddenly come out of the fog into bright moon-
light, to see range after range of hills at their feet above
the mist; beyond this, the Atlantic, the great globe itself;
above their heads a sky glorious with moon and the full
company of stars. The description ends with the sight of
a break in the mist, "a blue chasm, a fracture in the va-
pour" the 1805 text says; this is the 1850 description:

> through a rift—
> Not distant from the shore on which we stood,—
> A fixed, abysmal, gloomy breathing-place,
> Mounted the roar of waters, torrents, streams,
> Innumerable, roaring with one voice!
> Heard over earth and sea and in that hour,
> For so it seemed, felt by the starry heavens.
>
> [56–62]

1805 adds one touch to that:

> in that breach
> Through which the homeless voice of waters rose,

> That deep dark thoroughfare, had Nature lodg'd
> The Soul, the Imagination of the whole.

The whole universe is drawn together in this emblem, the last and most all-embracing union of inner and outer forms. This is the chasm of the mind, no abstraction but a breathing-place and a power involving the entire universe. Wordsworth goes on to say so, and it is one of the marvels of this last book that his philosophical discourse here, in the 1850 text, is as powerful and beautiful as the emblem itself.

> When into air had partially dissolved
> That vision, given to spirits of the night
> And three chance human wanderers, in calm thought
> Reflected, it appeared to me the type
> Of a majestic intellect, its acts
> And its possessions, what it has and craves,
> What in itself it is, and would become.
> There I beheld the emblem of a mind
> That feeds upon infinity, that broods
> Over the dark abyss, intent to hear
> Its voices issuing forth to silent light
> In one continuous stream; a mind sustained
> By recognitions of transcendent power,
> In sense conducting to ideal form,
> In soul of more than mortal privilege.
>
> [63–77]

Commentary here becomes impertinent; but we might notice that Wordsworth is saying in his own way what Coleridge said about thinking, that it was self-observation; notice also that the poet's image of the mind draws close to an image of God. A line or two later the poem continues:

> The power, which all
> Acknowledge when thus moved, which Nature thus

To bodily sense exhibits, is the express
Resemblance of that glorious faculty
That higher minds bear with them as their own.
This is the very spirit in which they deal
With the whole compass of the universe:
They from their native selves can send abroad
Kindred mutations; for themselves create
A like existence.

[86–95]

This is the last and most enigmatic of the "strange muta-
tions" of the world of which Edgar spoke in *King Lear,*
and an epitome of evolution: the entire universe as the
narrative of the mind. Wordsworth goes on reassuringly
to speak of the ordinariness of that mind, its capacity to
make use of all its store of everyday life, its humanity.
Then he speaks the logical conclusion of what he has been
saying so far:

Such minds are truly from the Deity,
For they are Powers; and hence the highest bliss
That flesh can know is theirs—the consciousness
Of Whom they are, habitually infused
Through every image and through every thought.

[112–16]

This is not lip service to religion added in later life. It
is in 1805 as well, which says explicitly, "hence religion,
faith" (xiii.111). What it is is an incredibly bold hypothesis
concerning the relation between nature, mind, and God.[59]
If we do not pursue this, it is not because it is unimpor-
tant (the same thing is true of the great political themes
and books of *The Prelude* [60] which I have omitted here).
It is because this is a branch of the Orphic inquiry we
cannot hope to deal with yet. But it is waiting for those
who can, with a power that can in some sort match the
power Wordsworth here conjures and commands.

Keeping to our own limited methodology, we have one or two things more to see. The poem after this great magnificence (and it is no accident that the later version has more of this than the earlier) quiets down, as epic tends to do at its close; and on the way, Wordsworth adds a note or two upon imagination, which has now come to appear as "the main essential Power," as 1805 says (XIII. 289). The poet says that this is what we have been tracing all along:

> This faculty hath been the feeding source
> Of our long labour;
>
> [1850, XIV.193]

the object and the means, in that image, of this long research. He goes on:

> This spiritual Love acts not nor can exist
> Without Imagination, which, in truth,
> Is but another name for absolute power
> And clearest insight, amplitude of mind,
> And Reason in her most exalted mood.

This is Wordsworth's later comment upon his own sense that imagination was an unsatisfactory term, because it made a division where none was. In the last resort logic and postlogic are a united faculty; the union of the stone and the shell is taken further, and further than we can follow it with our present halting psychologies. To this fusion Wordsworth admits love, as part of the methodology of thought:

> Imagination having been our theme,
> So also hath that intellectual Love,
> For they are each in each, and cannot stand
> Dividually
>
> [206–9]

Love is part of the nature of the mind and its workings and powers, as the Orphic tradition has always maintained; and it is to the mind that we are finally directed in this poem, as the point at which nature is to work her further transformations, the mind which, for all Wordsworth's passion for nature, is given unquestioned precedence, in its beauty, its fabric, and its future, all of which are, Wordsworth says, divine.

So ends Wordsworth's Orphic song, taking its place in the evolution of the research that poetry conducts into the nature of mind and world. It is Keats who can sum up for us:

> We "feel the burden of the Mystery". To this point was Wordsworth come, as far as I can conceive, when he wrote "Tintern Abbey" and it seems to me that his Genius is explorative of those dark Passages. Now if we live, and go on thinking, we too shall explore them—he is a Genius and superior [to] us, in so far as he can, more than we, make discoveries and shed a light in them—Here I must think Wordsworth is deeper than Milton—though I think it has depended more upon the general and gregarious advance of intellect, than individual greatness of Mind.[61]

Keats is right; however great the Orphic vision, there is always more to be done.

7

Mythology, like the severed head of Orpheus, goes on singing even in death and from afar

IN THE *Sonette an Orpheus* we meet the Orphic research in an unprecedented form. Up till now the figure of Orpheus has been a general clue to what was going on in Orphic minds, but the figure appears as sideways and glancing illumination rather than as cynosure, and the work has usually been steady and prolonged. It was so with Wordsworth. His research into the mind took the form of a long inquiry into a long and steady process, and in him Orpheus is associated with epic. With Rilke we have something entirely different. Instead of a long process we have a sudden lyric spasm concentrated into a mere moment of time in which this extraordinary Orphic explosion takes place, and from which issues Part I of the *Sonette an Orpheus.*

I am going to take Part I of these Sonnets, and it alone, as the climax of Rilke's mythological work and his true Orphic pronouncement. Part II, which followed at a slightly more leisurely rate the bursting-forth of Part I, is much more diffuse (you can see it in the rhythms even and it is longer than Part I, twenty-nine sonnets as against twenty-six), philosophizing, and commentational; we shall

use it as occasional comment but no more. Part 1 was writ-
ten within three days, between February 2 and 5 in 1922,
and what it would mean to write twenty-six beautifully
shaped sonnets in three days will perhaps be fully ap-
preciated only by those who have tried to write even one
careful sonnet; eighteen working hours upon one such is
nothing, to speak from my own experience. What Rilke
produced was a work of art in which scarcely any changes
were needed and which has form as a whole, quite apart
from the individual units. A fully Orphic sonnet stands
at the beginning and the end of the series, the only two
which deal exclusively with the traditional myth. Within
this work Rilke's Orphic task is accomplished. But not
merely what he says but the phenomenon is significant
too. The figure of Orpheus occasions here twenty-six son-
nets upon the modern Orphic theme, and also an extraor-
dinary spurt of energy and fertility in the living organism.
We have, as we go forward, to remember and hold to both.

Rilke himself is self-contradictory about the whole ex-
perience, which involved, over those three weeks, the com-
pletion of the *Duineser Elegien* as well. He knew himself
to be full of contradictions, which he wished to preserve
intact.[62] It is useful to realize this from the start, for it
makes him an unreliable guide to himself, and we have
been much too ready to take over his self-interpretations,
which are only partial. He is in this respect quite unlike
Wordsworth. Wordsworth knew in general very well what
he was about, and can tell us. Rilke cannot. His letters
over the years show a mind tenacious of its purpose but
for the most part groping blindly forward, deeply per-
plexed at its own bewilderment and long spells of im-
potence. Once he likens himself, in words that remind
one of Goethe and his concept of his own mental organ-
ism, to something growing out in radiate form from a
center, but he adds, "And in this no other person may

watch him, his nearest and dearest particularly, for he may not even do so himself" [63]—and this from one of the most conscientiously introspective minds imaginable. So also, in that much-quoted letter to his Polish translator, Witold von Hulewicz, of November 13, 1925, he says, "And is it *I* who may give the Elegies their right explanation?" and then goes on to give an explanation of Elegies and Sonnets which is endorsed again and again in critical works on these poems. But Rilke's statements are frequently as ambiguous as his poetry may be, and it is best to recognize this frankly.

Of the *Sonette an Orpheus* we find Rilke saying first of all that they were dictation, "perhaps the most mysterious . . . enigmatic dictation I have ever held through and achieved." [64] The idea of dictation is not new to Rilke. In 1920 he had written a series of poems which he called *Aus dem Nachlass des Grafen C.W.*, choosing to believe or make believe that they had come to him by dictation from one who was dead. [65] It implies a theory of poetic inspiration which is ultimately that of possession by a power in some sense other than the self. It removes inspiration, poetic or otherwise, from the ordinary run of human experience and ranges it among extrahuman or suprahuman experiences. This is a notion of inspiration which to some extent poets have fostered, but it is not helpful. It runs counter to the constant declarations of great poets that they are not different from other people; counter also to the whole Orphic tradition as we have traced it out here, in which poetry is a part of the great general endeavor of thinking and inquiry. Inspiration, whatever it may be, is at the root of science and all true thinking, and it should be possible to keep such an experience as Rilke's within the great current, as an interesting but not exceptional example of something which forms part of the way in which the human organism of

mind and body thinks and learns. (At another level al-
together, it is worth observing that Catholic theology of
inspiration in the Scriptures does not entail a concept of
"direct dictation" by the Holy Spirit, but rather a process
which, divine though it is, conforms to normal human ways
of thinking, learning, and writing.)

The experience which Rilke called dictation and to
which the term "inspiration" is frequently applied by
critics, consists in an apparently sudden access of power
and fertility resulting from the apprehension by the mind
(in this case a recognition, though sometimes it may be an
invention that is called for) of a figure which synthesizes
a great deal of earlier material already experienced and
learned, and held ready in the mind. Put in this way, the
experience tallies with what we know of cases of scientific
discovery, and with what we call having an idea. We know
that such discoveries and ideas do not appear out of no-
where, despite the dramatic suddenness with which they
may make themselves known [66] to the recipient mind, and
it is interesting to find Rilke saying this about his own
experience. When sending the *Sonette an Orpheus* to a
friend at the end of the momentous February of their com-
position, he says in the accompanying letter, "Here, it
seems to me, things have taken on form which date from
a long way back . . . Much that could gradually and
perfectly smoothly illuminate itself, and alongside, close
alongside, the immediate and direct elements which be-
came clear to me from the very first moment of the under-
taking." [67] This poetic experience too, like those other
experiences in thought to which it may be closely akin,
was the result of preparatory and prefiguring work within
the organism. In organic change and growth there can be
no absolute disjunction between what precedes and what
follows. Yet novelty does ensue, and it may be that it is
as some sort of organic change that we could visualize an

idea, in Rilke's case or elsewhere. It is this sort of change which the *Sonette* exhibit, and it is exciting to find Orpheus at the heart of the situation.

The Orpheus who so suddenly broke into Rilke's poetry in 1922—"the 'Sonnets to Orpheus' . . . stormily imposed themselves (they were *not* in my plan)" Rilke says in the von Hulewicz letter—was not a complete newcomer. He was, as we have seen, in Rilke's mind and poetry eighteen years earlier. The Orpheus of *Orpheus. Eurydike. Hermes* is a preliminary marker in a succession of happenings in Rilke's mental life. This earlier poem was not just, we remember, a retelling of the mythological narrative. There seemed then to be a change going on inside the myth itself, as it and mind worked on one another, toward the third and last stage of the story. In 1904 Rilke is, in his own terms, fore-thinking or pre-thinking what he is not yet capable of thinking—*Vor-denken* he calls it,[68] an admirable phrase which makes it unnecessary to entertain any notion of unconsciousnesses or subconsciousnesses in the mind. Now in 1922 what was there forethought can be taken up, added to all that has been thought and learned in the intervening years, and given new and more vital shape. In 1922 Rilke comes through Orpheus to his real theme.

For the real theme is not Orpheus himself. When one asks oneself the rather naive question what the Sonnets are really about, the answer is surprising. They are not *about* Orpheus, with the exception of the first and last sonnets of Part I, which tell the Orphic story. They are addressed *to* Orpheus. They are also intended by their author to be a memorial to Wera Ouckama Knoop, a young girl, a dancer, who had recently died and whose story he had been reading just before the Sonnets broke upon him. They are not, however, with the exception of one sonnet in each part, *about* her either. They commemorate her. When it comes to the point, there is only one theme that can be thought of as common to them all, with their widely varied subject matter (stars, animals, fruit and flowers, machines, the spring, and so on). This theme, the true subject of the *Sonette,* is metamorphosis.

It is characteristic of Rilke and his contradictions that in the end his subject matter proves to be abstract. His "thing-piety," a devotion to objects large or small, living or nonliving, in all their detail and individuality,[69] which reaches its height in the *Neue Gedichte* of 1907 and 1908, has obscured from us how abstract a poet he is, though the Elegies proclaim it all the way through, and explicitly in the Ninth, where "things" are to be "said" to the Angel who in Rilke is an abstract personification of power and intelligence at an infinite degree, supposedly purified of any theological taint in the concept. Earth, it says here, is to reach its fulfillment by becoming invisible within the human mind:

> Erde, ist es nicht dies was du willst: *unsichtbar*
> in uns erstehn?

a message taken up in Rilke's letters more than once.[70] (It is helpful here to remember Mallarmé, Rilke's immediate predecessor in the Orphic line, and what he was trying to do in the way of making the world disappear in his poetry.) Rilke's passion for abstraction tends to vaporize his poetry; also, at times, the criticism which is written about that poetry, much of which is philosophising to an excessive degree. This is a misfortune, for Rilke is a lyric poet through and through, by vocation. Immediately, though, we need to be clear about what that means. It does not mean that he is precluded from thinking by such a vocation. Not in the very least. An Orphic lyrist is not a gusher of imagery and sentiments. What it does mean is that he must do his thinking strictly in lyric, in concentratedly poetic, postlogical, mythological terms. It is at this exact point that Orpheus and Rilke meet and soar together.

We can see now how the Sonnets come to be the consummation of that union of myth and mind foreshadowed in 1904. There are hints of Rilke's negative tendencies still in them, though more in Part II than in Part I. Even in Part I the abstractness may become obtrusive (as in 12, for instance), but Rilke is blessed in his key figures. The girl brings with her two real forms of metamorphosis, dancing and death; and in the myth Rilke's theme fuses perfectly with his figure. Here once for all the Orphic myth comes into its own, a vast improvement on the angels of the Elegies, figures which do nothing for the mind. Now also we can see the reason for that tentative move in the earlier poem toward the third stage of the story. These Sonnets rise to their triumphant ending in Sonnet 26, celebrating Orpheus in death and destruction and what came after. Comment and statement are needed no more. Here Orpheus undergoes, or to put it another way, becomes metamorphosis himself, passing through an agony of dismemberment into earth and water and stars and so into the elements and all living things, in which henceforward the Orphic song and power abide. So, and only so, by means of this third figure of the myth itself, is the lyric thinker enabled to pursue, in terms which yet are wholly poetic, a highly abstract and difficult inquiry into metamorphosis in nature, to which he too, as body and mind, is subject.

This is Rilke's task in the line of Orphic research. Once again, as in Goethe and Wordsworth, the poet's life is involved, though Rilke's involvement is different from theirs. His Orpheus is not merely a figure of transformation in nature but also a marker of a mutation point in the development of the poet's nature. Once again, too, nature is to include mind, and the organic metamorphoses must be interpreted in those terms. The myth itself says this, for besides the bodily reintegration with the universe in the cycles of life and death, there is the figure of the head, the lyre, the speech and singing which also return to the elements and yet persist in their own forms. It seems that in Wordsworth and Rilke two different rhythms of total organic growth are being studied. Wordsworth was intent upon the "origins and progress of his mind." The growth of organisms and minds, however, can be thought of in different ways. One such way is to see growth as a steady process, involving change, of course, but slowly and gradually. Another way is to see it in terms of varying degrees of transformation, as plant-stuff is transformed in leaf and flower, those metamorphoses which Goethe watched in his pursuit of a transformational morphology that was to include humanity as well.

This is the way in which Rilke will work, for whom, as we have seen, "life is self-transformation." His own mind works so; and he will work on this subject. Orpheus of the third figure attends him at both points, and what this means is very important. In these poems myth in its most intrinsic and traditional form is reclaimed from the over-specialization into which Freudian psychology and Frazerian anthropology might narrow it. It is not solely the expression of erotic drives in the individual, nor of fertility rites in society. Not denying those two perhaps kindred motives, which it carries along with it, myth in the form of Orpheus (who is, we may remind ourselves, myth thinking about myth) is reinstated by the poet at the heart of the organism's process of growing and learning. What Rilke suggests in and through Orpheus is a morphogenesis of the organic life of the mind, an Orphic epistemology whose dynamic is that of metamorphoses in a continuum.

His preoccupation with metamorphosis (the word *Met-*

amorphose is in evidence in his work as early as 1907) [71] links him especially closely with two of his Orphic ancestors, Ovid and Goethe. Ovid he seems to have known and valued early.[72] He shares with him the concern with metamorphosis itself, the commanding position of Orpheus, the building in of sex as part of the methodology, of which we shall see more in a while, and there is a pure and beautiful Ovidian echo in II.12:

> Und die verwandelte Daphne
> will, seit sie lorbeern fühlt, dass du dich wandelst in
> Wind.

> (And Daphne, translated,
> in her laurelling self-awareness wants you to turn
> yourself into wind.)

This sonnet as a whole is a commentary on the main Ovidian theme. The German language has borrowed *Metamorphose* from the Greek, but it has two words of its own that fall within this range of meaning. They appear here as nouns, *Wandlung* and *Verwandlung,* in the first two lines:

> Wolle die Wandlung. O sei für die Flamme begeistert,
> drin sich ein Ding dir entzieht, das mit Verwand-
> lungen prunkt;

> (Be absolute for change. O be fervent for flame,
> in which a thing leaves you for good as it flaunts its
> transmutings)

and the nouns are answered by the verbs in the last two lines already quoted: *wandeln,* which contains a sense of both movement and change, and *verwandeln,* which means "to transform." When Rilke discovers another Orphic ancestor, Hölderlin, in 1914, and writes a poem to him,[73] he will apostrophize him as "O du wandelnder Geist, du wandelndster!", the most changing spirit of them all, and will give him for his image the moon, which shows forth those two senses of the word, movement and change both.

When we come to the other great Orphic ancestor Rilke owns to, Goethe, we find that Rilke's relationship to him constitutes in itself a metamorphosis. It seems to have begun in 1910. In that year Rilke writes to Anton Kippenberg, "I read Goethe all through the journey, (I was alone all the time), the *Tag- und Jahreshefte;* starting from this point, as with the Diaries, I get really close to him, and he bears with me then, just as if this was how things were meant to be." [74] It is borne out by the later references to Goethe in the letters that it is the Orphic Goethe who effects the rapprochement; not the Goethe of the great set pieces but the observing self-taxonomic and scientific Goethe in his Ovidian research. (Kretschmar in his *Goethe und Rilke* says that Rilke had known Goethe early, as a literary figure, reading *Die Wahlverwandschaften* at the age of sixteen, then later, *Wilhelm Meisters Lehrjahre;* then reacted against him during the period of production of the *Stundenbuch, Neue Gedichte* and *Malte Laurids Brigge.*) [75] In August 1911 Rilke visited Weimar, encouraged by the Kippenbergs, who played a large part in Rilke's education here. A month later he is saying in a letter to another friend, "Goethe was for the first time propitious." [76] In February 1912 Rilke says in a letter to Lou Andreas-Salomé, "The ban against him [Goethe] was already broken in July," and he goes on to discuss, with a sense of fellow feeling and an admission of how much it had moved him, the *Italienische Reise.* A year and a half later he is quoting to the same correspondent one of Goethe's *Venezianische Epigramme* and adding, "I need to realize that greatness is not superhuman exertion but naturalness." [77] His relationship with the Orphic Goethe progresses to 1919, when, six months before he wrote his essay *Ur-Geräusch* as Kretschmar points out, that essay with its splendidly Goethean prefix [78] (*Geräusch* is noise, but in the form of muted murmur or rustle—an *Ur-*rustling) he is reading the *Metamorphose der Pflanzen*, as he tells Lou Andreas-Salomé in a letter of February 21. He runs through as if by instinct the whole of Goethe's Ovidian and taxonomic work—the journals, the Italian Journey, the *Metamorphose der Pflanzen*, the lyric poems.[79]

Yet during these intervening years Rilke is not merely tracing out the Ovidian metamorphic line in others, nor merely thinking about it himself. His life is caught up in it as well. One poem of his, written in 1914, shows this particularly well. It is called *Wendung,* which is a turning or turning-point. In this meditation the poet reconsiders his entire living methodology. The poem is quiet, not very well-known. It is, I think, one of the most just and beautiful poems Rilke has written.

"Lange errang ers im Anschauen," it begins— Long he wrested out what he wanted by effort of looking. *Anschauen* is a favorite word of Goethe's: observation, contemplation, the long, deep, exact, loving looking of the morphologizing eye. Indeed the poem as a whole, with its concentration and the short irregular lines, reminds one insistently of the *Harzreise*. In Rilke as the poem advances it is first to the stars that the looking is directed, wrestling with them till they are brought to their knees, or alternatively the observer kneeling to look and receive a glimpse of a godhead, a sleeping smile. There is already a flexibility of effort and receptivity, and in the next paragraph (if that is the right word) of the poem there is a suggestion of an almost Wordsworthian interchangeability of inward and outward forms—towers and landscapes—in the looker's mind. The poem goes on:

Tiere traten getrost
in den offenen Blick, weidende,
und die gefangenen Löwen
starrten hinein wie in
    unbegreifliche Freiheit;
Vögel durchflogen ihn grad,
den gemütigen; Blumen
wiederschauten in ihn
gross wie in Kinder.

Beasts took comfort and came
into that open glance, for pasture,
captive lions stared in
as into ungraspable freedom;

birds flew straight through it,
it, the consenting; flowers
gazed back into the glance,
big as in children's.

  Und das Gerücht, dass ein
    Schauender sei,
rührte die minder,
fraglicher Sichtbaren,
rührte die Frauen.

  And the rumor, a seer was here,

stirred the less visible things,
the less certainly visible things,
stirred the women.

And then comes a passage saying this is not enough. Wherever he is, a stranger in strange rooms, something abroad in the air deliberates over his heart and passes sentence that love is lacking. He continues:

Denn des Anschauens, siehe,
    ist eine Grenze.
Und die geschautere Welt
will in der Liebe gedeihn.

For, see, there's a limit to look-
    ing.
And the much-looked-at world
wishes to blossom in love.

Werk des Gesichts ist getan,
tue nun Herz-Werk
an den Bildern in dir,
    jenen gefangenen; denn du
überwältigtest sie: aber nun
    kennst du sie nicht.
Siehe, innerer Mann, dein in-
    neres Mädchen,
dieses errungene aus
tausend Naturen, dieses
erst nur errungene, nie
noch geliebte Geschöpf.

Face-work is finished,
do now the heart-work
on those pictures imprisoned
    within you; for you
mastered them, yes: but, as of
    now, you don't know them.
Behold, oh innermost man, your
    innermost maiden,
fought for and won from
thousands of natures, she that was
only won up till now, and never
    as yet
a creature beloved.

This poem, coming almost halfway between the two Orpheus occurrences in Rilke's work, sums up what is going on. It is about metamorphosis. In it the poet enjoins a further metamorphosis upon himself, a moving on from observation to some deeper, more loving and more human interpretation which the poem speaks of as "heart-work." Yet there is continuity here too, for the poem reverts to one after another of Rilke's abiding subjects—stars, landscape, lions, birds, flowers, women. It is also prophetic, in that final glimpse of some kind of inner feminine principle as the means by which the new understanding might be achieved. All this waits for the *Sonette,* and we see in this poem something of what an individual poem always is in the life of the poet, a metamorphosis or true *Wendung* yet embedded in a continuum, complete in itself but preparing always some further metamorphosis in the future.

The process continues with Rilke right up till the last moment before the Orpheus Sonnets were to make their startling entrance. In his collected poems, three short lyrics appear [80] which were written on January 31 and February 1, the last gathering, preparatory, prefiguring work before the Orphic outburst began on February 2.

The first of these three, "Solang du Selbstgeworfnes fängst," is, like *Wendung,* self-admonition. (I make no apology for paraphrasing these poems; they are important for what they say, and to recognize this does them no violence.) The poet sees his task here as a game of ball, an image that will recur in the *Sonette,* in II.8. It is of no use, he says, to play by yourself and to catch the ball you have yourself thrown up in the air. Rilke uses the pronoun *du,* the familiar "you," in this poem, not as a sign of self-division but because the admonition concerns others besides the poet. You must suddenly find yourself catching the ball thrown to you by an eternal girl-playmate, "eine

ewige Mit-Spielerin." Only then is the ability to catch
(Rilke turns the poem most elegantly upon the child's
pride and sense of achievement in his ability to catch a
ball) a power, and a power not of your own but of the
world. If you were to have strength and enterprise enough
to throw it back, or better still, he says, to throw it straight
back before you knew you needed either, then and only
then would you be truly joining in the game. Out of your
hands the meteor comes and hurtles into its spaces.

The second is a tiny playful cycle [81] of three sets of verses,
written to accompany a drawing which Rilke himself made
of foliage and a lyre growing out of one another. He is so
close to Orpheus here as to be really tantalizing; but Or-
pheus is still two days off. The first of the three complains,
lightly yet feelingly, of the imposition of speech and song
in the face of the perfection of hearing (*Ur-Geräusch* was
a celebration of the sense of hearing, insufficiently appre-
ciated, Rilke thought, in modern poetry); in face also of
the lovely silence of the myths in the woods, Narcissus or
Artemis. The vignette he drew captures his own question-
ing: Is the lyre really to come out of the trees or to melt
back into them? In the second and third sets of verses it is
the lyre as visual shape that he plays with in a series of
conceits which grow, one feels, out of his actual limning
of the lyre. It is interesting to see Rilke, like Goethe, tak-
ing to the drawing pencil, and of course the two do resem-
ble each other in their lifelong interest in, and sympathy
with, the visual arts. Here in the second and third parts of
this tiny cycle of poems, the lyre after the hand has bent
it into shape out of twigs and branches becomes the horns
of a gazelle but without a head under them—"wo ist das
Haupt?"—the rounded hips of a woman, a vase or pitcher
in the potter's forming hand.

The circle is drawing in. In these two January 31st
poems we have already a great deal: the shadowy woman

who is to explain the world, who *is* the world in some sense, so that only though her, in a reciprocal relationship of action and passivity, can one fully participate and find a power which in the end becomes a shooting star; the lyre growing out of trees and leaves, the animals, woman—real woman here, a real, sexual being—and that tension between hearing and the uttering of language where also the myths are.

It is this last theme which is taken up by the third of these lyrics, "Wann wird, wann wird, wann wird es genügen," which precedes the Sonnets by only twenty-four hours. It repeats the complaint about the necessity of utterance in man. Speech here becomes noise, endless, filling the entire universe. Why, when such masters of human speech have come among us, must we keep on with new attempts? Books, too, are part of the hubbub—Rilke compares them to incessant peals of bells and bids us rejoice if between two of them we get a glimpse of quiet sky or an angle of evening earth. Men have made more din than all the storms and all the seas. What reserves of silence there must be in the universe for the cricket to have remained audible to us at all, for the stars to seem silent in a sky so much cried to! Rilke ends:

> Redeten uns die fernsten, die alten und ältesten Väter!
> Und wir: Hörende endlich! Die ersten hörenden
>   Menschen.
>
> (Time out of mind it was us our fathers and fore-
>   fathers spoke!
> And we: Hearers at length! The very first men to be
>   hearers.)

At this point Rilke is calling in question the whole language tradition from the Ancients onward, with the great minds that have worked in it. He questions books as part of that tradition, seeing an antagonism between books and nature, between language and nature, between the virtue of silent hearing and the dubious gift of speech. It is like Wordsworth, in *The Prelude* and the *Power of Sound;* there Wordsworth answers his own questions, affirmatively for language, but here Orpheus is going to answer them, on Rilke's behalf, and in the near future. For all of these seeming antagonisms are only waiting the Orphic resolution soon to come.

8

Thrace also has much that is essential to one who intends to dance—Orpheus, his dismemberment and his talking head that voyaged on the lyre

.

WHETHER it was Orpheus or Rilke who chose the sonnet cycle as the form of this inquiry, the choice was a good one. It permits repeated lyric utterance, yet at the same time gives a certain length and a serial quality. It is interesting, too, in the history it brings with it, for in Europe it is traditionally where love, intellect, and lyric meet. The rigorous sonnet form is helpful to this alliance, and certainly proves helpful to Rilke. With his consummate craftsmanship, the result of years of devotion, he responds wonderfully to its formal challenge—it is possible to count over a dozen metrical variations in the *Sonette an Orpheus*. It is likely that Rilke's genius was at its best when held fairly closely within certain fixed and formal bounds. (Where I quote from the *Sonette* I am going to put in a translation. There have been a great many translations of these poems already. Mine are, as I have said before in similar circumstances, rough ones, and they are, please, not to be taken in a high or solemn spirit. They were done as much for enjoyment as for any other reason, and I believe that a certain lightness of approach may fit Rilke better than an excess of reverence.)

The three figures of the Orpheus myth, in the succession in which we have been using them here, are going to be our guide to this, the last work we shall be concerned with. The first sonnet of Part 1 contains the first figure; the last sonnet contains the third. Between the two lies the figure of Eurydice, etherealized in death but a woman still.

We will start with Sonnets 1 and 2. They set the whole thing moving; then the series runs on to 11, after which it pauses. There will be another pause later, after 20, the two pauses marked by a correspondence of the figure in each, that of a horse. Yet there is metamorphosis in that figure itself, for the first occurrence asks "Separation?" while the second says "integration" within the whole Orphic cycling of the universe, including nature and mind.

This is Sonnet 1:

Da stieg ein Baum. O reine Übersteigung!
O Orpheus singt! O hoher Baum im Ohr!
Und alles schwieg. Doch selbst in der Verschweigung
ging neuer Anfang, Wink und Wandlung vor.

Tiere aus Stille drangen aus dem klaren
gelösten Wald von Lager und Genist;
und da ergab sich, dass sie nicht aus List
und nicht aus Angst in sich so leise waren,

sondern aus Hören. Brüllen, Schrei, Geröhr,
schien klein in ihren Herzen. Und wo eben
kaum eine Hütte war, dies zu empfangen,

ein Unterschlupf aus dunkelstem Verlangen
mit einem Zugang, dessen Pfosten beben,—
da schufst du ihnen Tempel im Gehör.

(And a tree mounted up—serene surmounter!
O Orpheus sings! Tree, in the ear how high!
And everything fell still. But new encounter
was in that stilling, to move and modify.

Turned into silence, beasts left lair and covert,
came pushing through the bright untangled wood,
and not for wariness, it was discovered,
nor yet for cunning were they being so good,

rather for hearing's sake. Roar, howl and boom
they felt at heart was little. Where was no room
to take this in—a den, scarcely a hovel,

woven of darkest longing, where you grovel
under and in past doorposts quivering tense—
you made them temples in their hearing-sense.)

We start with the sense of hearing, just as we did in Wordsworth's *Power of Sound,* the ear which opens into the labyrinth within the head, within the body which is also mind and which is the kingdom of living and dead. It is here within, quite as much as in the outside world of action (though that is here too in the thronging beasts of the wood) that the Orphic transformations are to begin. First, the human ear and mind respond, and the great tree is raised there by the power of the song. Scaled down as it is to the due level of lyric expression, this is still essentially an epic vision, the new ordering of things already in existence but dark and tangled, which is how ancient thought conceived of creation,[82] seeing it not as a bringing of something out of nothing but as a harmonizing of what was already there, a deeply human rather than super-human way of looking at things. After the human response come the animals, and their sense of hearing too is to be

transformed, from the animal level up to the level of the
human, is to become acceptable to them in the form of
poetry, because they recognize it as a continuation of forms
of their own, thus giving rise to no antagonism—neither
malice nor fear. This transformation which poetry is to
effect will move on into the greater world of social achieve-
ment and beauty which the idea of "Temple" brings with
it. Orpheus is here once more at the true Ovidian point of
metamorphosis or *Metamorphoses,* the evolutionary trans-
formations of the lower orders of nature up through man
into the works of society; for temples are not animal
refuges or human dwelling places called into being under
the stress of need. They are places of communal grace.

This is one turning point in the poem. There is another,
having to do with silence and speech or song. Nature falls
silent, so the first four lines say, but not now for desire to
be rid of the human voice, even at its loveliest, as Rilke
had seemed to desire in the pre-Orpheus poems. Rather
it falls silent for love of that voice as Orpheus sings. Silence
is here not an ultimate but a condition in which better
sounds can be abroad than the inarticulate crying of the
creatures. So we are not merely at the Ovidian, we are also
at the Baconian Orphic point, where nature may be made
to speak [83]—a human language. Orpheus, however, is not
merely poetry but myth as well. Rilke sets this essential
figure of myth, firmly and from the beginning, at the work-
ing point of transformation between the mind and nature,
and we shall meet the myths in general as we go forward
through the Sonnets, in the form of the classical gods who
turn up in strange and significant places.

In Sonnet 2 of Part 1 Rilke begins his own Orphic
speech. As we move on to it, we shall see that for these
poems metamorphosis is not only their theme, it is their
working dynamic. We cannot expect them to proceed in
a simple series by gradual development; instead we un-
dergo metamorphosis at once:

Und fast ein Mädchen wars und ging hervor
aus diesem einigen Glück von Sang und Leier
und glänzte klar durch ihre Frühlingsschleier
und machte sich ein Bett in meinem Ohr.

Und schlief in mir. Und alles war ihr Schlaf.
Die Bäume, die ich je bewundert, diese
fühlbare Ferne, die gefühlte Wiese,
und jedes Staunen, das mich selbst betraf.

Sie schlief die Welt. Singender Gott, wie hast
du sie vollendet, dass sie nicht begehrte,
erst wach zu sein? Sieh, sie erstand und schlief.

Wo ist ihr Tod? O, wirst du dies Motiv
erfinden noch, eh sich dein Lied verzehrte?
Wo sinkt sie hin aus mir? . . . Ein Mädchen fast . . .

(And what came out of it—almost a girl,
From undivided joy of lyre and song,
And through her springtime veils her body pearled,
And in my ear she laid herself along.

And slept in me. Her sleep was all-that-is.
The trees I've always thought miraculous things,
The meadow sensed, the sensible distances,
And all my own frequent self-wonderings.

She slept the world. O singing god, explain
How you perfected her she overstept
Waking, of choice? First came to be, then slept.

Where is her death? O will you catch that strain
Before your song itself becomes a ghost?
She sinks from me . . . where to? . . . a girl
    almost . . .)

Before we single out anything here, we have first to see what an extraordinary thing has happened. There was an "it" or a "this" in the eleventh line of the first sonnet, *dies,* meaning not any one thing but the whole phenomenon or process, all that was going on. It was this that there was no room for till Orpheus made it. The "this" is the Orphic metamorphosis itself. Now that "it," with the same meaning, is here in the first line, in the elided *es* of *wars,* it was. "It" is the entire postlogical process, the power of Orpheus; and what Rilke does with it, most astonishingly, is to turn it into a woman. The poem marvels at its own audacity—"*fast* ein Mädchen wars," it was almost a girl, the little phrase inverted to make the lovely answering cadence of the last line, "ein Mädchen fast." The girl is the power, the dynamic, the form of thinking, the speech and song, for she comes forth from song and lyre. She is bodily sense and its hearing, and her sleep is all the world—trees, fields, the human mind. And unless one sees this, it is quite possible to read these sonnets through without realizing how new and exciting this is.

Here is the first metamorphosis of the Orpheus myth in this cycle, from the first to the second figure. These two will now be elaborated up till the last sonnet but one, which will answer this one in being about a woman, and then all will be gathered in the last sonnet and the third figure. This is as near to Eurydice as we come in Part I. (She makes one entrance, by name, in II.13, "Sei immer tot in Eurydike"—be forever dead in Eurydice.) Instead of obsessing the poetry as she tended to do in *Orpheus. Eurydike. Hermes,* she is dispersed into a beautiful balance, not lost but spread abroad. This can be seen clearly in another poem, *Gegen-Strophen,*[84] one of many Rilke wrote on the subject of women, which was begun in 1912 and finished in 1922. In the part written later there are these lines:

Blumen des tieferen Erdreichs,
von allen Wurzeln geliebte,
ihr, der Eurydike Schwestern,

where women become blossoms of the deeper parts of the world, the beloved of all roots, Eurydice's sisters. It is like the Eurydice of 1904, "made root already," not now a dead weight of return to the kingdom of death but a circling of the cycles of vegetative life where women may be, most closely and livingly, in touch with the dead. (Flowers and women will continue circling through the *Sonette;* see particularly II.7.)

Eurydice is here in the shadows. But the "Mädchen fast" of this sonnet, shadowy though she too may be, is a real human being, the young girl to whose memory the work is dedicated. Wera brings with her her womanhood, her death; also, in time as we shall see, her dancing. It is not a mere metaphor of sex and of death who enters but the true living-and-dead figure, a mortal indeed in every sense. With her, sex and death are seen not only as part of the fate of the organism but as part of the interpretative methodology.

If we think that we know about sex and death, together with the reasons why poets connect them, because Freud has told us, we shall go hopelessly astray. We know little of either yet, even as physical facts, let alone as mental ones. What we have to realize is that there are sound reasons for connecting them which are not psychiatric but biological. It has been said by scientists that the two of them entered the world together. So long as an organism reproduces itself by simple fission, death is an irrelevance. As soon as there is differentiation of sex and reproduction on those terms, with the corresponding individualization of the organism, death follows.[85] It is this deep biological connection which Rilke inquires into, as Keats also did.

Rilke sees both sex and death not as incidents but as con-
tinuing states in the life of the human organism, and asks
the profound question: what effect do these two have on
the life of the mind? [86]

In this second sonnet, where both make their appear-
ance, sex is not spoken of directly. It is here, however, in
the delicate and ghostly eroticism of the image, the faint
bodily appearance of the girl, her passage into the physical
sense of the man, her sleep. It is a kind of mating at the
point where body passes over into mind, and part of the
postlogical investigation of that very point. The poem
says, as Rilke says elsewhere, that where there is union of
male and female in the mind, there the universe is. We
need a biological understanding (and Jung will not do)
of the conjunction and alternation of sex in the individual
mind, and of the "unendliche Paarung" of Rilke's own
phrase in ii.9. There were clues toward such a study in
Novalis, but it still waits to be made. We have glanced
already at Rilke's insistence on the female nature of crea-
tion, mental as well as physical. He goes on to suggest
that in time a comprehension of this may have a deeply
humanizing effect upon heterosexual relationships, seen
at length as relations not simply between man and woman
as opposites but between human beings.[87] The third Duino
Elegy, of 1913, is devoted to this subject, in a postlogical
setting in which the fearful Neptune, river-god of the
blood, appears at the very spring and fountainhead of
physical desire in the man. Rilke indicates that the way to
this more human understanding may be through attention
to the feminine quality of the organism.

Meanwhile Rilke turns to the other aspect of his in-
quiry, to death as a human phenomenon. In Sonnet 5 it
too is seen through Orpheus not as fixity but as movement,
not the memorial tablet but the roses blossoming in their
season. Then in 6, again through Orpheus, the unity of
human living and dead is figured. Here the dead inhabit

the house as much as the living do, and this Sonnet ends with Orpheus praising household objects, vessels or jewelry, whether they be in the household of the living or in that of the dead which is the grave.[88] For these are the objects traditionally buried with the dead, and the poet suggests a transformation of our attitude to this and other ancient ritual practices connected with the dead; for perhaps they are not only primitive customs but, seen with the eye of postlogic, genuine and profound biological insights not yet fully realized.

The metamorphosis continues. Death is not dust, stone, and silence; in 7 it is already, through Orpheus, becoming vineyard and grape and moving toward human language in such words as *Stimme,* voice, *Lügen,* lies, *Bote,* messenger, or *Rühmung,* praise.[89] The two merge beautifully in the first eight lines of Sonnet 10, where Rilke remembers what he had seen of the old stone coffins of antiquity, in Rome used as conduits and filled with water's "wandelndes Lied," that wavering modulant song, in Provence turned into troughs of wild flowers alive with bees and butterflies. In both, the dead are already moving back to speech, and Rilke greets in them "the reopened mouths which have already learned what it means to be silent."

Sonnets 11 and 12 are difficult and important. The first asks the question: Is there no constellation of Horse and Rider? Rilke sets up two extremes, the stars and a mental image (which is of course exactly what a constellation is, a fusion of those two) and tries to bridge them by postulating a unity between real horse and real man. The vision does not succeed; the poem falls back into separation, between man and beast, between star and the figure alone, which is all we are left with at the end, enjoined to believe *that* for the time being, if we cannot do more. Sonnet 12 reasserts *Geist* and *Figur,* the mind or spirit which binds us, the figures in which we truly live. But it comes down to earth, literally, and we progress from mind and figure at the beginning, through relations between mind and mind which Rilke figures by radio aerials, to the earth of peasant and summer and seed growing. So the way is prepared for Sonnet 20 and its beautiful white horse, remembered by Rilke from his Russian travels twenty years before. Sonnet 12 moves us from mental figure to earth. Sonnet 20 closes that circle, for in it one of earth's loveliest and earthiest creatures ("dieser Stolz aus Erde" Rilke called the horse) is offered back to Orpheus, who is in his turn, being a myth, a figure of the mind.

The theme of language and the organic life which shows itself in sex and fertility, flower and fruit, is taken further now. First an exercise is performed upon this alone, in 13, where word and fruit are merged with an exquisite sensuous exactitude in their narrow bodily meeting place, the mouth.[90] Apple, pear, banana, gooseberry speak in the mouth, yet gradually become nameless in the taste, which must then be resaid, "Wagt zu sagen, was ihr Apfel nennt," dare to say what you call "apple."

(One lovely gloss to this solidarity of words and plants occurs in 21. There the earth is figured as a child anxious to say all the poems she knows by heart. That is fancy, charming but no more. At the end, however, comes this:

> und was gedruckt steht in Wurzeln und langen
> schwierigen Stämmen: sie singts, sie singts!
>
> (and what is printed in roots and long
> difficult stems, she sings it, she sings it!)

Roots and stems—those are the very words we use technically and probably unthinkingly in philology, and it is admirable to see them revert, in a poet's mind, to their plant nature, which is at one with their word nature, in a postlogical and biological etymology.)

Already in 13 the fruit was said to speak "life and death in the mouth," and in 14 this fruit-language metamorphosis is expanded to include the ancestral past of the fruit which is also ours, our common ground as you might say.

> Wir gehen um mit Blumen, Weinblatt, Frucht.
> Sie sprechen nicht die Sprache nur des Jahres.

> (We have to do with flower, vineleaf, fruit.
> They speak a language not of this year only.)

They come from the dead whose bodies fatten the land in an intimate fusion, and the poem moves into an extraordinary image of ancestors sleeping not merely at the tree roots but with them in the sexual sense, the German preposition *bei* carrying both meanings, with the fruits as halfway things sent up to us, the living, out of the overplus of the dead and their dumb and griping embraces with prehuman organic life.

The fruit tree next becomes the genealogical or family tree binding dead and living in ceaseless reproduction in both kingdoms.[91] Sonnet 15 takes this forward into society and language, as Ovid did also:

> Zu unterst der Alte, verworrn,
> all der Erbauten
> Wurzel, verborgener Born,
> den sie nie schauten.
>
> Sturmhelm und Jägerhorn,
> Spruch von Ergrauten,
> Männer im Bruderzorn,
> Frauen wie Lauten . . .
>
> Drängender Zweig an Zweig,
> nirgends ein freier . . .
> Einer! O steig . . . O steig . . .
>
> Aber sie brechen noch.
> Dieser erst oben doch
> biegt sich zur Leier.

> (All things that blindly grow,
> Their hidden cause:
> The Old One far below,
> Gnarled in the roots.
>
> Helmet and hunting-horn,
> Ancients' wise saws,
> Man-wrath in brothers born,
> Women like lutes . . .
>
> Though shoot on shoot press on
> Freedom's not won . . .
> Yes, there! oh higher . . . higher.
>
> Now that too snapped and gone.
> Only the topmost one
> Curves and is lyre.) [92]

After this, immediately, with 18, the machines come in, "der Maschinenteil," the machine part of the social and modern world, entering here as a new sound which Orpheus is questioned about. This is not intrusion, not a mistaking by a poet of his lyric vocation. This is the classic Orphic tradition, from Bacon and his Mechanical Arts onward, and what Rilke has to say about machines is remarkable. They are dealt with in Sonnets 22–24. They would have had a run of four consecutive sonnets had Rilke not taken a dislike to the original 21 and substituted for it the little spring fantasy we have already mentioned. The reject stands in his later poems,[93] however, and is not uninteresting. It argues about what is new and what is old, saying that he who is all for novelty is bound to be soon brought to silence:

> Denn das Ganze ist unendlich neuer
> Als ein Kabel und ein hohes Haus,
>
> (For the All is infinitely newer
> Than a cable or a skyscraper)

and he goes on to add that the oldest fires of all are the stars, while the newer fires go out, and we are not to suppose our longest transmission shafts turn the wheels of the future, "denn Aeonen redet mit Aeonen," aeon speaks with aeon as deep calleth unto deep, and more than we realized has already happened. (It is strange how often Rilke catches a Goethean echo in what he says—he certainly does so here.)

Sonnets 22 and 23 speak of aeroplanes and flight: speed in itself alone is not the way into the future. Sonnet 22 ends with a lovely triplet, offset against the aeroplane and its hasting:

> Alles ist ausgeruht:
> Dunkel und Helligkeit,
> Blume und Buch.

Everything is rested through and through, completely re-
laxed, has had its sleep out—darkness and light, flower
and book. To come on these immediately after those swift
machines, in contrast and yet still in close relation to
them, makes a beautiful synthesis, everything turning in
the turning cycles of season and nature (books here being
as much a part of nature as they were in Wordsworth) to-
ward a new metamorphosis which 23 proposes for flight
itself, whose true possibilities for life and imagination
have not yet been realized.

With 24 the machines take a new, final, and exceed-
ingly interesting turn in Rilke's mind: they are related
to the gods, technology to mythology, and the difficulties
the former causes us are set down here, by implication,
to our increasing alienation from mythology. The sonnet
suggests there is a true connection we have failed to main-
tain. We think we have outstripped the gods by steel and
wheels and straight-engineered roads, but the fire im-
prisoned in our steam-boilers is the former fire still (of
the Titans and Vulcan perhaps?), and in our separation
from them we have merely become like swimmers who
have swum on and on only to find their strength is going.
This Sonnet is akin to II.19, where the god is linked with
gold in the bank, as if there too were a world subject to
mythology. "Dichtung der Finanzwissenschaften"—Novalis
hinted at it; "Nur dem Göttlichen hörbar," Rilke says,
audible only to the god are the proceedings of money.
There is a glimpse here of yet another extension of post-
logic, into a mythology which might be at the base of the
processes and thinking in technology and economics.

The one theme we have left to look at before coming
to the last Orphic figure is the dance. It enters as a lan-
guage of the body, akin to word language as we can see
in the pairing of 13, where apple is to be named, with 14,
where orange is to be danced. What it figures is the whole
dynamic of life, in nature and society. (This is enlarged

upon in II.18.) And the dance now gathers up all the themes and sets a symmetry on the whole work, for the next to last sonnet in each Part corresponds. Each is about a girl and dancing, and is addressed explicitly, by Rilke himself, to Wera. Sonnet 28 in Part II is much the better poem. In it the dead dancer, still almost a child, is bidden to come and go, like Orpheus himself in 1.5, perfecting the dance figure into a figure of stars. The dancer's motion is said to date from that primordial moment when Orpheus and the lyre were first heard, and to this high celebration and central point all the beauty of her steps was directed, part of the true hearing in nature which began when Orpheus sang. (There is playfulness in this poem too; the dancing girl is a little astonished if a tree takes a long time to make up its mind to go along with her, in the hearing and the dance.) So here are the dead girl, the dance, the figures of the myth, the hearing of nature, the power of poetry and the stars.

In 1.25 Rilke tries to deal with the real dancing girl's real illness and death, and cannot; but in the still-figuring first stanza there are two interesting lines. In line 2 the dead girl is called by the poet "a flower whose name I do not know," where flowers, language, death, and woman meet. Then in line 4 she becomes "schöne Gespielin des unüberwindlichen Schreis," beautiful playfellow of the cry that is to prevail. This is a difficult line, and we may understand it better if we remember that playmate in Rilke's pre-*Sonette* verses who was the universe and the poet's partner; and then turn to II.26, which is about cries in the universe, birds' cries, children's cries (as Rilke had been complaining in another of those verses that the universe was overfull of crying and noise). In this sonnet in Part II, the cries are to be regulated by Orpheus. He as singing god is asked to order the criers so that they may wake into a rushing stream carrying along with it

the head and the lyre. This is the only place in Part II
where the third Orphic figure is mentioned, and it seems
as if in this hint in 1.25 we look forward to that final meta-
morphosis.

This is Sonnet 26:

Du aber, Göttlicher, du, bis zuletzt noch Ertöner,
da ihn der Schwarm der verschmähten Mänaden befiel,
hast ihr Geschrei übertönt mit Ordnung, du Schöner,
aus den Zerstörenden stieg dein erbauendes Spiel.

Keine war da, dass sie Haupt dir und Leier zerstör.
Wie sie auch rangen und rasten; und alle die scharfen
Steine, die sie nach deinem Herzen warfen,
wurden zu Sanftem an dir und begabt mit Gehör.

Schliesslich zerschlugen sie dich, von der Rache gehetzt,
während dein Klang noch in Löwen und Felsen verweilte
und in den Bäumen und Vögeln. Dort singst du noch jetzt.

O du verlorener Gott! Du unendliche Spur!
Nur weil dich reissend zuletzt die Feindschaft verteilte,
sind wir die Hörenden jetzt und ein Mund der Natur.

(Worshipful one who sang on to the end, while the storm
Of gathering Maenads swept round you, your scorn to re-
        pay,
You in your beauty outmastered their cries into form:
Out of destruction your structuring melodies play.

Lyre and head were immune from that murderous crowd,
However much in their fury they struggled and burned;
All of the stones they flung at your heart, sharp edges,
        were turned,
As they met you, to gentle things and with hearing en-
        dowed.

Lusting for vengeance, at last they made you their prey,
But in the crags and the lions still lingered your sound,
And in the trees and the birds. You sing there today.

You are the god who is lost—most boundless of clues!
Only since hatred undid you and spread you around
Are we true hearers, a mouth for nature to use.)

This is the end of Rilke's inquiry into postlogical thought
as living metamorphic process. Orpheus, dead, is re-em-
bodied into the dynamic of nature at every level, which
sings of him henceforward: the methodology of postlogic
is a part of, and at one with, natural process. And it is
we, human beings with our hearing and our language-as-
poetry, who are the clue to what is going on. Rilke asks
an immense question: what if all the dynamics in the nat-
ural world, up to and including those of human society,
are clues to, or hieroglyphics of, the methodology of think-
ing, special attention to be paid to sex (which is here in
its full human complication, witness the "verschmähten
Mänaden," the Maenads Orpheus rejected) and to life and
death in their intimately connected dynamic relationship?
It can be seen dimly here how psychology, anthropology,
and poetry offer the basis for an immensely extended
Ovidian biology of thinking.

We have now only to attend to the ending of the myth;
for where Rilke leaves Orpheus in the final sonnet is not
the end of the story. It is Ovid in the *Metamorphoses* who
completes the cycle. Book xv ends with the apotheosis of
Rome in the person of the dead Caesar shooting up into
heaven as a star; the crowning social form, as Ovid saw
it, returning by right among the primordial forms of the
stars. Rilke also, in his pre-*Sonette* poem saw a meteor
shooting from the hand up into its own place, while the
Sonette speak of the human voice being lifted among the
stars in 1.8, of a possible connection between a mental

figure and the stars in 1.11, of dance as akin to the stars in 11.28. Critics have pointed out how often Rilke's poetry moves toward the stars.[94] As early as *Orpheus. Eurydike. Hermes* there was a sky of stars, but they were the landscape of mourning called up by Orpheus in his grief and were distorted. In the Tenth Elegy, Rilke returns to this image, naming there his own imaginary constellations for a sky of pain. Strangely and significantly, we are told, *Head and Lyre of Orpheus* figured in the original draft among these star clusters, but was later struck out.[95] Rilke does not answer the question: why this connection between figures and stars? The myth itself, however, makes a suggestion.

Figures of the mind may be thought of as being the terminus of one end of the scale of nature. The stars, those infinitely remote elemental fiery powers, are at the other. Between the two lies the whole range of form, in the energy of matter and the energies of mind. Interpretation is given this for its task. So the Orpheus myth ends with two things: the affirmation of the unity of all the forms in nature, between the galaxies and the mythological lyre —the power of the human mind figuring in its own characteristic function of language—which joins them; and there is also the floating, singing head, which is poetry and thinking, prophetic and unquenchable.

9

The world is young: the former great men call to us affectionately

THE ORPHIC VOICE attests a tradition and a method of thinking. The tradition is constant. What is important about it is that it is not history, cold and embalmed, but a living invitation. If the tradition means anything, it means that here is a marvelously adapted instrument for ordinary people to use in understanding their universe and themselves. It can and should enliven every situation in which thinking in words is going on—literature, criticism, education, many more. Indeed they need enlivening. It is not a matter for specialists, but for people, as the voices themselves insist. That is why they have felt their task to be so important.

The method, the postlogic, is a way of using mind and body to build up dynamic structures (never fixed or abstract patterns) by which the human organism sets itself in relation to the universe and allows each side to interpret the other. The mind's relation to its structure or myth is inclusive and reflexive. It is not detached; the working mind is part of the dynamic of the system, and is united, by its forms, with whatever in the universe it is inquiring into. The process of making the interpretative myths is carried on in language, and the structure of language in its dynamic with the mind both conditions and is conditioned by the mutual interpretation. The body is an essential part of the method. The method bears a close relation to sex and fertility. Love is a necessary part of its working. Its aim is the discovery of the world, and it is this which gives it all the beauty it has.

I have used the word "postlogic" in this study, but it is time now to return to the true term, which is "poetry," though I hope by now a little filled out, or cleared of the misunderstandings we have allowed to grow up around it. It has come into this study as drama, as epic, as didactic verse, as lyric. You can use it in any form, since this is its deep purpose, and according to whatever level of achievement you can reach. There is no need to think that only superlative poetry has any right to survive or that lesser work is not good and useful in our common explorations. It lies to everyone's hand and we have to return to it, not as a vague ornament of life but as one of the great living disciplines of the mind, friendly to all other disciplines, and offering them and accepting from them new resources of power.

On this the Orphic voices have made a beginning for us.

PART V
Working Poems for The Orphic Voice

IT HAS BEEN all along the theme of this work that poetry is a form of thought. Once this is accepted it need not be surprising that, in the course of the thinking, poems presented themselves from time to time as working instruments in the inquiry. Anyone trying this method of research will probably find, as I did, that the mind knows, in poems, a little more than it knows it knows, so that a poem will often tell the thinking mind where to look next. These hints, clues, and statements are what follow. They appear here in the order in which they, and the book, were written.

1

Poet to Scientist

Yours the intensity of perfect mind,
   The virgin light no prism can dispart,
The lattice where true tenses are declined.

Your instruments are crystals and cold beams,
   And the integrities of head and heart
Solemnize marriage at their last extremes.

Loving's our work, it seems; but where's the nerve
   To conjugate your white near-infinite speed
With my wet rainbow's broken-colored curve?

Yet by your light I find: Idea's bed,
   Where at full stretch of soul our thoughts may breed,
Is ultra-violet and infra-red.

2

Orpheus I

To sightlessness is love consigned,
And if it love, the thinking mind
Consents no less to being blind;

So the musician at the strings,
Withdrawn from all surrounding things,
Attends to what the music sings:

> *Orpheus descends, as he was taught,*
> *Toward his dear remembered thought,*
> *But lost in seeing what he sought.*

Intensity surpassing sight,
Shadows of sensing hands invite
The concentration of delight

In all whose thought and love, compact,
Feel with a long and fingering tact
For outline of an artifact:

> *Orpheus in minds undoes the curse*
> *That splits us into prose or verse;*
> *And, shaping, finds the universe.*

3

Orpheus II

> There is a long music.
> It comes from a severed head
>   Clutched in the tree roots.
>
> The voyage down-river
> Was traced by the mouth that bled
>   Its undrowned singing.
>
> Mysterious if that skull,
> All its dark sayings are said
>   For innocent people.
>
> Should you ask understanding,
> Go living, my soul, to the dead,
>   And see what happens.

4

Data

Poem is something that is made,
    The ruined house under the rain
Whose sky-bound staircase balustrade
    Ends in the infinite inane;

With everything five wits contain,
    Poem is something that is made,
Gaslight through foul or shattered pane,
    When heart begins to be afraid;

No smallest fact but must be laid
    Along the grain the nerves provide;
Poem is something that is made,
    Together with the world outside;

Tables and chairs and cold and pain,
    So still and shapely, have obeyed;
Sense is the senses' one refrain:
They neither falter nor explain:
That is the burden of the brain:
    Poem is something that is made.

5

Words and Stars

If God had spoken stars in the beginning,
Man's mind no less obeyed its tendencies,
Astronomers soon busy underpinning
Grammar and syntax of those sentences;

Astrology could offer only fancy,
The incantation and the sophist's trick;
Poets divined, in place of necromancy,
Superlative sidereal rhetoric.

To logic, metaphor is mere annoyance;
Lone image is anarchical and shoddy;
Their dialectic offers no advance.

What speculation in that high flamboyance?
What wedding heavenly mind to heavenly body,
The figure in the discourse and the dance?

6

Ways and Means

Only angelic thoughts may climb that ladder,
Dancing to God, through skies of milk and madder,
          Logic's ascension.
Others must greenly grow, sprung tendrils hoping
Trellis of air, Jack's beanstalk slowly groping
          Its own extension.
Far off I see Heaven's ultimate arbors shine,
Where line and leaf geometries combine,
          Metamorphosis
Of metaphor's and dialectic's loss:
Chaste frame of silver squares, and all across,
          Passion of roses.

7

Thinking

Whatever thinks the crystal, has been taught
      Perfected plan,
    Can flawlessly rehearse
    Much of the universe.
This is a harder thought:
      To be a man.

Plant-thought designed
      The intricated mesh,
    Giving itself the power
    To realize leaf and flower.
Man only feels his mind
      In-fibrilled in the flesh.

Beast-thoughts have grace,
      Whose body is their brain.
    Man-thought lies buried deep
    Where dumb the organs sleep.
Gleams struggle to his face;
      Then blind again.

Mind—fluted gem,
      Flushed trumpet-vines where dart
    Exquisite long-tongued words,
    Hawkmoths and hummingbirds—
O choose, rather than them,
      Man's heavy heart.

8

The Two Methods

I have sat down with the Entities at table,
Eaten with them the meal of ceremony,
And they were stamped with jewels, and intuned
         God's ordered praises.

But now the Activities hand me to the dancing,
Brown naked bodies lithe and crimson-necklaced,
And tambourines besiege the darkened altars,
         In what God's honor?

9

Bud and Trivium

Never again lay ear against a shell:
　　Already something stirs, or so it seems.
Listen only to stones who cannot tell,
　　They sleep so fast, their stiff inaudible dreams,
Whispered through walls of bone into your skull.

For yesterday a bud began to speak.
　　(So young? but offshoot of a classic line
Half-infinite to our poor Latin and Greek,
　　Each plant a slip of immemorial vine,
And even more than we, both young and old.)

Conservative in what it had to teach,
　　The mode Socratic and the theme Scholastic,
Actions and figures as implicit speech,
　　From which organic *Trivium* green and plastic
As its own substance it deduced ourselves.

Showed three relations: first that of survival,
　　The *Dialectic* in the thorn and claw,
Bodily argument with every rival
　　As the inflexible ruling of the law.
Here Darwin stopped—but there are two to come:

For *Rhetoric* plays with natural selection,
　　Hyperbole swims and flies in red and gold;
Ingenious living similes for protection,
　　Beauty's unnecessary manifold;
And *Grammar* is the dance of living form.

Was this once known and framed to education,
    High ancient code, we fools have lost the clues?
Master-vision or mere hallucination,
    Organon bedded crackling like a fuse
In the damp innocence of a crinkled bud?

Suppose it opens as we wait before it,
    A huge gold circle with a face and eyes,
Would it begin to speak? best to implore it,
    "Moon, make no mouth whose monstrous prophecies
Blow like God's horns as we go down to dust"?

Or would it simply show, in slow dilating,
    Plato and Aristotle closely curled
Inside a yellow roseleaf, speculating
    That language is the nature of the world,
And all philosophy a flowering thought?

Fierce, honey-throated, formalized, prolific,
    Anticipate in our most human powers,
The poet but a speaking hieroglyphic
    In one whole universe of continual flowers,
Shall we run weeping, throw away our life?

Or gather little children in a ring,
And blossom into oracles and sing
That mind and word is every living thing?

10

Ideas

The coming of new forms
Is priestly and war-like; doubled they campaign,
Ringing, besiege the head with holy storms,

Till shouts and trumpets crack
The glassy air; fortifications spill,
And we lie open, to fury and to sack,

And then to all the expanses of the plain,
The world's wide landscape suddenly appears,
And nine huge stars waiting above the hill
Will march through walls of clay-dust to the brain
And camp there, silent, leaning on their spears.

11

Orpheus III

> He sees over his shoulder
>   Flowers, not her;
> Scarcely a second older,
>   For still they stir;
> Not asphodel but colder,
>   And sharp as myrrh.
>
> Half-roused from holy sleeping
>   Their pallor flames
> To urge upon his keeping
>   A lover's claims.
> Sunlit he stumbles, weeping,
>   To give them names.

12

Orpheus IV

> Let him chord up the stars,
> Sweeten the salt sea,
> Answer with his heartstrings
> For our sterility—
>   *So the wild women cried,*
>   *And Orpheus died.*
> Stars were strung to sound,
> Waves turned red,
> And the wild women appeased
> Went home to supper and bed.
> Far out, what echoes brood
> One ravished head?

13

Genesis

Poet by poet launched upon that sea.
This was before the moon was, or the land.
Everything in a moving patience waited
To be created—

Solitary were they borne
On those immense waters
Breathing and profound
(How many drowned),
The mind, the Mind,
Under this presence contemplated—

In darkness but for stars
That crowded, jostled, stabbed and showered and rang,
The tideless ocean tingled and pulsated,
A million working surfaces for light,
And by those influences impregnated—

Of World and Mind
Poet by poet said
No thing is only dead
And nothing unrelated.

Notes

SOURCES OF SECTION HEADINGS:

PART I

1. Robert Browning, *Essay on Percy Bysshe Shelley.*
2. Fenollosa, quoted by Donald Davie in *Articulate Energy,* Appendix.
3. Lucian on "The Dance." Quoted by E. Louis Backman in his work on *Religious Dances,* London, 1952. (The ascription of this piece of writing to Lucian is doubtful.)
4. The *Phaedrus* in the Jowett translation.
5. Vico, *Scienza nuova,* in the Michelet version, Bk. IV, chap. 7.
6. Teilhard de Chardin, *Le Phénomène humain,* Pt. IV, chap. 3.
7. John Middleton Murry, *GOD: An Essay in Metabiology,* Pt. I.

PART II

1. Schelling, quoted by Sir Herbert Read, *The True Voice of Feeling,* Pt. II, Essay 1.
2. Middleton Murry, *Keats and Shakespeare,* chap. 10.
3. Sir John Harington, *A Briefe Apologie of Poetrie,* prefaced to his translation of the *Orlando Furioso,* 1591.
4. Bacon, *The Advancement of Learning,* Bk. II.
5. *A Midsummer Night's Dream,* Act V, Scene 1.
6. Robert Hooke, *A Discourse of Earthquakes,* in the *Posthumous Works.*
7. Hooke again.
8. Carlyle, *Heroes and Hero-Worship,* "The Poet as Hero."
9. Coleridge, *Lectures on Shakespeare.*

PART III

1. Dryden, Preface to the *Fables.*
2. D'Arcy Thompson, *On Growth and Form,* chap. 1.

3. A. O. Lovejoy, *The Great Chain of Being,* chap. 9.
4. Emerson's essay "Intellect" in the first series of *Essays.*
5. Coleridge, *Lectures on Shakespeare.*
6. Emerson's essay on Goethe in *Representative Men.*
7. Erasmus Darwin, Interlude 3 in *The Loves of the Plants.*
8. Ruskin, preface to the second edition of *Modern Painters.*
9. Taine, *La Fontaine et ses fables,* Pt. II, chap. 2.

PART IV

1. Shelley, *Prometheus Unbound,* Act III, Scene 3.
2. Blake's *Milton,* Bk. II.
3. Milton, *Areopagitica.*
4. Friedrich Schlegel, *Gespräch über die Poesie.*
5. Coleridge, from *Inquiring Spirit,* ed. Kathleen Coburn.
6. Emerson, *The Natural History of Intellect.*
7. C. Kerenyi, Prolegomena to Jung and Kerenyi, *Introduction to a Science of Mythology.*
8. Lucian, *The Dance,* trans. A. W. Harmon. (See note to Pt. I, Sec. 3, above.)
9. Emerson, essay on Goethe in *Representative Men.*

Part I

1. *Werke,* ed. Schröter, Munich, 1927 (*Einleitung in die Philosophie der Mythologie*), Vorlesung 3, Hauptband 6, p. 54.
2. Classic statements of this view can be found in Comte, Renan, and Lévy-Bruhl.
3. *The Botanic Garden* (London, 1791), "Advertisement," p. 5.
4. Erwin Schrödinger, *What Is Life?* (Cambridge, 1951), p. 79; Agnes Arber, *The Mind and the Eye* (Cambridge, 1954), p. 41; C. Lloyd Morgan, *Mind at the Crossways* (London, Williams and Norgate, 1929), pp. 1 ff.; J. H. Woodger, *Biology and Language* (Cambridge, 1952), p. 8; K. Koffka, *Principles of Gestalt Psychology* (London, Kegan Paul, 1935), p. 64.
5. Buffon, *Oeuvres philosophiques,* ed. Piveteau (Paris, 1954), p. 9: "L'inconvénient est . . . de vouloir soumettre à des loix arbitraires les loix de la Nature, de vouloir la diviser dans des points où elle est indivisible." Cuvier, *Le Règne Animal distribué d'après son Organisation* (Paris, 1817), p. 4.
6. *Problems of Life* (London, 1952), pp. 155–59.
7. See particularly Max Wertheimer in *A Source Book of Gestalt Psychology,* ed. Willis D. Ellis (London, Routledge, 1938), p. 3: "The problem has not merely to do with scientific work—it is a fundamental problem of our times. Gestalt theory is not something suddenly and unexpectedly dropped upon us from above; it is, rather, a palpable convergence of problems ranging throughout the sciences and the various philosophic standpoints of modern times." See also pp. 10, 15.
8. In *Zur Morphologie: Die Absicht eingeleitet.*
9. Goethe puts the point well: "A man born and bred up to the so-called exact sciences does not find it easy to realize, perched as he is on the heights of his own rationality, that there might also exist an exactitude of the imagination working through the senses, without which art would be simply unthinkable" (*Aphorismen und Fragmente, Werke,* Zürich, 1952, *17,* 779).
10. See Michael Polanyi, *Personal Knowledge* (London, Routledge,

1958), passim. Also Woodger, *Biology and Language*, p. 60: "In view of the popularity of science in these days it is deplorable that it is so little understood, even by those actively engaged in it."

11. Particularly *The Philosophy of Symbolic Forms*, Vol. 2, *Mythical Thought*, Yale, 1955; and *The Problem of Knowledge*, Yale, 1950.

12. Seventh ed. (Paris, 1922), pp. 79, 448.

13. These phrases are from Max Planck, *The Universe in the Light of Modern Physics* (London, 1937), p. 61; Fred Hoyle, *The Nature of the Universe* (New York, 1950), p. 6; Polanyi, *Personal Knowledge*, pp. 123 ff.

14. Cassirer, *Philosophy of Symbolic Forms*, 2, 55: "All mere properties or attributes must for myth ultimately become bodies"; also p. 59: "while the true tendency of scientific, analytic-critical thinking is toward liberation from this substantial approach, it is characteristic of myth that despite all the spirituality of its *objects* and *contents*, its 'logic'—the *form* of its contents—clings to bodies." Cf. also William Robertson Smith, *Lectures on the Religion of the Semites* (London, Black, 1927), p. 18: "It may be affirmed with confidence that in almost every case the myth was derived from the ritual, and not the ritual from the myth."

15. Cf. Schelling (n. 1 above), p. 58: "Wir gehen auf die Meinung zurück, dass die Mythologie überhaupt eine *Erfindung* sey."

16. Newman's *An Essay on the Development of Christian Doctrine* adopts this as a working principle from the theological point of view.

17. The development of this kind of thinking is one of the great themes of Bergson. See for instance *La Pensée et le mouvant* (Paris, Alcan, 1934), p. 164: "Nous disons que le changement existe, que tout change, que le changement est la loi même des choses . . . mais ce ne sont là que des mots, et nous raisonnons et philosophons comme si le changement n'existait pas." This essay is dated 1911.

18. Ed. Nicolini (Bari, 1936), pp. 318–19. The Latin is as follows: "Hinc nos, si non felici, certe pio ausu, de principiis humanitatis, cuius studium philologia est, ex necessariis argumentis a corrupti hominis natura desumptis disserere hoc libro decrevimus, et ita philologiam ad scientiae normam exigere." There is a plea for philology in this same sense in Renan, *L'Avenir de la science;* Renan is familiar with Vico, of course, and mentions him.

19. "Perception was accounted for until fairly recently in terms of sensation and association, but now perceptions are viewed as

organized mental structures selectively taken from the unstructured stimulus field." Aubrey Lewis, quoted by Woodger, *Biology and Language,* p. 266.

20. See Polanyi, *Personal Knowledge,* on the act lying behind all assertions, on which they ultimately depend.

21. In *Crise de vers, Divagations.*

22. *L'Avenir de la science,* in *Oeuvres complètes,* ed. Psichari (Paris, 1949), *3,* 830. He goes on: "Depuis que nous avons dressé une carte de la science, nous nous obstinons à donner une place à part à la philologie, à la philosophie; et pourtant ce sont là moins des sciences spéciales que des façons diverses de traiter les choses de l'esprit."

23. Cf. Owen Barfield, *Poetic Diction* (London, Faber, 1928), pp. 88–89: "There is a strong tendency in the Greek language . . . to make itself felt as a living, muscular organism rather than as a structure; and it is quite in harmony with this that the terminology of grammar, most of which is derived from the Greek, should have originated in so many cases as physical or physiological metaphor."

24. *Man on his Nature* (Cambridge, 1940), pp. 269, 185.

25. Ibid., p. 179: "The mind is utilitarian. By evolution it is bound to be so. Each step of its development has had to justify itself *ad hoc.*"

26. Chapter 3 of Wellek and Warren's *Theory of Literature* (New York, 1949) is helpful on this subject.

27. New York, Harper, 1930, p. 125.

28. *Romanticism and the Modern Ego* (Boston, Little Brown, 1943), p. 76.

29. *GOD: Being an Introduction to the Science of Metabiology* (London, Cape, 1929), p. 45.

30. *The Itinerant Ivory Tower* (Yale, 1953), p. 243.

31. *GOD,* p. 46.

Part II

1. See D. G. James, *The Dream of Learning, An Essay on "The Advancement of Learning," "Hamlet" and "King Lear"* (Oxford, 1951), p. 35: "Bacon . . . was one of the first of the moderns; his vision of things was creative of, and is better understood in the light of, what came after him . . . And so it is, I think, with Shakespeare."

2. For details about this consult J. A. K. Thomson, *Shakespeare and*

the Classics, London, 1952; and, more generally on mythology, Douglas Bush, *Mythology and the Renaissance Tradition in English Poetry,* Minnesota, 1932; and Franck L. Schoell, *Études sur l'humanisme continental en Angleterre à la fin de la renaissance,* Paris, 1926.

3. Benjamin Farrington in his preface to *Francis Bacon: Philosopher of Industrial Science* (London, Lawrence and Wishart, 1951), protests rightly: "The book which Francis Bacon called *The Great Instauration* came to be called by the name of one of its parts, *Novum Organum.* As I have urged, this is a serious distortion."

4. The translation is Spedding's. The edition used throughout is *The Philosophical Works of Francis Bacon* (hereafter referred to as *Philosophical Works*), ed. Robertson, London, 1905.

5. He has been claimed by Marx and others as one who "anticipated an alteration in the means of production, and the practical subjugation of nature by man, as a result of the altered mode of thought." Farrington, *Francis Bacon,* pp. 174–75.

6. "He was not, after all, clear as to what he was about," James says in *The Dream of Learning,* p. 8. Cf. Macaulay in his essay "Lord Bacon," in *Critical and Historical Essays* (1843): "we think that the nature of his services is often mistaken, and was not fully understood even by himself."

7. The views of Ellis and Spedding are to be found in the *Philosophical Works,* in the general introduction and the preface to the *Parasceve* respectively. The other sources are Thomas Sprat, *History of the Royal Society of London,* 4th ed. London, 1734, to which Cowley's Ode serves as preface; Joseph de Maistre, *Examen de la philosophie de Bacon,* Paris, 1836; Thomas Fowler, *Bacon's Novum Organum,* Oxford, 1878; Dean Church, *Bacon,* London, 1888; J. M. Robertson, editor's introduction to *Philosophical Works;* L. L. Whyte, *Accent on Form,* London, 1955.

8. *Examen,* p. 365.

9. By de Maistre, Macaulay, James, and Fowler by implication.

10. As in Sir Samuel Garth's preface to the translation of Ovid's *Metamorphoses.*

11. Cf. Robertson's Note, *Philosophical Works,* p. 820: "To the anthropological or psychological study of myth the best modern guides are Tylor, Mannhardt, Frazer . . ."; and Robert Graves, *The Greek Myths* (Penguin Books, 1955), *1,* 22: "A true science of myth should begin with a study of archaeology, history and comparative religion, not in the psycho-therapist's consulting room."

12. Walter Pater in his essay on Pico in *The Renaissance* (1873) claims that Bacon's phrase of man as the interpreter of nature really belongs to Pico.

13. See *Hymne an die Götter Griechenlands*.

14. Michael Polanyi, "The Stability of Beliefs," *British Journal for the Philosophy of Science, 3* (1952), 218–19, says: "I hold that the propositions embodied in natural science are not derived by any definite rule from the data of experience, and that they can neither be verified nor falsified by experience according to any definite rule. Discovery, verification and falsification proceed according to certain maxims which cannot be precisely formulated and still less proved or disproved, and the application of which relies in every case on a personal judgment exercised (or accredited) by ourselves. These maxims and the art of interpreting them may be said to constitute the premisses of science, but I prefer to call them our scientific beliefs." Goethe says in the *Aphorismen und Fragmente* that in science nothing can really be *known*, it all has to be *done*.

15. See Rachel Trickett, "The Augustan Pantheon: Mythology and Personification in Eighteenth Century Poetry," *Essays and Studies* (London, 1953), pp. 71–87.

16. There is also of course a Catholic tradition of hostility to myth. Prynne found the Early Fathers of the Church very helpful in this respect.

17. Gosson says: "By writing of untruthes they are open liers." Prynne says: "It is dangerous, it is sinfull, therefore, to applaude such Playes, admit such Poemes, which may withdraw us Christians from our God." They are in his view, "a means to revive that Heathenism and propagate that Idolatrie, which the light and power of the Gospel hath long since abolished." Later, however, Prynne puts in a saving clause for Ovid, or at least "some parts of Ovid where he is not obscene." Addison in No. 523 of *The Spectator* says on the subject of mythology: "I do hereby strictly require every person who shall write on this subject to remember that he is a Christian, and not to sacrifice his catechism to his poetry." And if that is half-jesting, the following is perfectly serious, "And it is no doubt a sad proof of universal degeneracy, that the *Metamorphoses* of an *Ovid* are preferred in our schools, to the sacred *Realities* of *Moses* and the *Prophets*." This is C. de Coetlogon's Introduction to Quarles' *Emblems*, reissued London, 1777. Earlier this same writer speaks of the "fabulous knowledge . . . and frivolous tales of heathenish science."

18. After Puttenham, not until Herder will Orpheus be given so central a place in learning. With Herder, Orpheus is the inventor of letters, music, the seven-stringed lyre, natural lore, magic, prophecy, astrology, and in especial, theology, poetry, and law. *Älteste Urkunde des Menschengeschlechts, Sämtliche Werke*, ed. Suphan (Berlin, 1883), *6*, 397.

19. Included in J. E. Spingarn's *Critical Essays of the Seventeenth Century*, Oxford, 1908.

20. Goethe says very sensibly in the *Farbenlehre* (Historische Teil, Dritte Abteilung): "Man kommt zwar den wackern Personen früherer Zeiten darin zu Hilfe, dass man sie vom Verdacht der Zauberei zu befreien sucht; aber nun täte es gleich wieder Not, dass man sich auf eine andere Weise ihrer annähme, und sie aus den Händen solcher Exorzisten abermals befreite, welche, um die Gespenster zu vertreiben, sichs zur heiligen Pflicht machen, den Geist selbst zu verjagen."

21. Sandys adds, "a way not untrod by the sacred Pen-men," and says later, in his Commentary on the Tenth Book, "Such Moses among the Hebrewes, among the Grecians Orpheus." So we come round to Pico's synthesis again.

22. See L. P. Wilkinson, *Ovid Recalled* (Cambridge, 1955), for a tracing of some of these influences. The writer says of Shakespeare in particular that he "draws on every book of the Metamorphoses, and there is scarcely a play which shows no trace of its influence, which is found particularly in the lighter scenes . . . All the Elizabethan poets borrowed from Ovid, but it was Shakespeare who knew best how to value him" (pp. 410, 423).

23. This is a favourite phrase of Bacon's: it occurs three times—in the *Advancement*, Bk. ii, the *De Augmentis*, Bk. ii, chap. 13, and in the Preface to *De Sapientia Veterum*.

24. For this series of opinions see Macaulay's essay on Bacon; Spedding's preface to the *De Sapientia Veterum* in the *Philosophical Works;* C. D. Broad, quoted by Douglas Bush (n. 2 above), p. 241, "Bacon wasted much time and ingenuity in showing that some mute inglorious Newton had hidden the true principles of Natural Philosophy in the story of *Pan*." The sympathetic commentator, as indeed nearly always, is Farrington, *Francis Bacon*, p. 76.

25. It is perhaps necessary to explain that the *De Augmentis Scientiarum* is Bacon's enlarged version, in Latin, of what he had already set out, in English, in *The Advancement of Learning*. He made a bad guess in assuming that Latin would continue to be the language

of scholarship, and so translated his work into it, adding to it as he went. The dates of the two publications are 1605 and 1623.

26. "Circumstances, and a certain bias of mind, have led me to take interest in such riddles, and it may well be doubted whether human ingenuity can construct an enigma of the kind which human ingenuity may not, by proper application, resolve." So says one of the characters in *The Gold-Bug*. Poe's opening to *The Murders in the Rue Morgue* is interesting also in this connection.

27. *Shakespeare's Imagery* (Cambridge, 1935), p. 17.

28. The Elizabethan taste for allegorical explanations of myth, catered to by works such as those of Natalis Comes, is to some extent responsible. Douglas Bush (n. 2 above), p. 31, quotes Marston,

> Reach me some poets' index that will show
> *Imagines Deorum,* Book of Epithets,
> Natalis Comes, thou I know recites
> And makest anatomy of poesy.

Chapman made considerable use of Comes.

29. He is of course sometimes identified with the rival poet in Shakespeare's Sonnets. There is a reference to the School of Night in *Love's Labour's Lost*. Chapman's *The Shadow of Night* came out in 1594; *Love's Labour's Lost* is conjecturally dated 1594–95, and *A Midsummer Night's Dream* 1594–98.

30. This labyrinth which is at once question, evidence, and answer is a very profound figure. E. Louis Backman in *Religious Dances in the Christian Church and in Popular Medicine* (Allen and Unwin, London, 1952), says (p. 70) that on a labyrinth or puzzle pattern in the church of St. Savino, Piacenza, stood the inscription, "This labyrinth reveals the structure of the world." Robert Hooke will use the image; so will Erasmus Darwin. See the discussion on the relationship between question and evidence in Polanyi, *Personal Knowledge*, p. 30.

31. He originally called it Maximus, not Masculus, but toned the title down later. Bacon's emblematic titles are part of his method and of his gifts. They are akin to the names he gives his Instances in *Novum Organum*, Bk. II—of the Door, of the Lamp, of the Twilight; or wonderful working phrases such as Circle Learning or the characterization of Memory as Pre-notion and Emblem. It has become customary among Bacon's commentators to call these "quaint" (Fowler, Macaulay) or "fantastic" (Farrington). They are in fact imaginative and mythological in the most positive sense.

32. There is an interesting passage on what Bacon calls "Circle Learning" in *Valerius Terminus,* chap. 8, "that use by way of supply of light and information which the particulars and instances of one science do yield and present for the framing or correcting the axioms of another science in their very truth and notion."

33. The adoption of this tone is usually held to have been an experiment on Bacon's part. See Robertson, *Philosophical Works,* p. xv.

34. *Complete Works,* ed. Ellis and Spedding, *3,* 329-30.

35. Wilkinson, *Ovid Recalled,* connects the *Metamorphoses* particularly with *A Midsummer Night's Dream* and *The Tempest.* For Shakespeare as a thinker through sleep and dream, see Victor Hugo in his long essay on Shakespeare, Pt. II, Bk. IV, *Oeuvres complètes* (Paris, Hetzel and Quantin, n.d.), Vol. 2 of *Philosophie,* p. 304: "Disons plus, là où il rêve, il pense encore; avec une profondeur autre, mais égale." See also Donald Davie, *Articulate Energy* (London, Routledge, 1955), p. 51: "Sleep is seen, as Shakespeare sees it, to be an energy."

36. *Lectures on Shakespeare and Milton* (London, 1883), p. 290.

37. In *The Tempest* too the spirit Ariel comes near to having human feelings as Puck could never do. See Act V, Scene 1. The loving friendship between Prospero and Ariel, compared with the colder connection between Oberon and Puck, is another of the added richnesses of the later play.

38. Another of Bacon's wonderfully imaginative titles. It has the general meaning of "Preparative," but a special one of the day of preparation for the Jewish Sabbath, and in that sense it appears in the Douay version of the New Testament.

39. Cf. Lamarck, *Philosophie zoologique* (Paris, 1809), p. 12: "La nécessité reconnue de bien observer les objets particuliers a fait naître l'habitude de se borner à la considération de ces objets et de leurs plus petits détails, de manière qu'ils sont devenus, pour la plupart des naturalistes, le sujet principal de l'étude. Ce serait cependant une cause réelle de retard pour les sciences naturelles . . . si ceux qui se livrent à une pareille étude dédaigneront de s'élever à des considérations supérieures." The kind of natural history these minds descry may still be set down, as Bacon would say, as deficient. See also Teilhard de Chardin, *Le Phénomène humain* (Paris, Éditions du Seuil, 1955), p. 246, where the writer speaks of "ce point de vue, qui est celui de la future Histoire Naturelle du Monde."

40. So Goethe says to Eckermann, "I think of the earth, with its encircling atmosphere, under the figure of a great living creature, engaged in an endless breathing in and breathing out" (*Gespräche mit Eckermann*, entry for April 11, 1827). Also Teilhard de Chardin, passim. This is probably a characteristic of the ways of working of Orphic minds in science.

41. See, for instance, the fable of Atalanta in *De Sapientia Veterum;* or *Novum Organum*, Bk. I, Aphorisms 95 and 99, where Bacon distinguishes between experiments of light and those of fruit and gives primacy to the former. There is a clear statement in Aphorism 5 of the *Parasceve:* "It would be an utter mistake to suppose that my intention would be satisfied by a collection of experiments of arts only with the view of thereby bringing the several arts to greater perfection."

42. Bacon's signature is attached to the record of the examination under torture of Father John Gerard, S. J., in April 1597. Bacon was one of the official Lords Commissioners who had to be present. *The Autobiography of a Hunted Priest*, John Gerard, trans. Philip Caraman (New York, 1952), p. 106 n.

43. Who writes their play? Peter Quince is encouraged by Bottom (III.1) to write a prologue, and it is he who eventually speaks that composition, presumably his own work, at the performance. Similarly, when Bottom wants to express his own vision he says he will ask Peter Quince to make a ballad of it (IV.1).

44. Notes to the New Shakespeare Edition of *A Midsummer Night's Dream* (Cambridge, 1924), p. 102.

45. Judge Learned Hand, *The Spirit of Liberty, Papers and Addresses* (New York, Knopf, 1952), p. 16.

46. From *A General Scheme or Idea of the Present State of Natural Philosophy*, included in *Posthumous Works* (London, 1705), pp. 43–61.

47. Essay 9 of Section 2 (London, 1866), pp. 325–26: "He has shown and established the true criterion between the ideas and the *idola* of the mind—namely, that the former are manifested by their adequacy to those ideas in nature, which in them and through them are contemplated . . . Bacon names the laws of nature, ideas; and represents what we have . . . called facts of science and central phenomena, as signatures, impressions and symbols of ideas."

48. See, on Bacon's method in this respect, Whyte, James, and Farrington.

49. In *Philosophical Works*.

50. Ellis, Spedding, and Robertson, all of whom are friendly to Bacon, point this out turn by turn in their respective editorial comments in the *Philosophical Works.*

51. *Posthumous Works,* pp. 6–7.

52. Pt. II, Bk. I.

53. Vol. 2 of the Michelet edition, p. 33.

54. Cf. his conversation with Falk, 1826: "At the same time he laid it down as a principle that Nature accidentally and as it were willy-nilly blurts out many of her secrets. Everything has been let out at some point only not in the places where we expect it . . . It is because of this that our knowledge of Nature has its riddling, sibylline, incoherent character" *(Goethe im Gespräch,* Leipzig, 1907, p. 253).

55. Hugo, *Shakespeare,* Pt. II, Bk. I; Coleridge, *Lectures on Shakespeare,* Sec. I; Goethe, *Dichtung und Wahrheit,* Vol. 2, Bk. XVI.

56. Coleridge, *The Friend,* Essay 11.

57. Quoted by Carlyle, *Heroes and Hero-Worship,* Lecture 3, "The Hero as Poet." See also Middleton Murry's *Shakespeare* (London, Cape, 1936), pp. 287, 289: "We must take the plunge into meaningful nonsense: Shakespeare *is* Life, uttering itself . . . In this sense we may say that the flower utters the plant and the earth and the rain and the sun which nourish it."

58. Both these passages are from *Lectures on Shakespeare,* Section 1.

59. John F. Danby, *Shakespeare's Doctrine of Nature* (London, Faber, 1949), p. 15. See also James, *The Dream of Learning,* and Carlyle, *Heroes and Hero-Worship.*

60. Danby's whole book (see above) is admirable in its discussion of this. See also Robert B. Heilman, *This Great Stage* (University of Louisiana Press, 1948), p. 11: "It seems safer to assume, as a working hypothesis, that when there is repeated speculation upon nature, the play is to that extent an essay upon nature."

61. Dr Johnson confessed that he could not bear to reread the last act until he had to annotate it for his edition of the play. The Nahum Tate happy-ending version held the stage for 150 years. The old play of *King Leir* ended happily, and the histories are not wholly tragic; it is Shakespeare who chooses to depart from them. (R. C. Bald, intro. to Crofts Classics ed. of *King Lear,* New York, 1949, p. vi.) Our involvement in the play is discussed by Danby, p. 181: "We occupy the same heath as Lear and are fellow agents and patients. Sympathy with Lear's sufferings will not explain this turn. Nor is it a case of daydream identification with

a hero. What happens is that the root of the mind is reached and activated." Middleton Murry also, in *Shakespeare,* p. 19, says: "In Shakespeare we seem to watch Nature involved in her destiny of self-discovery; and since this is a process which cannot be merely watched, we ourselves are caught up in it."

62. Cf. Spurgeon, *Shakespeare's Imagery,* on the subject of *King Lear:* "every kind of bodily movement, generally involving pain, is used to express mental and abstract as well as physical facts."

63. The answer is staggering. Lear calls him "blind Cupid." "The sign over a brothel," say the notes to the Penguin edition of the play (ed. G. B. Harrison). Yet Cupid is not only the god of "love," licit or illicit, as in our shrunken mythology, but the Eros who in the Orphic hymns creates the world, and on whom Bacon comments in his *De Principiis*—On Principles and Origins according to the Fables of Cupid and Coelum.

64. If *King Lear* is prehistory and legend, it is also fairy tale. It is impossible to narrate the fable of the play without its sounding like the conventional opening to a fairy tale; Middleton Murry has pointed this out. Myth is brought in further by the references to classical myths—Apollo, Jupiter, etc.—and the mention of fairies (IV.6).

65. We are not concerned with the truth and prayer functions of language here, but they are vital to the play and to poetry itself. Kent, Cordelia, and the Fool carry forward language-as-truth. Kent introduces language-as-prayer, and Edgar picks this up later. The logicians are precluded from certainty of truth, their system appealing not to truth but to consistency. Thus Regan begs Edmund, "Tell me but truly, but then speak the truth" (v.1), but receives no assurance. The affirmation of language-as-prayer in the play, particularly in Lear and Gloucester, does not mean that the prayers will be answered. Here, too, logical conclusions are not dodged.

66. *Schriften,* ed. Kluckhohn and Samuel (Leipzig, n.d.), 2, 331, 350.

Part III

1. I have simplified here. The second part of the poem was actually published first, anonymously, in 1789.

2. In the *Anti-Jacobin* in 1798. The interesting thing is that while the excellent parody of the style holds firm, the ridicule of the subject matter seems now, in the light of modern knowledge, to

vindicate Darwin. Here is one of the parodists' notes to Canto i: "Upon this view of things it seems highly probable that the first effort of Nature terminated in the production of Vegetables, and that these being abandoned to their own *energies*, by degrees detached themselves from the surface of the earth, and supplied themselves with wings or feet, according as their different propensities determined them in favour of aërial and terrestrial existence." We do now indeed think something of this sort happened; of course it sounds absurd.

3. Cambridge, 1941, chap. 2, pp. 62 ff. See also chap. 1, p. 23, for a discussion of Goethe's first acquaintance with Orpheus.

'4. See particularly his work *Ideen zur Philosophie der Geschichte der Menschheit*, 1784 (Suphan edition, Vol. 13). He speaks there of the globe as an immense workshop or laboratory directed toward the organization of differing forms (p. 47).

5. Vol. 1, Bk. x.

6. Critics insist on it also. For instance, Gundolf in *Goethe* (Berlin, 1922), p. 671, says that with two or three other poems they are the most concentrated formulation of Goethe's *Weltanschauung* that we have. Ermatinger in *Goethe und die Natur* (Zürich and Leipzig, 1932), p. 31, calls these verses the most cryptic Goethe ever wrote and says that they deal with the metamorphoses of man. Emil Staiger in his intro. to the first volume of Goethe's poems in the Gedenkausgabe (Zürich, 1950), pp. 748–49, says that the *Urworte* are an attempt to put the whole sense of existence into a single poem.

7. See particularly the essay on Bacon in *The Friend*, and the Shakespeare lectures. Coleridge is very shrewd about Bacon—"no man was ever more inconsistent" (*Table Talk*, October 3, 1830)—but there is no holding back on the final assessment: "in the persons of . . . Shakespeare, Milton and Lord Bacon were enshrined as much of the divinity of intellect as the inhabitants of this planet can hope will ever take up its abode among them" (*The Friend*, intro. to Vol. 3).

8. The last poet to be admitted to the Society that I know of was Byron. He was elected in 1816, but left England permanently a few months later, so that his membership never became an active one. I owe this information to Mr. John Jump.

9. "Il n'est peut-être aucun inventeur dont on puisse moins indiquer les précédens," Michelet says in the intro. to Vico's works, selected

and translated, which Michelet had published in Paris in 1835. It is difficult in England to get hold of an English translation of his works; the Michelet is still the most accessible.

10. H. P. Adams, *The Life and Writings of Giambattista Vico* (London, Allen and Unwin, 1935), p. 71. This is an excellent and sympathetic introduction to Vico and his work.

11. See Vico's *Autobiography*, translated by M. H. Fisch and T. G. Bergin (Cornell, 1944), pp. 83, 84.

12. Croce in *The Philosophy of Giambattista Vico*, trans. R. G. Collingwood (London, 1913), p. 271, gives details of the Hamann-Herder connection. Herder refers to Vico in *Briefe zu Beförderung der Humanität*, Sammlung 10, 1797 (Suphan edition, Vol. 18, p. 245), in a rather dull passage. Cassirer discusses this line of influence in *The Problem of Knowledge*, chap. 18. The Goethe reference is dated March 5, 1787, in the *Italienische Reise*.

13. See *The Philosophy of Symbolic Forms*, Vol. 2, intro. and *The Problem of Knowledge*, chap. 18.

14. *The Idea of History*, Oxford, 1946, p. 71: "in the late eighteenth century . . . German scholars discovered Vico and attached a great value to him, thus exemplifying his own doctrine that ideas are propagated not by 'diffusion,' like articles of commerce, but by the independent discovery by each nation of what it needs at any given stage in its own development."

15. Adams, *The Life and Writings of Giambattista Vico*, p. 219.

16. *1*, 412, and *2*, 196, in the Michelet edition.

17. Croce, p. 60; Adams, p. 120.

18. In *Notes, Theological, Political and Miscellaneous*, ed. Derwent Coleridge, London, 1853: "Note on the Treatise 'De Cultu et Amore Dei' of Emmanuel Swedenborg," September 22, 1821.

19. *Essays*, Second Series, Boston, 1860: Essay 1, "The Poet," p. 25.

20. Ibid., pp. 38–39.

21. The three genealogies are from (1) *Essays*, Second Series, Essay 1, p. 10; (2) ibid., p. 36; (3) *Representative Men* (Boston, 1860), section on Swedenborg, p. 104.

22. *Table Talk*, entry for September 1, 1832.

23. *Representative Men*, essay on Swedenborg, p. 133: "The universe is a gigantic crystal . . . The universe in his poem suffers under a magnetic sleep, and only reflects the mind of the magnetizer . . . All his types mean the same few things. All his figures speak one speech."

24. It is interesting that the real unraveller of hieroglyphs, Cham-

pollion, shows all the flexibility of the true poet and scientist. See his *Précis du système hiéroglyphique des anciens Égyptiens* (Paris, 1828), particularly chap. 10.

25. Second ed. Cambridge, 1942, Vol. 1, p. 411.

26. Cassirer, *The Problem of Knowledge*, p. 127: "Linnaeus was not only a brilliant observer but an indefatigable and inexorable logician as well, and it was said of him that he was possessed at times by a veritable mania for classification. The urge to codify and arrange phenomena has never been so strongly developed in any other great naturalist." A. J. Wilmott, "Systematic Botany from Linnaeus to Darwin," in *Lectures on the Development of Taxonomy*, Linnean Society (London, 1950), p. 34: "Linnaeus was a collector and codifier."

27. See A. J. Boerman, "Carolus Linnaeus: A Psychological Study," *Taxon* (Utrecht, 1953), 2, 145–56: "Another point that deserves our attention is his pronounced artistic temperament" (p. 148). See also Knut Hagberg, *Carl Linnaeus*, trans. from the Swedish by Alan Blair (London, Cape, 1952), pp. 60–65.

28. In the intro. to Pt. III of the *Philosophie zoologique*, Lamarck asks whether we must not consider "si les idées, la pensée, l'imagination même, ne sont que des phénomènes de la nature, et conséquemment que de véritables faits d'organisation; il appartient principalement au zoologiste, qui s'est appliqué à l'étude des phénomènes organiques, de rechercher ce que sont les idées, comment elles se produisent . . . et comment encore des actes de pensées et des jugemens multipliés peuvent faire naître *l'imagination,* cette faculté si profonde en création d'idées."

29. From *Amoenitas Academici*, Vol. 10, ed. Schreber, Erlangen, 1790. Hagberg in his biography of Linnaeus gives an account of the list and its contents, p. 187.

30. On account of his concern with internal structure, Cuvier has sometimes been ranked above Linnaeus. See P. Flourens, *Analyse raisonnée des travaux de Georges Cuvier* (Paris, 1841), "Éloge historique de M. Cuvier" (1834), p. 4: "il est évident que ce qui avait manqué à Linnaeus et à Buffon, soit pour classer les animaux, soit pour expliquer convenablement leurs phénomènes, c'était de connaître assez leur structure intime ou leur organisation." Sainte-Beuve seems to demand of Cuvier that he should himself have recognized the connection between science and art. In *Premiers Lundis* (Paris, 1886), he discusses Cuvier's reception to the Académie Française, where he took the poet Lamartine's place and had

to make the customary panegyric upon his predecessor. Sainte-Beuve says: "M. Cuvier est un homme de génie lui-même; arrivé à ces hauteurs de la science où elle se confond presque avec la poésie, il était digne de comprendre et de célébrer le poëte philosophique qui, dans l'incertitude de ses pensées, avait plus d'une fois plongé jusqu'au chaos, et demandé aux éléments leur origine, leur loi, leur harmonie: Aristote pouvait donner la main à Platon. Il nous coûte d'avouer qu'il est resté au-dessous de sa tâche" (p. 315). Cassirer says in *The Problem of Knowledge*, p. 131: "The knowledge of a single form, if it is really to penetrate to the heart of the matter, always presupposes a knowledge of the world of forms in its entirety. Systematic biology, therefore, as understood and practiced by Cuvier, was no mere device of classification and arrangement that can be easily apprehended, but a disclosure of the very framework of nature herself."

31. Quoted in the "Life of Gray" prefaced to the poet's *Works*, by J. Mitford (London, 1847), pp. lxx, lxxv.

32. Quoted by Charles Eliot Norton, *The Poet Gray as a Naturalist* (Boston, 1903), p. 18. The drawings as reproduced are exquisite in their exact detail. Part of Gray's work on Linnaeus, so Mitford says, consisted in turning the Swedish sage into Latin hexameters.

33. Linnean Society lectures on taxonomy (n. 26 above), pp. 72–74.

34. Ibid., p. 37.

35. Gustave Theodor Fechner, *Nanna, oder Über das Seelenleben der Pflanzen;* in the foreword the author says that in his searches for a title for his book he thought of *Flora* or *Hamadryas,* but rejected the first as too botanical, the second as too stiffly antiquarian and too much restricted to trees. He found the name of Nanna, Baldur's wife, in the German poet Uhland. Fechner quotes poetry and myth as precedent for his standpoint, and speaks of a deep spring of poetry in nature itself.

36. This is quoted verbatim, with complete approval in each case as an example of the true nature of science, by Poe in *Eureka* and Michael Polanyi in *Personal Knowledge.*

37. Second ed., London, 1897 (the first ed. was 1889), p. 300. The idea of Nature as a poem is repeated: "In Nature's workshop but a shaving, Of her poem but a word, But a tint brushed from her pallette, This feather of a bird!" Then, fourteen lines later, "What then must be the poem, This but its lightest word!"

38. The four references are *Schriften,* ed. Kluckhohn and Samuel, *3*, 183; *1*, 32; *2*, 322, 325.

39. Ibid., 2, 346.

40. "A state of Spirit . . . analogous to mine own when I am at once waiting for, watching, and organically constructing and being constructed by, the *Ideas*, the living Truths . . ." *Inquiring Spirit: a New Presentation of Coleridge from His Published and Unpublished Writings*, ed. Kathleen Coburn (London, 1951), p. 214.

41. There is an indirect reference to Orpheus in Pt. 1, chap. 2. More interestingly still, Novalis' notes for the completion of the novel, never finished, show that he meant to identify his hero's death with the death of Orpheus. See Walter Rehm, *Orpheus: Der Dichter und die Toten* (Düsseldorf, Schwann, 1950), p. 100.

42. From *Schriften*, 2, 326; 3, 272, 290. One of Novalis' own collections of thoughts is called *Blütenstaub* or pollen.

43. *The Elements of Botany*, trans. Hugh Rose from the *Philosophia Botanica* (London, 1775), pp. 282, 334. A case could be made out for Linnaeus as a poet in his own right. His biographer Hagberg says, "The task which professional writers have often set themselves, namely, to describe the sexual act in beautiful resounding words . . . is here admirably accomplished by Linnaeus. In his presentment a floral radiance is even shed upon the vital animal functions. This can only be attained by a writer who is a poet by nature" (*Linnaeus*, p. 65). Other passages in Linnaeus suggest the same thing—this, for instance, from Vol. 4 of the *Systema Naturae*: "*Mollusca*: Are naked, furnished with tentacula or arms, for the most part inhabitants of the sea; and by their phosphorous quality, illuminate the dark abyss of waters, reflecting their lights to the firmament. Thus what is beneath the water corresponds with that which is above."

44. Each has his own protagonists too. Thus we find C. E. Raven in *John Ray, Naturalist* (Cambridge, 1942), p. 200, saying, "It could easily be argued that Ray in fact laid down lines of classification more in accord with genuinely scientific and evolutionary principles than those of his illustrious successor," i.e. Linnaeus.

45. *The Elements of Botany*, trans. James Hewetson (London, 1849), pp. 526–27, 530.

46. Section 20, p. 512. The passage is particularly interesting because it leads into a discussion of the variability of flowers as an instance of evolution at work, "the perpetual progress of all organized beings from less to greater perfection existing from the beginning of time to the end of it! a power impressed on nature by the great father of all" (p. 515).

47. *Darwiniana* (London, 1902), p. 26.

48. Essay entitled "The Progress of Science" in *Methods and Results*, London, 1904.

49. What is a fact? "Das Höchste wäre: zu begreifen, dass alles Faktische schon Theorie ist," Goethe says in *Aphorismen und Fragmente*, Gedenkausgabe (Zürich, 1952), *17, 723*. Whether in a matter of fact or opinion, Charles Darwin seems to have had a considerable barrier in his mind against his grandfather's work. He appears in the *Origin of Species* only in a footnote in the "Historical Sketch" preceding the 1872 edition: "It is curious how my grandfather, Dr. Erasmus Darwin, anticipated the views and erroneous grounds of opinion of Lamarck in his *Zoonomia*, published in 1794."

50. *Darwiniana*, p. 25. Huxley returns to this subject later: "Long occupation with the work has led the present writer to believe that the 'Origin of Species' is one of the hardest books to master." [Footnote: "Sir J. Hooker writes, 'It is the very hardest work to read, to profit, that I ever tried.' "]

51. *Darwinism*, p. 461.

52. The first quotation is from *Methods and Results*, p. 6, the second from Huxley's *Scientific Memoirs*, ed. Foster and Lankester (London, 1898), *1, 311*.

53. *Methods and Results*, pp. 60, 62. Huxley's pursuit of logic at times betrays him out of a scientific attitude. The contrast with another type of scientific mind can be seen in the passage where he relates how Clerk Maxwell told him that two atoms can occupy the same space simultaneously. Huxley goes on, "I am loth to dispute any dictum of a philosopher as remarkable for the subtlety of his intellect as for his vast knowledge; but the assertion . . . appears to me to violate the principle of contradiction, which is the foundation not only of physical science but of logic in general. It means that A can be not-A."

54. *Darwiniana*, pp. 245, 246.

55. Ibid., pp. 72, 248–49.

56. Ibid., p. 93. The passage is also characteristic of Huxley in that it goes on to suggest a genetic origin for inanimate matter in embryological terms, a lovely reversion to the Baconian metaphor of generations, and quite un-Darwinian.

57. See *Geschichte meines botanischen Studiums*, written in 1817 and reworked in 1831, appended to the *Metamorphose der Pflanzen*.

58. See Anna Seward's *Memoirs of the Life of Dr. Darwin* (London, 1804) for this and subsequent details.

59. The proper name of the Lunatics was the Lunar Society, so called because it met at the full moon to enable members to see their way home. For particulars see James Venable Logan, *The Poetry and Aesthetics of Erasmus Darwin* (Princeton, 1936), p. 15.

60. *Erasmus Darwin* by Ernst Krause, trans. W. S. Dallas, London, 1879.

61. In *Biographia Literaria*, chap. 1, Coleridge says: "I remember to have compared Darwin's work to the Russian palace of ice, glittering, cold, and transitory." In No. 6 of the *Philosophical Lectures*, ed. Kathleen Coburn, London, 1949, pp. 213–14, he says: "He [Darwin] told me he had some wish to employ a young man of a metaphysical turn to read the books of all former philosophers to him and to give him a syllabus of their opinions which he was not acquainted with. 'For,' says he, 'I can reconcile the whole to my system and I think it will be doing a great service to confute them when I establish the great doctrine of physics and the understanding of man.' This took place with a man who was deemed a great philosopher some time ago and I believe in the hospitals and elsewhere you may hear his name now, and there was a time when he was a great poet likewise. Both the one and the other appear to have been in rapid decay." In private Coleridge is yet more positive: "and I absolutely nauseate Darwin's Poem" he says in a letter to John Thelwall, May 13, 1796. Yet he read the poem, and its notes, in considerable detail, as Livingston Lowes traces out in *The Road to Xanadu*.

62. Opinions differ very widely on the question of Goethe's status as a scientist. Cassirer, for instance, makes great claims for his scientific standing in *The Problem of Knowledge* (pp. 137 ff.), while Sherrington considers it negligible. The question is discussed fairly fully in Agnes Arber's *Goethe's Botany*, Chronica Botanica, 10, No. 2 (1946), 67 ff.

63. Quoted by Adolph Hansen, *Goethes Morphologie* (Giessen, 1919), p. 127.

64. *Goethe im Gespräch* (Leipzig, 1907), p. 252. Date before 1826.

65. There is an amusing sequel to this account. Apparently Miss Seward did in fact pen some verses on the occasion, which the Doctor then quietly purloined and incorporated in *The Botanic Garden* without any acknowledgment, to Miss Seward's considerable indignation.

66. *Gedenkausgabe* (Zürich, 1950), *17*, 699: "Bei Ovid ist die Analogie der tierischen und menschlichen Glieder im Übergang trefflich ausgedrückt." See also Darwin's *Phytologia,* Sec. 7, p. 108.

67. By Ermatinger. See n. 6 above.

68. That strange fantastical scientist of Goethe's own time, Oken, uses much this same metaphor. In his *Lehrbuch der Naturphilosophie* (2d ed. Jena, 1831) he says, "Natural philosophy is therefore a divine philology or a divine logic" (p. 15). Later he says: "The artificial systems of plant classification stand in the same relation to the plant kingdom as a lexicon does to language. The hitherto so-called 'natural' systems, which really ought to be called merely 'methodical' systems, stand in the same relation to the plant kingdom as ordinary grammar does to language. But the true system of plant classification must bear the same relation to the plant kingdom as philosophic or genetic grammar bears to language" (p. 218). Later commentaries on this man are interesting. He figures in one of Emerson's Swedenborg genealogies. Shaw in the preface to *Back to Methuselah* says of him: "Oken defined natural science as 'the science of the everlasting transmutations of the Holy Ghost in the world.' . . . The man who was scientific enough to see that the Holy Ghost is a scientific fact got easily in front of the blockheads who could only sin against it." Agnes Arber in *The Natural Philosophy of Plant Form* (Cambridge, 1950), says, "his extravagant nature philosophy is illumined here and there by flashes of genuine insight" (p. 158).

69. *The Friend.* This and the subsequent passages are from Sec. 2, Essay 6.

70. In a recent article in *The Sunday Times* in England, in connection with the centenary of the *Origin of Species,* Rebecca West claims Ovid outright as the poet-founder of evolution as a way of thinking.

71. This is not a break but a sequence. The poet, as Orpheus or Amphion, is the builder of cities. Cf. Carlyle, *Sartor Resartus,* Bk. iii, chap. 8: "Not only was Thebes built by the music of an Orpheus; but without the music of some inspired Orpheus was no city ever built, no work that man glories in ever done."

72. I am indebted for information on the predominance of Orphic elements in the *Metamorphoses* to Wade C. Stephens, who very kindly put at my disposal his dissertation for the Ph.D. Degree at Princeton University, entitled "The Function of Religious and Philosophical Ideas in Ovid's Metamorphoses," 1957.

73. Darwin knew *Paradise Lost* well enough to steal from it. The line, "And sweet, reluctant, amorous delay" turns up shamelessly in *The Temple of Nature*.

74. See notes to poems in Vol. 2 of the *Festausgabe* of Goethe's *Werke*, p. 440. The so-called Nature Ode or Fragment, whether it be by Goethe or by Tobler under Goethe's influence, is flat on the whole and of no use here. See Arber, *Goethe's Botany*, and Trevelyan, *Goethe and the Greeks*, for a discussion of this latter work.

75. *Goethe im Gespräch*, p. 176. Conversation with von Müller and Riemer, May 29, 1814.

76. In a most interesting passage on this subject, in *Aus meinem Leben, Fragmentarisches. Spätere Zeit*, he says this: "I have never encountered a more presumptuous human being than myself, and since it is I who bear witness to this, it shows that what I say is true. I never thought of anything as still to be attained, rather that I possessed it already. They could have set a crown on my head and I should have taken it for granted. And yet all the time I was just a human being like any other, and just because of this. Only the fact that I tried to do justice to the things I took on that were beyond my strength, and tried to deserve the things I received that were beyond my deserts—this and this alone distinguished me from an out-and-out madman."

77. From *Über die neue Ausgabe der Goetheschen Werke*, 1816; *Tag- und Jahresheften*, 1807; *Ferneres in Bezug auf mein Verhältnis zu Schiller;* conversation with von Müller, and with Soret, 1832, both from *Goethe im Gespräch*, pp. 306, 311.

78. *Goethe im Gespräch*, p. 95; conversation with Riemer, August 2, 1807.

79. See *Notiz* of 1809 to the novel.

80. Novalis early in Pt. II of *Die Lehrlinge zu Sais* speaks of the spectrum as if it were an instrument of the mind.

81. See Arber, *Goethe's Botany*, passim, and *The Natural Philosophy of Plant Form*, chap. 4; Hansen, *Goethes Morphologie*, p. 21; Cassirer, *The Problem of Knowledge*, p. 140.

82. I have borrowed bits of this translation from that given in Magnus, *Goethe as a Scientist*, New York, Schuman, 1949 (originally published 1906), p. 82. The passage is so important I give the original: "Ich war völlig überzeugt, ein allgemeiner, durch Metamorphose sich erhebender Typus gehe durch die sämtlichen organischen Geschöpfe durch, lasse sich in allen seinen Teilen auf gewissen mittleren Stufen gar wohl beobachten und müsse auch noch da aner-

kannt werden, wenn er sich auf der höchsten Stufe der Menschheit ins Verborgene bescheiden zurückzieht."

83. Emil Staiger, in the notes to Goethe's poems in the *Manesse-Bibliothek der Weltliteratur*, 2, 480, says very beautifully that the poem is to effect this final transformation in the two, and so takes its place in the metamorphic process of nature. I am in general indebted to these notes.

84. Ibid., p. 487.

85. Samuel Butler's *Life and Habit* suggests such a possibility, and it might offer a different development of taxonomic and morphological thought from that offered by Charles Darwin in his would-be fixing of the Linnaean system in serial, historical time, which he took to be the consummation of the Linnaean vision of natural classification. See on this subject Arber, *The Natural Philosophy of Plant Form*, pp. 162–63.

86. *Der Untergang des Abendlandes* (Munich, Beck, 1923), intro. p. 67 n., and chap. 2, p. 132. The Goethe quotation is given as from the *Nachlass*. Rilke recommends Spengler and his "überragende Bedeutung" to Katharina Kippenberg in a letter of March 7, 1919.

Part IV

1. I have borrowed this translation from the version given in the translation of Rilke's *Sonnets to Orpheus* by J. B. Leishman (London, Hogarth Press, 1949), notes on the First Part, p. 149. The letter is to Frau Wunderly-Volkart.

2. *Shakespeare*, Pt. III, Bk. II: "Or ce mouvement est un fait d'intelligence, un fait de civilisation, un fait d'âme; et c'est pourquoi celui qui écrit ces lignes n'a jamais employé les mots *romantisme* ou *romantique*."

3. I have taken this term from Michael Polanyi, who gives *Personal Knowledge* the subtitle "Towards a Post-Critical Philosophy."

4. In his 1888 preface to these plays Renan says, "*Coriolan* et *Jules César* ne sont pas des peintures de moeurs romaines; ce sont des études de psychologie absolue."

5. Fourth ed. (Paris, 1864), sec. 1, pp. 66, 69.

6. See, for instance, Lance Whyte, "The Growth of Ideas," *Eranos-Jahrbuch 23* (Zürich, 1955), p. 370: "But there is as yet no philosophical anthropology, no history of human consciousness, no adequately grounded natural history of ideas." And Michael Polanyi, *Personal Knowledge*, Pt. IV, pp. 387, 399: "Biology can be ex-

tended by continuous stages into epistemology . . . I would expect, on the contrary, that biology would gain greatly in scope and depth by addressing itself more candidly to the fundamental features of life."

7. *Collected Letters*, ed. Griggs (Oxford, 1956), 2, 830; to Southey, July 29, 1802. Wordsworth was raised on Bacon's work. Mary Moorman in *William Wordsworth: The Early Years, 1770–1803* (Oxford, 1957), to which in general I am much indebted, says that in school "the boys were made familiar with the name of Francis Bacon and with the more experimental and 'scientific' approach to knowledge which had been gaining ground during the last two centuries" (pp. 56–57). Elsewhere in this work (especially pp. 582–85), Wordsworth's attitude to science is discussed. The writer takes the view that Wordsworth shows a "lack of imagination about the scientist's task," particularly the taxonomic side of it. I would prefer to put it that he was opposing, as Goethe did, a rigid or mechanically logical approach in favor of a more post-logical one, closer to the true nature of science. But Wordsworth may well, in his isolation as time went on from the living science of his day, have withdrawn into increasing suspicion of it.

8. *Collected Letters, 1*, 320–21. Letter to Joseph Cottle, early April 1797. The passage is preceded by a mention of Milton.

9. Moorman, p. 367; but see also chap. 18, regarding the series of epic themes in *The Prelude*. "Significantly, he aims at completing Milton" (p. 607).

10. Garrod, *Wordsworth* (Oxford, 1923), p. 27, quotes Hazlitt as saying, "Milton is his great idol and he sometimes dares to compare himself with him." Garrod adds, "The comparison, as Hazlitt quite well knew, was not so absurd as he would have us suppose." Moorman, pp. 506–7, quotes a letter from Lamb to Manning, February 15, 1801, in which he talks of a letter from Wordsworth, "with a deal of stuff about a certain Union of Tenderness and Imagination, which in the sense he used Imagination was not the characteristic of Shakespeare, but which Milton possessed in a degree far exceeding other Poets: which Union, as the highest species of poetry, and chiefly deserving that name, 'he was most proud to aspire to'; . . . After one has been reading Shakespeare twenty of the best years of one's life, to have a fellow start up, and prate about some unknown quality, which Shakespeare possessed in a degree inferior to Milton *and somebody else!!*" Lamb's real indignation comes right through the humor.

11. From *Kunst und Altertum,* included in *Maximen und Reflex-ionen,* in *Gedenkausgabe* (Zürich, 1949), *9,* 508; and conversation with Sulpiz Boisserée and Anton Thibaut, September 20, 1815, *Goethe im Gespräch,* p. 193.

12. *The Art of Wordsworth* (London, 1952), pp. 41–42, 55. See also Moorman, p. 609: "Yet during the next two years Wordsworth did indeed write an epic, of which the 'hero' is himself and the story that of his own spiritual adventures, discoveries, and sufferings. *The Prelude* is the only kind of epic he could ever successfully have written."

13. Letter to Sir George Beaumont, April 11, 1805. *Early Letters,* ed. Selincourt (Oxford, 1935), p. 489.

14. See C. M. Bowra, *From Virgil to Milton* (London, Macmillan, 1945), p. 246, and elsewhere.

15. Ibid., pp. 15, 58.

16. This is most beautifully said by an anthropologist writing on epic—G. R. Levy, *The Sword from the Rock* (London, Faber, 1953): "Thither he drove the spear, and Hector fell in the dust. *Then you and I and all of us fell down* . . . In this climax, unlike the earlier duels, the two heroes have drawn into themselves the whole fate of camp and city" (p. 191).

17. Published in Vol. 5 of *Poetical Works of William Wordsworth,* ed. Selincourt and Darbishire (Oxford, 1949), appendix A. I am indebted to the Moorman biography of Wordsworth for directing me to this "little-known poem," as the author calls it there.

18. Rilke, *Letters, 1892–1910,* tr. Greene and Norton (New York, Norton, 1945), letter to Clara Rilke (June 26, 1907), *1,* 287.

19. Rilke, *Briefe an einen jungen Dichter* (Leipzig, Insel-Verlag, n.d.), p. 11; February 17, 1903.

20. See *Briefwechsel mit Katharina Kippenberg* (Wiesbaden, Insel-Verlag, 1954), letters of December 11, 1915, and February 7, 1917, pp. 155, 215.

21. Ibid., letter of August 17, 1919; and *Letters,* Vol. 1, letter to Clara Rilke, June 24, 1907, p. 287.

22. *Briefwechsel mit Lou Andreas-Salomé* (Zürich and Wiesbaden, Insel-Verlag, 1952), letters of August 10, 1903, p. 99; May 12, 1904, p. 161; May 13, 1904, pp. 166–67; October 19, 1904, p. 192.

23. *Briefe an einen jungen Dichter,* letter of August 12, 1904, p. 47.

24. *Letters,* Vol. 1, letter to Clara Rilke, June 28, 1907, p. 289; and to Friedrich Westhoff, April 29, 1904, p. 151.

25. *Briefe an einen jungen Dichter,* July 16, 1903, p. 25.

26. The phrase, from a letter of Wordsworth's, is quoted in Mary Moorman's biography, p. 260. The same writer also quotes Coleridge as writing in a letter to Thomas Poole in 1799: "but dear Wordsworth appears to me to have hurtfully segregated and isolated his being. Doubtless his delights are more deep and sublime; but he has likewise more hours that prey upon the flesh and blood" (pp. 435–36).

27. "Of all the men I ever knew, Wordsworth has the least femineity in his mind. He is *all* man" (*Inquiring Spirit,* ed. Coburn, p. 296).

28. See the introductions to the companion volumes of translation of the Duino Elegies and the Sonnets, by Leishman and Spender and by Leishman respectively, London, Hogarth Press, 1952, 1949.

29. See *Poetical Works of William Wordsworth,* ed. Selincourt (Oxford, 1944), Vol. 2, notes, p. 526.

30. The whole poem is reminiscent of Milton. Barron Field, writing to Wordsworth on December 17, 1836, says of this poem, "Milton should have written it when blind."

31. It is not surprising that the opening of St. John's Gospel should haunt Orphic poets: one remembers Goethe and Valéry on it, among others. There is a very brief and very wise discussion of Rilke's disjointed relation to the Logos in Rudolf Kassner's introduction to *Rainer Maria Rilke und Marie von Thurn und Taxis: Briefwechsel,* Vol. 1, Zürich, Insel-Verlag, 1951.

32. See G. R. Levy, *The Gate of Horn: A Study of the Religious Conceptions of the Stone Age, and Their Influence upon European Thought* (London, Faber, 1948), p. 52: "Both the winding path, and the rope or clue, appear in European tales of entry into an actual or subjective spiral maze [*footnote:* Cf. the kitten who unwinds the ball of wool before Alice penetrates the looking-glass, and the fatal spindle of the Sleeping Beauty] and with these savage analogies before us it does not seem unreasonable to connect such a pathway between the two worlds, both with the winding entrance signs of the Palaeolithic caves, and with the choice of intricate and difficult passages to their inner sanctuaries." Also p. 159, concerning mazes and labyrinths: "The primitive conception of the divine body as the road travelled by itself and by its seeker, will again be recalled in the Australians' interpretation of their ground drawings, as will its possible origins in Palaeolithic cave religion." In her other work, *The Sword from the Rock,* this writer specifically links Wordsworth's *Prelude* with ancient figures, p. 138, n. 1: "In the Greek version of Ut-napishtim's story of the Flood Xisu-

thros has to bury his archives before the waters are loosed, just as
the Arab has to bury the symbols of poetry and mathematics be-
fore the pursuing sea in *The Prelude*. Had Wordsworth read
Berossus?" He may have done, of course; but I think the con-
nection is postlogical and goes far deeper than scholarship.

33. Rilke took the title from a work of art in the Naples museum;
see *Letters*, Vol. 1, postcard to Clara Rilke, December 2, 1906. The
edition of Rilke's poems used throughout is *Gesammelte Werke*
(Insel-Verlag, 1956), Vols. 1 and 2.

34. See, for instance, "It is so natural for me to understand *girls and
women;* the deepest experience of the creator is feminine" (*Letters*,
Vol. 1, November 20, 1904, p. 181); "I, who could never get along
with men . . ." (*Briefwechsel, Thurn und Taxis, 1,* 54, August
5, 1911); "I often think that what is possible between two human
beings is not really very much in the long run; everything that is
infinite is inside the individual" (Ibid., p. 42, May 31, 1911). The
celebration of death is to be found from the *Stundenbuch* to the
Duino Elegies. Kassner, in his introduction to the Thurn und
Taxis collection of letters already cited, has wise things to say
about this death doctrine of Rilke's ("Sie hat etwas knabenhaft
Hastiges an sich, sie scheint reif, ist unreif," p. xvii) as also about
the whole relation of Rilke to psychoanalysis.

35. See Levy, *The Sword from the Rock*, p. 121: in myths of dis-
covery "such heroes were apt to win their ultimate renown for
mental rather than for physical achievement."

36. Ibid., p. 101. The writer describes how the ancient myth of
cosmic enmity between father and son "has given rise in modern
times to new myths of interpretation," adding in a footnote, "Cf.
Freud's Myth of the Murdered Father in *Totem and Tabu.*"

37. The contrast, in tone and helpfulness, in some modern work,
such as Mircea Éliade's *Patterns of Comparative Religion,* is
heartening.

38. The edition is that of Selincourt, Oxford, 1933.

39. Freud has an interesting comment on this question in his essay
"The Relation of the Poet to Day-Dreaming," *Collected Papers,*
Vol. 4, London, Hogarth Press, 1950. He says on p. 177: "The rela-
tion of phantasies to time is altogether of great importance. One
may say that a phantasy hovers between three periods of time—the
three periods of our ideation . . . So past, present and future are
threaded, as it were, on the string of the wish that runs through
them all."

40. Oxford edition, p. 246.

41. The heroic shield occurs later in the poem also. "I had approach'd, like other Youth, the Shield / Of human nature from the golden side / And would have fought, even to the death, to attest / The quality of the metal which I saw" (x.663–66).

42. Rachel Levy in *The Sword from the Rock* gives three main subjects of epic poetry, the battle for creation, the quest of the lost, and the third, heroic, type, based on wars of migration (pp. 85–86). It is not fanciful, I think, to see in *The Prelude* notes of all three.

43. Bk. iv.71; x.659; xi.42; xiii.269, 408, 418.

44. See, for instance, J. Z. Young, *Doubt and Certainty in Science: A Biologist's Reflections on the Brain* (Oxford, 1951): "In some sense we literally create the world we speak about. Therefore our physical science is not simply a set of reports upon an outside world. It is also a report upon ourselves and our relations to that world, whatever the latter may be like" (p. 108).

45. Wordsworth sees truth itself as a living thing, not a dead idol. He says in Bk. viii, line 430: "ye who are fed / By the dead letter, miss the spirit of things, / Whose truth is not a motion or a shape / Instinct with vital functions, but a Block / Or waxen Image which yourselves have made, / And ye adore."

46. Logic in isolation may become an idol also (see preceding note). In xi.123, Wordsworth says, "There comes a time when Reason, not the grand / And Simple Reason, but that humbler power / Which carries on its no inglorious work / By logic and minute analysis / Is of all Idols that which pleases most / The growing mind." Earlier (x.844) he speaks of minds that "sacrificed / The exactness of a comprehensive mind / To scrupulous and microscopic views / That furnish'd out materials for a work / Of false imagination." One recalls Lévy-Bruhl, Valéry, and Poe, each of whom understood in his own way about idolatry in the mind.

47. See the passage from the *Friend* quoted above in Pt. ii, Sec. 8.

48. xii.234.

49. iv.303.

50. This Orphic vision appears also in Novalis' *Die Lehrlinge zu Sais,* in the second part. One recalls the strange saying, "My Father works hitherto, and I work," in John 5:17. The Word works in the works of creation.

51. Cf. "the Creature, / Sensuous and intellectual as he is, / A twofold Frame of body and of mind" (xi.168).

52. The phrase about the differences hid in all exterior forms sug-

gests Bacon's "latent configuration," while the whole passage ac-
cords with Goethe's scientific method.

53. Quoted by Selincourt, notes, p. 265.

54. II.180, 370, 374.

55. XII.252.

56. The dream works on classic Freudian structural, though not in-
terpretative, principles.

57. There are two passages where Wordsworth connects explicitly
childhood and power. The first is v.531: "our childhood sits, /
Our simple childhood sits upon a throne / That hath more power
than all the elements. / I guess not what this tells of Being past, /
Nor what it augurs of the life to come; / But so it is." The second
is XI.329, "Oh! mystery of Man, from what a depth / Proceed
thy honours! I am lost, but see / In simple childhood something
of the base / On which thy greatness stands." A few lines later he
speaks of his own childhood as "the hiding-places of my power."
Rilke with his abiding nostalgic preoccupation with childhood is
on much less sure ground here.

58. v.579.

59. This is not to be labeled, or confused with, pantheism. Mircea
Éliade, in *Patterns in Comparative Religion* (New York, Sheed and
Ward, 1958), discusses this matter very helpfully. In the conclusion,
p. 459, he says, "Some of the highest religious experiences identify
the sacred with the whole universe . . . That this is more than a
simple idea classed, rightly or wrongly, as pantheist, is shown by the
words of Léon Bloy speaking of the . . . 'mystery of Life, which is
Christ. *Ego sum Vita.* Whether the Life is in man, animals or plants,
it is always Life . . .' It is clear that this is not 'pantheism' in our
sense, but what we might call 'panontism.'" This is not to deny the
boldness of the theological thinking in Wordsworth's poem. It is
matched only, in my experience, by Teilhard de Chardin's *Le
Phénomène humain*, Pt. IV and epilogue.

60. He deals with these on the same postlogical terms. Cf. IX.102,
"Whence the main Organs of the public Power / Had sprung,
their transmigrations when and how / Accomplish'd, giving thus
unto events / A form and body . . ."

61. *Letters,* ed. Forman, letter to John Hamilton Reynolds (May 3,
1818), p. 143.

62. A passage from Rilke's diary, November 3, 1899, runs: "I fear
within me only those contradictions that tend towards conciliation.
That part of my life, where they could join hands, must be very

narrow. My contradictions ought rarely to know of one another and then only through rumour." Quoted by F. W. van Heerik-huizen, *Rainer Maria Rilke: His Life and Work*, trans. Fernand G. Renier and Anne Cliff (London, Routledge, 1951), p. 121.

63. *Letters*, Vol. 1, letter to Clara Rilke (May 8, 1903), p. 105.

64. In a letter to Xaver von Moos, April 20, 1923. I have taken this Englishing from *Sonnets to Orpheus*, trans. M. D. Herter Norton (New York, Norton, 1942), which, with J. B. Leishman's translation of the same work, I have frequently consulted.

65. In the *Nachwort* to the individual edition of these poems (Insel-Verlag, 1950), p. 37, Rilke is quoted as saying, "es war sehr merk-würdig, die Feder wurde mir buchstäblich 'geführt.' "

66. There is good precedent for the conscious use of personification in the language in which one talks about ideas. Goethe spoke of them to Eckermann as the free children of God who stand before us and say "Here we are!" There is also Valéry's *Chant de l'idée-maitresse* in *Mélange*, where the Idea is indeed the master-mistress of a passion.

67. *Briefwechsel mit Katharina Kippenberg* (February 23, 1922), p. 455.

68. *Briefwechsel mit Lou Andreas-Salomé* (February 20, 1914), p. 327. The whole passage is interesting: "Und vielleicht ist alles *Phal-lische* (wie *vor*-dachte ich im Tempel von Karnak, denken konnt ichs noch nicht) nur eine Auslegung des menschlich heimlich-Geheimen im Sinne des offen-Geheimen der Natur. Ich kann das aegyptisches Gott-Lächeln gar nicht erinnern, ohne dass mir das Wort 'Blütenstaub' einfällt."

69. ". . . if they would not lose the power to rejoice as deeply in a birch leaf or in the feather of a peacock or the pinion of a hooded crow as in a great mountain range or a splendid palace. The small is as little small as the big—is big." *Letters*, Vol. 1, letter to Hel-muth Westhoff (November 12, 1901), p. 59. The attitude is like Wordsworth's "looking for the shades of difference." Hugo von Hoffmannsthal's *Der Brief des Lord Chandos*, written in 1902 but supposed to be set in the year 1603, is an interesting commentary to this and to much else in Rilke. Donald Davie deals with it in *Articulate Energy*.

70. See especially that much-publicized letter to the Polish trans-lator. It is given in full in the Leishman translation of the Sonnets, introduction, p. 17, and in M. D. Herter Norton's version, notes, pp. 131 ff. Rilke is connected at this point not only to Mallarmé,

a poem by whom is among those Rilke translated into German, but to Valéry also, his nearest and closest Orphic friendship. As Hans-Egon Holthusen points out in his *Rilkes Sonette an Orpheus: Versuch einer Interpretation* (Munich, 1937), pp. 19–21, "Auch Valéry ist ein Verwandler." He differs from Rilke, however, in that his transformations tended to be mathematical. Rilke's imagery for his own transformations was organic from the beginning. He speaks in a letter to Lou Andreas-Salomé of August 10, 1903, of his need to find the "smallest basic element, the cell," of his art.

71. See, for instance, stanza 1 of *Aus dem Kathedralen-Kreis, Notre-Dame-de-Paris*, of this year (*Gesammelte Werke*, Vol. 2, p. 350). Also letter to Paul Zech, September 12, 1907, where Rilke speaks of "the unerring recognition of my metamorphoses through your eyes."

72. About Rilke's connection with Ovid there are incidental intelligences in Else Buddeberg, *Rainer Maria Rilke, eine Innere Biographie* (Stuttgart, Metzler, 1954), p. 403, "die viel frühere Kenntnis der Ovidschen Metamorphosen"; and in J.-F. Angelloz, *Rainer Maria Rilke, l'évolution spirituelle du poète* (Paris, Hartmann, 1936), p. 32, n. 1: "L'amie qui s'est occupée de l'installation à Muzot nous signala ces deux faits susceptibles d'avoir contribué à inspirer les Élégies: l'admiration de Rilke pour les *Métamorphoses* d'Ovide et la présence d'une image représentant Orphée, qu'elle lui avait offerte." The most circumstantial is in Erich Simenauer, *Rainer Maria Rilke: Legende und Mythos* (Berne, 1953), p. 739, n. 12, which refers to the Rilke *Lettres à Merline* and says Rilke read the *Metamorphoses* in the French translation.

73. *An Hölderlin, Gesammelte Werke,* Vol. 2, p. 93.

74. *Briefe* (Wiesbaden, Insel-Verlag, 1950), Vol. 1 (letter of February 11, 1910), p. 279.

75. *Goethe und Rilke* (Dresden, 1937), pp. 19–21.

76. *Briefe*, Vol. 1 (letter to Hedda Sauer, September 28, 1911), p. 314.

77. The two references are *Letters,* Vol. 2 (letter of February 19, 1912), p. 58; and *Briefwechsel mit Lou Andreas-Salomé* (letter of October 13, 1913), p. 312.

78. Kretschmar, *Goethe und Rilke*, pp. 69 ff. Rehm in his *Orpheus* (p. 521) makes a connection between Goethe's *Urworte: Orphisch* and Rilke.

79. We know Rilke particularly loved the *Harzreise im Winter*.

80. *Gesammelte Werke*, 2, 132–35.

81. Playfulness as a genuine element in Rilke's poetic make-up

should not be underestimated. It shows plainly in many of the occasional poems, in German and French. In this also he resembles the Mallarmé who used to address envelopes to his friends in little riddling verses which found, one hopes, an ingenious postman.

82. Levy, *The Sword from the Rock*, p. 117: "In all ancient thought creation means the arrangement into form of what is already alive."

83. It is interesting, in this connection, that one of the sonnets in Pt. II deals with the torture of the rack, in a judicial situation—quite inadequately, as II.11 deals with its theme of killing. These are subjects (and suffering is among them, despite Rilke's pronouncements about that) from which Rilke shut himself out, by the life he led and its effects on him.

84. *Gesammelte Werke*, 2, 136.

85. See, for instance, Von Bertalanffy, *Problems of Life*, p. 49, and Polanyi, *Personal Knowledge*, p. 387.

86. *Letters*, Vol. 1, letter to Baroness Schenk zu Schweinsberg (November 4, 1909), p. 353: "The hour of dying, which wrests this insight from everyone, is only one of our hours and not exceptional: Our being is continually undergoing and entering upon changes that are perhaps of no less intensity than the new, the next, and next again, that death brings with it." *Briefe*, Vol. 1, letter to Franz Xaver Kappus (July 16, 1903), p. 51: "denn auch das geistige Schaffen stammt von dem physischen her, ist eines Wesens mit ihm und nur wie eine leisere, entzücktere und ewigere Wiederholung leiblicher Wollust."

87. *Briefe*, letter to Kappus, as above, p. 52: "Und auch im Mann ist Mutterschaft, scheint mir, leibliche und geistige, sein Zeugen ist auch eine Art Gebären, und Gebären ist es, wenn er schafft aus innerster Fülle. Und vielleicht sind die Geschlechte verwandter, als man meint, und die grosse Erneuerung der Welt wird vielleicht darin bestehen, dass Mann und Mädchen sich, befreit von allen Irrgefühlen und Unlusten, nicht als Gegensätze suchen werden, sondern als Geschwister und Nachbarn und sich zusammentun werden als *Menschen*." Also letter to Kappus (May 14, 1904), p. 80: "Dieser Fortschritt wird das Liebe-Erleben, das jetzt voll Irrung ist, (sehr gegen den Willen der überholten Männer zunächst) verwandeln, von Grund aus verändern, zu einer Beziehung umbilden, die von Mensch zu Mensch gemeint ist, nicht mehr von Mann zu Weib."

88. A poem of Rilke's of 1907 (*Gesammelte Werke*, 2, 30) gives buried treasure as one of a series of almost taxonomic images of what it means to be a young girl: "Ein junges Mädchen: das ist wie ein

Schatz, / vergraben neben einer alten Linde; / da sollen Ringe
sein und Goldgewinde, / doch keiner ist erwählt, dass er sie finde:
/ nur eine Sage geht und sagt den Platz." (The girl is also com-
pared in this poem to a star and to fallen rain.) It is as if at this
Orphic point of death-and-life woman retained her importance as
presence and possibly clue.

89. *Rühmen,* the concept of praising as the poet's task, has seemed
very important in Rilke. It plays a considerable part in the Elegies
and in other poems, notably, "Oh sage, Dichter, was du tust?—Ich
rühme," of 1921. But to isolate praising like this as the poet's es-
sential task is misleading. The poet obviously should love and
affirm all the universe, and be grateful to the Maker of it. But
poetry's task is not to be so simplified, including as it does the task
of discovering, learning, teaching, foretelling, thinking, tending
and fostering the good estate of language. Nothing is gained by
muddling poetry with liturgy.

90. Language and food meet again in 11.20, where a language for
fish is suggested by the poet looking at their odd faces when cooked
and on the table.

91. It reminds one deeply of Valéry's *Le Cimetière marin.*

92. Women become lutes in this sonnet, just as before they were lyres.
Thus Rilke identifies women in bodily terms (cf. *Die Laute* in the
second part of the *Neue Gedichte*) with the two traditional musical
instruments of Orpheus.

93. *Gesammelte Werke,* 2, 135.

94. See Holthusen, *Rilkes Sonette an Orpheus,* pp. 33–34: "Immer
wieder überschreiten die Bilder der Sonette die bloss irdische
Natur des Symbols und manifestieren sich in der kosmischen Figur
des Sternbildes."

95. Rehm, *Orpheus,* p. 525. There is one place in Rilke where the
lyre is among the stars—in "Depuis quand nous te jouons" of
1926 (*Gesammelte Werke,* 2, 632). It says, "Comme la lyre, tu
devais etre / rendue aux constellations!"

Index

The notes following page 421 have not been indexed.

Abercrombie, Lascelles, 302
Academy of Sciences (Stockholm), 189
Adams, H. P., 184
Adanson, Michel, 200; *Familles des plantes*, 213
Aeschylus, 281
Analysis vs. synthesis, 29–31, 32
Andreas-Salomé, Lou, 380, 381
Anthropology, 64, 288, 327, 334–36, 402
Anthropomorphism, 262, 352
Apollo, in Orpheus myth, 3, 333; and Christ, 65
Arber, Agnes, 49, 50, 193, 221, 262; *Goethe's Botany*, 229
Aristotle, 60, 61, 101, 108, 144, 145, 187
Arnold, Matthew, 8
Art: and science, split between, 7; plastic, 29; union of nature and, 124–25; various meaning of, 125; liberal, 126; mechanical arts, in Shakespeare, 127, 128–33
Ascham, Roger, 72, 75; *Toxophilus*, 71
Auden, W. H., 334

Bacon, Francis, 5, 50, 56, 63, 68, 76, 77, 79, 91, 113, 116, 117, 142, 157, 159, 166, 171, 175, 179, 180, 183–85, 187, 188, 192, 194–96, 202, 203, 206, 215–18, 223, 224, 243, 247, 263, 299, 334, 348, 354, 356, 357, 364, 390, 398; Orpheus myth in, 57–58, 59, 61, 72, 75, 82–86, 89, 100–1, 103, 142; characteristics of work, 59–60; disagreement on nature of his method, 60; the myth-maker, 61; a poet who did not trust poetry, 62, 110; comments on disrepute of myth, 71; time in, 101, 105; poetry as learning, 106; on philosophy, 107–10; betrayal of poetry, 109–10; doctrine of forms, 134–36; attacks Aristotelian logic, 144–45; *Abecedarium Naturae*, 146; *The Advancement of Learning*, 26, 84, 94, 95, 106, 107, 117, 120, 135, 146; *Catalogue of Particular Histories by Titles*, 121, 127; *Cogitationes de Scientia Humana*, 126; *De Augmentis Scientiarum*, 71, 74–75, 81, 84, 106, 120, 121, 125, 135, 143, 146; *De Principiis*, 145; *De Sapientia Veterum*, 58, 82, 92–96, 98, 103, 108, 109, 147; *Descriptio Globi Intellectualis*, 102, 109, 120, 124; *Essays*, 83; *Filum Labyrinthi sive Formula Inquisitionis*, 98, 126; *Historia Ventorum*, 118; Idols of the Theatre, 109–10; *Magna Instauratio*,

455

Bacon, Francis (*continued*)
57, 62, 83, 97–99, 103, 106, 118,
119, 144, 146–47; *New Atlantis*,
102, 180; *Novum Organum*, 16,
57, 75, 100–3, 109, 118, 119, 135,
136, 141–44, 148, 150, 155, 180,
182, 295, 304; *Parasceve*, 118, 120,
123, 125, 126, 128, 147; *Sylva Syl-
varum*, 97; *Temporis Partus
Masculus*, 101, 108; *Valerius
Terminus*, 97, 102, 104–5, 134,
136, 146
Barzun, Jacques, 50
Behaviorists, 11–12
Beowulf, 305
Bergson, Henri, 45
Bertalanffy, L. von, 10
Biology, 10, 312; from the poet's
point of view, 42–48; character-
istic of biological thinking, 43;
needs poetry, 44–45; of thinking,
287–88, 325–26, 336, 402
Blake, William, 50, 242; *The Mar-
riage of Heaven and Hell*, 300;
Milton, 297
Boas, George, *Our New Ways of
Thinking*, 50
Body. *See* Mind
Boisserée, Sulpiz, 229
Bonstetten, Charles Victor de, 199
Botany, 253–54; Coleridge on, 231
Buffon, Georges L. L. de, 10, 213
Butler, Samuel, *Evolution Old and
New*, 221

Cardan, Jerome, 187
Carlyle, Thomas, 221
Cassirer, Ernst, 15, 16, 18, 50, 182,
183
Caxton, William, *Eneydos*, 132
Cervantes, Miguel de, *Don Quix-
ote*, 356
Chapman, George, 85, 89, 91;
Bussy D'Ambois, 87; *A Justifica-
tion of Perseus and Andromeda*,
86; *The Shadow of Night*, 88
Chardin, Teilhard de, 44, 49, 195
Christian theology, 66
Church, Dean, 60
Cipher, 88, 89, 186. *See also* Hiero-
glyphic
Coleridge, Samuel Taylor, 5, 113,
138, 150–54, 179, 182, 185, 186,
188, 205, 221, 230, 231, 251, 262,
282, 289, 297, 299, 304, 313, 314,
345, 348, 367; *Aids to Reflection*,
350; *The Friend*, 138, 350; *Kubla
Khan*, 240; Preface to *Lyrical
Ballads*, 289–91; *To William
Wordsworth*, 291–92
Collingwood, R. G., 182, 183
Comte, Auguste, 18, 45, 195; *Cours
de philosophie positive*, 16
Cornelius Agrippa, 187
Cowley, Abraham, 60, 180; *A Prop-
osition for the Advancement of
Experimental Philosophy*, 180
Croce, Benedetto, 182, 184
Cuvier, Georges L. C. F. D., 10, 194;
*Le Règne Animal distribué
d'après son organisation*, 196, 197

Dance, 399–400; and ritual, 29
Dante, 187, 283, 299, 305, 334;
Divine Comedy, 302
Darwin, Charles, 31, 173, 174, 182,
200, 334; *The Descent of Man*,
215–16; *Origin of Species*, 215–18
Darwin, Erasmus, 5, 50, 80, 171,
172, 179, 199, 218, 220, 221, 223,
225, 231, 236, 255; on poetry and
science, 7; Orpheus myth in, 173–
76, 178, 247, 251–52; *The Bo-
tanic Garden*, 173, 220, 237–38,
241, 242, 244; "The Cultivation
of Broccoli," 238–39; *The Econ-
omy of Vegetation*, 224, 241, 242;
The Loves of the Plants, 196,
208–9, 224, 228, 241, 245; *Phyto-
logia*, 209, 214, 220, 227, 238; *The*

Temple of Nature, 173, 220, 224, 238, 240, 244–52, 360; *Zoonomia,* 200, 215, 220

Day, Thomas, *Sandford and Merton,* 220

De Quincey, Thomas, 355

Death, 393–95

Delille, Jacques, *Les Trois Régnes de la nature,* 196–98

Deucalion, 358

Dialectic, 30–33

Dream, 75, 106, 109; Bottom's, 114, 133, 149; in Shakespeare, 110–14; in *The Prelude,* 355–58

Eckermann, Johann Peter, 221, 260

Edgeworth, Richard Lovell, 220

Eleusinian Mysteries, 174, 175

Eliot, T. S., 8

Ellis, Robert Leslie, 60

Emerson, Ralph Waldo, 5, 171, 185, 202, 221, 222, 362; on Swedenborg, 186–90; *Essays,* 186; "Man Thinking," 192; "Nature," 186–87, 192, 206; *Representative Men,* 186, 221–22

Empedocles, 187

Epic poetry, 302–8, 371; as postlogic, 301–4; *The Prelude* as, 302–9, 343, 356

Euclid, 357

Eurydice: in Orpheus myth, 3, 51, 79, 88, 174, 209, 223, 251, 309, 310, 323, 326, 392; in Rilke, 329–31, 332–33, 392–93; in Wordsworth, 332

Falk, reports Goethe conversation, 227

Falstaff, on honor, 25

Farrington, Benjamin, 60

Faustus, 125

Fechner, Gustav Theodor, *Nanna,* 200–1

Form: and content, 39–40; in language, not separable from content, 39–40; as poetry, 139; as metamorphosis, 348. See *also* Formal systems, Forms

Formal systems, of languages, five types of, 29, 39

Forms, 33, 36–37; Bacon's concept of, 116, 117, 119, 134–39, 141–43, 154; in *Midsummer Night's Dream,* 139–41; in *The Prelude,* 348, 352–53, 367. See *also* Gestalten

Fowler, Thomas, 60

Frazer, Sir James George, 378; *The Golden Bough,* 17, 334, 335

Freud, Sigmund, 209, 331–34, 378, 393

Fuseli, Henry, 242

Galileo, 68, 147

Galton, Samuel, 220

Genius, 260–62, 283–84

Geometry, 350

Germany: biology and philosophy in, 43; Shakespeare in, 179

Gestalt psychology, 9, 10–12, 45, 50

Gestalten, 11, 37, 203, 274

Gilgamesh, 305

Goethe, Christiane von, 267

Goethe, Johann Wolfgang von, 5, 8, 45, 50, 51, 65, 80, 111, 150, 151, 171, 172, 179, 182, 199, 203, 218–23, 227, 228, 236, 251, 253, 286, 299, 312–14, 327, 341, 353, 362, 372, 377, 379, 380, 398; on poetry and science, 7; main theme as biologist, 10; on *Gestalt,* 11; Orpheus myth in, 176–79; travels to Italy, 257, to Switzerland, 257–58; his behavioral morphology of poetic genius, 260–61; five great powers of organic life, 274; concept of *Urpflanze,* 177, 178, 225, 264, 274; *An Attempt to Explain the Morphology of Plants,* 262; "Atmosphäre," 255–57;

Goethe, Johann W. von (*cont.*)
Dichtung und Wahrheit, 178,
228, 259; *Episteln*, 259; *Farben-
lehre*, 262; *Geschichte meines
botanischen Studiums*, 223, 226–
27, 259; *Gott und Welt*, 254,
255–56, 266; "Howards Ehrenge-
dächtnis," 255; *Italienische Reise*,
219, 225–26, 257, 264, 380; *Kunst
und Altertum*, 269; *Metamor-
phose der Pflanzen*, 200, 220, 223,
254, 262–65, 266, 267, 381; *Meta-
morphose der Tiere*, 263–65, 266,
268; *Morphologie*, 178; *Römische
Elegien*, 220; *Selbstschilderung*,
230, 258–59; *Shakespeare und
kein Ende*, 153; *Die Skelette der
Nagethiere*, 264; *Urworte: Or-
phisch*, 177, 178, 265, 266, 269–
74, 360; *Venezianische Epi-
gramme*, 380; *Die Wahlverwand-
schaften*, 262, 380; *Wilhelm Mei-
sters Lehrjahre*, 380; "Wohl zu
Merken," 255
Golding, Arthur, 80
Gosson, Stephen, *Schoole of Abuse*,
68
Grammar, 34–36, 285–86; com-
plexity of, 34; mythological, 35;
reflexives, 40
Gray, Thomas, 199
Greeks, 175; biology began with,
46; mythology of, 64; science of,
103

Hallier, Hans, 200
Hamann, Johann Georg, 182
Hayata (Japanese botanist), 200
Hazlitt, William, 297
Heraclitus, 187
Herder, Johann Gottfried von, 16,
150, 182, 230; *Aelteste Urkunde
des Menschengeschlechts*, 177;
Über der Ursprung der Sprache,

178; *Von deutscher Art und
Kunst*, 142, 153
Hieroglyphic, 84–86, 97, 98, 100,
148, 189–90
Hölderlin, Friedrich, 64–66, 67, 70,
312, 379; *Der Einzige*, 65; *Die
scheinheiligen Dichter*, 66; *Rilkes
Sonette an Orpheus*, 335–36
Holthusen, Hans-Egon, *Rilkes
Sonette an Orpheus*, 335–36
Homer, 72, 175, 356, 362; *Iliad*, 302;
Odyssey, 342
Hooke, Robert, 5, 138, 147–49, 181
Howard, Luke, 255, 256
Hugo, Victor, 5, 150, 151, 179, 286,
288; *Shakespeare*, 280–85
Hulewicz, Witold von, 373, 375
Humboldt, F. H. A., Baron von, 187
Hutchinson, Evelyn, 49, 50
Huxley, Thomas Henry, 215, 216,
218

Imagination: vs. intellect, 19, 25,
30; Hugo on, 283–84; Puttenham
on, 76; Theseus on, 115–16; in
The Prelude, 369
Intellect, vs. imagination, 19, 25,
30

Jalabert, Buffon's letter to, 213
James, William, 60
Johnson, Samuel, 220
Jung, Karl, 332, 394
Jussieu, Adrien de, 194; *The Ele-
ments of Botany*, 213–14
Jussieu, Antoine Laurent de, 194;
Genera Plantarum, 213

Keats, John, 50, 297, 393; extract
from *Letters*, 370; *On Sitting
Down to Read King Lear Once
Again*, 156
Kepler, Johannes, 187, 201, 216
Kippenberg, Anton, 380

Knoop, Wera Ouckama, 375, 393, 400

Krause, Ernst, 220

Kretschmar, Eberhard, 381; *Goethe und Rilke,* 380

Lamb, Charles, 297

Lamarck, Chevalier de, 45, 194; *Philosophie zoologique,* 43

Lamartine, Alphonse, 286

Langer, Suzanne, 49

Language, 6, 29, 30, 34–35; as poetry, 6, 7–10, 30, 287, 402; as science, 6, 7–10, 12, 30, 44, 287; surpasses its users' power of exegesis, 22; a misunderstood instrument, 23; as activity, 27; myth in process of, 35; in Midsummer Night's Dream, 131–32; nature as, 151, 183, 206, 222; in *King Lear,* 164–65. *See also* Formal systems, Words

Leibniz, Gottfried Wilhelm von, 187

Leishman, J. B., 314

Lévy-Bruhl, Lucien, 31, 45, 81, 335; *Les Fonctions mentales,* 17–18

Linnaeus, Carolus, 5, 47–48, 50, 172, 173, 181, 186, 188, 192–93, 195–99, 208–10, 213–15, 217, 218, 223–28, 230, 231, 236, 251, 253, 255, 259, 263, 266, 267, 272, 312; *Deliciae Naturae,* 195; *Philosophia Botanica,* 211, 212; *Systema Naturae,* 191, 211–12

Linus, 72

Logic, 39, 369; as mythologizing activity, 38; Bacon's proposed reform of, 116, 117, 119, 143–49, 150, 157; in *King Lear,* 159–61, 164–65; symbolic, 193; a language of nature, 358

Logos, 70, 324

London, 359

Love, in Goethe, 267–68, 271, 273; in Novalis, 208, 209; in Shakespeare, 112–13; intellectual, in *The Prelude,* 369

Loves of the Triangles, 173, 240

Lucian, 21

Macaulay, Thomas Babington, 60

Maenads, in myth of Orpheus, 3, 333, 402

Maistre, Joseph Maria de, 60, 61, 194

Mallarmé, Stéphane, 5, 32, 273–74, 282, 287, 288, 325, 376; *Autobiographie,* 280, 281; *Un Coup de dés,* 284

Malory, Sir Thomas, 308

Marx, Karl, *Das Kapital,* 182

Mathematics, 7, 8, 10, 29, 36, 38, 39, 44; vs. words, 19, 25. *See also* Geometry

Metamorphosis, 229–30, 348, 360, 388, 396–97; in Rilke, 377–83. *See also* Goethe, Ovid

Metaphor, 7, 9, 26, 31, 32, 39; importance of, 6

Methodology, 4, 257, 274, 289, 291, 293, 339, 345–46, 348, 350–51, 359, 360–61, 369, 402, 404

Michelet, Jules, 182, 183

Milton, John, 5, 50, 68, 80, 179, 231, 334, 341, 356; Orpheus myth in, 69, 300; *At a Solemn Music,* 324; *Il Penseroso,* 69; *L'Allegro,* 69, 326; *Lycidas,* 69; *Paradise Lost,* 69, 70, 251, 294, 297, 300, 302, 303, 307–9, 341, 344

Mind: vs. body, 25, 36–37, 326; body-mind as generator of forms, 28; and language, 34–35

Moorman, Mary, *William Wordsworth,* 308

Morphology, 172, 199, 201, 255, 260, 261, 355

Müller, Max, 17

Murry, John Middleton, 49, 50;
  Metabiology, 50

Musaeus, 72

Music and rhythm, 29

Myth, mythology, 7, 27, 35, 38–41,
  46, 198, 377; importance of, 6;
  modern use of word, 15–17;
  Bacon's use of, 57; as the activity
  between mind and language in
  poetry, 57; truth of, 67–70; three
  ways of studying, 82–84; as hiero-
  glyphic or cipher, 84–86; in
  Chapman, 87, 89; in Shakespeare,
  88–92; in Bacon, 92–99; in *King
  Lear*, 158–59; as interchange of
  nature and thought through lan-
  guage, 187; Renan's view, 285;
  Shelley's use of, 298–99; in *The
  Prelude*, 344–45. *See also* Or-
  pheus myth

Natural history: Bacon's project
  for, 116, 118–19, 120–21, 133, 151–
  52, 155–56; Linnaeus' view of,
  191

Natural phenomena, in *Midsum-
  mer Night's Dream*, 121–22

Nature: as theme of *Midsummer
  Night's Dream*, 119; unity of art
  and, 124–25; Bacon's "inquisi-
  tion" of, 126–27; as language,
  151, 206, 222; seen as language
  and myth, 183; in *King Lear*,
  155–57, 163

Newman, John Henry, 68; *The
  Grammar of Assent*, 34

Newton, Sir Isaac, 283

Noah, 358

Novalis, 5, 168, 184, 201–2, 221, 394,
  399; *Fragmente*, 203; *Heinrich
  von Ofterdingen*, 208; *Die Lehr-
  linge zu Sais*, 202–8, 209

Oken, Lorenz, 187

Orpheus, 8, 26, 187, 310, 319, 321,
323, 326, 330, 335, 360; patron of
  discovery, 20; song in *King Henry
  VIII*, 56; favorite figure of Eng-
  lish Renaissance, 57; fusion of
  poetry and philosophy, 202. *See
  also* Orpheus myth

Orpheus myth: three parts to, 3;
  in various authors, 5; as tradition
  to be traced, 5, 22; concerned
  with power and fate of poetry,
  40–41; as reflection of myth in its
  own mirror, 41; poetry thinking
  about itself, 47; poetry and nat-
  ural history meet in, 48; as
  imaginative framework for book,
  51; in Bacon, 57–58, 59, 61, 72,
  75, 82–86, 89, 100–1, 103, 127,
  142; in Shakespeare, 58–59, 91,
  128; in Milton, 69, 300, 334; in
  Sprat, 72; in Sidney, 72; in Put-
  tenham, 76; in Chapman, 87; in
  Erasmus Darwin, 173–76, 178,
  247, 251–52; in Goethe, 176–79;
  in Ovid, 233, 235; in nineteenth
  and twentieth centuries, 279 ff.;
  in Wordsworth, 309–10, 316–27,
  335–36, 338–70; in Rilke, 327–36,
  376–86, 388–403

Orphic: "casualties," 68; cult, 233;
  genius, 171–72, 287; journey,
  309, 310, 323 ff., 327, 333; method,
  see Methodology; mind, 172,
  209, 221–23, 231, 241, 243, 254,
  257, 259, 304, 312, 371; power,
  318, 319; quest, 323; question, 4,
  6, 289, 291, 293, 297, 305; search,
  327; spirit, in eighteenth century,
  179; tradition, 259, 275, 286, 288,
  352, 362, 370, 373; vision, 190,
  206, 370; voice, 203, 280, 300, 309,
  310, 356, 362, 364, 404, 405, de-
  grees of, 181

Ovid, 57, 79, 80, 88, 110, 175, 186,
  228, 230, 231, 244, 245, 255, 266,
  267, 269, 295, 312, 348, 362–64,

379, 381, 397; Orpheus myth in, 3, 233, 235; *Metamorphoses*, 80, 138, 185, 229, 231–36, 247, 251, 252, 268, 273, 283, 323, 360–61, 390, 402

Oxford English Dictionary, quoted, 132

Parable, in Bacon, 100, 103
Paracelsus, 187
Paul, Saint, 104
Pentateuch, 229
Philology, 34, 285–86; according to Vico, 24
Pico della Mirandola, 64, 65, 67, 70, 75, 79; *De Dignitate Hominis*, 65
Plato, 108, 175, 187
Plutarch, 187
Poe, Edgar Allan, 85, 274; on poetry and science, 7; *Eureka*, 61, 62, 262, 284; *Mellonta Tauta*, 62
Poetic genius, Goethe's comments on, 260–61. *See also* Genius
Poetry, 7, 13–19, 22, 39, 288; power of, 3–5; language as, 6, 7–10, 30, 287, 402; contemporary, 8, 51; vs. science, 19, 25, 30; relation between science and, 289–91; puts language to full use, 46; usefulness, 46–47; truth the object of, 66–67; truth of, 71–72; and philosophy, 72–74, 109–10, 202; as learning, 106, 109; Bacon's view of, 106–9; the first natural speech, 183; as living activity, 259; genius as, 283; Renan's view, 285; as postlogic, 405, *see also* Postlogic. *See also* Epic poetry
Poincaré, Henri, 18, 284
Polanyi, Michael, 49, 50, 193, 221; *Personal Knowledge*, 22, 32, 40
Postlogic, 57, 105, 123, 124, 126, 133, 148–50, 153–55, 164, 166, 168, 171, 184, 195, 203, 213, 214, 216–

18, 224, 227, 235, 243, 244, 254, 262, 274, 284, 286, 287, 301, 335, 347, 348, 355, 358, 359, 364, 365, 369, 392, 400, 402, 404, 405
Pound, Ezra, 80
Priestley, Joseph, 220
Proteus myth, 126
Prynne, William, *Histriomastix*, 68
Psychology, 64, 288, 312, 331–36, 402. Gestalt, *see* Gestalt psychology
Puritans, 68
Puttenham, 284; Orpheus myth in, 76; *The Arte of English Poesie*, 71, 76
Pythagoras, 175, 187, 233

Quadrivium, 73, 126

Ralegh, Sir Walter, *History of the World*, 132
Rawley, Dr., 97
Ray, John, 191, 212; *The Wisdom of God Manifested in the Works of Creation*, 199
Read, Sir Herbert, 49; *Studies in Romantic Poetry*, 50
Religion, 68, 368
Renaissance, English, 5, 50, 57, 64
Renan, Joseph Ernest, 5, 17, 171, 179, 282, 288; *Caliban*, 286, 287; *De l'Origine du langage*, 178, 287; *L'Avenir de la science*, 45, 68, 182, 194, 281, 285–88; *L'Eau de Jouvence*, 286; *Vie de Jésus*, 286, 287
Reynolds, Henry, 81; *Mythomystes*, 77–80, 107
Rhetoric, 30–33
Richards, I. A., *Science and Poetry*, 7
Rilke, Rainer Maria, 5, 51, 80, 221, 281, 282, 310–15; Orpheus myth in poetry, 327–36, 376–86, 388–403; *Aus dem Nachlass des Grafen C. W.*, 373; *Duineser Elegien*, 311, 314, 372, 373, 394; *Gegen-Stro-*

Rilke, Rainer Maria (*continued*)
  phen, 392; *Malte Laurids Brigge*,
  380; *Neue Gedichte*, 327, 376,
  380; *Orpheus. Eurydike. Hermes*,
  327–34, 375, 392, 403; "Solang du
  Selbstgeworfnes fängst," 383–84;
  Sonette an Orpheus, 50, 280, 281,
  314, 315, 325, 331, 336, 371–80,
  383, 387, 388–403; *Stundenbuch*,
  380; *Ur-Geräusch*, 381, 384;
  "Wann wird, wann wird, wann
  wird es genügen," 385; *Wendung*,
  381–83
Robertson, J. M., 60
Romanticism, 282
Rome: in Rilke, 395; mythology
  of, 64
Rosicrucianism, Darwin's myths of,
  242
Ross, Sir Ronald, 201
Royal Society, 74, 138, 180, 199
Ruskin, John, 257

Sainte-Beuve, Charles Augustin, 45,
  196; *Nouveaux Lundis*, 194
Salisbury, Lord, 92
Sandys, Edwin, 81; trans. *Metamor-*
  phoses, 75, 79
Schelling, Friedrich W. J. von, 6,
  16, 50, 65, 182, 183, 186, 187, 254
Science, 13–19, 32, 44, 103, 212, 288;
  language as, 6, 7–10, 12, 30, 44,
  213, 287; logic in, 8–9; biological,
  10, 12; vs. poetry, 19, 25, 30; re-
  lation between poetry and, 289–
  91; art vs. utilitarian science, 47;
  theology and poetry as fellow
  disciplines of, 66–67
Selden, John, 187
Selincourt, E. de, 341
Seward, Anna, 220, 237, 240, 241,
  243, 244; *Memoirs of the Life of
  Dr. Darwin*, 223, 227–28
Sex and fertility, 209–10, 249, 267–

68, 273, 286, 288, 292, 330–31,
  393–94, 396, 402, 405
Shakespeare, William, 5, 50, 51, 63,
  80, 151, 171, 172, 179, 188, 199,
  223, 226, 231, 290, 296, 299, 312,
  326, 348, 353, 362; Orpheus myth
  in, 58–59; Herder on, 142, 153;
  King Henry VIII, 56; *King Lear*,
  57, 140, 155, 157, 158–68, 210, 216,
  356, 368; *A Midsummer Night's
  Dream*, 88–91, 110–17, 121–23,
  127, 128–33, 139–41, 149, 155, 159,
  210, 224, 243; *The Tempest*, 110,
  113, 155, 157, 224, 286, 287; *The
  Two Gentlemen of Verona*, 58;
  The Winter's Tale, 124–25
Shaw, Airy H. K., 200
Shaw, George Bernard, 297; *Back
  to Methuselah*, 221
Shelley, Percy Bysshe, 5, 138, 282,
  289, 358; use of myth, 298; *De-
  fence of Poetry*, 31, 61, 280, 299;
  Prometheus Unbound, 281, 297–
  300; *The Revolt of Islam*, 299
Sherrington, Sir Charles Scott, 44
Sidney, Sir Philip, 50, 71, 75, 76,
  79, 106, 318; Orpheus myth in,
  72; *Apologie for Poesie*, 68, 72–
  74
Sonnet cycle, 387
Spedding, James, 60, 71, 147
Spender, Stephen, 314; *The Making
  of a Poem*, 7
Spengler, Oswald, 274
Spinoza, Baruch, 223, 226
Sprat, Thomas, 60, 75, 79, 106, 176,
  180, 195, 334; Orpheus myth in,
  72; *History of the Royal Society
  of London*, 72–74
Spurgeon, Caroline, 85
Staël, Madame de, 254
Strauss, David Friedrich, 17, 183
Swedenborg, Emanuel, 5, 50, 181,
  209, 210; Orphic vision of, 184–

90; Emerson on, 186–90; *Camena Borea*, 185; *Daedalus Hyperboreus*, 185; *Oeconomia Regni Animalis*, 185, 187; *On the White Horse Mentioned in the Apocalypse*, 189; *Principia Rerum Naturalium*, 185

Taxonomy, 172, 186, 188, 191, 193, 194, 199, 201, 203, 210, 217, 218, 227, 230, 255, 264–65, 268, 355

Taylor, Thomas, *The Mystical Initiations*, 175

Tennyson, Alfred Lord, *In Memoriam*, 337

Themes of book, 339

Theology, in relation to science and poetry, 66–67; doctrine of inspiration in, 374

Thinking, thought: prelogical, 17, 81; scientific, 17–19; logical vs. imaginative, 19; in England, *1600–1610*, 55; postlogical, *see* Postlogic; Orphic tradition of, 404

Thompson, D'Arcy, 236; *On Growth and Form*, 10, 139, 191–92

Thurn und Taxis, Princess von, 313

Time, in Bacon, 101–2

Trevelyan, Humphry, *Goethe and the Greeks*, 177

Trickett, Rachel, 69

Trivium, 30, 34, 73, 126

Urania, 69, 246, 251, 294, 300

Utnapishtim, 358

Valéry, Paul, 8, 85, 288, 325

Vico, Giambattista, 5, 50, 150, 175, 181, 286, 354; *Diritto universale*, 24; *Scienza nuova*, 16, 182–84

Virgil, *Aeneid*, 229, 233, 302, 304

Wagner, Richard, 297

Wallace, Alfred Russell, 216; *Darwinism*, 201

Warburton, Bishop, 224; *The Divine Legation of Moses*, 174–75

Watt, James, 220

West, Rebecca, 49, 50

Whyte, Lance, 49, 50, 60, 221

Wilmott, A. J., 200

Wilson, Dover, 129

Words: vs. mathematics, 19, 25; as meaning and history, 23; as mental activity, 24–25; Mechanicals' use of, 131–32. *See also* Language

Wordsworth, William, 5, 80, 231, 282, 289, 327, 334, 372, 377, 378, 381, 399; Orpheus myth in, 309–10, 316–27, 335–36, 338–70; *The Excursion*, 293–96, 303, 306, 338, 341, 346, 365; *Lyrical Ballads*, 347, Preface to, 289–91, 335; *On the Power of Sound*, 316, 320–26, 362, 386, 389; "Poems of the Imagination," 316, 317, 320; *Power of Music*, 316, 317–20, 323; *The Prelude*, 205, 251, 252, 279–80, 291–93, 297, 301, 302, 304, 306, 308, 314, 316, 318, 323, 325, 336–70, 386; *The Recluse*, 251, 293, 302, 305–8, 311, 313, 323, 342; *The Reverie of Poor Susan*, 317

OTHER NEW YORK REVIEW CLASSICS

For a complete list of titles, visit www.nyrb.com.

RENATA ADLER Speedboat

AESCHYLUS Prometheus Bound; translated by Joel Agee

ROBERT AICKMAN Compulsory Games

LEOPOLDO ALAS His Only Son *with* Doña Berta

CÉLESTE ALBARET Monsieur Proust

DANTE ALIGHIERI The Inferno; translated by Ciaran Carson

DANTE ALIGHIERI Purgatorio; translated by D. M. Black

JEAN AMÉRY Charles Bovary, Country Doctor: Portrait of a Simple Man

KINGSLEY AMIS Lucky Jim

KINGSLEY AMIS The Old Devils

U.R. ANANTHAMURTHY Samskara: A Rite for a Dead Man

IVO ANDRIĆ Omer Pasha Latas

HANNAH ARENDT Rahel Varnhagen: The Life of a Jewish Woman

ROBERTO ARLT The Seven Madmen

WILLIAM ATTAWAY Blood on the Forge

W.H. AUDEN (EDITOR) The Living Thoughts of Kierkegaard

W.H. AUDEN W. H. Auden's Book of Light Verse

ERICH AUERBACH Dante: Poet of the Secular World

EVE BABITZ Slow Days, Fast Company: The World, the Flesh, and L.A.

DOROTHY BAKER Young Man with a Horn

J.A. BAKER The Peregrine

S. JOSEPHINE BAKER Fighting for Life

HONORÉ DE BALZAC The Unknown Masterpiece *and* Gambara

VICKI BAUM Grand Hotel

SYBILLE BEDFORD A Legacy

SYBILLE BEDFORD A Visit to Don Otavio: A Mexican Journey

MAX BEERBOHM The Prince of Minor Writers: The Selected Essays of Max Beerbohm

STEPHEN BENATAR Wish Her Safe at Home

FRANS G. BENGTSSON The Long Ships

WALTER BENJAMIN The Storyteller Essays

ALEXANDER BERKMAN Prison Memoirs of an Anarchist

GEORGES BERNANOS Mouchette

MIRON BIAŁOSZEWSKI A Memoir of the Warsaw Uprising

ADOLFO BIOY CASARES The Invention of Morel

ROBERT MONTGOMERY BIRD Sheppard Lee, Written by Himself

PAUL BLACKBURN (TRANSLATOR) Proensa

CAROLINE BLACKWOOD Great Granny Webster

LESLEY BLANCH Journey into the Mind's Eye: Fragments of an Autobiography

RONALD BLYTHE Akenfield: Portrait of an English Village

HENRI BOSCO Malicroix

NICOLAS BOUVIER The Way of the World

EMMANUEL BOVE Henri Duchemin and His Shadows

EMMANUEL BOVE My Friends

MALCOLM BRALY On the Yard

MILLEN BRAND The Outward Room

ROBERT BRESSON Notes on the Cinematograph

DAVID BROMWICH (EDITOR) Writing Politics: An Anthology

SIR THOMAS BROWNE Religio Medici and Urne-Buriall

DAVID R. BUNCH Moderan

JOHN HORNE BURNS The Gallery

ROBERT BURTON The Anatomy of Melancholy

DINO BUZZATI Poem Strip

INÈS CAGNATI Free Day

MATEI CALINESCU The Life and Opinions of Zacharias Lichter

GIROLAMO CARDANO The Book of My Life

DON CARPENTER Hard Rain Falling

J.L. CARR A Month in the Country

LEONORA CARRINGTON Down Below

LEONORA CARRINGTON The Hearing Trumpet

BLAISE CENDRARS Moravagine

EILEEN CHANG Little Reunions

EILEEN CHANG Love in a Fallen City

FRANÇOIS-RENÉ DE CHATEAUBRIAND Memoirs from Beyond the Grave, 1768–1800

UPAMANYU CHATTERJEE English, August: An Indian Story

NIRAD C. CHAUDHURI The Autobiography of an Unknown Indian

ELLIOTT CHAZE Black Wings Has My Angel

ANTON CHEKHOV Peasants and Other Stories

ANTON CHEKHOV The Prank: The Best of Young Chekhov

GABRIEL CHEVALLIER Fear: A Novel of World War I

JEAN-PAUL CLÉBERT Paris Vagabond

RICHARD COBB Paris and Elsewhere

COLETTE The Pure and the Impure

CARLO COLLODI The Adventures of Pinocchio

D.G. COMPTON The Continuous Katherine Mortenhoe

IVY COMPTON-BURNETT Manservant and Maidservant

BARBARA COMYNS The Vet's Daughter

ALBERT COSSERY Proud Beggars

HAROLD W. CRUSE The Crisis of the Negro Intellectual

ASTOLPHE DE CUSTINE Letters from Russia

JÓZEF CZAPSKI Lost Time: Lectures on Proust in a Soviet Prison Camp

JÓZEF CZAPSKI Memories of Starobielsk: Essays Between Art and History

LORENZO DA PONTE Memoirs

ELIZABETH DAVID Summer Cooking

L.J. DAVIS A Meaningful Life

AGNES DE MILLE Dance to the Piper

VIVANT DENON No Tomorrow/Point de lendemain

MARIA DERMOÛT The Ten Thousand Things

DER NISTER The Family Mashber

TIBOR DÉRY Niki: The Story of a Dog

G.V. DESANI All About H. Hatterr

ANTONIO DI BENEDETTO The Silentiary

ALFRED DÖBLIN Berlin Alexanderplatz

HEIMITO VON DODERER The Strudlhof Steps

JEAN D'ORMESSON The Glory of the Empire: A Novel, A History

ARTHUR CONAN DOYLE The Exploits and Adventures of Brigadier Gerard

CHARLES DUFF A Handbook on Hanging

BRUCE DUFFY The World As I Found It

DAPHNE DU MAURIER Don't Look Now: Stories

ELAINE DUNDY The Dud Avocado

G.B. EDWARDS The Book of Ebenezer Le Page

JOHN EHLE The Land Breakers

CYPRIAN EKWENSI People of the City

MARCELLUS EMANTS A Posthumous Confession

EURIPIDES Grief Lessons: Four Plays; translated by Anne Carson

J.G. FARRELL The Siege of Krishnapur

ELIZA FAY Original Letters from India

KENNETH FEARING The Big Clock

FÉLIX FÉNÉON Novels in Three Lines

M.I. FINLEY The World of Odysseus

THOMAS FLANAGAN The Year of the French

BENJAMIN FONDANE Existential Monday: Philosophical Essays

SANFORD FRIEDMAN Conversations with Beethoven

MARC FUMAROLI When the World Spoke French

WILLIAM GADDIS The Recognitions

BENITO PÉREZ GÁLDOS Tristana

MAVIS GALLANT The Cost of Living: Early and Uncollected Stories

GABRIEL GARCÍA MÁRQUEZ Clandestine in Chile: The Adventures of Miguel Littín

LEONARD GARDNER Fat City

WILLIAM H. GASS On Being Blue: A Philosophical Inquiry

THÉOPHILE GAUTIER My Fantoms

GE FEI Peach Blossom Paradise

JEAN GENET The Criminal Child: Selected Essays

ANDRÉ GIDE Marshlands

ÉLISABETH GILLE The Mirador: Dreamed Memories of Irène Némirovsky by Her Daughter

FRANÇOISE GILOT Life with Picasso

NATALIA GINZBURG Family *and* Borghesia

NATALIA GINZBURG Valentino *and* Sagittarius

JEAN GIONO Hill

JEAN GIONO The Open Road

JOHN GLASSCO Memoirs of Montparnasse

P.V. GLOB The Bog People: Iron-Age Man Preserved

ROBERT GLÜCK Margery Kempe

NIKOLAI GOGOL Dead Souls

EDMOND AND JULES DE GONCOURT Pages from the Goncourt Journals

ALICE GOODMAN History Is Our Mother: Three Libretti

A.C. GRAHAM Poems of the Late T'ang

HENRY GREEN Nothing

HENRY GREEN Surviving

WILLIAM LINDSAY GRESHAM Nightmare Alley

HANS HERBERT GRIMM Schlump

EMMETT GROGAN Ringolevio: A Life Played for Keeps

VASILY GROSSMAN Life and Fate

VASILY GROSSMAN Stalingrad

LOUIS GUILLOUX Blood Dark

OAKLEY HALL Warlock

PATRICK HAMILTON The Slaves of Solitude

PETER HANDKE Slow Homecoming

ELIZABETH HARDWICK The Collected Essays of Elizabeth Hardwick

L.P. HARTLEY The Go-Between

NATHANIEL HAWTHORNE Twenty Days with Julian & Little Bunny by Papa

ALFRED HAYES The End of Me

PAUL HAZARD The Crisis of the European Mind: 1680–1715

ALICE HERDAN-ZUCKMAYER The Farm in the Green Mountains

GILBERT HIGHET Poets in a Landscape

YOEL HOFFMANN The Sound of the One Hand: 281 Zen Koans with Answers

HUGO VON HOFMANNSTHAL The Lord Chandos Letter

RICHARD HOLMES Shelley: The Pursuit

ALISTAIR HORNE A Savage War of Peace: Algeria 1954–1962

GEOFFREY HOUSEHOLD Rogue Male

BOHUMIL HRABAL Dancing Lessons for the Advanced in Age

DOROTHY B. HUGHES In a Lonely Place

RICHARD HUGHES A High Wind in Jamaica

INTIZAR HUSAIN Basti

MAUDE HUTCHINS Victorine

YASUSHI INOUE Tun-huang

DARIUS JAMES Negrophobia: An Urban Parable

HENRY JAMES The New York Stories of Henry James

TOVE JANSSON The Summer Book

RANDALL JARRELL (EDITOR) Randall Jarrell's Book of Stories

DIANE JOHNSON The True History of the First Mrs. Meredith and Other Lesser Lives

UWE JOHNSON Anniversaries

DAVID JONES In Parenthesis

JOSEPH JOUBERT The Notebooks of Joseph Joubert; translated by Paul Auster

ERNST JÜNGER The Glass Bees

ANNA KAVAN Machines in the Head: Selected Stories

MOLLY KEANE Good Behaviour

HELEN KELLER The World I Live In

YASHAR KEMAL Memed, My Hawk

WALTER KEMPOWSKI All for Nothing

MURRAY KEMPTON Part of Our Time: Some Ruins and Monuments of the Thirties

ROBERT KIRK The Secret Commonwealth of Elves, Fauns, and Fairies

ARUN KOLATKAR Jejuri

TÉTÉ-MICHEL KPOMASSIE An African in Greenland

SIGIZMUND KRZHIZHANOVSKY Unwitting Street

GIUSEPPE TOMASI DI LAMPEDUSA The Professor and the Siren

D.H. LAWRENCE The Bad Side of Books: Selected Essays

CAMARA LAYE The Radiance of the King

GERT LEDIG The Stalin Front

MARGARET LEECH Reveille in Washington: 1860–1865

PATRICK LEIGH FERMOR A Time of Gifts

NIKOLAI LESKOV Lady Macbeth of Mtsensk: Selected Stories of Nikolai Leskov

SIMON LEYS The Hall of Uselessness: Collected Essays

GEORG CHRISTOPH LICHTENBERG The Waste Books

DWIGHT MACDONALD Masscult and Midcult: Essays Against the American Grain

CURZIO MALAPARTE The Skin

JANET MALCOLM In the Freud Archives

JEAN-PATRICK MANCHETTE The N'Gustro Affair

OSIP MANDELSTAM The Selected Poems of Osip Mandelstam

THOMAS MANN Reflections of a Nonpolitical Man

OLIVIA MANNING Fortunes of War: The Balkan Trilogy

JAMES VANCE MARSHALL Walkabout

GUY DE MAUPASSANT Like Death

HENRI MICHAUX Miserable Miracle

JESSICA MITFORD Hons and Rebels

NANCY MITFORD Voltaire in Love

KENJI MIYAZAWA Once and Forever: The Tales of Kenji Miyazawa

PATRICK MODIANO In the Café of Lost Youth

FREYA AND HELMUTH JAMES VON MOLTKE Last Letters: The Prison Correspondence

MICHEL DE MONTAIGNE Shakespeare's Montaigne; translated by John Florio

HENRY DE MONTHERLANT Chaos and Night

BRIAN MOORE The Lonely Passion of Judith Hearne

ALBERTO MORAVIA Contempt

JAN MORRIS Conundrum

GUIDO MORSELLI Dissipatio H.G.

MULTATULI Max Havelaar, or the Coffee Auctions of the Dutch Trading Company

ROBERT MUSIL Agathe; or, The Forgotten Sister

ÁLVARO MUTIS The Adventures and Misadventures of Maqroll

FRIEDRICH NIETZSCHE Anti-Education: On the Future of Our Educational Institutions

SILVINA OCAMPO Thus Were Their Faces

IONA AND PETER OPIE The Lore and Language of Schoolchildren

IRIS ORIGO A Chill in the Air: An Italian War Diary, 1939–1940

LEV OZEROV Portraits Without Frames

ALEXANDROS PAPADIAMANTIS The Murderess

CESARE PAVESE The Selected Works of Cesare Pavese

LUIGI PIRANDELLO The Late Mattia Pascal

DAVID PLANTE Difficult Women: A Memoir of Three

ANDREY PLATONOV Soul and Other Stories

J.F. POWERS The Stories of J.F. Powers

ALEXANDER PUSHKIN Peter the Great's African: Experiments in Prose

QIU MIAOJIN Last Words from Montmartre

PAUL RADIN Primitive Man as Philosopher

GRACILIANO RAMOS São Bernardo

GREGOR VON REZZORI Memoirs of an Anti-Semite

JULIO RAMÓN RIBEYRO The Word of the Speechless: Selected Stories

TIM ROBINSON Stones of Aran: Pilgrimage

MAXIME RODINSON Muḥammad

MILTON ROKEACH The Three Christs of Ypsilanti

GILLIAN ROSE Love's Work

CONSTANCE ROURKE American Humor: A Study of the National Character

RUMI Gold; translated by Haleh Liza Gafori

TAYEB SALIH Season of Migration to the North

JEAN-PAUL SARTRE We Have Only This Life to Live: Selected Essays. 1939–1975

ARTHUR SCHNITZLER Late Fame

GERSHOM SCHOLEM Walter Benjamin: The Story of a Friendship

DANIEL PAUL SCHREBER Memoirs of My Nervous Illness

JAMES SCHUYLER What's for Dinner?

SIMONE SCHWARZ-BART The Bridge of Beyond

LEONARDO SCIASCIA To Each His Own

ANNA SEGHERS The Dead Girls' Class Trip

PHILIPE-PAUL DE SÉGUR Defeat: Napoleon's Russian Campaign

GILBERT SELDES The Stammering Century

VICTOR SERGE Memoirs of a Revolutionary

VARLAM SHALAMOV Kolyma Stories

CHARLES SIMIC Dime-Store Alchemy: The Art of Joseph Cornell

MAY SINCLAIR Mary Olivier: A Life

WILLIAM SLOANE The Rim of Morning: Two Tales of Cosmic Horror

WILLIAM GARDNER SMITH The Stone Face

SASHA SOKOLOV A School for Fools

BEN SONNENBERG Lost Property: Memoirs and Confessions of a Bad Boy

VLADIMIR SOROKIN The Queue

NATSUME SŌSEKI The Gate

JEAN STAFFORD Boston Adventure

FRANCIS STEEGMULLER Flaubert and Madame Bovary: A Double Portrait

GEORGE R. STEWART Names on the Land
GEORGE R. STEWART Storm
STENDHAL The Life of Henry Brulard
ADALBERT STIFTER Motley Stones
JEAN STROUSE Alice James: A Biography
ITALO SVEVO As a Man Grows Older
MAGDA SZABÓ The Door
JÁNOS SZÉKELY Temptation
ANTAL SZERB Journey by Moonlight
SUSAN TAUBES Divorcing
ELIZABETH TAYLOR You'll Enjoy It When You Get There: The Stories of Elizabeth Taylor
TEFFI Other Worlds: Peasants, Pilgrims, Spirits, Saints
GABRIELE TERGIT Käsebier Takes Berlin
HENRY DAVID THOREAU The Journal: 1837–1861
ALEKSANDAR TIŠMA Kapo
TATYANA TOLSTAYA White Walls: Collected Stories
LIONEL TRILLING The Liberal Imagination
YŪKO TSUSHIMA Woman Running in the Mountains
MARINA TSVETAEVA Earthly Signs: Moscow Diaries, 1917–1922
KURT TUCHOLSKY Castle Gripsholm
IVAN TURGENEV Virgin Soil
RAMÓN DEL VALLE-INCLÁN Tyrant Banderas
JULES VALLÈS The Child
MARK VAN DOREN Shakespeare
CARL VAN VECHTEN The Tiger in the House
SALKA VIERTEL The Kindness of Strangers
ELIZABETH VON ARNIM The Enchanted April
EDWARD LEWIS WALLANT The Tenants of Moonbloom
ROBERT WALSER Little Snow Landscape
MICHAEL WALZER Political Action: A Practical Guide to Movement Politics
REX WARNER Men and Gods
SYLVIA TOWNSEND WARNER Lolly Willowes
LYALL WATSON Heaven's Breath: A Natural History of the Wind
MAX WEBER Charisma and Disenchantment: The Vocation Lectures
C.V. WEDGWOOD The Thirty Years War
SIMONE WEIL On the Abolition of All Political Parties
SIMONE WEIL AND RACHEL BESPALOFF War and the Iliad
HELEN WEINZWEIG Basic Black with Pearls
GLENWAY WESCOTT The Pilgrim Hawk
EDITH WHARTON Ghosts: Selected and with a Preface by the Author
KATHARINE S. WHITE Onward and Upward in the Garden
PATRICK WHITE Riders in the Chariot
T.H. WHITE The Goshawk
JOHN WILLIAMS Augustus
JOHN WILLIAMS Stoner
HENRY WILLIAMSON Tarka the Otter
ANGUS WILSON Anglo-Saxon Attitudes
RUDOLF AND MARGARET WITTKOWER Born Under Saturn
RICHARD WOLLHEIM Germs: A Memoir of Childhood
FRANCIS WYNDHAM The Complete Fiction
JOHN WYNDHAM The Chrysalids
STEFAN ZWEIG Chess Story
STEFAN ZWEIG The Post-Office Girl